# JANDAVLATTEPA

The Excavation Report for Seasons 2002–2006

## VOL. 1

*Results of excavations conducted by Charles University in Prague and
Institute of Archaeology, Academy of Sciences of Uzbekistan in Samarqand*

Editors
KAZIM ABDULLAEV
LADISLAV STANČO

CHARLES UNIVERSITY IN PRAGUE
KAROLINUM PRESS 2011

Reviewed by: Mgr. Alžběta Danielisová, Ph.D.
Mgr. Karel Nováček, Ph.D.

KATALOGIZACE V KNIZE – NÁRODNÍ KNIHOVNA ČR

Jandavlattepa I / Ladislav Stančo (ed.). – 1st ed. – Prague: Karolinum, 2011
Vydavatel: Univerzita Karlova v Praze
ISBN 978-80-246-1965-1

902.2 * 902:904 * 94(396) * (575.1)
– archeologické výzkumy – Uzbekistán
– archeologické nálezy – Uzbekistán
– Baktrie – dějiny
– Džandavláttepa (Uzbekistán: archeologická lokalita)
– kolektivní monografie
– excavations (archaeology) – Uzbekistan
– antiquities – Uzbekistan
– Bactria – history
– Jandavlattepa (Uzbekistan: archeological site)
– collective monographs

902 – Archeologie [8]
930.1 – Archaeology [8]

# Contents

## *Acknowledgements*

We would like to thank all those who have contributed to the appearance of this publication, and who have also permitted the research project itself to take place – in particular, those institutions that provided finance. This was in large part Charles University, which financed the project for its duration, through the following grants: GA UK 292/2001/A-HN/FF "The influence of Hellenistic art in Asia on the basis of archaeological sources" and 473/2004/A-HN/FF "Bactria in the age of the Greeks, Sakas and Kushans." In addition, the Faculty of Arts of Charles University contributed by awarding numerous grants to students taking part in the project, as well as by financing the preparatory work for this publication in 2007 (an internal grant for a research paper entitled "Late Ancient Bactria in the light of evidence of the material culture.") The Faculty of Arts, specifically the Institute for Classical Archaeology, also provided institutional support, including part of our technological equipment, while the institute's directors, Jan Bouzek and Iva Ondřejová, provided their full support to our endeavours. In 2004 the Fund for the Development of Higher Education funded student participation in the project through the grant no. 1827/2004 "Continuity and discontinuity in the settlement of northern Bactria in ancient times."

We are also very much indebted to the staff of the Archaeological Institute of the Academy of Sciences of Uzbekistan in Samarkand for their support and aid, above all to the former director of the institute, Timur Shirinov. We are also very appreciative of the help and kindness to our hosts and friends in the village of Akkurgan, to Shadmon Ergashev, caretaker of local museum, his daughter, who was occasionally our doctor and his granddaughter Dilbar, our truehearted cook. The same gratefulness deserve those people from the villages of Saitabad and Akkurgan, who assisted us in the exhausting fieldwork.

We would like to thank Mr. Škoda and Mr. Sanytrák from the company Foto Škoda, who supported us in the initial phases of the project, above all by providing photographic materials and holding promotional exhibitions. We are greatly indebted to Mr. Haruštiak, the director of the company Eriell, who provided us with significant support in 2006. Throughout the period of the research he lent us a new all-terrain vehicle and helped us in all sorts of ways. We should also like to convey our thanks to the representatives of the Czech Embassy in Tashkent – the Consul, Mrs. Deňková, for her help in 2002–3, and above all the Ambassador, Mr. Aleš Fojtík, and his wife for their availability, frequent help and significant contribution to the success of the expedition in 2006.

We would also like to thank those who helped us with the final work on the publication, including Valerie Talacko for translating texts from Czech into English, and Antonio Arias, who corrected the texts submitted in English. Beside the editors mentioned on the front page, Jan Kysela helped much both with preparation of this volume and of the online database.

Finally, the Czech participants would like – from their part – to thank our closest colleagues and friends, Kazim Abdullaev, who first initiated this joint project, and Shapulat Shaydullaev for all the care he lavished on us, and both of them for the large amount of advice with which they provided us as they introduced us to Central Asian archaeology. We can never sufficiently thank our friend and colleague Alisher Shaydullaev, for all his dedication and hard work.

# Introduction

*Ladislav Stančo*

After the long period of almost exclusively Soviet scholarly interest caused by the political situation, Central Asia became a forefront of international archaeological research early in the 90's. Several respected archaeological teams have established gradually their projects throughout post-Soviet republics of Central Asia, including Uzbekistan. In 2002 this effort was joined by a small Czech-Uzbekistani team aiming to start archaeological investigation of northwestern part of ancient Bactria, particularly the area of Sherabad oasis. The preparatory season 2001 led to the decision to start the trial excavations on the Jandavlattepa, the major site of the oasis, located close to the town of Sherabad itself (Maps 1 and 2). This stage of our research was intended as initial step for gaining detail knowledge of the settlement structure and chronology of the Sherabad oasis as a whole.

The main goals of our project on the site of Jandavlattepa were as follows:

1. to refine the chronology of the site as well as of the region (Sector 02)
2. to obtain archaeological material sufficiently complex to enable us to study various aspects of culture and society of Late Kushan a and Kushano-Sasanian periods (Sectors 06, 07, 08 and 20)

In this respect, one of the main concerns of the present publication is to present some freshly gained data in the field of Bactrian archaeology of Pre-Islamic periods and to shed some more light on different aspects of understanding its material culture especially during transitional period between Kushan period and early medieval times.

During the process of excavations on Jandavlattepa a large amount of archaeological material and data was unearthed and accumulated. Both co-editors decided early at the beginning of the joint work to publish all the material as soon as possible and the term of five years after termination of the excavations was firmly set as the deadline. Herewith we try to fulfil, at least partly, our erstwhile undertaking. The present title, however, is far from being complete publication of our results. It represents just a pilot volume, which will be ensued by two other books in the near future. This one presents primarily the description of the process of excavation in the Sector 20, the Citadel, and its results, as well as several thematic studies of concrete groups of artefacts (see Structure of the publication below). The reader can expect a similar description of the Sector 07, i.e. upper Shakhristan, (L. Grmela, J. Halama, L. Stančo et alii) as well as a thorough study of ceramics from the Sectors 07, 08 and 20 in the second volume (M. Odler and L. Stančo) and a complete publication of vast material from the Sector 02 (stratigraphical trench, K. Abdullaev) and final conclusion in the third volume respectively. As the site of Jandavlattepa representing the core of the settlement structure in the Sherabad oasis did not function in a vacuum, we would like to analyse its position, spatial relations with the other sites of the oasis and dynamics of the oasis' settlement structure in general in yet another volume.[1]

## Structure of the publication

This publication has been divided into three parts. The first part contains a brief general description of the site and the history of its excavation, as well as geographical and topographical notes. The second, core, part contains a description of the archaeological situations in the various sectors. These descriptions have been grouped into three units, corresponding to their physical distribution over the site. The first unit is the area of the so-called Citadel, or sector 20. The second is the area of the lower town, or *Shakhristan*, comprising sectors 04, 07 and 08. Sectors 02 and 06 ought to be included here, but the material from sectors 07 and 02 in particular is extremely extensive,

---

[1] We focused on this aspect during our subsequent project, for some preliminary notes on this subject cf. Stančo 2009 and Danielisová – Stančo – Shaydullaev 2010.

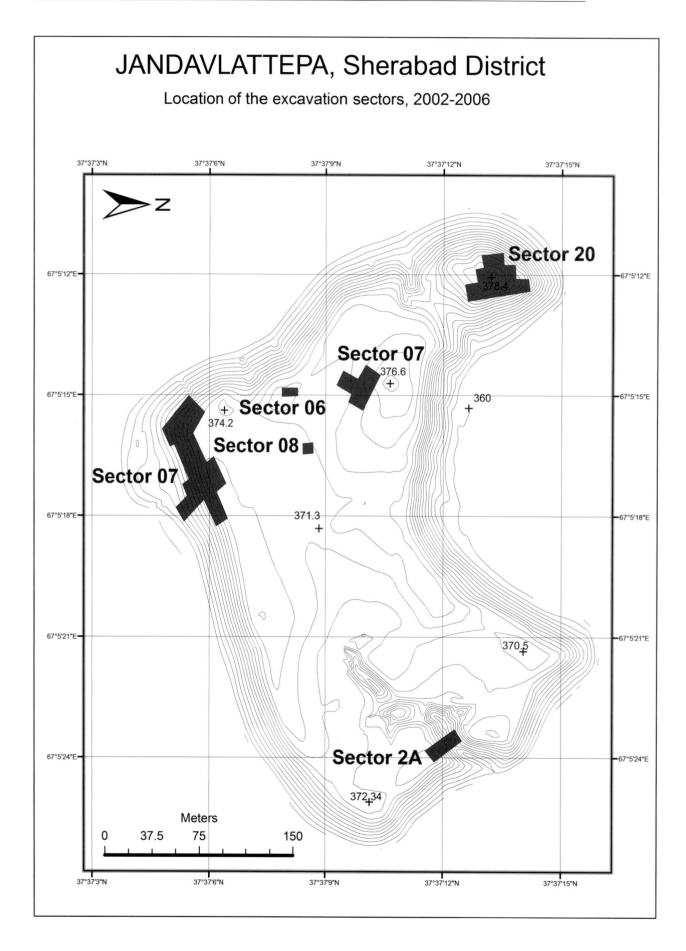

**Fig. 1** General plan of the site.

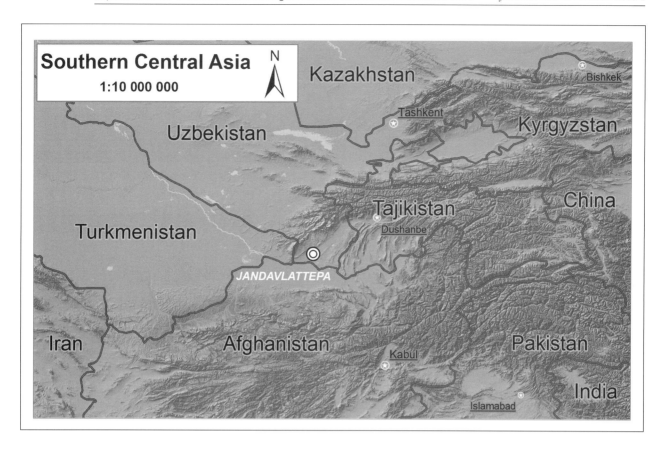

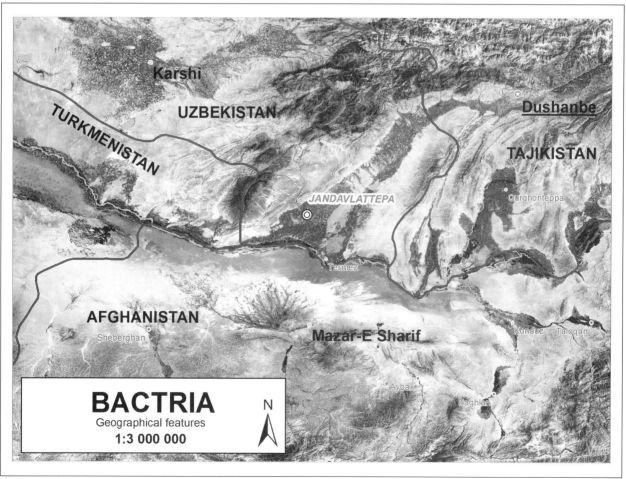

**Map 1 and 2** Location of the site in southern Uzbekistan and main geographical features of Bactria.

and the plan is to publish it in separate volumes. The third is a description of sector 30, an area outside the *tepa* itself, where preliminary exploration took place. The overall map shows the location of the sectors in the site (fig. 1).

The third part of the publication consists of studies devoted to various groups of finds: coins, textile-making implements, weapons and tools, jewellery and clay figurines.

At the end of the book, in addition to a bibliography, is placed a list of all small finds, with references to depictions of them in drawings and photographs, and to the places in the text where special attention is paid to these finds.

# 1. The site and its environs

## 1.1 General remarks and description of the landscape

*Kazim Abdullaev*

Southern Uzbekistan is characterised by alternating mountain ridges and river valleys (Maps 1, 2 and 3). The valley of the river Surkhan Darya (after which the whole region – Viloyat – is named) is exceptional in terms of both its dimensions and the landscape variability. It begins roughly in the district of the modern village of Dekhanabad where the Great Uzbek Highway passes along the river Kan (a left-bank tributary of the river Kichik Ura Darya).

In this tract, the road rises steadily up to the Chakchak pass (near Akrabat). Beyond the village of Akrabad, there is a watershed between the basins of the river Guzar Darya and that of the river Sherabad Darya, one of the important tributaries of the Amu Darya. Here, the mountains – the southwestern spurs of Baysun Tau – do not attain extraordinary heights but have fairly sharp outlines. The picturesqueness of

the mountains is enhanced by the presence of variegated rocks – white, greenish and red. A particularly striking visual effect is produced by the slightly inclined yellowish-white limestone slopes. Easily eroded by torrents of mud and water, they have been shaped into deep and narrow valleys. The main road hugs the slopes of the Sarymas ridge and subsequently emerges into the Shurob Say valley.

After the confluence of the salt-water river Shurob Say ("Salty Water" in Tajik) and the fresh waters of the Machay Darya, which rises in the Baysun Tau Mountains, the waters of the Sherabad Darya become salty. The Sherabad Darya valley, stretching from north to south, is shaped by one of the principal tributaries of the Amu Darya, which rises in the southern spurs of the Hissar mountains, in Baysun Tau. After passing through picturesque foothills (fig. 1.1, *1*), the river enters the plain after the Kangi

**Fig. 1.1, 1** Piedmont landscape in the river valley of Sherabad Darya, photo L. Stančo.

# Surkhandarya Province of Uzbekistan
# Southern Part

1:1 000 000

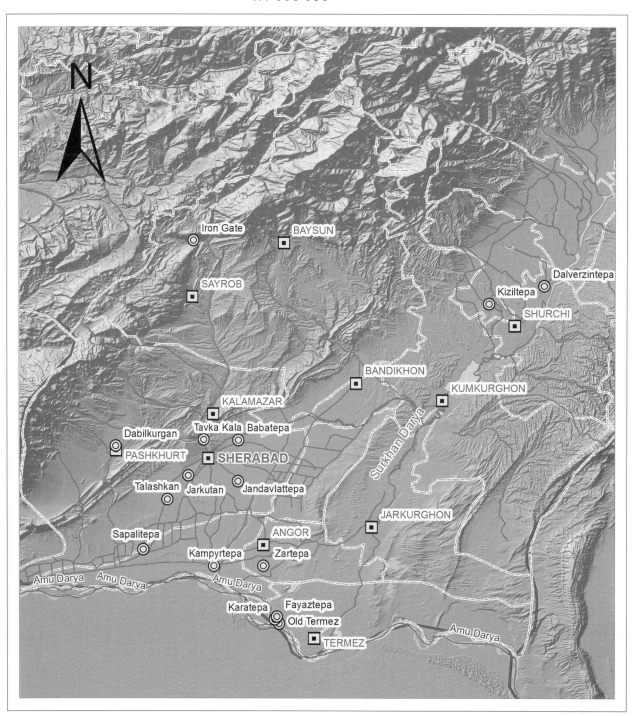

## Legend

◎ Archaeological sites      ------- District borders

▫ Towns

—— Rivers and irrigation channels

**Map 3** North-western Bactria, location of the site of Jandavlattepa in southern Uzbekistan.

14

foothills approximately in the outskirts of the modern regional centre, the town of Sherabad.

Archaeologists have detected human habitation in this region since the upper Palaeolithic era. The finding of remains of Neanderthal boy in the cave of Teshik-Tash near the Machay district is one of the earliest testimonies to human presence.

The archaeological sites located in the river's alluvial plain (fig. 1.1, 2) can be dated to various periods, and testify to human settlement in the territory from the most ancient times. The territory of the Sherabad oasis formed part of the ancient historical and cultural region of Bactria. Without entering into details of the question of the borders of Bactria mentioned in cuneiform rock inscriptions from the 6th century BC, it should be noted that the northern limits of Bactria included the territory north of the river of Amu Darya – Oxus.[1]

This is confirmed by basically all categories of artefacts, which show cultural development along common lines, with common tendencies and, it appears, from common sources (both north and south of the river). In any case, the territory north of the river Amu Darya/Oxus up to the spurs of Baysun Tau (i.e. the southern spur of the Hissar ridge) is considered by more and more scholars to be a uniform cultural region.[2] At Baysun Tau a system of defensive constructions has been identified by archaeologists, in-

cluding a monumental fortification wall near modern Darband. Archaeological surveys of the sites within the Sherabad oasis testify to the presence an advanced culture in the area as early as the Bronze Age. It is in this region that monuments such as those at Sapallitepa and Jarkutan were unearthed and investigated. Excavations by Uzbekistani archaeologists indicate ancient societies with complex and particular forms, and a highly developed material and spiritual culture.

At the site of Jarkutan, in particular, excavations of the ancient settlement revealed the initial stage of development of proto-urban cultures and traces of cultural ceremonies of which elements would reappear subsequently in a religious doctrine close to Zoroastrianism. So, for example, the sacred terrace discovered at Jarkutan, with its precise lay-out composed around the Chokhortag, makes the complex comparable to well-known monuments in Iran (Bard-e Nishande, Takht-e Suleyman, Nush-e Jan).

One of the interesting features of the Sherabad oasis is the continuity of settlement, with sites surviving from one archaeological period to another. So for example, the final phase of Jarkutan, in the late Bronze and Early Iron Ages, apparently continues in a number of other neighbouring sites in the oasis (Talashkan 2, Kuchuktepa, Pshaktepa etc.). It is therefore likely, going by excavations of the lowermost levels

**Fig. 1.1, 2** Typical landscape in the irrigated lowlands of Sherabad District, photo L. Stančo.

---

[1]    There is some discrepancy among ancient writers as far as the northern limits of Bactria (Bactriana) are concerned. Traditionally, they place the border on the Oxus river (Arr., VII, 5, 1–2; Strabo, XI, II, 2; Ptol., VII, II, I). This opinion seems to prevail down to the 4th century AD, judging from the work of Ammianus Marcellinus who appears to follow the tradition set by Ptolemy quoted above (Amm. Marc., XXIII, 6, 57). Among modern scholars, it was W. Tomaschek who placed the border on the Hissar ridge (cf. Tomaschek 1877, pp. 28–31).

[2]    Masson 1968, pp. 14–26; Staviskiy 1976, p. 74; Staviskiy 1977, p. 36ff; Abdullaev 1997, pp. 54–60.

of Jandavlattepa (with fragments of painted pottery), that the beginning of human presence in the site is connected with a period of dwindling human activity in a number of other sites, including Jarkutan.

The history of archaeological research into this period in Central Asia may be subdivided into four stages. In the archaeological literature the first stage is traditionally connected to the pre-revolutionary period (before 1917) and is characterised by the investigations of military topographers and engineers, and also local history amateurs.

The second stage, preceding the Second World War (until 1941), is associated with the first archaeological expeditions organized by the main museums of the Soviet Union and Departments of the Academies of Union Republics (Museum of the History of Eastern Culture, the State Hermitage, Termez Complex Archaeological Expedition), led by such outstanding scholars as B. P. Denike, M. E. Masson, and others. The most fruitful period in the history of archaeological research in Bactria is that following the Second World War – the third period.

At this time the right-bank part of Bactria was studied by large expeditions such as that of the Leningrad Department of the Institute of Archaeology of the Academy of Sciences of the USSR (now the Institute of History of Material Culture of the Russian Academy of Sciences), headed by V. M. Masson; that of the Institute of Archaeology of the Academy of Sciences of the USSR (Institute of Archaeology of

the Russian Academy of Sciences) under the direction of G. A. Koshelenko; that of the Institute of Archaeology of the Academy of Sciences of the Uzbek SSR (now the Institute of Archaeology of the Academy of Sciences of Uzbekistan) led by A. A. Askarov; the Southern Tajik Archaeological Expedition under the leadership of B. A. Litvinski.

A big contribution to the research into Kushan culture was made by the expedition of the Uzbek Art History Institute under the direction of G. A. Pugachenkova. Important roles in the studies of Kushan culture were played by the works of such scholars as L. I. Albaum, E. V. Rtveladze, A. M. Mandelshtam, B. J. Stavisky and others.

It should be noted that archaeological expeditions from France, Italy and Japan worked simultaneously in the territory south of Amu Darya (Afghanistan). Particular mention should be made of the activities of the French Archaeological Mission (MDAFA) directed by such outstanding scholars as A. Foucher, d. Schlumberger and P. Bernard. Their discovery and lengthy excavations of the Greek city of Ay Khanum made a significant contribution to the understanding of Hellenistic cultures in Central Asia. Another expedition on the territory of Afghanistan was the Soviet-Afghan expedition led by I. T. Kruglikova and later by V. I. Sarianidi. The various publications that followed these excavations were invaluable in enlarging our knowledge of the history of the ancient culture of Bactria.

# 1.2 General description of the site, history of research

*Ladislav Stančo*

## Location

Position: GPS – measured from the topmost point of the Shakhristan (former Soviet topographical point, 37.619720°, 67.087370°).

37.619050° E 67.088536° N (source: GoogleEarth)
Straight lines of distance to related archaeological sites:

A) Regional importance: to Tafka Kala 13.6 km[1]; to Talashkan 16.5 km; to Kampyrtepa 23.8 km; to Fayaztepa 38 km; to Old Termez 40.3 km; to Zurmala 41.5 km; to the Iron gate (Darbant) 65.5 km; to Dalverzintepa 86 km.

B) Interregional importance: to Baktra 96 km; to Ai Khanum 211 km; to Sogdiana (Yerkurgan) 190 km, (Marakanda) 227 km; to Merv (Gyaur Kala) 432 km; to Khwarazm (Ayaz Kala) 711 km, (Toprak Kala) 718 km; to Sirkap (Taxila) 673 km; Kashgar 802 km.

The site of Jandavlattepa is located in an intensely irrigated and cultivated plain close to rather deep riverbed of the Sherabad River (Uzb. Sherobod Darya), 7.67 km from the town of Sherabad, the district headquarters (Map 3). The river[2], itself, flows 780 m to the east of the site (fig. 1.2, *1*). Nowadays, most of the surrounding fields are used for the cultivation of cotton, and the whole area is interwoven with irrigation ditches[3]. This flat plain dominates the whole southern horizon while the northern and north-western views are dominated by the ranges and foothills of the Kougitang and Baysoun Mountains. Lower ridges of Haudag hills rise also on the east side, separating the valleys of Sherabad Darya and Surkhan Darya. Jandavlattepa commands the area being strategically well located only 10km from the outflow where the Sherabad River leaves the mountains. At one time, when travelling from Sogdiana to Bactria (as understood in the prevailing view of modern scholarship), the first large settlement of letter on the way was Jandavlattepa.

## Dimensions

General surface area including slopes: 72,820 sq. m; Shakhristan[4] – upper surface 40,203 sq. m; Citadel – upper surface 920 sq. m.
Maximum length SE to NW: 416 m
Maximum length NE to SW: 341 m

The height of the Citadel above the surrounding cotton fields is about 20 m, while the height of the Shakhristan varies between 12 and 18 m. The highest point, the top of the Citadel, lies at an elevation of 378.4 m above sea level, while the elevation of the original topographical point on the top of the Shakhristan is marked on the Soviet-era topographical plan at 376.6 m.

Judging simply by its dimensions, we are inclined to classify the site of Jandavlattepa in the Graeco-Bactrian and Kushan periods as a small fortified town or "townlet", in Russian terminology the term "Городище" is favoured. Its extent in the earlier periods, i.e. in the Achaemenid and the Early Iron Age, is hard to determine in the present state of research.

## Shape

The ground plan of the site has a strange polygonal shape, which resembles a deformed rectangle. Irregularities, especially the inward curve in the northern part, are hard to explain. While theories concerning large-scale erosion inflicted by the earlier riverbed of the Sherabad River or the building of the settlement

---

[1]  All distances are measured as the crow flies.

[2]  The river is actually almost not existent at present, especially in the summer and autumn time, being reduced to a tiny stream by the extensive use of its waters for irrigation of the cotton fields. Rough picture of the river as it used to be can be gained some 10 km upstream, just before Sherabad Darya leaves the piedmont steppe and rocky ranges.

[3]  It is only relatively recently, however, that the landscape in the immediate surroundings of Jandavlattepa gained this character. In the 1960s, large areas on the right bank of the Sherabad Darya were uncultivated and looked more like a steppe. The considerable increase in the area under crops in recent decades has had a very negative effect on the state of archaeological sites, especially burial grounds, rabats and smaller *tepas*, and thus contributed to a significantly distorted picture of the historical landscape. See Chapter 4, Concluding remarks.

[4]  For definitions of the individual parts of the tepa, see below in "Shape."

**Fig. 1.2, 1** Sherabad Darya close to the Jandavlattepa, photo L. Stančo.

in a backwater of its earlier course are rather unlikely[5], another theory, that the site had grown gradually and spontaneously in the earlier periods of its occupation[6] and that its shape was respected also in later, let us say, historic periods, make more sense.

The site (*tepa*) could be divided into two principal parts: Citadel and Shakhristan. Both terms are borrowed from Russian and local archaeological terminology. The Citadel refers to the smaller, separate, usually higher, part of the settlement with some specific function either religious or defensive or representative. The term "Shakhristan" indicates the lower town, larger as a rule, primarily functioning as living and craftsmen quarters.

The slopes of the tepa are very steep, except for the southern part (see excavations in Sector 04, Chapter 2.1). The surface of the lower town (Shakhristan) is rather flat and descends slightly from west to east (fig. 1.2, 2). Almost the whole surface of the plateau is covered by shallow depressions indicating the slumps of the cavities of recent grave pits. These loose-soil depressions are covered with more

luxuriant vegetation, grass and dry little shrubs. To the contrary, the surface of the Citadel is uneven (figs. 1.2, *3*\* and 1.2, *4*\*).[7]

Unlike many other sites in Surkhan Darya, little can be said about the extent and character of those parts of the settlements, which arose in the vicinity of the main tepa outside the town walls because of the extensive cultivation of the area (fig. 1.2, 5). For the results of our preliminary survey, see Chapter 2.4.

**Name**

The historical name(s) of the site is, unfortunately, not known to us. Unlike several other sites in Bactria, there have not yet been any proposals to identify it with some names recorded in historical sources, in particular Chinese. The meaning of the name Jandavlattepa refers to the personal name indicated by the courteous preposition *jan* or *jon* (meaning "soul" in Turkic languages; *davlat* means "power" or "state"), while *tepa* (elsewhere also "tepe"), needless to say, means artificial mound like the Near Eastern *tell*. In publications, it is possible to find several differ-

5 Huff – Pidaev – Chaydoullaev 2001, p. 219; besides the other reasons, the main argument against such theories is the existence of traces of human activities (buildings) in the assumed course of the river and the absence of characteristic landscape features, such as a distinct fault or riverbed in the area. Despite this, on the high right bank of the present riverbed, between the river itself and Jandavlattepa, it is possible to find small archaeological sites and structures, which would have otherwise been completely washed away by the moving watercourse.
6 Huff 1997, p. 84.
7 The figures marked with * are attached only on accompanying disc while the others are included both on the CD and in this printed version.

**Fig. 1.2, 2** Jandavlattepa, view from north, photo L. Stančo.

ent transcriptions of the name. V. M. Masson, Sh. Pidaev and E. V. Rtveladze used Джандавлат-Тепе in their Russian publications, but Sh. Pidaev utilized also another version, namely Жандавлаттепа. D. Huff used to write Džandaulattepe in his German articles. A. Schachner uses Džandaulat-Tepe (English text) and Djandaulat-Tepe or Džandavlatepe (German text). A French publication utilizes one more option – Djandavlat Tepe.[8] To make matters

more confused, we ourselves had initially used other transcriptions (Russian Джандавляттепа, English Djandavlattepa), and the quite accurate Czech transcription Džandavláttepa is still used.[9] After all this, these days we tend to use the English transcription, Jandavlattepa, because it is the best phonetic transcription. Note that Pidaev intentionally used the name of Джандавлаттепа for the neighbouring site of Pachmaktepa initially.[10]

**Fig. 1.2, 5** Jandavlattepa, view from south, photo L. Stančo.

---

[8]  Masson 1974; Pidaev 1973; Pidaev 1974; Pidaev 1978, p. 22; Rtveladze 1974; Huff 1997; Schachner 1995/1996, pp. 154 and 159; Schachner 2003–2004; Huff – Pidaev – Chaydoullaev 2001, p. 219.
[9]  Abdullaev – Stančo 2003; Abdullaev – Bohach – Stancho 2003; Abdullaev – Stančo 2004a; Stančo 2003; Stančo 2006a.
[10]  Pidaev 1973, p. 78, note 1.

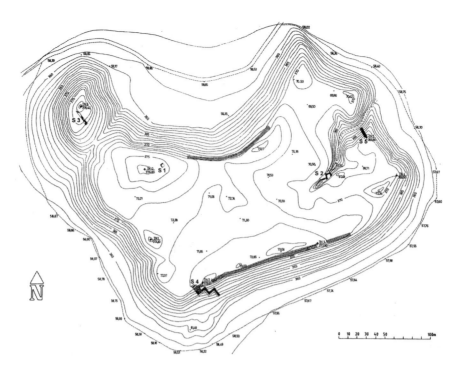

**Fig. 1.2,6** Jandavlattepa – topographical plan with marked locations of trenches of Uzbek-German excavations (1993), according to Huff 1997, Abb. 2.

**History of research**

The first registered and published surface prospecting of Jandavlattepa and its vicinity was undertaken by the Bactrian Archaeological Expedition under Shakir Pidaev in spring, 1972, even though the main interest focused on the neighbouring site of Pachmaktepa. The results of the survey were published in 1973 and 1974.[11] However, the description of the site given in the latter article contains several mistakes. For example, the site is located to the southeast not the northeast of the town of Sherabad. The site code B-38 is used, whereas, in the same book, another code (B-33) is utilized by Rtveladze (see below). Pidaev assumed the town gate to be at the eastern end of the site, with even two towers flanking it. The fact of the matter is that neither the gate nor the towers were found in this area (as a result of excavation in Sector 2a). A depression at the eastern spur was not a gateway but a natural phenomenon created by the waters of seasonal rain. However, Pidaev was then quite accurate in his determination of the site chronology. He correctly considered the middle of the first

millennium AD to be the end of occupation. His assumption, that the beginning of occupation was in the Achaemenid period, has been revised by excavations quite recently.[12]

Almost identical data are given in a short description of the site in Rtveladze's list of the sites, which was published in the same volume.[13] Jandavlattepa here is marked as site B-33.

Rtveladze assigned it to the second type of his third group (examples include Khaytabad-tepa, Besh-kopa and Dergiz-tepa), which is a walled settlement with a surface area between 5 and 10 ha, including Citadel, defending towers and moat. Surprisingly, Rtveldze and Khakimov describe the site in detail in yet another – earlier – article.[14] Short description of the site is given also by V. M. Masson, who besides the other mistakes inverted cardinal points.[15]

In his overview of Kushan settlements in Northern Bactria Sh. Pidaev classifies Jandavlattepa among the sites of his third type, i.e. sites larger than 6 ha and smaller than 15 ha.[16] Pidaev stresses that it is only site of this size in the Sherabad oasis.

---

[11]　Pidaev 1973, pp. 77–82; Pidaev 1974, pp. 32–33.
[12]　New finds, specifically painted pottery date the beginning of earlier activity to the period of the Late Bronze and Early Iron Ages, cf. Abdullaev – Stančo 2010.
[13]　Rtveladze 1974, pp. 77–78.
[14]　Rtveladze – Khakimov 1973, pp. 13–14. Among the other information they note that "its surface is over 5 hectares, the longer side is oriented NE-SW, the Citadel (40×40; height 13–14m), stands near the NW corner of the ancient settlement site and is separated from it by a gully up to 12m wide; the plan of the lower town is polygonal with a sharp curve in the NW side. Its maximum dimensions are 280m in length, 200m in width (130m in the area of the curve). Height varies from 7m in the SE part up to 10m in the NW. The crests of the walls are poorly pronounced. The site's slopes are abrupt, and in the NE there are some sharp gullies, especially in the centre where the gate was most probably sited. The overall extent of the site, measured from the extreme NW point of the Citadel to the SE corner of the lower town is 360 m". In the surroundings of Jandavlattepa, to the SE and SW, the remains of buildings in the form of small hills have been noted, the remains of small farms..." (reduced).

The site had to wait for twenty years for the real archaeological excavations to begin, when Jandavalttepa was chosen as the main objective of the German-Uzbek archaeological expedition in 1993. These excavations started as part of a joint project between the German Archaeological Institute in Berlin and the Archaeological Institute of the Uzbek Academy of Sciences in Samarqand, better known results of which come from digs at the site of Jarkutan. The team led by Dietrich Huff and Shakir Pidaev wisely chose the starting points for the survey and actually anticipated and inspired the choice of the Czech-Uzbekistani successors eight years later. Five trenches were opened: S1 (Schnitt 1) on the highest point of the Shakhristan, S2 on the northern slope of the western part of an erosion-made depression or flume (ovraq) in the eastern part of the site, S3 on the summit of the Citadel, S4 at the southern edge of the site and finally S5 on the southern slope of the ovraq (fig. 1.2, 6). Their particular results, as far as are known to us (they were never fully published), we will discuss in respective chapters of this and following volume. Among their small finds, a very interesting clay figurine of Bodhisattva is worth mentioning[17] (see below in this volume the separate study on clay figurines from Jandavlattepa, chapter 3.4). Unfortunately, despite the promising results of the excavations, the first season became the last. D. Huff justifies this with logistic difficulties, the lack of manpower in particular.[18]

Thus far, the last chapter of the story has been written by the Czech-Uzbekistani archaeological expedition. Collaboration originated in 2001 as a joint project of the Archaeological Institute of Academy of Sciences of Uzbekistan in Samarqand and the Institute for Classical Archaeology, Charles University in Prague. The pilot season took place the next year, in 2002. Since then, every year, a four to six-week-long excavation campaign under the direction of Kazim Abdullaev and Ladislav Stančo has been organised (fig. 1.2, 7). The huge amount of archaeological material and data collected in five seasons obliges us to make it public. Let this volume be the starting issue of publications which shall present this data.

**Fig. 1.2, 7** Czech-Uzbek team on the excavations in 2005.

---

[15] Masson 1974, pp. 5–6.
[16] Pidaev 1978, p. 22.
[17] Huff 1997, Abb. 4; Mkrtychev considers this figurine to be a depiction of a god or hero inspired by the iconography of Avalokiteshvara, see Mkrtychev 2007, p. 482.
[18] Huff 1997, p. 87.

## Bibliography
### (Introduction and parts 1.1 and 1.2)

Abdullaev, K. (1997): O severnykh rubezhakh gosudarstvennoy granitsy Baktrii v ellinisticheskuyu epokhu, *Rossiyskaya arkheologiya*, 1997, 4, pp. 54–60.

Abdullaev, K. – Stančo, L. (2010): Arkheologicheskie raboty na Dzhandavlattepa v 2006 godu, in: *Arkheologicheskiye Issledovaniya v Uzbekistane 2006–2007 goda*, Samarkand, pp. 18–23.

Danielisová, A. – Stančo, L. – Shaydullaev, A. (2010): Preliminary report of the archaeological survey in Sherabad Dsitrict, South Uzbekistan in 2009. *Studia Hercynia* XIV, pp. 67–90.

Huff, D. (1997): Deutsch-Uzbek Ausgrabungen auf dem Džandaulattepe und in Džarkutan, Süduzbekistan, 1993–1995. *Mitteilungen der Berliner Gesellschaft für Anthropologie, Ethnologie und Urgeschichte*, 18, pp. 83–95.

Masson, M. E. (1968): K voprosu o severnykh granitsakh "velikykh Kushan." *Obshchestvennyye nauki v Uzbekistane*, 1968, 8, pp. 14–26.

Masson, V. M. (1974): Problema drevnego goroda i arkheologicheskiye pamyatniky severnoy Baktrii, in: *Drevnyaya Baktriya*, ed.: Masson, V. M., Leningrad, pp. 3–13.

Mkrtychev, T. K. (2007): *Buddiyskoye iskusstvo Sredney Azii I–X vv*. Moskva: Akademkniga.

Pidaev, Sh. P. (1973): Otkrytiye novogo pamyatnika serediny I tysyacheletiya do nashey ery. *Obshchestvennyye nauki v Uzbekistane* 11/1973, pp. 77–82.

Pidaev, Sh. P. (1974): Materialy k izucheniyu drvnikh pamyatnikov Severnoy Baktrii, in: *Drevnyaya Baktriya*, ed.: Masson, V. M., Leningrad, pp. 38–40.

Pidaev, Sh. (1978): *Poseleniya kushanskogo vremeni severnoy Baktrii*. Tashkent.

Rtveladze, E. V. – Khakimov, Z. E. (1973): Marshrutnyye issledovaniya pamyatnikov severnoy Baktrii, in: Pugachenkova, G. A., ed., *Iz istorii antichnoy kul'tury Uzbekistana*, Tashkent, pp. 10–34.

Rtveladze, E. V. (1974): Razvedochnoe izuchenie Baktriyskych pamyatnikov na yuge Uzbekistana, in: Masson, Vadim Michailovich, ed., *Drevnyaya Baktriya*, pp. 74–85. Leningrad: Nauka.

Stančo, L. (2009): The activities in Uzbekistan in the 2008 season: testing the Google Earth programme as a tool for archaeological prospecting. *Studia Hercynia* XIII, pp. 115–122.

Staviskiy, B. Ya. (1976): O severnykh rubezhakh Kushanskoy Baktrii, in: *Istroriya i kul'tury narodov Sredney Azii*. Moskva.

Staviskiy, B. Ya. (1977): *K yugu ot zheleznykh vorot*. Moskva.

Tomaschek, W. (1877): *Zentralasiatische Studien, Centralasiatische Studien I. Sogdiana*, Wien.

# 1.3 Jandavlattepa: complete bibliography (– 07/2010)

Abdullaev, K. – Boháč, L. – Stančo, L. (2003): Arkheo-logicheskie raboty na Dzhandavlattepa Sherabadskogo rayona Surkhandarinskoy oblasti, in: Arkheologicheski-ye Issledovaniya v Uzbekistane 2002 god, pp. 15–20.

Abdullaev, K. – Stančo, L. (2003): Djandavlattepa: Prelim-inary report of the 2002 excavation season. *Studia Her-cynia* VII, 165–168.

Abdullaev, K. – Stančo, L. (2004): Arkheologicheskie raboty na Dzhandavlattepa, in: *Arkheologicheskiye Issle-dovaniya v Uzbekistane 2003 god*, pp. 19–25.

Abdullaev, K. – Stančo, L. (2004b): Jandavlattepa: Prelim-inary report of the 2003 excavation season. *Studia Her-cynia* VIII, 156–160.

Abdullaev, K. – Stančo L. (2004c): Excavation of Jandav-lattepa, Sherabad District, Northern Bactria. *Circle of Inner Asia Art* 19/2004: 3–10.

Abdullaev, K. – Stančo, L. (2005): Jandavlattepa: Prelimin-ary report of the 2004 excavation season. *Studia Her-cynia* IX, pp. 273–275.

Abdullaev, K. – Stančo, L. (2006): Arkheologicheskie raboty na Dzhandavlattepa v 2004–2005 gg. Sherabad-skiy rayon Surkhandarinskoy oblasti, in: *Arkheologic-heskiye Issledovaniya v Uzbekistane 2004–2005 gody*, Tashkent, pp. 12–22.

Abdullaev, K. – Stančo, L. (2007): Jandavlattepa 2006. Preliminary excavation report. *Studia Hercynia* XI, pp. 157–159.

Abdullaev, K. – Stančo, L. (2010): Arkheologicheskie rabo-ty na Dzhandavlattepa v 2006 godu, in: *Arkheologicheski-ye Issledovaniya v Uzbekistane 2006–2007 goda*, Samar-kand, pp. 18–23.

Huff, D. (1995): An Unusual Type of Terracotta Figurine from North Bactria, in: *In the Land of Gryphones*, ed.: Invernizzi, A., Torino, pp. 269–273.

Huff, D. (1997): Deutsch-Uzbek Ausgrabungen auf dem Džandaulattepe und in Džarkutan, Süduzbekistan, 1993–1995. *Mitteilungen der Berliner Gesellschaft für Anthropologie, Ethnologie und Urgeschichte*, 18, pp. 83–95.

Huff, D. – Pidaev, Ch. – Chaydoullaev, Ch. (2001): Uzbek-German archaeological researches in the Surkhan Darya region, in: *La Bactriane au carrefour des routes et des civi-lisations de l'Asie centrale*. Actes du colloque de Termez, 1997. Paris, pp. 219–233.

Masson, V. M. (1974): Problema drevnego goroda i ark-heologicheskiye pamyatniky severnoy Baktrii, in: *Drev-nyaya Baktriya*, ed.: Masson, V. M., Leningrad, pp. 3–13.

Pidaev, Sh. P. (1973): Otkrytiye novogo pamyatnika serediny I tysyacheletiya do nashey ery. *Obshchestvennyye nauki v Uzbekistane* 11/1973, pp. 77–82.

Pidaev, Sh. P. (1974): Materialy k izucheniyu drvnikh pamyatnikov Severnoy Baktrii, in: *Drevnyaya Baktriya*, ed.: Masson, V. M., Leningrad, pp. 38–40.

Rtveladze, E. V. (1974): Razvedochnoe izuchenie Baktriys-kych pamyatnikov na yuge Uzbekistana, in: *Drevnyaya Baktriya*, ed.: Masson, V. M., Leningrad, pp. 74–85.

Rtveladze, E. V. (1982): Ob areale i chronologii sasan-idskich zavoyevanii v severnoy Baktrii – Tokharistane (po dannym numismatiky). *Obshchestvennyye nauki v Uzbekistane* 1/1982, pp. 47–54.

Rtveladze, E. V. – Khakimov, Z. A. (1973): Marshrutnyye issledovaniya pamyatnikov severnoy Baktrii, in: *Iz istorii antichnoy kul'tury Uzbekistana*, ed. Pugachenkova, G. A., Tashkent, pp. 10–34.

Schachner, A. (1995/1996): A Special Kind of Pattern Bur-nished Decoration on Late Kushan Pottery in Bactria and Afghanistan. *SRAA* 4, 151–159.

Schachner, A. (2003–2004): Die Keramik der Grabungen 1993 am Džandavlattepe, Süd-Uzbekistan. *Archäologi-sche Mitteilungen aus Iran und Turan* 35–36, 335–372.

Stančo, L. (2003): Džandavláttepa – Předběžná zpráva o archeologickém výzkumu v roce 2002, in: *Orientalia Antiqua Nova* III, 121–124 (Czech).

Stančo, L. (2005): Současná archeologie severní Baktrie. *Auriga* XLVII, 54–64 (Czech).

Stančo, L. (2006a): Antropomorfně zdobený džbánek z Džandavláttepa. *Studia Hercynia* X, pp. 106–110 (Czech).

Stančo, L. (2006b): Pozdně antická severní Baktrie, in: *Orientalia Antiqua Nova* VI, ed. Pecha, L. VI, pp. 73–78 (Czech).

Stančo, L. et alii (2006): Jandavlattepa 2005. Preliminary excavation report. *Studia Hercynia* X, pp. 167–172.

# 2. Excavations

## Methods

Our expedition explored the Jandavlattepa site using standard archaeological excavation methods. Emphasis was placed on detailed analysis of individual archaeological features, a gentle approach and above all on precise primary documentation, with a view to interpreting the results as correctly as possible and to the planned publication of a complete context database (see below). The settlement site was thus explored using square trenches of 4 by 4 metres, for ease of producing drawn documentation to a scale of 1:20. The areas explored were analysed layer by layer. Walls of unfired brick were largely left *in situ*, and were only taken apart in a very few well-founded cases. Given limited financial resources and the difficulty of using them when on site, we were unfortunately unable to use some natural science methods that would have improved our knowledge of the site still further. In particular, this concerns the collection of ecofacts. When there were clear organic remains in the layers, samples were taken, but they have not yet been further analysed.

## Labelling system for the sectors explored

The areas (sectors) explored were labelled using ordinal numbers, to aid orientation in documentation, contexts and finds. These labels have no internal order, and do not correspond, for example, to the network of squares. They were allotted during the first season that we worked on the site, and followed from the numbering given to the exploratory trenches by a previous German-Uzbek team, so that there would be no confusion. The geodesic measurement of the site took place later, and the labelling of the areas stayed the same. Originally, too, the individual numbers always referred to one – usually square – trench. If a sector had more than one square, each was labelled with a letter in addition to the number, and more numbers were added later. For example, *Sector 07* was originally opened as just one exploratory trench, later labelled 07A, to which were later added Squares 07B, 07C, 07D and 07E – located in a series – while parallel rows of Squares were labelled 09, 10, 11 and 12, plus letters. They all form, however, part of sector 07.

Essentially, then, our expedition explored seven sectors: 02a, 04, 06, 07, 08, 20 (fig. 1) and 30. Sector numbers beginning with 0, or squares with labels beginning with 0 or 1, are situated in the Shakhristan, while numbers beginning with a 2 indicate squares in the Citadel. A 3 at the start indicates an area outside the *tepa* itself.

## Documentation system – codes

To describe contexts, finds and ceramics, and for ordering and classifying, we use a simple coding method, set up in such a way so that it can be used to create a database. The codes are above all spatial indicators, so that it is possible to read from the code the precise location of the given unit. The code is used both in its full form and (more often) in its shortened form. In its full form the code might look like this: "Džt04.20C002.4." Džt is an abbreviation of the Czech transliteration of the name of the site, while 04 indicates the year 2004. The subsequent data is part of the shortened code: 20C is the number of the square/trench, and 002 is the ordinal number of the context in that square. Finally, the last figure is the ordinal number of the fragment of ceramic vessel in that context. Usually only the shortened code "20C002" will be used for the context, maybe with an indicator in the form of an Arabic numeral for ceramics and a Roman numeral for other small finds. The context code may also be accompanied by a letter "c" or –"f," the former specifying the context as a building construction – i.e. a wall, floor, pavement and so on, the latter any sort of hollow feature, i.e. cuts such as a construction cut, a moat, a supply or waste pit and, of course, a grave pit.

## Database

The primary data was continuously documented using a system of forms, which were then transferred into electronic form. This created a database that contained, as far as possible, all the available data on archaeological contexts, ceramics and small finds from the Czech part of exploration of Jandavlattepa. As this publication is being prepared, work on the database is also being completed. After conversion into GIS form the database will be published online. Our aim is that it should contain information – above all, primary, descriptive information – on all the features and artefacts from the site. The database's penetrable system will allow it to be further added to and expanded to include newly-gained knowledge (such as the planned analysis of metals and a study of human and animal bone remains). It will also be expanded to include links to literature. A similar complex publication of the data from the part of the exploration that was undertaken by Uzbek archaeologists is currently under negotiation. Current state of simple online database is accessible from http://arcis.ff.cuni.cz/.

*Ladislav Stančo*

# 2.1 Excavations in Sector 20, the so-called "Citadel"[1]

*Ladislav Stančo*

The Citadel is situated in the north-western spur of the site and represents also its highest point (378.4 m above sea level). It is only part of Jandavlattepa, which is separated from the main body of the tepa by a shallow depression (fig. 2.1, *1*). This separation was not formed by secondary erosive processes caused by seasonal rain and wind, but was created intentionally by human activities. The ground plan of the Citadel resembles a trapezoid. The slopes of the Citadel are quite steep and very difficult to climb (fig. 2.1, *2*). The surface area of the summit measures slightly more than 900 m², the base of the mound including the depression about 6100 m². The Citadel was strongly affected by erosion. Therefore, no architectural remains were initially visible on the surface. However, the north-central part of the summit was slightly raised compared to the rest. For the local herdsmen, it is so far the best point from which they can keep an eye on their flocks.

## 2.1.1 The excavations

The first archaeological investigation of the Citadel was undertaken in 1993 by a German-Uzbek

**Fig. 2.1, 1** Jandavlattepa with the Citadel on the left, view from west, photo L. Stančo.

team. One trial trench (marked as S3 – Schnitt 3) was opened in the south-central part of the site and was shaped like a prolonged rectangle oriented from southeast to northwest. Some means of communication between Citadel and Shakhristan (a bridge or causeway) had been expected in this place.[2] Unfortunately, the results of those digs were never fully published. Thus, we have only a vague statement that *"auf dem Zitadellenhügel wurden die Reste eines kleinen islmischen Heiligtums angeschnitten, das auf starken Aschenschichten, wahrscheinlich von Signalfeuern herrührend, steht, beides neuzeitliche Kulturschichten. Darunter kam eine kushanzeitliche Bebauung mit Lehm-*

**Fig. 2.1, 2** Citadel of Jandavlattepa, view from north, photo L. Stančo.

---

1  We have borrowed this term from Russian although its meaning in English is linked exclusively with fortification. The real functions were various and changed over time, see Conclusion below in this chapter.
2  Huff – Pidaev – Chaydoullaev 2001, p. 219.

**Fig. 2.1, 3** Progress of the excavations on Citadel (Sector 20), September 2004, photo L. Stančo.

*ziegelwänden zutage, in der Vorratsgefässe, Spinnwirtel, Steingeräte und einige Münzen gefunden wurden."*[3] Quite recently, an article has appeared devoted to the pottery from these digs.[4]

The Czech-Uzbekistani team investigated this important part of the tepa during the 2004 season and worked there also in 2005 and 2006. The research lasted, all in all, for 55 working days (2004 – 14 days, 2005 – 25 days, and 2006 – 16 days). Four Czech archaeologists took part in the excavations: Ladislav Stančo (head of the team, 2004–2006), Kristýna Urbanová (2004, 2005), Petra Belaňová (2005, 2006) and Jan Kysela (2005, 2006). Ten to fifteen local workers supported us in the fieldwork. Besides the people mentioned above, who are responsible for primary documentation in the field, both drawings of sections and plans and photography, large group of students of Classical Archaeology in Prague help to digitize the drawings in frame of school subject "Archaeological practice" from 2006 to 2010.

The reasons for the choice of this research objective are obvious from the description above. The Citadel is a prominent part of the site, being compact and clearly defined. We expected the existence of a prominent building or at least a simpler or rather more coherent building development than we had run into in the lower town. The information we had from the German-Uzbek trench was not satisfactory. Hence, it was decided to proceed in a different way.

**Excavation progress**[5]

Our original aim was to uncover the external walls of any building from the last stage of regular occupation and to gain some chronologically sensitive material for classifying the site. Thus, we opened three parallel squares (20C, 20D, 20E) on the northeastern edge of the summit (fig. 2.1, 3). The trenches were actually not proper squares but rectangles and measured 3 × 4 m. We could not start with regular squares, as we had done, because of the steep slope of the Citadel, since the difference in height between the western

and eastern sections would have been too great. Between the trenches we left baulks, each 1 m wide. The depths of the squares varied between 1 and 2 m.

The results of these trial digs were so interesting and successful that four other "squares" in the same line (20B, 20F, 20G, 20H) were subsequently opened in the same season in order to uncover all the eastern edge of the Citadel (fig. 2.1, 4).

The remains of the monumental external wall were found in five of these seven squares (except 20B and 20H). Moreover, behind another control block to the west, a second row of trenches was opened (20N, 20R) at the same time. This second row consisted of proper squares 4 × 4 m, which was completed the next season (2005) by opening squares 20O, 20P (only the eastern half), 20Q and 20S (only the eastern half). Several baulks or parts of such were removed in order to make some situations clear (the baulks between 20R and 20S, 20R and 20G, 20S and 20H, 20Q and 20P). At the same time, two more squares (20Y and 20Z) were excavated further to the west, creating the third row. As we found the remains of the northern external wall of the building in squares 20N and 20Y, we continued digging, following its direction to the west. Thus, Squares 21D, 21O and 21P were opened in 2006. Parts of the northern wall were traced in all these squares. Another question, the inner disposition of the building, we tried to resolve by opening Squares 21E, 21F (see the general ground plan). Altogether we worked in 20 squares (or half-squares) and examined a total surface area of 312 m², which is approximately one third of the Citadel's summit surface (fig. 2.1, 5).

**Fig. 2.1, 4** Progress of the excavations on Citadel (Sector 20), October 2004, photo L. Stančo.

## 2.1.2 Description of the archaeological situation

As was already stated above, the Citadel is a quite compact formation. The archaeological situation will be shortly described as a whole here, and subsequent

---

3  Huff 1997, p. 84.
4  Schachner 2003–2004.
5  The detailed description of the excavation progress in this sector, square by square, see below in this chapter.

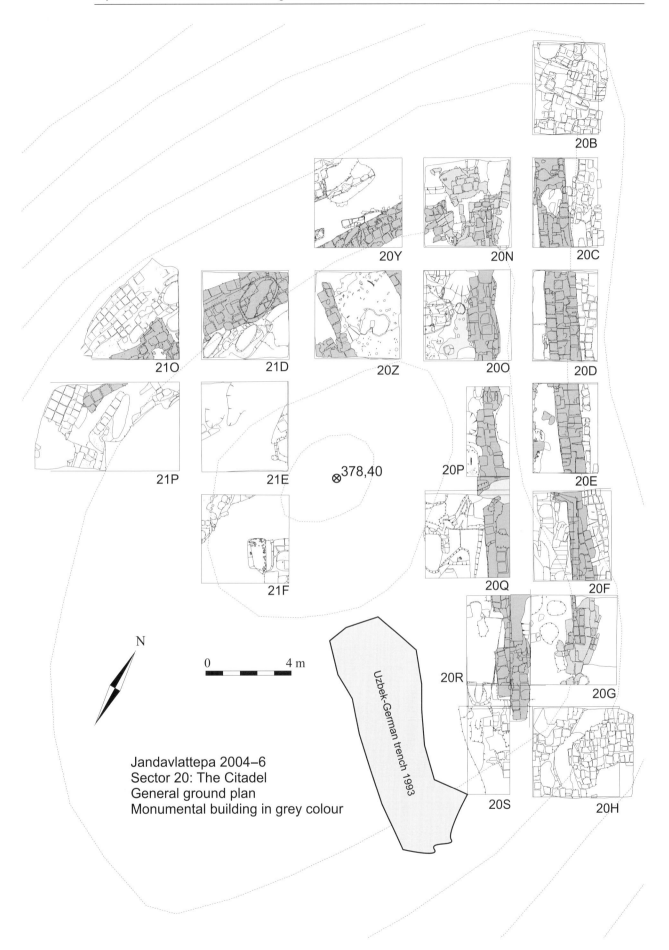

20B

20Y

20N

20C

21O

21D

20Z

20O

20D

21P

21E

⊗378,40

20P

20E

21F

20Q

20F

N

0          4 m

20R

20G

Jandavlattepa 2004–6
Sector 20: The Citadel
General ground plan
Monumental building in grey colour

Uzbek-German trench 1993

20S

20H

**Fig. 2.1, 5** Sector 20 – general ground plan of the excavations of the monumental building.

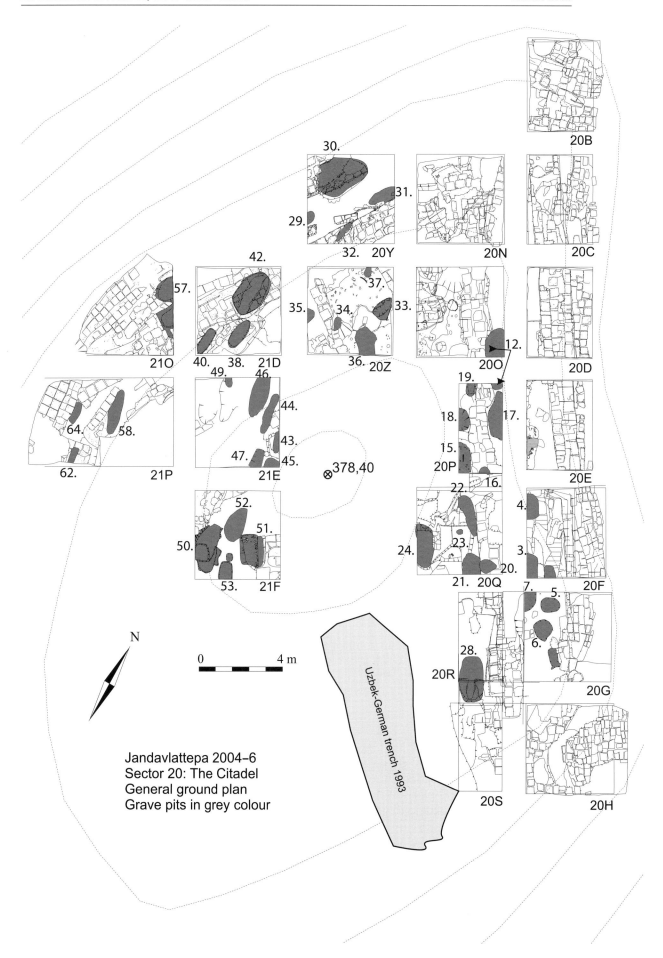

N

0       4 m

Jandavlattepa 2004–6
Sector 20: The Citadel
General ground plan
Grave pits in grey colour

**Fig. 2.1,6** Sector 20 – general ground plan with modern-time grave pits.

chapters will discuss some special features found in single squares. This chapter is intended as an exact factual description of the situation. For our general interpretations see the last subheading "Conclusion."

## 2.1.2.1 Surface layer

The entire surface of the Citadel is covered with an eroding surface layer. Its thickness varies between several cm on the slopes and about 20 cm on the summit. A detailed survey showed several thin constituent layers of this stratum, but there is no need to deal with them separately, as they originated through identical processes, by the regular influence of heavy seasonal rains. As the soil and human artefacts in the stratum were gradually removed by the rain and were mixed up, we use finds from this layer only for typological comparisons or simple presence/absence examination of these items on the site, but not for the purpose of chronology. Although this layer was the uppermost, several younger features were also found, especially grave pits (see below). The soil consistency was dusty and loose, with a colour that was grey to greyish-brown, depending on the measure of desiccation. Surface layers comprise all contexts labelled with a code ending in 001: 20B001, 20C001, 20D001, 20E001, 20F001, 20G001, 20H001, 20N001, 20O001, 20P001, 20Q001, 20R001, 20S001, 20Y001, 20Z001, 21D001, 21E001, 21F001, 21O001, 21P001, 21P(z)001.

## 2.1.2.2 Grave pits

Like the Shakhristan, the Citadel summit is covered by dozens of grave pits, connected with the use of the *tepa* as a graveyard in modern and maybe also in late medieval times (fig. 2.1, 6). However, unlike the Shakhristan, the Citadel has not been used for this purpose recently. Still, the local people, at least the older generation, consider the summit of the Citadel to be some sort of sacred place with the tomb of an *imam* (leader of a mosque and the community in Islamic society). The description given by the German-Uzbek team (see above) may be given to this structure,

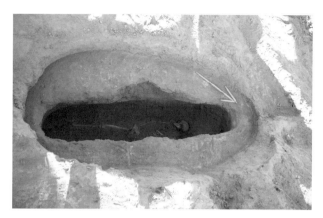

Fig. 2.1,8 Grave pit of the type P2 (double), context no. 21P003/004f, photo J. Kysela.

but we can neither confirm nor refute the existence of such a tomb or even shrine, as we left the central highest point untouched. Our reasons for this were practical rather than pious since we needed to preserve a permanent measuring point exactly on this spot.

We identified basically two main types of grave pits. The first could be called a primary (P) grave, the second one a secondary (S) or "careless" grave. The primary grave pits were those typical of local Muslim funeral rites. Among them we could distinguish two separate groups. The first is a simple pit – P1 (tab. 2.1, 1:3; fig. 2.1, 7; fig. 2.1, 67).

The second – P2 (fig. 2.1, 8) is a double pit of the same sort as most of the graves on the Shakhristan, i.e. upper shallow, wide pit and lower deeper, narrow pit. Both of them are oriented more or less from south (legs) to north (head) with the face of the deceased turned to the west or southwest, to Mecca. The depths of the pits are various. Some of them are quite shallow, down to 50 cm, while the other pits are almost 2 m deep. As a rule, no offerings were deposited in the graves. Sometimes several potsherds were found in the soil filling the pit, but they are certainly of earlier date and have nothing in common with the graves.

The second type is of a different nature. These graves actually had no proper pits but are only small, shallow hollows with unclear outlines. The term "secondary" grave refers to the second inhumation of previously

Fig. 2.1,7 Grave pit of the type P1 (simple), context no. 20Y011/20Y012f, photo J. Kysela.

Fig. 2.1,9 Grave pit of the type S (secondary), context no. 21F006/007f, photo J. Kysela.

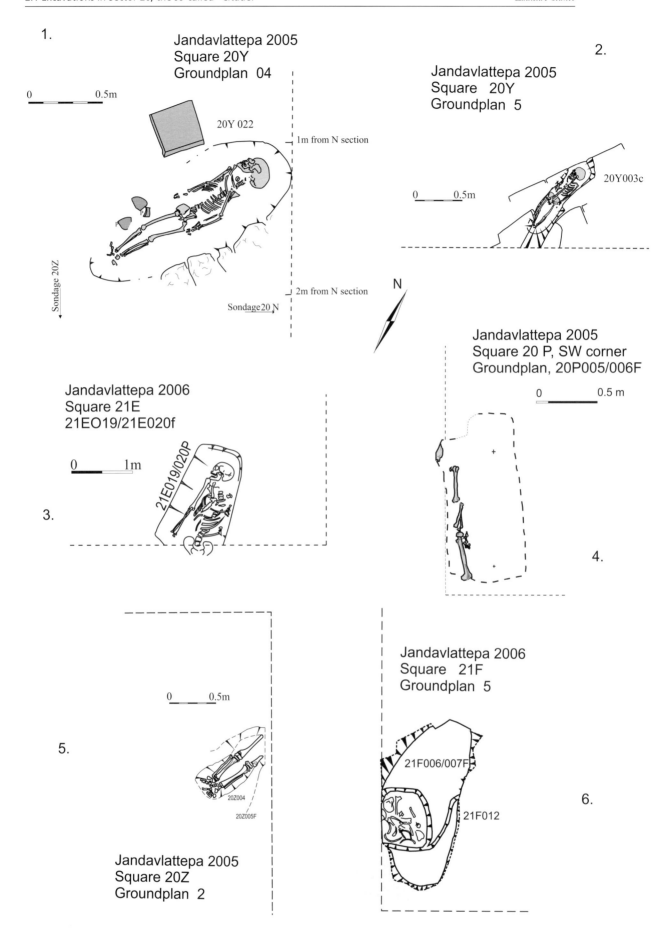

1.

Jandavlattepa 2005
Square 20Y
Groundplan 04

0        0.5m

20Y 022

1m from N section

2m from N section

Sondage 20Z

Sondage20 N

2.

Jandavlattepa 2005
Square  20Y
Groundplan  5

0        0.5m

20Y003c

N

Jandavlattepa 2005
Square 20 P, SW corner
Groundplan, 20P005/006F

0          0.5 m

Jandavlattepa 2006
Square 21E
21EO19/21E020f

0        1m

21E019/020P

3.

4.

5.

0        0.5m

20Z004

20Z005F

Jandavlattepa 2005
Square 20Z
Groundplan  2

Jandavlattepa 2006
Square  21F
Groundplan  5

21F006/007F

21F012

6.

**Tab. 2.1, 1:** 1. Ground plans of selected grave contexts in sector 20, drawing by J. Kysela (1-3, 6), K. Urbanová (4, 5).

## Description of the graves

| no. | context filling / pit | length upper / lower | width upper / lower | depth | orientation | type | note |
|---|---|---|---|---|---|---|---|
| 1. | 20E003 and 20E007/20E008f | 2.0 | 0.8 | 0.6 * | south – north | P | excavated only upper part of the filling |
| 2. | 20E018/20E019f | --- | --- | --- | --- | S | unclear |
| 3. | 20F005/20F009f | 1.2 | 0.6 | 0.6 * | south – north | P | excavated only upper part of the filling |
| 4. | 20F010/20F011f | --- | 0.9 | 0.4 | --- | P | partly excavated, visible in western section |
| 5. | 20F012/20F013f 20G006/20G007f | 0.4** 1.0** 2.4 | 0.76 1.0 | 0.8* 0.7* | south – north south-southeast – north-northwest | P | excavated only upper part of the filling; reconstructed length 2.4 m |
| 6. | 20G004/20G005f | 1.1 | 0.96 | ---* | --- | P1 | |
| 7. | 20G011/20G012f | 1.0** | 0.6** | 0.8* | --- | P1 | |
| 8. | 20H003/20H004f | 1.15 | 0.7 | ---* | south-southeast – north-northwest | P1 | |
| 9. | 20N006/20N007f | 2.1 | 0.6 | 1.1 | south-southeast – north-northwest | P1 | |
| 10. | 20N010/20N011f | --- | --- | --- | --- | P1 | unclear shape |
| 11. | 20N012/20N013f | 0.65** | 1.0 | 0.7* | --- | P1 | uncertain |
| 12. | 20O004/20N005f 20P017/20P018f | 1.2** 0.2** 2.4 | 0.6** 0.4** | 0.6* 1.0* | south-southeast – north-northwest | P | reconstructed length 2.4 m |
| 13. | 20O006/20O007f | 2.2 | 0.7 | 0.7* | south-southeast – north-northwest | P1 | lower part covered by a matting |
| 14. | 20O011/20O012f | 1.55 | 1.0 | 0.9 | --- | P1 | irregular shape |
| 15. | 20P005/20P006f | 1.4** | 0.65** | 0.4* | south-southeast – north-northwest | P2 | piece of wood covered lower part of grave (<0.3 m) – bier? tab. 2.1, 1:4 |
| 16. | 20P010/20P011f 20Q014/20P015f | 0.3** 0.42 | 0.54 0.4 | 0.18 0.1 | south – north --- | P1 | reconstructed length 1.72 m |
| 17. | 20P012/20P013f | 2.2 | 0.7** | 0.7* | south-southeast – north-northwest | P | |
| 18. | 20P015/20P016f | 1.0** | 0.5 | 0.28* | --- | P | |
| 19. | 20P019/20P020f | 0.6** | 0.48 | 0.22 | south-southeast – north-northwest | P | |
| 20. | 20Q004/20P005f | 0.8 | 0.7 | --- | --- | S | |
| 21. | 20Q006/20Q007f | 1.16** | 0.8 | 0.6 | south-southeast – north-northwest | P1 | |
| 22. | 20Q009/20Q010f | 2.1 | Max. 0.7 | 0.3 | south-southeast – north-northwest | P1 | fig. 2.1, 67 |
| 23. | 20Q020/20Q021f | 0.3 | 0.26 | 0.1 | --- | S | |
| 24. | 20Q022/20Q023f | 2.1 | 0.9 | 1.0 | south-southeast – north-northwest | P1 | |
| 25. | 20Q031/20Q032f | --- | --- | --- | --- | S | unclear pit |
| 26. | 20R007/20R008f | 0.6 | 0.4 | 0.2 | southeast – northwest | P1 | shallow pit, resembles a secondary grave |
| 27. | 20R009/20R010f | --- | --- | --- | --- | S | unclear pit with a careless child grave, probably secondary |
| 28. | 20R012/20R013f | 2.2/1.5 | 1.2/0.36 | 0.55+ 0.22 | south – north | P2 | southern part of the pit unearthed in control block 20R/S |
| 29. | 20Y005/20Y006f | 0.6** | 0.42 | --- | --- | P1 | |

| no. | context filling / pit | length upper / lower | width upper / lower | depth | orientation | type | note |
|-----|----------------------|---------------------|---------------------|-------|-------------|------|------|
| 30. | 20Y007/20Y008f | 2.2/065 | 1/0.42 | --- | southwest – northeast | P2 | lower pit marked as context 20Y017/018f |
| 31. | 20Y011/20Y012f | 1.5 | 0.6 | Min. 0.4 | south – north | P1 | tab. 2.1, 1:1 |
| 32. | 20Y023/20Y024f | 0.95 | 0.4 | 0.2 | south – north | P1 | tab. 2.1, 1:2; fig. 2.1, 7. |
| 33. | 20Z004/20Z005f | 0.6** | 0.3 | 0.1 | south – north | P1 | tab. 2.1, 1:5 |
| 34. | 20Z008/20Z009f | 0.3 | 0.22 | 0.1 | --- | S | |
| 35. | 20Z011/20Z012f | 0.6** | 0.6 | | | | |
| 36. | 20Z013/20Z014f | 1.3** | 0.6 | 0.1** | southeast - northwest | P1 | |
| 37. | 20Z015/20Z016f | 0.5** | 0.35 | 0.15 | south-southeast – north-northwest | P1 | |
| 38. | 21D002/21D003f | 2.8/2.0 | 1.3/0.6 | 1.5 | south – north | P2 | |
| 39. | 21D009/21D010f | 0.28** | 1.2 | 0.7 | --- | P1?? | |
| 40. | 21D020/21D021f | --/0.75** | --/0.42 | 0.45 | south – north | P2 | |
| 41. | 21D023/21D024f | 0.4** | 0.64 | 0.36 | --- | P1 | |
| 42. | 21D025/21D026f | 2.16/2.1 | 1.16/0.46 | 0.66+0.42 | south – north | P2 | |
| 43. | 21E002/21E003f | 1.0 | 0.3** | 0.3 | --- | P1 | child grave |
| 44. | 21E004/21E005f | 1.9 | 0.4 | 0.7 | south – north | P1 | pieces of wood and textiles covered the pit |
| 45. | 21E007/21E008f | 0.7** | 0.4** | 0.6 | --- | P1 | |
| 46. | 21E010/21E011f | 1.8 | 0.9 | 0.65 | south-southeast – north-northwest | P1 | |
| 47. | 21E019/21E020f | 0.9** | 1.1 | 0.7 | south – north | P1 | tab. 2.1, 1:3 |
| 48. | 21E021/21E022f | 0.45 | 0.35 | 0.12 | --- | S | fig. 2.1, 93 |
| 49. | 21E031/21E032f | 0.4** | 0.34 | 0.2* | southeast – northwest | P1 | |
| 50. | 21F006/21F007f | 2.24/0.8 | 1.15/0.6 | 0.54+0.2 | south-southeast – north-northwest | P2 | tab. 2.1, 1:6; fig. 2.1, 9 |
| 51. | 21F010/21F011f | 2.2/1.24 | 1.26/0.82 | 0.58+0.63 | south-southeast – north-northwest | P2 | |
| 52. | 21F016/21F017f | 1.44 | 0.78 | 0.16 | south – north | P1 | simple child grave |
| 53. | 21F021/21F022f | 0.94** | 0.76 | 0.56 | south-southeast – north-northwest | P1 | simple child grave |
| 54. | 21F026/21F027f | 1.04** | 0.1** | 0.48 | south-southeast – north-northwest | P1 | |
| 55. | 21F028/21F029f | 0.96 | 0.6 | 0.1 | south – north | P1 | simple child grave |
| 56. | 21F030/21F031f | 0.56 | 0.4 | 0.1 | --- | S | |
| 57. | 21O007/21O008f | 0.9** | 1.1 | 0.4* | south – north | P1 | |
| 58. | 21P003/21P004f | 2.4/2.16 | 1.34/0.7 | 0.6+0.3 | south – north | P2 | fig. 2.1, 8 |
| 59. | 21P009/21P010f | 0.56**/0.3** | 0.8/0,4 | 0.2/--* | south-southeast – north-northwest | P2 | |
| 60. | 21P011/21P012f | 0.94**/--- | 0.5**/--- | 0.2*/--- | --- | P2 | pieces of wood covered the pit |
| 61. | 21P020/21P021f | 1.06** | 0.52** | 0.4 | south-southeast – north-northwest | P1 | |
| 62. | 21P(z)002/21P(z)003f | 0.63** | 0.35 | 0.18 | south – north | P1 | |
| 63. | 21P(z)007/21P(z)008f | 1.5** | --- | 0.7* | south – north | P2 | |
| 64. | 21P(z)010/21P(z)011f | 1.04 | 0.4 | --- | south – north | P1 | |

\* measured to the level reached not to the actual bottom of the pit

\*\* measured only excavated part, incomplete

buried and again dug out remains (fig. 2.1, *9*). It probably happened in cases when grave-diggers found older graves and did not want or were not allowed to stop digging, and so went on, dug out the remains and buried them in a disorderly manner somewhere else. On that account, the secondary graves usually contained only small amounts of bones not complete skeletons.

Very similar to the secondary graves were also some child graves. They were shallow and irregular as though dug out in a hurry. Most likely there were not any funeral rites performed.

Regardless, it was not a rule since we know regular child graves from both the Citadel and the Shakhristan.

Many grave pits were not fully uncovered because our aim was to clarify the ground plan of the ancient building not to search the modern graves. Thus, we basically uncovered those pits that were placed in appointed areas to be excavated deeper in general. Therefore, in some cases, we were not sure whether the pit was actually a grave or not. These examples are included here because all the external features were in accordance with the characteristics of the known graves. Due to the excavation strategy, which focused on the larger structures (i.e. buildings not graves) their measurements are not complete (especially the length, sometimes the width).

Since a special chapter devoted to the study of all anthropological material from Jandavlattepa is intended to be included in the second volume of the excavation report, the characteristics of the remains are omitted here.

An interesting picture is provided by simply counting the grave pits in the various parts of the area excavated (squares). The largest number of grave hollows – seven – is found in squares 20Q, 21E and 21F. There are also seven in trench 21P, but this is of course two metres longer. In the excavated half of square 20P there were six, and five each in the neighbouring squares, 20Z and 21D. In 20Z there were only four graves. Several squares had three grave pits: 20F, 20G, 20N, 20O and 20R. In 20E there were two, while squares 20H and 21O had one each. There were no grave pits at all in squares 20B, 20C, 20D and 20S. These totals clearly show that that there was a marked concentration of graves in the central part, around the highest point of the elevation, in other words around the supposed imam's grave. This would correspond to local tradition, since it was said here to be propitious to bury the dead as close as possible to the holy man's grave.

### 2.1.2.3 Destruction layers

Below the surface layer, layers of loose to medium-settled soil with many fragments of mud-bricks usually appeared. Depending on the steepness of the slope these two layers were more or less intermingled.

The low quality of building materials and techniques used added to the substantial damage of the architectural remains. As most parts of the walls fell down the slopes of the Citadel, the destruction layers related to the last building phase are quite thin.

**2.1.2.3.1**    The most obvious destruction layer was that which formed the upper part of the preserved walls. It originated due to wind and frost erosion after the collapse of the upper walls but before the sedimentation of the surface layer, in other words, in the period when the remains of the walls were exposed and probably visible above the surface. There are no finds in these layers except for the accidental items mixed in the mud-brick material itself.

**2.1.2.3.2**    Surprisingly, we rarely encountered layers of fallen walls or bricks. The reason for this was already mentioned above, being that most parts of the buildings (at least of the last building phase) fell down from the Citadel or were gradually washed away. Examples of fallen walls are those of contexts 20D008c and 20O020.

**2.1.2.3.3**    Very interesting layers of lightweight but strangely cohesive soil.

Over a large part of the area uncovered in the Citadel we found a characteristic filling that was appeared at various levels, although none of them high above the floor of the last phase of construction. It comprised a single layer, atlthough in some parts it was composed of a group of layers, of which the individual components were very similar to each other. In terms of colour, it was dominated by white to whitish-grey, with an ochre to ochre-brown admixture. During analysis, the material in these layers divided into largish bits and areas that did not crumble or fall apart, and were remarkably light. Many of the macro admixtures were reminiscent of the straw used as opening material in bricks. Even without chemical analysis, it was clear that this was a deposit with a notable component of organic material. An explanation of how it came to be there is more a matter of interpretation. It may be the remains of collapsed ceilings or roof coverings, made, in the local tradition, of wooden circles, sticks, reeds and other plant material, smeared with clay. The connection with collapsed ceilings is accentuated by the

**Fig. 2.1, 10** Level of the Floor. no. 1 and the deposits of an organic character, Square 20E, photo L. Stančo.

fact that this layer is found together with burnt layers. These are above all layers 20C011, 20D002, 20E002, 20F002, 20F004 and 20Q011. An example of the situation in square 20E (fig. 2.1, *10*) shows the relationship between the level of the floor (Floor. no. 1, see below) and the deposits of an organic character that are described here. The spatial border here is at a level of 375.90 m, above sea level, while 5 m to the north in square 20E it is between 375.80 and 375.90 m.

### 2.1.2.4 Layers of ash or burned soil

Layers with an abundance of cinders and ash or layers of burnt soil occur in several places in the Citadel, and are a reflection of several independent phenomena. The most numerous group of layers of which fire played a role in the creation and character is found in the immediate surroundings of the highest point of the elevation. These are contexts 20Q013, 20Q017, 20Q018, 21E015, 21E017, 21E024, 21E028, 21F002 and 21F013. Context 20Q013 can be identified with 21E015 and 21F013, and others are certainly also connected. It is not clear how this group of layers was created. Regular burning (probably of wood) must have played a part, with longish intervals between the burnings (the interlayers are relatively marked). The burning took place over a considerable area, at least 5 × 3 m. This phenomenon occurs only a few decimetres under the surface; in other words, it is a relatively recent affair, probably from the mediaeval, or, even more likely, the modern era. The same is true of the burnt layer 20R002 with cinders and grains of corn, and of other layers of a similar nature in the same square, 20R006 and 2R016 (more of an admixture of larger cinders). The character of the burnt and compacted layers in squares 20O and 20Z is of an entirely different nature. This is above all contexts 20O13c, 20O014, 20O015 and 20O19, which is identical to 20Z021. This phenomenon may have been caused by parts of ceiling constructions that collapsed during a fire, plus the subsequently burnt floor. There are also some separate and probably random phenomena, consisting of smallish deposits containing cinder and ash, such as contexts 20B003, 20C013, which is identical to 20D007, 20F003, 20P003, 21F004, 21F018 (only the bottom part of the context, undifferentiated during the excavation of a small area).

### 2.1.2.5 Architecture

The architectural remains of the last period of long-term occupation on the Citadel are rather poorly preserved. Nevertheless, it is possible to describe the general features of a monumental building or, at least, its fundaments. By chance, we found probably the best-preserved part of the building just at the very beginning of the dig. As the uncovering of this building was our primary objective, we did not endeavour to reveal much of the earlier structures. We had planned to work on a larger area but only as deep as necessary. In spite of this, traces of earlier structures were found here and there, and we gathered a considerable amount of data, encouraging our future interest.

**Building material[6]**

Among the building remains on the Citadel, three basic types of brick could be distinguished. All of them were made of clay and differed only in size, form and quality.

The **first** and most common type was a square mud-brick measuring 40 × 40 × 10 cm.[7] This size was never exact. In some cases, slightly smaller and rarely bigger mud-bricks occurred. The size varied between 38 × 38 and 41 × 41 cm. Thickness seldom reached 11 cm. The material consisted of sloppily floated clay, and the brick itself seemed to be badly, perhaps insufficiently, sun-dried. In consequence, the quality of the product was very low. We ascribe the poor state of preservation of the building partially to this scant work. Similarly, the walls made of these mud-bricks were usually of lesser quality. It was almost impossible to remove a complete, unbroken brick of this type. Consequently, the study of the brick marks is rather limited. The eroded mud-bricks were friable and looked like grit (fig. 2.1, *11*).

The **second** type was also a square mud-brick. Its size varied between 30 and 32 cm, thickness 11 to

**Fig. 2.1, 11** First type of mud-brick, Square 20N, photo L. Stančo.

---

6   For overview of typical building materials and techniques see Baimatova 2008, pp. 31–43 or Kaim 2002, pp. 17–32.
7   See Pugachenkova 1978, p. 29 for examples of utilisation of mudbricks of this (and similar) size on different sites in different periods: Ay Khanum – 4th–3rd centuries BC, Karabagtepa – 2nd century AD and other sites (Dal'verzintepa itself, Khayrabadtepa). She states, evidently correctly, that the size of the mudbrick is not sufficient for datation of given context. The mudbricks of this size (40 × 40 × 10–11 cm) occur however in case of Dal'verzintepa predominantly in contexts of 1st–2nd century AD (*Dal'verzintepe – kushanskiy gorod na yuge Uzbekistana* 1978, p. 232).

**Fig. 2.1, 12** Example of burnt-brick dated to Late Kushan period, small find no. 20Z018c.II, photo L. Stančo.

12 cm. Unlike the material of the previous type, the clay was well floated and the brick appears to have been well dried (fig. 2.1, 16 lower part). The final product was a compact, solid and cohesive mud-brick. The quality of the walls made of these mud-bricks was in accordance with the quality of the bricks themselves. If the wall was not damaged intentionally, then this second type survives in a much better condition than the first type. Even today, removing these bricks is relatively easy. We know of second hand utilization of these two-thousand-year-old mud-bricks by local people on other sites.

The **third** type is the so-called *pakhsa*, i.e. the large frustum block also made of dried clay. We cannot say much about its size, for no block of this type was ever fully uncovered on the Citadel. *Pakhsa* could be mistaken with pisé, clay-made platforms of various sizes, which were not constructed of blocks but as a whole.

Besides the three basic building blocks, we encountered also other sizes: 34–38 × 34–38 × 11 cm (walls 21P015c, 21Pz012c) and 34–35 × 34–35 × 11 cm (walls 21Pz009c, 21Pz013c).

**Fig. 2.1, 13** Example of burnt-brick dated to Middle Ages, Square 20G, photo L. Stančo.

In addition to mud-bricks, *burnt bricks* were also used although seldom. Unfortunately, none of the examples on the Citadel (found in Squares 20Z and 20Y) were found in original construction context, and we do not know much about their original use (see below details about the floor), (fig. 2.1, *12*).

One exceptional construction was found: part of a pavement made of small boulders measuring up to 20 cm (Squares 21D and 21F, see below). As only a small part of the surface was uncovered, little can be said about its original function.

**Fig. 2.1, 14** Example of burnt-brick dated to Middle Ages, Square 20Q, above the grave pit 20Q022/023f, photo L. Stančo.

A special use of burnt bricks we encountered in connection with the recent grave pits. They functioned apparently as a cover for the narrow grave shafts (there are, in other cases – especially in Shakhristan – also small boulders, sherds of storage vessels or organic material used for the same purpose). These bricks are usually smaller in size than the others (23 × 23 × 8 cm, see fig. 2.1, *13*). They seem to represent spolia from some medieval Muslim structures standing originally nearby. The burnt bricks of such size are not attested among finds from contexts prior to Middle Ages. Best examples were found in square 20G, and were connected with grave contexts 20G004/20G005f and 20G0011/20G0012f in particular. Similar situation repeated in the Sqaure 20Q, where one such brick was found above the grave no. 20Q022/023f (fig. 2.1, *14*).

**Building remains**
1. Monumental representative building (figs. 2.1, *5* and 2.1, *20*)

By its extent, it is so far the most important remnant of the building activities on the Citadel. After three seasons of excavations, a substantial part of this building can be described. The monumental building was constructed of mud-bricks of the First type: 40 × 40 × 10 cm. In addition to the poor quality of the bricks themselves, its construction was carried out carelessly as well. The outside walls consisted of three rows of mud-bricks. Between them unusually wide

**Fig. 2.1, 15** Best preserved part of the Wall "A" in Square 20D, photo L. Stančo.

gaps were left. We measured gaps up to 10 cm wide. The same clay material used for the bricks was used as a mortar. Thus, the width of the wall including two gaps reached almost 1.5 m.

We subsequently uncovered the eastern and northern section of the building. The eastern part consisted of two long walls constructed alongside each other to a length of 25 m. They created a corridor or a passageway almost 2.4 m wide (measured in Area 20E–20P, 2.3 m measured in Area 20C–20O). The easternmost wall, called "Wall A," is actually the outer wall of the building. It comprises the following contexts: 20C006c, 20D003c, 20E004c, 20F008c, and 20G003c. The inner collateral "Wall B" comprises contexts: 20N004c, 20O009c, 20P014c, 20Q003c, 20R005c, 20G010c and probably also 20H008c. The building was badly damaged as a whole but the area of the supposed south-eastern corner was worse in this respect. Here, both Walls A and B completely disappeared over the course of time.[8] In the baulk between 20S and 20H, the last (fundamental) row of mud-bricks of the latter is visible. Therefore, we cannot say much about the southern part of the monumental building, which has been extensively damaged by erosion. Thus, we were not able to uncover the ground plan of the whole building. This was even more unfortunate in the area where some kind of communication (a ramp, a bridge) between the Citadel and the lower town was expected.

The north-eastern corner was found in Square 20C in a bad state of preservation because it was damaged by two pits. From this point, the northern external "Wall C" continued to the west. Surprisingly, both

walls formed not a right but an acute angle (70°). On the northern side no collateral inner wall was found, in other words, the corridor was not planned to frame an interior. The outside northern wall was almost 20 m long, or its preserved and uncovered part at least, and its other characteristics corresponded with the eastern wall. Wall C comprises the following contexts: 20C007c, 20N008c, 20Y003c, 21D028c, 21O005c 21P014c, 21Pz005c. In Square 20N, one rare example of a brick stamp (or so-called production stamp) was also found, or more precisely a negative of a mark imprinted in the mortar, resembling the Russian letter Ж (fig. 2.1, *11* right lower corner and ground plan fig. 2.1, *57*, detail in fig. 2.1, *58*).[9]

In fact, we found only the fundaments of the monumental building. Wall A, in its best-preserved part (square 20D and 20E, see fig. 2.1, *15*), had a height of only six mud-bricks. Elsewhere, we have three, two, or only one last base row of the mud-bricks remaining of the fundaments. The same is to be said of Walls B and C. Therefore, nothing can be said about the upper constructions: windows, vaults, stairs, or a second floor with the roof of this building. The fundaments themselves were built on a substructure, which were actually the remains of older building activity (details see below, see also fig. 2.1, *16*). The preceding building was no doubt abandoned and fell into ruin some time before the construction of the monumental building.

The elevation of the footing bottom (foundation seam) of the building is most precisely established in Square 20E (375.23) for Wall A, in Squares 20Q (375.95) and 20R (376.05) for Wall B and in Squares 20Y (375.09)[10] and 21P (375.42) for Wall C. We have also some less precise figures for Wall C in Square 20N (375.35) and 21O (375.08). It is quite obvious that the fundaments of the outer walls (A and C) were placed much deeper than in the case of inner Wall B. The difference is almost 1m. The explanation is quite

**Fig. 2.1, 16** Fundaments of the Wall "A" built on a substructure – remains of older building activity, Square 20D, photo L. Stančo.

---

8   The same heppend to some parts of the "Building A" on the site of Tchingiztepa, Old Termez (its last period), which is dated similarly to the last period of occupation on the Citadel of Jandavlattepa, see Leriche – Pidaev 2007, p. 194.

9   See similar imprints after removed mudbricks within the cultic complex on Tchingiztepa, Old Termez, shaped as Greek letter Φ, Leriche – Pidaev 2007, p. 201, fig. 18. For the discussion about the purpose of these marks in the architecture of Bactria see Lecuyot – Rapin 2000 and Kaim 2000.

10  This figure was not measured at a level where the proper masonry begins but approximately 30 cm below it, where the foundations were formed like the filling of the gaps between the ruins of the earlier structures. Regular masonry appeared at an elevation of 375.35–375.40.

simple: that most of Wall B was founded on the massive substructure of an earlier pakhsa structure.

## Interior or later rebuilding?

As we had uncovered the eastern and northern walls of the building, we were interested in its inner disposition. Several squares were opened just to answer this question (20O, 20Q, 20Z, 21E and 21F). Curiously, the results of these digs made the situation rather more complicated than vice-versa. None of the discovered walls stratigraphically linked with the monumental building were not directly connected in construction with any of the Walls A, B or C. Yet, some walls could be perceived as part of the inner disposition, specifically contexts 20Z007c, 20Z017c and 20O020. First of all, the orientation of these walls was at a right angle to Wall C. Also, the bricks were of the same size and quality as those of the monumental building (42 × 42 or 42 × 41 or even 42 × 36 × 10–11 cm). Unfortunately, the proper joint of the walls did not remain. The quality of the masonry was even worse than that of the main walls and their stratigraphy testified to a rather later date. More important was the fact that Floor No. 2 (context 20O024c) stretched under the ruins of Wall 20O20, and so the floor is of an earlier construction than this. We can assume the original con-

struction of Walls "D" (20Z007c), and "E" (20Z017c, and 20O020 respectively) to be at a time after the monumental building lost its original function and its inner space was divided by several partition walls. Thus, the second building phase of the monumental building could be determined. Walls "D" and "E" together with Wall "C" form a room measuring at least 2.6 m × 4.3 m (11.18 square meters). A substantial part of this situation was uncovered in Square 20Z. Here, the best-preserved part of the floor was unearthed (see below).

In the course of the excavation, four more structures, "N" (context 21P022c), "O" (context 21P006c), "V" (context 21E033c) and "W" (context 21F028c), were found linked with this situation. All of them were located in the western part of the monumental building in Squares 21E, 21F and 21P. Here again, the common features of all these structures are those of poor quality in masonry, narrow walls, oblong shapes of the mud bricks and their atypical sizes, height and adequate or perpendicular orientation to each other.[11] It is obvious that the walls form a room measuring at least 2.75 × 4.6 m (12.65 square meters). As the dimensions, orientation, height and quality of the masonry in both cases ("Room D-E-C" and "Room N-O-V-W") are equal, we suppose that they are two parts of one period of building activity.

**Fig. 2.1, 17** Floor no. 1, Square 20E, context no. 20E006c, photo L. Stančo.

---

[11] Walls "O" and "V" go from east to west, while "N" and "W" go from south to north, i.e. are perpendicular to them.

The surface in the interior of "Room N-O-V-W" seemed to be compacted, especially in Square 21P, between the fundaments of Walls "N" and "O" (context no. 21P002). From a formal point of view, this may well have been the floor or at least its fundament.

A previous analysis of the structures inside the monumental building showed that they evidently differ from the walls of the monumental building in most general characteristics. Due to this, and due to the fact that no distinct joints of exterior walls and interior divisions were found, we suppose a successive origin of these constructions: Walls A, B and C in the first stage and Walls D, E, N, O, V and W in the second stage, after the collapse or other substantial change in the existence of the monumental building.

### The floors

As has already been stated above, the building was in a very poor state of preservation. Largely only the foundations were uncovered. Nevertheless, several fragments of floor were found in some squares.

**Floor No. 1.** Only two squares – 20E and 20F – in the eastern part revealed fragments of a floor. The larger fragment, a strip of 26–56 cm × 210 cm in the south-western corner of Square 20E, formed context 20E006c (fig. 2.1, 17). It is, however, of very poor quality, being a compacted limy surface mixed with potsherds. This floor was damaged by some pits (20E008f and 20E009f). The elevation of this floor varied between 375.80 and 375.92. Another frag-

ment of the floor was found in the north-western corner of Square 20E at an elevation of 375.75. The low quality of its construction led us initially to suppose that this floor was built later than the building itself. We assumed we had here the level of the late period of utilization of the Citadel. This guess was proved unsubstantial by the following excavations. Compared to the low quality of mud-bricks and masonry with respect to a larger part of the floor in Square 20Z, we now believe that this could easily be a fragment of the original floor of the building, more accurately of the corridor between Walls A and B.

A second fragment of the same floor was found in a similar position in the next square, 20F, and is marked with context number 20F006c (fig. 2.1, 50). Its size was 20–30 × 140 cm and elevation varies between 375.98 and 376.11. Like in Square 20E, here a small part of it was also unearthed in the north-western corner (10–20 × 48 cm), in this case at elevation 375.97–375.99.

**Floor No. 2.** By its extent (280 × 40–180 cm)[12], a far more important fragment of floor was uncovered in Squares 20Z and 20O. The best-preserved fragment of this floor is context 20Z018c in the centre of the northern half of Square 20Z (fig. 2.1, 18). The floor here was constructed of two layers: the lower was made of compacted pottery fragments (mainly of storage pot shards) and the upper of fine clay. Most of the pottery consisted of rims of storage pots (pithoi or s.c. "*khumcha*")[13] with shapes

**Fig. 2.1, 18** Floor no. 2, Square 20Z, context no. 20Z018c, photo L. Stančo.

---

[12] Including only the main part of the floor with a pottery shard layer and excluding those parts without it.
[13] Cf. similar situation which was encountered in the R-6 trench of the site of Zartepa, see Zav'yalov 2008, p. 42 and ris. 8.

typical of the 4th century AD. They help to broadly date the construction of the building. The sizes of the fragments are very different, with the biggest rim of a storage jar being a length of 40 cm. Two complete bricks and one fragmentary baked brick were found on the surface of the floor. They did not make up any apparent construction and we cannot say for what purpose they were actually used. They measure 32 × × 32 × 4 cm. One could imagine that they were originally part of the pavement in this room, but a question mark must be placed after this statement. The level of the shards was at elevation 376.16 – 376.18. The backed bricks were placed directly on it (elevation 376.18 – 376.21).

The second part of the same floor was unearthed in adjoining Square 20O and was marked as context 20O024c. Its surface measured 45–110 × 320 cm in the best-preserved area, but this floor probably covered almost all the western half of Square 20O originally. The elevation of the lower shard layer corresponded very well with that of 20Z018c and varied between 376.11 and 376.15.

In both squares, the floor was burned by an extensive fire. In addition, the layers above the floor exhibited traces of heavy fire. Several explanations for this situation could be put forth. Perhaps a burning roof fell on the ground at the time of a violent destruction of the building complex.

**Floor No. 3**. A third area with a floor connected with the monumental building was found in the north-eastern corner of Square 20Q and subsequently in the baulk between 20Q and 20P. Unlike the previous examples, this one (20Q035c) was constructed in a different way. No traces of a lower pottery shard layer were documented here. This fragment of floor consisted only of a thin layer of lime-wash and measured 40–140 × 110 cm. It descended slightly eastwards to a presumed opening or doorway in Wall B (20Q003c). Its elevation in the western part was 376.30, while in the eastern end, close to the eastern section, only 376.18. Either this decline was intentional or arose in the course of time due to the slight movement of soil on the slope. The former possibility seems more likely to us. It could have been the floor of a passageway connecting two rooms with different elevations, more precisely the outer corridor (between Walls A and B) and inner rooms of the building.

**Floor No. 4**. This structure differs radically from the previous examples. It is more rather a pavement than a floor in the right meaning of the word, being constructed of small river boulders with an average length of 10 cm, the biggest of which had a size of 20 × 15 cm. Two cases of such pavement were documented on the Citadel, contexts 21D012 (140 × 50 cm) (fig. 2.1, *19*) and 21F032c (150 × 20–70 cm). As none of them were removed, the actual thickness of the pavement is not known to us. The character of this construction and ob-

**Fig. 2.1, 19** Pavement (floor no. 4), Square 21D, context no. 21D012, photo L. Stančo.

vious dissimilarity from the usual interior floor make evident that this pavement floored either an exterior courtyard or a passage. Both fragments of pavement were about 9 m away from one another, but their average elevation was almost identical: 21D012 (376.20) and 21F032c (376.10). Without further excavation we cannot find out whether these two fragments are parts of one large structure or two different structures laid down in the same time period.

A comparison of all the floors described above within the monumental building, despite the differences in their constructions, shows clearly, that all of them were built at almost an identical elevation. Therefore, we assume they all belong to the same period of occupation of the Citadel and let us say to the initial phase of the existence of the monumental building. Little doubt remains in the case of Floor No. 3 (20Q035c), which could be connected with Floor No. 5 (20O013c; see below) by both its character and elevation, and thus could represent the later phase of occupation of this building. One context (21P002) is not included among the previous register because its identification as a floor is not certain. It was obviously a horizontal level of compacted clay (at elevation 376.28–376.33), but its surface was not treated in a way typical for local floors. This context, however, could be understood as a simpler floor or fundament for a floor.

**Plaster**

During the excavations we searched for any traces of plaster or roughcast on the walls of the monumental building because its use in the architecture of Central Asia in the Kushan period is well attested. In spite of the fact that a considerable part of the walls was uncovered, no evident trace of plaster was found. As many fragments of plaster were found in other parts or other strata of Jandavlattepa, we suppose that this absence was not caused by improper excavation methods but by the quality of the building itself. The walls were either not plastered at all – they could be easily the foundations placed under the surface – or were plastered with a low-quality material, which fell off entirely.

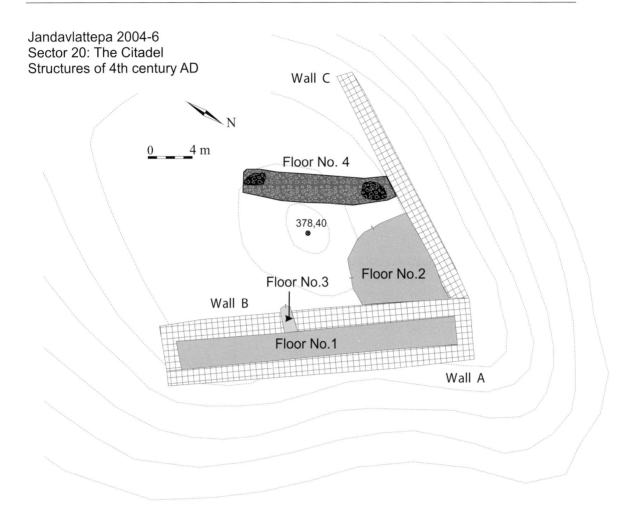

Jandavlattepa 2004-6
Sector 20: The Citadel
Structures of 4th century AD

Wall C

N

0    4 m

Floor No. 4

378,40

Floor No.3

Floor No.2

Wall B

Floor No.1

Wall A

**Fig. 2.1, 20** Sector 20 – reconstruction of monumental building.

## Constructions earlier than the monumental building

The monumental building described above represents the only well attested and thoroughly examined complex of stratigraphical units on the Citadel in the larger area (fig. 2.1, *20*). The earlier contexts were surveyed only partially. The largest body of these unearthed older constructions was the remains of the walls, which were used as a substructure for the foundations of the monumental building. Thus, while documenting the foundations we were able to trace a substantial part of the course of the earlier walls (fig. 2.1, *21*). Unfortunately, we know only the inner or outer faces of the majority of these walls.

The walls antecedent to the monumental building are of two major types. They correspond to the second and third type described above, i.e. their masonry consisted of well-dried, compact square mud-bricks (length 30–34 cm, thickness 11–12 cm) made of well-floated clay or the so called *pakhsa*, the large frustum blocks also made of dried clay.

At the eastern edge of the Citadel, a long part of the outer face of a wall was uncovered. It was later used as the building substructure of Wall "A" in almost its entire course. This structure could be traced even in those squares where Wall "A" was missing (20B and 20H), which means at both the northern and southern ends. If this earlier structure in Squares 20C, 20D, 20E, 20F and 20G could be understood as an outer wall of the otherwise unknown building in the same way as later Wall "A", then the remains of the structure uncovered in larger surfaces in Squares 20B and 20H exceed the simple description of a "wall." In other words, they do not constitute any distinct shape and their function could probably be explained as the reinforcement of building corners or possibly as part of some fortification masonry. The entire structure was made of square mud bricks and comprises contexts 20B005c, 20C008c (elv. 375.08)[14], 20D005c (elv. 375.36) (fig. 2.1, 16, lower part), 20E013c (elv. 375.15 – 375.29), 20H009c (in Squares 20F and 20G these contexts were not clearly distinguishable,

---

[14] Here the highest point of the surviving part of the wall is meant.

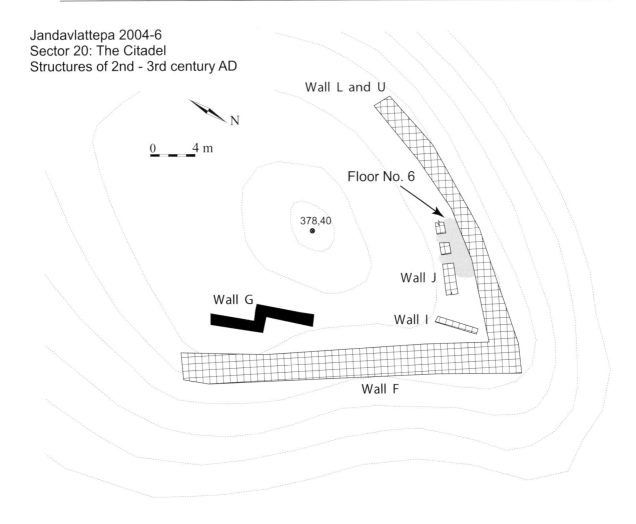

**Fig. 2.1, 21** Sector 20 – reconstruction of earlier buildings than the monumental one.

but the elevation of the preserved part in 20F – context no. 20F015c – is about 375.20). Because we did not remove Wall "A," we cannot say much about the thickness of this wall. The thickness of the massive construction in 20G and 20B, on the other hand, reached almost 2.5 m. In 20G, the elevation came up to 374.41 or 375.29 in different parts and, in 20B, varied between 374.56 and 375.14. In view of the fact that all values of the highest preserved points of the wall are within the range of 20 cm, it is possible to confirm the supposition of the levelling of the ruins of the older building in order to use them as a substructure for the new, monumental building.

Unlike the greater majority of the other constructions on the Citadel, this one was quite firmly dated by a find of four coins of the Great Kushans. These coins were found together in the gap between the mud-bricks of Wall 20C008c and were documented in context 20C004 by mistake (20C004.I, 20C004.II – fig. 2.1, *22*, 20C004. III, 20C004.IV).[15] The exact position of this find is marked on the ground plan of Square 20C (fig. 2.1, *37*).

A different picture appeared in the second row of squares. Whilst in Squares 20O and 20P, the level beneath the floor of the monumental building was never reached, in trenches 20Q and 20R the earlier constructions (Wall "G") were unearthed again (contexts 20Q033c and 20R017c). A secondary use as a substructure (for Wall "B" in this case) was the same, but originally, the wall was built of *pakhsa*, and its relation to the outer one was difficult to define. Unlike Walls "A" and "B" and also the earlier outer wall, this one was not a straight, long, simple wall, but created two corners in the small uncovered segment, i.e. in Squares 20Q and 20R, as is clearly seen on the general ground plan. The orientation of Wall "B" and the earlier *pakhsa* wall diverged from each other at an angle of 18°. This fact leads us to the conclusion that both buildings, in general, had different orientations. We found no floor related to this wall. It is necessary to state that Wall "G" could also have been constructed as a *pisé* because no gaps between *pakhsa* blocks were found.

---

15  These coins are by coincidence not included in the catalogue, chapter 3.5

**Fig. 2.1, 22** Coin of Great Kushans, small find no. 20C004.II, photo L. Stančo.

Some constructions antecedent to the monumental building were also found in Squares 20S on the one hand and 20N on the other. From their elevation and type of masonry and bricks themselves, they are related to the earlier building described above. In 20S, there was only a small fragment of architecture which could be easily linked to a massive construction adjacent to trench 20H. One of the three coins which were found in this square again supported the dating of these structures to the Great Kushan period (small find no. 20S002.III, see also chapter 3.5 cat. no. 61, interpreted as coin of Kaniska II by K. Abdullaev). The area to the west and south of 20S was excavated by the German-Uzbek team in 1993. Their results as a source of additional information concerning an earlier building phase are of no use to us because they were not fully published.

The situation at the other end of this row of squares is more complicated. Square 20N contained a large

area of heavily damaged mud-brick constructions. Only one segment, Wall "I," could be solidly ascribed to an earlier phase than that of the monumental building (context 20N009c). It is a 3.4 m-long part of a wall in the easternmost part of the trench uncovered under Wall "B." Its orientation from south to north fits very well with the *pakhsa* wall and the elevation at its highest point is 375.42. This wall was partially destroyed by Grave Pit 20N007f. Unfortunately, nothing can be said about the room enclosed by this wall because excavation work was postponed exactly at this stage. Thus, we know Wall 20N009c only from its top.

In this situation, with only scarce information about this building phase, we opened trench 20Y. The results of the digs here were most promising, as part of the monumental building was found, particularly Wall "C" (i.e. context 20Y003c), as was already described above. For an earlier phase, the structure uncovered under it was important and was once again utilized as its substructure. The importance of this context lay in its state of preservation and in that not only the walls but also a singular part of a floor and plaster were found. The preserved remains of Construction "J" consisted of three contexts: 20Y028c, 20Y025c, 20Y030c, which were actually one wall interrupted by two doorways (fig. 2.1, *23*).

The whole situation revealed several interesting details. Here, unlike the other parts of the earlier wall, Wall "C" was constructed not on the levelled old wall, but was placed inside the foundation trench, which was actually cut into the old wall. As a consequence, this wall of the monumental building was founded almost at the same elevation as the walls of the earlier building. The empty spaces, where the doorways

**Fig. 2.1, 23** Construction "J" as a substructure for the Wall C, Square 20Y, photo J. Kysela.

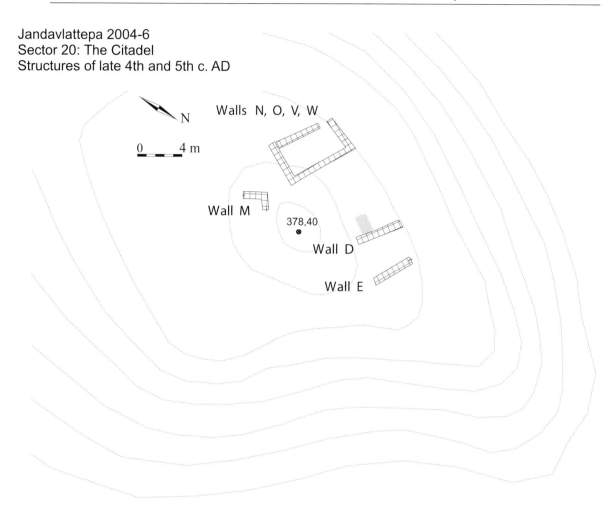

Jandavlattepa 2004-6
Sector 20: The Citadel
Structures of late 4th and 5th c. AD

**Fig. 2.1, 24** Sector 20 – reconstruction plan of walls later than monumental building.

originally led, were chaotically filled with mud-bricks. Here, with all probability Wall "C" represented the outer wall of the building. The earlier wall, on the contrary, was a mere division with two doorways leading northward, not outside, but into some interior room. How far to the north the floor of the earlier building, or that building itself, reached is difficult to answer, but definitely not much because the edge where the steep slope begins is less than two meters far away. The width of the eastern doorway (a gap between Walls 20Y028c and 20Y025c) was 0.80 m and the western doorway (a gap between Walls 20Y025c and 20Y030c) is 0.90 m.[16] The distance between both doorways, the length of Wall 20Y025c, was 1.10 m. Whether the doorways lead southwards to one or two more different rooms is impossible to determine at the present stage of the excavation. Although a good state of preservation of the walls was mentioned, it was not so for the height. Only four rows of mud-

bricks remained above the level of the floor, with elevations of 374.85 – 375.35 m. It is obvious that these elevations are in accordance with the elevations of the walls hitherto mentioned (fig. 2.1, 82).

The floor of the room (20Y020), as well as Walls 20Y025c and 20Y028c and floor of the doorway, were covered with lime plaster (20Y031c) consisting of several thin coatings separated from each other by mud-brick dust (fig. 2.1, 23 and 2.1, 82). While removing individual coatings, traces of straw were noticed. These coatings indicate a repetitive renovating of the plaster, the thickness of which was almost 2 cm in the end. Unlike the floors of the monumental building, there was no layer of packed potsherds under the plaster. Instead of this, a settled, greyish-green clay soil made up the base. The preserved surface of the floor measured approximately 3.0 × 1.1m. Nevertheless, just a smaller portion of it remained plastered. The elevation of the floor was 374.80, but the level of the floor in the door-

---

[16] Let us remark that the width of the doorway leading from Bastion No. 1 to the corridor in the southern part of the city wall (sector 04) was exactly equal (0.9 cm). This width seems to be typical one, as we can see in Zartepa (Zav'yalov 2008, p. 43, 44).

way was slightly higher at 374.95. It is likely that some kind of threshold was constructed here. It is remarkable that all three components – the floor, the walls and the threshold – were covered with the same plaster.

The question of the extent of this room could easily be answered by a reconstruction of Wall "L" (20Y021c). In Square 20Y, an approximately 3 m-long section of this wall was uncovered, which went parallel with "J." In addition, its masonry was of the same quality, with mud-bricks measuring 30–32 × 30–32 × 12 cm. Wall "L" was apparently the outer wall of the earlier building and together with Wall "J" formed an inner narrow corridor (1.1–1.2 m width) with plastered floor and walls. Only the fundament of this outer wall survived, which was, moreover, damaged by a grave pit (20Y018f).

A wall with very similar characteristics to Structure "L" was also uncovered in Square 21O. This 5.6 m-long fragment of wall ("U"; 20O006c) was relatively well-preserved. Despite its slightly different orientation, we surmise a direct relation between these two walls. In other words, Wall "U" is probably the same as Wall "L," which just changed its orientation somewhere between Squares 20Z and 21O, i.e. in an imaginary square 21C.

All structures thus far described in this chapter have had obvious mutual relations. Regardless, in Sector 20, several other walls were found in relation neither to the monumental building nor to the earlier complex. It is probably not an accident that such examples oc-

curred in the westernmost part of the excavations, in Trench 21P and its extension westward 21Pz.

## Constructions later than the monumental building

In addition to Walls D, E, N, O, V, W mentioned above, we found several other structures among the contexts on the Citadel which were definitely of later date than the monumental building (fig. 2.1, *24*).

Most important in this respect was a small fragment of a building discovered in the south-eastern corner of Square 21F (Wall "M," context no. 21F019c; fig. 2.1, *25*). This structure consisted of a short segment of wall made of *pakhsa* in its lower part (height 0.45 m) and of mud bricks in its upper part (height 0.45 m). It could be a similar case to the system of Walls D, E,

**Fig. 2.1, 25** Wall "M" or corner of a building of late phase, Square 21F, context no. 21F019c.

### Overview of all documented postholes:

| no. | context no. | diameter / length | depth | elevation (upper) | shape of pithead |
|-----|-------------|-------------------|-------|-------------------|------------------|
| 1. | 20O025f | 0.12 m | 0.10 m | 376,09 | circular |
| 2. | 20O026f | 0.125 m | min. 0.28 m | 376.15 | oval |
| 3. | 20O027f | 0.09 m | 0.135 m | | circular |
| 4. | 20O028f | 0.05 m | 0.10 m | | circular |
| 5. | 20O029f | 0.09 m | min. 0.17 m | | oval |
| 6. | 20O030f | 0.15 m | min. 0.25 m | 376.17 | oval |
| 7. | 20O031f | 0.16 m | 0.47 m | 376.20 | circular/oval (partly documented) |
| 8. | 20O032f | 0.10 m | 0.40 m | 376.15 | circular (partly documented) |
| 9. | 20O033f | 0.12 m | 0.14 m | | rather oval |
| 10. | 20O034f | 0.12 m | 0.08 m | 376.13 | circular |
| 11. | 20Z022f | 0.05 m | 0.125 m | | circular |
| 12. | 20Z023f | 0.125 m | 0.16 m | 376.01 | oval |
| 13. | 20Z024f | 0.16 m | 0.12 m | | prolonged oval |
| 14. | 20Z025f | 0.08 m | 0.05 m | 376.02 | circular |
| 15. | 20Z026f | 0.10 m | min. 0.2 m | 376.07 | circular |
| 16. | 20Z027f | 0.10 m | 0.035 m | | circular |
| 17. | 20Z028f | 0.10 m | 0.07 m | | oval |
| 18. | 20Z029f | 0.08 m | 0.06 m | 376.05 | circular |
| 19. | 20Z030f | 0.13 m | min. 0.05 m | 376.06 | irregular oval |
| 20. | 20Y033f | 0.12 m | min. 0.45 m | 376.49 | filled with 20Y032 |

N, O, V, and W, meaning a group of rooms / buildings which were constructed after the collapse of the monumental building and used its floors and pavements as a substructure without any specific levelling. Even the elevation fit this comparison well. However, two facts question such categorization with this group of architecture: the orientation of the walls, which differed considerably from the others, and the size of the bricks 36–38 × 36–38 × 9 cm, which was also slightly smaller.

*Floor No. 5.* A fragment of the "upper floor" in the southwest corner of Square 20O (context no. 20O013c) was found at elevation 376.56–376.74. Its size was 150 × 120 cm. Theoretically we can presume a relationship between this floor and Walls "D" and "E."

## Wooden structures (See table on the previous page)

The most evident remnant of wooden or wood-based structures in archaeological contexts (huts, etc.) is the posthole. However, postholes occur very seldom, according to the publications pursued in Northern Bactria and in Central Asia in general. Our knowledge of the purpose of postholes is, in accordance with this state of research, very low. A cluster of postholes was found in Squares 20O and 20Z.

As we can see, altogether twenty postholes were documented in Squares 20O and 20Z (10 in 20O and 9 in 20Z). They were distributed in the southern halves of these trenches. As far as we know, all of the postholes were dug in context 20O024c, into Floor No. 2 (fig. 2.1, *26*). The majority of these post-

**Fig. 2.1, 26** Cluster of postholes in Square 20O (dug in context no. 20O024c), photo K. Urbanová.

holes seemed to be placed in such a way that they formed a semicircle, as is clearly seen in the ground plan (figs. 2.1, *69* and *70*). While the extent of this context is not preserved northward, we can roughly estimate the circular shape of a whole structure with a diameter of about 5.6 m. It reminds one remotely of a modern yurt.[17] A supposed circular building would not fit well in the interior enclosed by Walls "B" and "C;" therefore, we presume that the wooden structure was constructed after the collapse of the monumental building but still before the rebuilding of this complex (walls D, E, N, O, V, W). With a fair amount of romanticism we can imagine the story: the monumental building was attacked and reduced to ashes by some nomadic tribe (e.g. Hephtalites) and their chieftain pitched his "yurt," a yurt-like shelter or a tent among the ruins.

## Overview of all building constructions in Sector 20[18]

### 1. Walls

| no. | context no. | overall mark[1] | documented length | documented width | documented height | size of the mud-bricks | elevation upper /lower | orientation (azimuth)[2] | quality of masonry | note |
|---|---|---|---|---|---|---|---|---|---|---|
| 1. | 20C006c, 20D003c, 20E004c, 20F008c, 20G003c | A | 24 m | 1.4 m (20D and 20C) | 0.8 m (20E)0.8 m (20D) | 40–42 × 40–42 × 10–11 cm | --/ 375.23 (20E) | SE-NW az. 330° | low | |
| 2. | 20N004c, 20O009c, 20P014c, 20Q003c, 20R005c, 20G010c, 20H008c (?) | B | 25 m | 1.5 m (20R) 1.4 m (20O) | 0.8 m (20O) 0.7 m (20R) | 40–42 × 40–42 × 10–11 cm | --/ 375.95 (20Q) --/ 376.05 (20R) | SE-NW, az. 330° | low | |
| 3. | 20C007c, 20N008c, 20Y003c, 21D028c, 21O005c 21P014c, 21P(z)005c | C | 20 m | 1.36 m (20Y) | 0.73 m (20Y) | 40–42 × 40–42 × 10–11 cm | 376.08 / 375.35 (20Y) --/ 375.42 (21P) --/ 375.35 (20N) --/ 375.08 (21O) | SW-NE az. 40° (20Y) az. 25° (21P) | low | |
| 4. | 20Z007c | D | 3.5 m | 0.6 m | 0.46 m | 42 × 41–42 or 36 × 10–11 cm | 376.58 / 376.12 | SE-NW az. 315° | poor | |
| 5. | 20Z017c, 20O020 | E | 3.5 m | min. 1 m (20Z) | 0.31 m (20Z) | 41–42 × 41–42 × 10–11 cm | 376.47 / 376.16 (20Z) | SE-NW az. 310° | poor | |
| 6. | 20B005c, 20C008c, 20D005c, 20E013c, 20H009c, also 20F015c (also 20G) | F | 34 m | 2.5 m (20G and 20B), Otherwise unknown | --- | 30–34 × 30–34 × 11 to 12 cm | 374.56–375.14 / -- (20B) 375.08 (20C) / -- 375.36 (20D) / -- 375.15–29 (20E) / - 375.20 (20F) / -- 374.41–375.29 /-- (20G) | SE-NW az. 330° (?) | high | documented only general outline |

---

[17] See Stronach (SD).
[18] Any wall, floor, pavement or other type of construction is included in this table.

| no. | context no. | overall mark[1] | docu-mented length | docu-mented width | docu-mented height | size of the mud-bricks | elevation upper /lower | orientation (azimuth)[2] | quality of masonry | note |
|---|---|---|---|---|---|---|---|---|---|---|
| 7. | 20Q033c, 20R017c | G | 8.3 m | --- | 0.5 m | --- | 376.07 / 375.56 (20R) 375.95 / 375.58 (20Q) | SE-NW, az. 350° | high | pakhsa / pisé ? |
| 8. | 20S004c | H | 3.1 m | --- | 0.4 m | 32 × 32 × 12 cm | 375.82 / 375.28 | az. 325° | high | |
| 9. | 20N009c | I | 3.4 m | --- | 0.25 m | 30–32 × 30–32 × 12 cm | 375.42 / -- | S-N az. 350° | high | documented only general outline on the bottom of the square |
| 10. | 20Y028c, 20Y025c, 20Y030c | J | 3.5 m | --- | 0.5 m | 30–32 × 30–32 × 12 cm | 375.35 / 374.85 (20Y) | SW-NE az. 50° | high | |
| 11. | 20E014c | K | 1.0 | 1.0 | --- | unclear | 375.04 / 374.92 | --- | unclear | documented only general outline on the bottom of the square |
| 12. | 20Y021c | L | 3.0 m | min. 1.4 m | 0.54 m | 30–32 × 30–32 × 12 cm | 374.92 / 374.36 | SW-NE az. 32° | high | possibly identical with "U" (21O006c) |
| 13. | 21F019c | M | 1.9 m | --- | 0.9 m | 36–38 × 36–38 × 9 cm | 377.00 / 376.10 | az. 150° | medium | |
| 14. | 21P022c | N | 2.5 m | 0.45 m | 0.31 m | 40–42 × 40–42 cm (?) | 376.17 / 375.86 | S-N, az. 11° | poor | make up corner with "O" |
| 15. | 21P006c | O | 2.7 m | 0.5 m | 0.31 m | 48 × 30 (?) | 376.45 / 376.14 | E-W. az. 110° | poor | make up corner with "N" |
| 16. | 21P015c | P | 2.2 m | 0.4 m | 0.47 m | 34–38 × 34–38 × 11 cm | 375.64 / 375.17 | S-N, az. 9° | medium | |
| 17. | 21P(z)012c | Q | 0.9 m | min. 0.5 m | 0.29 m | 38 × ? × 11 cm | 375.44 / 375.15 | S-N, az. 9° | medium | |
| 18. | 21P(z)009c | R | 2.6 m | 0.64 m | 0.34 m | 34–35 × 34–35 cm | 375.39 / 375.05 | S-N, az. 356° | medium | |
| 19. | 21P(z)014c | S | 1.7 m | 0.9 m | --- | 38–40 × 38–40 ×?cm | 375.17 / -- | S-N, az. 356° | low | |
| 20. | 21P(z)013c | T | --- | --- | 0.6 m | 35 × 35 × ? cm | 375.65 / 375.05 | E_W, az. 82° (?) | medium | |
| 21. | 21O006c | U | 5.6 m | min. 2.2 m | 0.83 m | 30–32 × 30–32 × 12 cm | 375.36 / 374.53 | S-N, az. 4° | high | possibly identical with "L" (20Y021c) |
| 22. | 21E033c | V | 1.1 m | 0.6 m | 0.35 m | 48 × 28 × 10 cm | 376.55 / 376.20 | E-W, az. 113° | poor | linked with "N" and "O", "W" (?) |
| 23. | 21F028c | W | 1.2 m | min. 0.45 m | 0.43 m | unclear | 376.91 / 376.48 | S-N, az. 35° (?) | poor | linked with "N" and "O", "V" (?) |

## 2. Floors

| no. | context no. | overall mark[3] | documented length | documented width | thickness | elevation highest / lowest | material | note |
|---|---|---|---|---|---|---|---|---|
| 24. | 20E006c, 20F006c | Floor No. 1 | 2.1 m (20E) 1.4 m (20F) 0.4 m (20F) | 0.26–0.56 m (20E) 0.2–0.3 m (20F) 0.1–0.2 m (20F) | | 375.92 / 375.80 (20E) 375.75 (20E) 376.11 / 375.98 (20F) 375.99 / 375.97 (20F) | compacted limy surface mixed with potsherds | |
| 25. | 20O024c, 20Z018c | Floor No. 2 | 2.8 m (20Z) 3.2 m (20O) | 0.4–1.8 m (20Z) 0.45–1.1 m (20O) | | 376.18 / 376.16 (20Z) 376.15 / 376.11 (20O) | two layers: the lower was made of compacted pottery fragments and the upper of fine clay | burned by fire |
| 26. | 20Q035c | Floor No. 3 | 1.1 m | 0.4–1.4 m | | 376.30 / 376.18 | thin layer of lime wash | |
| 27. | 21D012, 21F032c | Floor No. 4 | 1.4 m (21D) 1.5 m (21F) | 0.5 m (21D) 0.2–0.7 m (21F) | | 376.20 (21D) 376.10 (21F) | small river boulders with average length 10 cm | |
| 28. | 20O013c | Floor No. 5 | 1.5 m | 1.2 m | | 376.74 / 376.56 | | |
| 29. | 20Y020 | Floor No. 6 | 3.0 m | 1.1 m | 2 cm | 374.95 / 374.80 | lime plaster | plaster continues up to walls and inside the doorway |

## 2.1.3 Economic activities: storage and household industry

### 2.1.3.1 Storage & pithoi

A considerable amount of fragments of storage jars – *pithoi* – was found during the excavations, most of them intentionally used as part of Floor. No. 2, but only two examples of pithoi were found placed *in situ*. The first of them, more precisely its bottom with the lower part of the body, was unearthed in the north-eastern corner of Square 20N (fig. 2.1, *27*). This provenance seemed strange, especially in its relation to Walls "B" and "C," as this pithos was situated just outside their corner.

The second storage jar was found in the north-western corner of Square 20O. Here, too, only the lower body and bottom in several fragments were preserved. Such a provenance is closely connected with context 20O020, i.e. wall / destruction of Wall "E" (fig. 2.1, *28*).

It is supposable that, in the first case, the pithos was built into the floor, as in similar situations elsewhere. Usually, one third or even more of a vessel's height was hidden underground. At the site of Ak-tepe II (southern Tajikistan) one well-preserved storeroom with four complete *pithoi* was found. Although the description of this situation states, "In Trench III, part of the storeroom with storage jars standing on the floor was uncovered,"[19] the picture shows something else: the four vessels are actually built into the floor. At least one third of every *pithos*, in one case one-half, was hidden under the surface. Unambiguous proof is not given by the finding of a similar "*khumkhona*" (store room) at the site of Shodmon-kala in Kafirnigan val-

ley in southern Tajikistan. Here, several *pithoi* were unearthed, some of which were dug into the floor at diverse heights. In one case, almost all of a one-meter-high vessel was hidden.[20] In any case, both examples – Ak-tepe II and Shodmon-kala – show *pithoi* placed in the interior. It shall be added that these contexts are dated broadly to the Kushano-Sasanian period. A relevant analogy comes also from the second period of occupation of the site of Jigha-tepe in northern Afghanistan with material typical of the Late Kushan and Kushano-Sasanian periods. Again, a room with six pithoi half dug into the floor was uncovered.[21] While many similar examples exist[22], we perceive it as a common way of fixing storage vessels. In spite of this, different methods were also employed, as is clearly shown in the interior of a room in the 9th stratigraphical unit of the site of Chopli-depe in southern Turkmenistan. No fewer than 17 pithoi were placed directly on the floor. Fragments of mud bricks were laid around in order to fix them.[23]

We can conclude that our storage vessel in Square 20N was dug into the floor. Although no floor was found at the level of its bottom, we presume the existence of a potentially higher floor on level with one-third to one-half of the original height of the vessel, meaning at a level that was not preserved. There is only a slight indication in the case of Square 20N – a small fragment of lime plaster was found directly beside the storage vessel to the north. Its elevation of 375.53 corresponded very well with the elevation of the bottom of the pithos, which was 375.24. The vessel would have been dug into the floor some 0.29 m deep. This way of reconstructing this situation allows us to bring together the contexts of the pithos, the floor and probably also Wall "I" (20N009c). A question mark should

**Fig. 2.1, 27** *Pithos* unearthed in the north-eastern corner of Square 20N, photo L. Stančo.

**Fig. 2.1, 28** *Pithos* unearthed in the north-western corner of Square 20O, photo L. Stančo.

[19] Sedov 1987, p. 16 and ris. 3.
[20] Sedov 1987, p. 37 and ris. 18.
[21] Pugachenkova 1979, p. 71, ris. 7 and 8.
[22] Pugachenkova – Turgunov 1974, p. 69–71, ris. 5 shows another example of *khumkhona* found on Dalverzintepa (Dt-11), where the storage vessels were dug into the floor approximately 0.3m deep. This complex is well dated to the reign of Kanishka I. Authors mention several other store rooms, which were unearthed in Northern Bactria: Khatyn Rabat, Shortepa, Kampyrtepa and Dalverzintepa itself (with two examples).
[23] Pilipko 1985, p. 40–41, ris. 8.

be stressed at this point because the "floor" fragment is too tiny and was also omitted in the summary table of the floors above. Another interpretation is suggestible, that the fragment of lime plaster could be understood as mortar for the fixture of the pithos on the ground.

The second pithos, the example from Square 20O, was actually secured in this way. It was found amidst the remains of Wall "E," but after its removal it became clear that this pithos stood directly on the surface of Floor No. 2, and its bottom was fixed in the ground by mortar resembling lime plaster in its appearance (context no. 20O023c). The bottom of the pithos had a diameter of 45 cm and its elevation was 376.22. The stability of the vessel was secured by mud-bricks laid around it, either originally or some time later during the rebuilding of the interior.

### 2.1.3.2 Fireplaces & ovens

In Sector 20, many contexts with burned soil, coals and ashes occurred. On the other hand, a proper fireplace was as rare here as storage vessels. Even the context which could be interpreted as a fireplace was in close relation with the large burned layers and could have easily been missed. It was a circular feature (context no. 20O035f) situated in the central part of Square 20O close to Wall "B" and had a diameter of 0.5 m (figs. 2.1, *69* and *70*). Its depth is unknown because the fill – mostly ash (contexts 20O015 and 20O016) – was not removed entirely. The elevation of its upper surface was 376.12, and it was definitely related to Floor No. 2. The other simple fireplaces were uncovered in contexts 20O017f (fig. 2.1, *29*) and 21P007/008f. Concerning more sophisticated furnaces, we encountered neither ovens nor kilns in the excavated part of the Citadel. The same goes for small slag pieces, both ceramic and metal. In this vast area we found only six small pieces of slag (in Squares 20Y, 20Z, 21D and 21P). The presence of a production centre of pottery or metal in this place can, therefore, be excluded.

### 2.1.3.3 Household crafts: grind stones, loom weights, spindle-whorls

The secondary indicators of economic activity or household crafts present on the Citadel were the finds of grindstones, querns, loom weights and spindle-whorls. Among the small finds from Sector 20, five grindstones, quern stones or their fragments appeared, all of them in only two squares, 20Y and 20Z. Both examples of the lower concaves of the functional part of a grindstone (20Y022.I and 20Y027.II) were found above the level of Floor No. 6 (20Y020) and below the construction of Wall "C." Thus, they can be linked to an earlier period of occupation represented by Walls F, G, H, I and J. On the other hand, two quern stones (20Z002.I – fig. 2.1, *30* and 20Z002.II) were found in contexts distinctly linked to the late phase of occupation, the period of rebuilding of the monumental building. To be more precise, they are connected with Walls "D" and "E" in Square 20Z (fig. 2.1, *31*). Hence, they obviously come from the later stage of development. The third piece was in the same layer as one of the grindstones (20Y022), but this context emerged as the destruction of Wall "C" after its fall. Separate study on the grindstones and querns we prepare for the next volume.

The second group of artefacts, loom weights and spindle-whorls, which is perceived as evidence for textile production, is described in detail in the second part of this volume in a separate study by Urbanová.[24] To this, it should only be stated that at least one of these small finds was found in 13 of a total of 19 squares on the Citadel. There is no provenance with a specific cluster of spindle-whorls or loom weights. No square provided us with more than four finds. For that reason, a single textile-production place cannot be positively determined. The only hint of which, pointing to the northern part of the Citadel, was the finding of a raw piece of alabaster in Square 20O.

**Fig. 2.1, 29** Fireplace in southern part of Square 20O, (context no. 20O035f), photo L. Stančo.

**Fig. 2.1, 30** Quern stone (small find no. 20Z002.I).

---

24   See chapter 3.1, especially part 3.1.6 – Sector 20 concerning with the Citadel material.

**Fig. 2.1,31** Quern stone (small find no. 20Z002.I) in its original find context, photo L. Stančo.

**Fig. 2.1,32** Shallow open bowl with vertical rim, decorated with "sunburst pattern burnished", ceramics no. 20H007.1, photo L. Stančo.

### 2.1.3.4 Conclusion

Despite the large area excavated on the Citadel, only insignificant traces of economic activities were found. In contrast with the lower town, no traces of production complexes have been found on the Citadel. The only place with a partial accumulation of craft or production-related objects (grindstones, querns tones, spindle-whorls, loom weights, pithoi and maybe a fireplace) is the north-eastern corner of the Citadel summit. Therefore, we suppose the existence of some kind of production centre here, obviously intended to supply this complex with the most needed food and objects of daily use.

### 2.1.4 Small finds

During the excavations we uncovered several dozens of small finds. Most of them can be related to the Kushano-Sasanian period, therefore we can speak of almost pure Kushano-Sasanian context.[25] The finds show variability of the material culture in this period. Most common finds are the pottery fragments. Except the kitchen ware (large cooking pots), all other pottery is made on fast potter's wheel. Concerning table ware (we call it "fine ware/red slip ware" = FW/RSW), we have several basic shapes, among them: 1. shallow open bowl with vertical rim, decorated with "sunburst pattern burnished"[26] (fig. 2.1, *32*);

2. the high bowl with a slight narrowing in the half of its height, decorated in the similar way, but more simple, with only burnished vertical lines on the out side (fig. 2.1, *33*).

Significant shape among the storage vessels represents the type cited above: small pithos with striking neckband (Russian terminology says "khumcha," fig. 2.1, *34*).

Special kind of decoration should be noticed here: beside anthropomorphic jug[27] we have found strange zoomorphic application as well. It is animal head, frontally depicted, which is difficult to identify (tab. 3.4, 2:6; fig. 3.4, 18). Subjective opinions vary from donkey or camel to ram (*arkhar*). The pottery decoration differs evidently from that of lower town (Shakhristan). The fact, that the last phase on the Citadel and on the *Shakhristan* is different, is obvious. We miss the bowls decorated with lion's heads on the Citadel, for example, although they are wide spread in final phase of lower city. *Vice versa* there is no trace of above described "Citadel pottery complex" in these Shakhristan final layers. The catalogue of ceramics from the Citadel and its detailed analysis will be included in the next volume of this series.

The other small finds include loom-weights, spindle-whorls, fragments of glass vessels, glass-paste beads, stone beads, quern stones (grain stones), bronze and iron objects (knives, needle) and of course coins.[28]

**Fig. 2.1,33** High bowl with a slight narrowing in the half of its height, decorated with burnished vertical lines on the out side, ceramics no. 20O018.2, photo L. Stančo.

---

25  For the characteristics of the Kushano-Sasanian complex see Stančo 2006a.
26  The term has been taken from the Schachner 1995/1996.
27  See Stančo 2006b and Chapter 3.4 (tab. 3.4, 1–7; fig. 3.4, *20*) in this volume.
28  See special studies on given groups of small finds below in this volume.

**Fig. 2.1, 34** Small pithos ("khumcha") with striking neckband, ceramics no. 20O002.9, photo L. Stančo.

The coins are badly preserved and we are not able to attribute many of them exactly to particular rulers. Anyway, general characteristics of the majority indicate again the Kushano-Sasanian mints (see below in subhead Chronology).

## 2.1.5 Chronology

Over the course of excavations, a total of 33 coins were found, of which one is a modern-era Soviet coin, clearly from the 1920s (20R004.I). Two can be related to the period of the high to late Middle Ages, although there are doubts about the authenticity of this find (nos. 20Y007.II, 20Y014.I).[29] Earliest coin from the Citadel dates to Greco-Bactrian period and was attributed to Euthydemus by K. Abdullaev (no. 20Y002.VIII).[30] Ten bronze coins can be dated to the high to late Kushan period, in other words to the 2nd–3rd century AD (20C004.I, II, III, IV, 20S002.III, 20Y002.IX, 21E006.I, 21P003.I, 21P018.I, 21Pz004.II)[31] and one and single silver piece belongs to mint of southern Sogd (21E012.I, cf. Chapter 3.5, cat. no. 83). They mostly have a diam-

eter of over 20 mm (min. 21 mm max. 24 mm) and are between 4 and 5 mm thick. Although part of this thickness consists of a heavy layer of corrosion, these coins were made of more solid and better-quality metal than later coins. In some cases even without chemical cleaning the outlines of a standing ruler at an altar can be seen. Six of them have been classified by Abdullayev as coins of Kanishka II (around 229–247 AD) or Vasudeva II. (around 270–310 AD).[32] The remaining eighteen items are bronze coins that, for reason of their size, weight and state of preservation, belong to the Kushano-Sasanian period (20C001.I, 20N002.V, 20N002. VI, 20P002.I, 20Q001.2, 20Q001.7, 20Q002.IV, 20Q018.I, 20Q038.I, 20S002.I, 20S002.II. (Shapur II.), 21D001.II, 21D017.I, 21D019c.I, 21F001.IV, 21F010.II (Peroz ?), 21P001.II, 21P016.I).[33] Most of them are not clearly legible, and it is thus not possible to specify a particular ruler. We can, however, stress the significance of the finding of four coins from the Kushan period, found together in the gaps between the bricks of wall "F" in square 20C. In all likelihood they allow us to date this, the earliest phase of settlement traced so far in the Citadel, to the turn of the 2nd and 3rd centuries Ad. Further coins from this period were found in squares 20S, 20Y, 21E and 21P, and also in the western extension of the last-mentioned square, 21P(z). None of these contexts can be considered closed – in all cases, destruction was involved, and the placing of the coins there was secondary. From the large group of Kushano-Sasanian period coins, Abdullayev has classified coin 20S002.II as having been struck by Shapur II (around 309–379 AD), see chapter 3.5 cat. no. 115.

The fact that sixty percent of the coins found in the Citadel are of the Kushano-Sasanian type, and that they clearly predominate in contexts connected to the monumental building, allow this complex to be dated to the period from the second half of the 3rd century to the start of the 5th century. Without a precise attribution of individual coins we cannot be more precise about the chronology, above all in relation to the monumental building and later alterations and additions. All we can do is state in what order they come, on the basis of the archaeological situation and the stratigraphy of the architecture. In addition to coin finds from our excavations of the Citadel, Kushano-Sasanian coins from Jandavlattepa are also mentioned in the older literature.[34]

---

29  We suspected that workmen had brought them from elsewhere, since part of the motivation scheme consisted of small rewards for finds of coins in contexts; cf. Chapter 3.5 cat. nos. 134 and 135.
30  See Chapter 3.5 cat. no. 1.
31  Kanishka II: 20C004.I, 20D002.III, 20S002.III, 21E006.I, cf. Chapter 3.5, cat. nos. 60, 61, 70, 80; Vasudeva II: 20Y002.IX, 21P003.I, 21Pz004.II, cf. Chapter 3.5, cat. nos. 49, 59, 120.
32  See the catalogue of coin finds from Jandavlattepa in this volume, Chapter 3.5.
33  See the catalogue of coin finds from Jandavlattepa in this volume, Chapter 3.5, cat. nos. 93–97, 99, 101, 103, 105, 107, 108, 110–112, 115, 121.
34  Rtveladze 1982, p. 48, tab. 1, mentions 4 items.

To sum up, we have so far distinguished four basic phases of the Citadel's inhabitation or use. The first phase is connected with the so far oldest part of the architecture, constructed with the use of smaller and better-quality bricks. With the aid of coins, we may date it to the turn of the 2nd and 3rd centuries AD at the earliest. The second phase is the best documented. This is represented by a monumental building constructed of larger and lower-quality unfired bricks. Parts of the floors and paving connected to the building have also been preserved. Thanks to the wealth of Kushano-Sasanian coins found in these contexts, we may date the construction to the end of the 3rd, or more likely the first half of the 4th century Ad. There is also something of an intermediate phase when a wooden construction grew up in the northeastern part of the Citadel, reminiscent of a yurt in the shape of its ground plan and dimensions. The third phase is then the alteration of the large complex using bricks of an even worse quality; this may be dated to some time around the start of the 5th century, above all because of the absence of some ceramic forms typical of the later period. In the fourth and last phase of use, the Citadel no longer has a residential function, but a funeral one. The hillock is covered by a large number of graves of a clearly Muslim character, which cannot for now be clearly dated, although it can be assumed that they grew up in the late Middle Ages and especially in early modern period. During the modern era the Citadel, including the elevation, was also used as a place for the winnowing of grain with the help of the wind, as shown by the extensive accumulations of grains of corn in the layers under the surface of square 20R. Also related to this recent phase is the discovery of a Soviet coin from the 1920s, as well as part of the sole of a leather shoe.

## 2.1.6 Conclusion

The foregoing text provides the details of the different parts of our research. From our point of view we have to ask what the function of the Citadel was in this or that phase of existence that we have investigated, at least to a certain degree, by archaeological research across the area. From this angle, the Citadel of Jandavlattepa shows several characteristics of ostentatious residential architecture. A large part of its area in the late ancient period was clearly taken up by a monumental building of regular layout, with narrow corridors along the sides. Even if we have not excavated the surface of the Citadel as a whole and thus the completed ground plan of the

Citadel is not known to us, we can find typologically close parallels to this type of architecture within a group of so-called early medieval[35] "castles" (Russian "*zamok*"). These represented most probably seats of lesser local aristocrats comparable to a squire in the medieval Europe. The building on the top of Jandavlattepa's Citadel is not the only example situated in this way. For instance Zartepa shows another one, founded most likely along the same lines. Several examples of free-standing castles are described in Annaev's monograph.[36] For a study of the layout of the architectural complex of the Citadel compare study of Khmelnickiy.[37]

### 2.1.5.1 General comparison with other Citadels

As can be seen from the topographical plan, as well as by the whole of this chapter, Jandavlattepa is among the sites in Bactria that feature a separate, smaller part of the fortified settlement. In the Russian-language literature this is usually labelled a Citadel. Since this is a relatively common element in the morphology of extensive settlements, it is worth asking what function these Citadels had, and also comparing the different examples. A Citadel as a separate part of the settlement, or one that was clearly demarcated in relation to the "town" or "lower town" (*Shakhristan*) can be seen in a number of Bactrian sites from the ancient and late ancient period: Bactra, Dalverzintepa, Old Termez, Kampyrtepa, Zartepa, Khayrabad Tepa, Khaytabadtepa, Dilberjin, Dabilkurgan, Talashkan, Kulugshakhtepa, Babatepa and several others. In a certain sense this group might also be said to include Ai Khanoum and Takht-e Sangin, although here the separation of the upper part of the settlement might said to be the result of the formation of the terrain, something that could be – and, indeed, clearly was – an intentional choice. The basic variations are: placing the Citadel inside the town, for example in its centre (Dilberjin, Kampyrtepa[38]) or, as more often happened, in the corner of a regular layout (Khaytabadtepa, Dalverzintepa, Termez, Zartepa, Kulugshakhtepa). This second type of arrangement is reminiscent of the layouts of newly-founded or revived Seleucid cities, in which elevated or separated parts were earmarked as the royal *basilea* or governor's residence with a palace, gardens, shrines and so on.[39] Although such a function can definitely be ruled out for most of the Bactrian sites, it is clear that some of them were forming right at the time of Seleucid rule, and in this case we can surmise a use similar to that which we know from the Seleucid residential cities in Syria and Mesopotamia. The sites that can be

---

[35] "Early medieval" is to be understood as originated in the period between 5th and 7th century AD (i.e. pre-Arab period) according to the traditional chronology. Some of the castles could well be dated to the earlier periods, to the end of the 4th c. AD at least.
[36] Annaev 1988.
[37] Khmelnicky 2001.
[38] If we accept the reconstruction of the original layout of the site, as proposed by, for example, Azimov (2000, p. 36, ris. 4).
[39] See especially Held 2002.

included in this group are Ai Khanoum and Bactra. Old Termez and Kampyrtepa were forming during the same period, but their primary function, not only the function of the Citadel, was different. They appear to have served as points of protection on trade routes, and at places where the river Oxus could be crossed. The genesis of these specific sites also corresponds to this. For the period of the third and fourth century BC we can back up settlement in the Citadels of Kampyrtepa[40] and Old Termez, but not in the lower towns. It is clear that these sites grew up from a smaller fortified point with a clearly-defined function into extensive agglomerations of an urban type that reached their maximum size during the high Kushan period. In both these cases the specific arrangement of the settlement, as well as its very development, was dictated by the need to adapt to the banks of the rivers Amu Darya / Oxus. In the case of the Dalverzintepa, Khayrabadtepa, Zartepa, Kulugshakhtepa and Khaytabadtepa sites, the situation is different. The Citadel is an integral part of a more or less regular plan. It is clear here that this part was specifically earmarked, either during the foundation of the settlement or during the course of its development, and we have no reason to believe that it would have arisen earlier than the rest of the site. Such an assumption is difficult to prove, however, since the bottom layers of the Citadel have not in this case been archaeologically investigated. Some of the other sites listed have less regular layouts, or the division between the lower town and Citadel is not as obvious and clearly demarcated. These include Talashkan and Babatepa.

When we look at the topographical plan of Jandavlattepa it is clear that the site can be included in the second group analysed, but with a significant difference. The Citadel here may be on the edge of the site rather than in the middle, but it is not part of the inside of a regularly and geometrically arranged layout. Development here must have taken place in another manner, but it is hard to say why this was (see the General Description chapter). The key to understanding the morphological processes that led to such an arrangement is detailed all-over archaeological research, including of the earliest layers, but this is of course unthinkable on such an extensive scale in present.

Returning to the function of the Citadel as such, let us note the now thirty-year-old analysis of E.V. Rtveladze.[41] He believes that the main function of the Citadel was to act as a fortification, and that it also served as a place of last refuge. He doubts that the Citadel's founders chose to site it in the part of the settlement that was most exposed to enemy attack,

and believes that the Citadel was located in the place most difficult to access. As the last place of refuge for the town's inhabitants in the event of an attack, the Citadel was supposed to be protected not only by the lower town, but by its naturally-suitable position. The Citadel would thus have had to lie on the side from which attack was least likely, as is shown in the cases of Old Termez and Kampyrtepa, where the Citadels were on the river side. In view of the shape of the site and the location of the Citadel he compares Jandavlattepa with the sites of Karabagtepa, Babatepa and Ishanbobo. Rtveladze draws other conclusions from the size of the Citadel and its relationship to the other parts of the settlement. Here he includes Jandavlattepa in a group of sites which have Citadels that are much smaller than the settlements themselves. The area of the Citadel here is around 0.2 ha, and it thus comprises 1/30 or 1/35 of the settlement. Rtveladze thus assumes that in such a small area there could not have been several buildings with various functions, but that there was just one building: a well-fortified structure of a palace nature, which might have had one or several storeys. Such a building served as the place of last refuge for the inhabitants of the town in case of need. We should remember that Rtveladze is only comparing sites that lie in the Uzbekistani part of northern Bactria (Surkhandarya Province): Dalverzintepa (B-3)[42], Zartepa (B-5), Yalangtushtepa (B-93), Karaultepa (B-56), Jandavlattepa (B–33), Khaytabadtepa (B-49), Dergiztepa (B-67), Kampyrtepa (B-11), Babatepa (B-30), Aktepa (B-13), Khayrabadtepa (B-6), Arpapayatepa (B-54), no name tepa (B-51) and Ishanbobo (B-63).[43] We do not share the Rtveladze's opinion concerning refugial character of Citadel, however, at least for the Kushano-Sasanian period, for this Citadel had neither real fortification nor sufficient inner space to house more than several dozens of refugees. A simple comparison with Choresmian fortresses with the obvious refuge function, as are both the sites of Ayaz Kala I and III for instance, shows the real structure being able to fulfil such a need. For now, we keep the interpretation of the Citadel of Jandavlattepa in the Late Antique period as the seat of a lesser aristocratic family, commanding part of the once flourishing Sherabad Oasis.

## 2.1.7 A detailed description of research in sector 20

The squares that have been systematically uncovered in sector 20 are described here in the order in which we gradually opened them (fig. 2.1, 5).

---

[40]  Rusanov 2000, p. 19.
[41]  Rtveladze 1978, pp. 20–21.
[42]  Respective numbers of the sites ascribed to them by E. V. Rtveladze in a series of articles in the 1970s.
[43]  Rtveladze 1978, tab. 1 (p. 21).

N

0            1m

Square 20C

Square 20P

Jandavlattepa 2004
Square 20D
Groundplan 1

20D003c

20D006

20D005c

20D008c

Square 20E

**Fig. 2.1, 35** Square 20D, general ground plan, drawing by K. Urbanová.

The initial work on the Citadel took place in the 2004 excavation season, where on 16 September the systematic uncovering of the late ancient phase of the settlement was started. Fieldwork that year was carried out by Ladislav Stančo and Kristýna Urbanová, with Lucie Šmahelová, Jakub Halama and Štěpán Rückl helping with documentation.

**Square 20D** (figs. 2.1, 35 and 36)

Work started with the removal of the surface layer 20D001. Almost immediately below the surface we discovered the destroyed crowns of the walls, creating a layer of separated bricks, 20D004. After they were cleaned, we uncovered wall 20D003c (fig. 2.1, *15*) running north-south, in other words approximately paral-

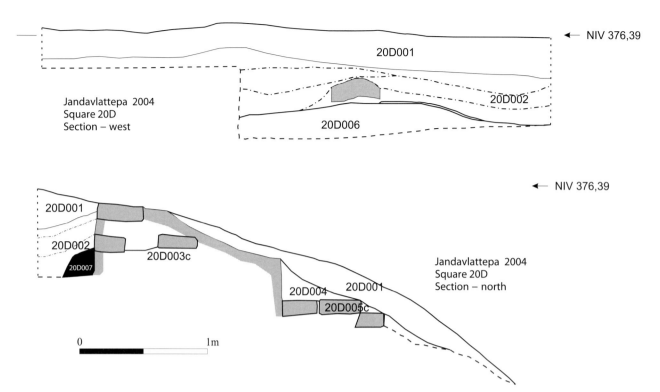

**Fig. 2.1, 36** Square 20D, western and northern section (profile), drawing by L. Stančo.

lel to the axis of our squares. By chance we managed to open the trenches in such a way that we captured both the wall itself and part of the inside of the building. On the other side, in the eastern parts of the trenches, in the layers under Wall "A," the remains can be observed of some sort of earlier architecture, probably part of the fortifications. It was labelled 20D005c (fig. 2.1, 16). This older construction phase seems to have used smaller, square bricks of 30 × 30 cm. A preliminary conclusion might be that this is a construction from the period of the Great Kushans, probably from the 2$^{nd}$ century Ad. To the west of wall 20D003c ("A"), in the inside of the building, a layer of light grey, dusty soil with the character of fine ash with white particles, 20D002, was found under the erosion layer. It could be divided into at least three further layers, but since we believe it is part of the same layering phenomenon, a single label has been reserved for this whole layer. In the southern part a large block of brickwork consisting of mud bricks, probably from the upper part of Wall "A" has fallen into this layer.

In the northern part, under 20D002, there is a loose layer of light brown dusty soil, 20D006, and at the northern section, right up against Wall "A," also a layer of cinders and ash, 20D007. We have yet to come across a floor in this square, although under 20D006 in the middle of the western section there is an accumulation of hard-packed fragments, similar to the situation in 20E. This feature requires clarification from further research, however.

Next to square 20D, square 20C was opened to the north, and square 20E to the south.

**Square 20C** (figs. 2.1, 37, 38 and 39)

In square 20C we once again removed the surface erosion layer, 20C001. Under it, over a large part of the area, was a layer of eroded mud bricks (labelled retrospectively 20C009) indicating under it a hidden fragment of Wall "A," here labelled 20C006c. Part of the wall in the northern half of the square was disturbed by two pits of unknown function (20C002 / 20C003f and 20C004/20C005f). Remains of bricks in the western section, labelled 20C007c, indicate that the smaller of the pits disturbed not only Wall "A" but also the north-eastern outside corner of the building (thus in the north-western corner of square 20C).

From the section we assumed that at this point there was a wall perpendicular to Wall "A," and we intended to show its existence and course by opening the neighbouring square (20N). As with the main Wall "A," here, too, above construction 20C007c there was a layer of eroded mud bricks, 20C010, in this case starting practically from the surface. In 20C, too, under Wall "A," in the eastern part of the trench an older construction could be noted, of the same type as in 20d. Here it is labelled 20C008c.

**Square 20E** (figs. 40, 41 and 42)

Trench 20E, in a southerly direction, contains the corner between Wall "A" and the western section, and so this square gave us more space to research the situation inside the building. Under the surface erosion layer, 20E001, in the southern half there is a light grey dusty ash-like layer with white particles, 20E002 (fig. 2.1, 10). It lies on top of an apparently inten-

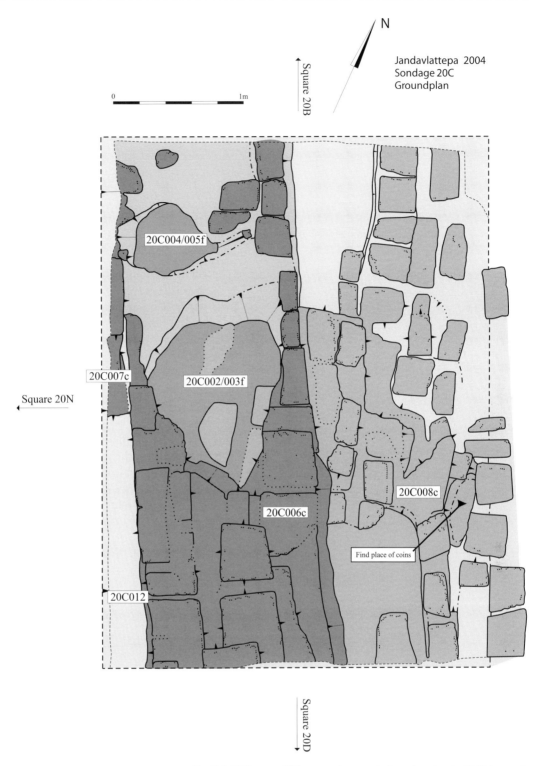

Jandavlattepa 2004
Sondage 20C
Groundplan

0                              1m

Square 20B

Square 20N

20C004/005f

20C007c

20C002/003f

20C008c

20C006c

Find place of coins

20C012

Square 20D

**Fig. 2.1, 37** Square 20C, general ground plan, drawing by K. Urbanová.

tionally compacted layer with a quantity of ceramic fragments, 20E006c (fig. 2.1, *17*). This layer of fragments forms some sort of floor, which is related to the monumental building and the main period of its use. Finds on this floor include, among other things, an interesting two-storey ceramic lamp (fig. 2.1, *43*), from which we took a sample of burnt material. The floor is disturbed between the western section and Wall "A" in the southern part by pit 20E008f, seem-

ingly a grave, which we have not yet investigated, with the exception of the upper part, filled with layer 20E003. The layer of filling, which we left largely in situ, is labelled 20E007. We did, however, clean out the large pit, 20E009f, in the north-western part of the square, which meant that we found the foundation seam of Wall "A" and under it came across brick constructions of an earlier building phase. However, the pit disturbed both the floor made of ceramic frag-

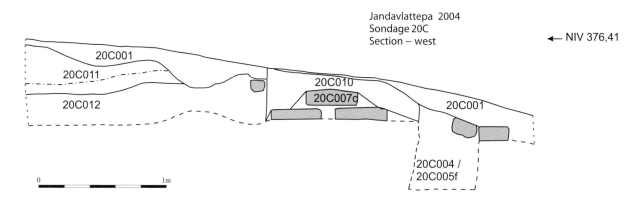

Jandavlattepa 2004
Sondage 20C
Section – west

← NIV 376,41

20C001

20C011

20C012

20C010

20C007c

20C001

20C004 /
20C005f

0                    1m

**Fig. 2.1, 38** Square 20C, western section (profile), drawing by L. Stančo.

**Fig. 2.1, 39** Square 20C, general view from south-west, photo L. Stančo.

ments and the situation under it, so we were unable to verify in this space whether there was another floor below it belonging to the building with Wall "A."

The filling of pit 20E009f forms in the upper part context 20E005, which is a layer of medium-brown rather non-cohesive soil, relatively well-packed and thus more difficult to remove. It contains small pieces of mud bricks, both smaller and larger fragments. In the upper part of the filling we found, in a small pit on a heap of such fragments, the skeleton of a small child, clearly incomplete. It was close to the surface, and it is thus likely that some of the bones were removed by erosion. What is certain is that it was not an ordinary burial with a funeral and all the requisites, but that the child was merely covered with a small amount of soil

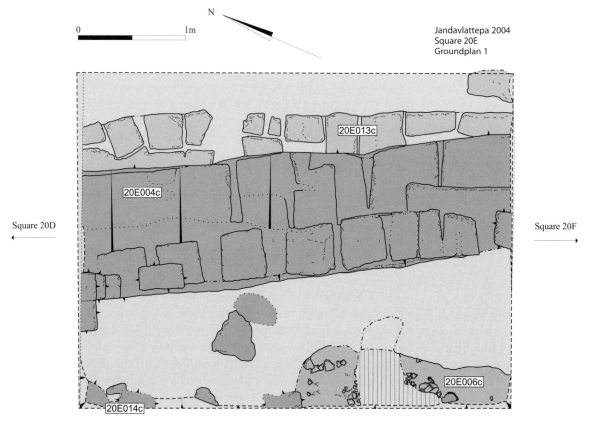

N

0                    1m

Jandavlattepa 2004
Square 20E
Groundplan 1

20E013c

20E004c

Square 20D

Square 20F

20E006c

20E014c

**Fig. 2.1, 40** Square 20E, general ground plan, drawing by K. Urbanová.

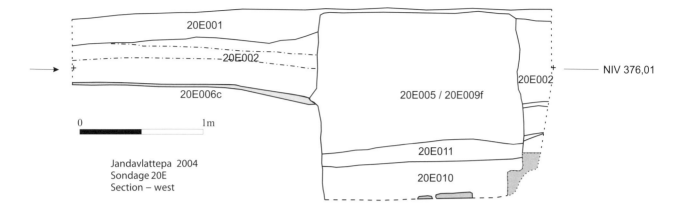

**Fig. 2.1,41** Square 20E, western section (profile), drawing by L. Stančo.

**Fig. 2.1,42** Square 20E, general view from north-east, photo L. Stančo.

in slipshod manner, without a pit of great size being dug. Layer 20E005 is divided from a layer of the same nature, 20E010 in the lower part of the pit, by a narrow layer, 20E011, which is similar to layer 20E002: it is light grey dusty soil of an ash-like character. It is possible that this is the same material as that of layer 20E002, poured in secondarily when pit 20E009f was being filled in. The different layers were very different to distinguish across the space, so this one was un-

**Fig. 2.1,43** Two-storey ceramic lamp, context no. 20E002.

fortunately removed together with the previous layer, 20E005. There are thus no separate finds from it. In the north-western corner layer 20E002 is once again visible in the section; it continues in the neighbouring square as 20D002. Here, too, it is really a complex of several layers of similar character, differing from each other merely in the quantity of white particles. Wall "A" itself here is numbered 20E004c, and for the greater part of its course is once again covered by a layer of eroded mud bricks, 20E012. The older construction phase of the "fortifications," of smaller mud bricks, is here labelled 20E013c.

**Square 20B** (figs. 44 and 45)

Work in square 20B was determined by its position lower down the slope. It was only logical that after the removal of the surface erosion layers, 20B001 and 20B002, destroyed constructions from the earlier phase of construction (mud bricks 30 × 30 cm) began to appear across the whole area. In this corner position, this might have been part of the fortifications, perhaps a bastion. We postponed the systematic excavation of this level until later. Layer 20B001 corresponds to the type of light grey erosion layer as found in the surrounding squares, while 20B002, which in many places connects to it or mixes with it, is a light brown, looser, soft soil that sits immediately on top of the remnants of structure 20B005c. The absence of Wall "A" in this square means there is an absence of the eroded bricks common to all the squares where we found "A." After being destroyed, the earlier construction phase clearly had lay as rubble for some time, open to the elements. Its cleaned remnants were then used as the basis for the construction of Wall "A" – indeed, of the palace – and thus remained preserved. Where the wall from the earlier phase remained bare, as here, the mud bricks must have suffered further erosion, but the steep slope helped ensure that loose and broken bits of brick were immediately washed away. Only compact brickwork remained here, flooded understandably by material from above. It is also

N

0    1m

Jandavlattepa 2004
Square 20B
Groundplan 1

20B004

20B005c

Square 20C

**Fig. 2.1,44** Square 20B, general ground plan, drawing by K. Urbanová.

clear that the mud bricks from the older construction phase, 30 × 30 cm in size, were made of better-prepared and finer clay. They also seem to have been dried better, since they resist erosion better and above all do not crumble, as the younger bricks (40 × 40 cm)

do. Under the northern edge of the construction from the older construction phase, there are then layers of a humusy nature – 20B003 and 20B004 – which, however, we analysed over too small an area (above all the south-eastern corner of the trench) and they did

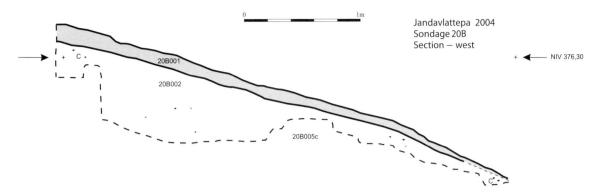

Jandavlattepa 2004
Sondage 20B
Section – west

+ ◄─── NIV 376,30

**Fig. 2.1, 45** Square 20B, western section (profile), drawing by K. Urbanová.

**Fig. 2.1, 46** Square 20F, general ground plan, drawing by K. Urbanová.

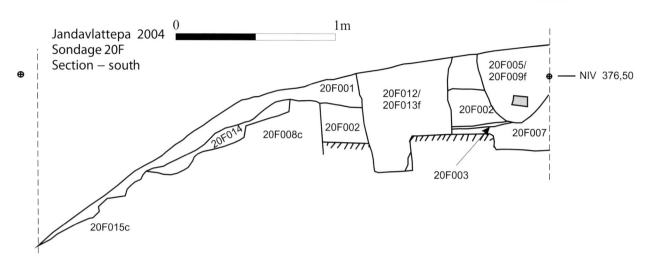

**Fig. 2.1, 47** Square 20F, northern section (profile), drawing by L. Stančo.

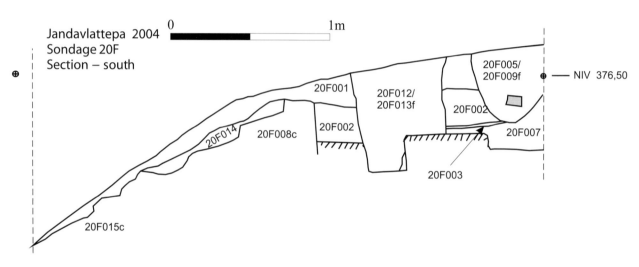

**Fig. 2.1, 48** Square 20F, southern section (profile), drawing by L. Stančo.

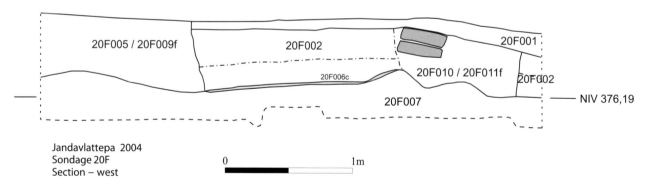

**Fig. 2.1, 49** Square 20F, western section (profile), drawing by L. Stančo.

not therefore provide us with much information, or, unfortunately, finds.

In an attempt to capture as far as possible the whole course of the eastern wall of the "palace" building ("A"), we gradually opened squares 20F, 20G and 20H, preserving the width of the control blocks as 1m. The state of the preserved wall was similar everywhere to that in square 20C. The upper rows of mud bricks are badly destroyed, especially those going down the slope.

**Fig. 2.1, 50** The floor no. 1 with large pot of Kushan-Sasanian period, context no. 20F006c, photo L. Stančo.

## Square 20F (figs. 2.1, 46, 47, 48 and 49)

In square 20F we once again removed the erosion layer, 20F001. Under it was the same light grey dusty layer of ash-like character with white particles (like 20E002); here it was labelled 20F002. Here, too, it could have been divided into further partial layers, but we kept the same numbering as in 20E. In this square 20F002 was disturbed by pits – in the south-west corner by a modern-era grave, 20F005/20F009f. Originally we thought that, in the sloping terrain, it was an ordinary layer, and it was only the southern section that revealed its true shape. It was only in this southern section that the bones were found, although the pit continues for about 1m further to the north. The bottom of the grave disturbs another layer (20F007, see below) which is under the level of the floor (20F006c), found in this square only in two fragments – in the western section in the central part and in the south-western corner. It is similar in character to 20E006c, and we may consider it one and the same phenomenon (fig. 2.1, *50*).

Between these two fragments of floor was the second of the two pits, which also disturb 20F002. Pit 20F010/20F011F, of unknown function, contained among other things fallen mud bricks in good condition, and is most visible in the western section. There is another pit, 20F012/20F013f, between the grave pit 20F009f and Wall "A" – 20F008c, well visible in the southern section. Here and there there was a burnt layer of black cinders and ash, 20F003, which we encountered in both the northern and southern sections. We removed the above-mentioned floor made of potsherds, or rather fragments from it, and began to analyse the heavily-packed layer of light brown soil with numerous fragments of mud bricks, which runs the whole width of the western section, whether under the floor or under the fillings of the pits. The crown of Wall "A" (20F008c) is once again covered by a layer of eroded mud bricks, 20F014, and unlike in the previous squares it was no longer possible here to establish the border between "A" and the older phase of construction, given the narrower

width of the square. The earlier phase has not yet been identified in this square for sure, but lower layer of compact clay (mudbricks?) in the eastern part of the square (context no. 20F015c) may well be identified with Wall F.

## Square 20G (figs. 2.1, 51 and 52)

Excavations in square 20G initially brought only further ambiguities and questions rather than answers to some of our questions regarding the shape of the whole building. We ascribe this to, among other things, the fact that the absolute height of the terrain is once again lower here, which means that Wall "A" is less well preserved here than in the more northern squares (q.v. 20B and above all 20H, where situation in this regard is even less favourable). In addition, the angle between Wall "A" and the western edge of the row of squares is also more open here, which means that the earlier construction phase once again cannot be traced in this square, although there is a larger area for excavating the inside of the (palace?) building. After removing the dusty surface erosion layer, 20G001, we found ourselves in a complicated situation in the western half, where 20G002, a thick layer with numerous large fragments of baked bricks that was clearly created by the destruction of the wall, was disturbed in many places by dug pits, probably all graves. Some of them, those in the northern section, continue from square 20F (20G011/20G012f). Pit 20G006/20G007f is clearly just a deeper part of the pit that also continues from 20F. Pit 20G004/20G005f, on the other hand, is captured only in the area itself. We decided not to excavate the bottom parts of these pits for the time being, but we believe that they probably also had the function of graves. As with the child's skeleton in 20E, they were probably rapid and haphazard burials, which the shape of the pits also suggests. Some of them were covered in the upper part by several baked bricks of small dimensions, typical of mediaeval Muslim architecture. The wall is not too well preserved in 20G, and is very difficult to trace in the southern half of the square in particular. The situation is partly disturbed by an extensive pit, 20G008/20G009f.

The situation in the western section compelled us to open another square (20R), this time in a westerly direction, not in the direction of the main wall. The reason was the presence of a large wall, which occurred after the removal of the destruction level, 20G002, in the northern section. While it was being straightened, part of the western section several centimetres thick fell down. The material fell from the edge of a wall of mud bricks, exactly the same in character as Wall "A." We assumed it was part of the same building. Of the two possibilities – that it was a wall perpendicular to "A" or that it was parallel to

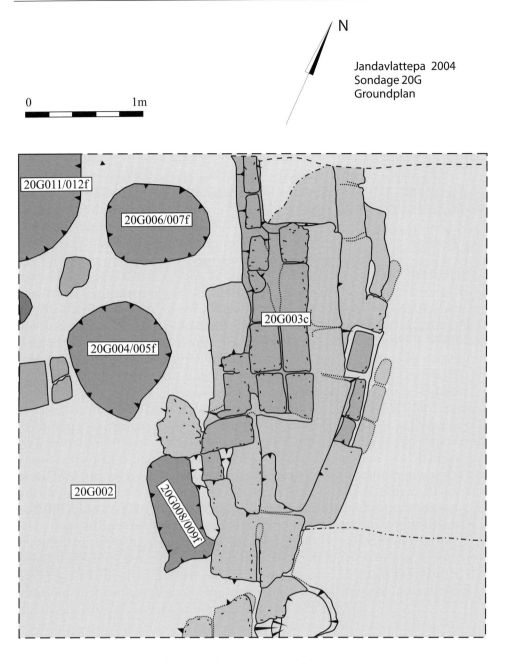

N

Jandavlattepa 2004
Sondage 20G
Groundplan

0          1m

20G011/012f

20G006/007f

20G003c

20G004/005f

20G002

20G008/009f

**Fig. 2.1, 51** Square 20G, general ground plan, drawing by K. Urbanová.

**Fig. 2.1, 52** Square 20G, general view from north-west, photo L. Stančo.

it – the second proved to be correct after square 20R was opened. We did not exclude a perpendicular wall initially, because the potential corner lay in the area disturbed by a series of pits – see above. The wall thus runs parallel to Wall "A," and thus, with a slight angle, runs into the western section. It is labelled 20G010c, and in all the trenches we give it the general name of wall "B."

**Square 20R – eastern half** (fig. 2.1, 53 and 72)

Excavations in square 20G led to the opening of trench 20R to the west, with a control block 1 m wide left. Given that an old trench from the German-Uzbek team in 1993 was located several metres further west, we were forced to limit the dimensions of trench 20R to 2 × 4 m. The aim of our work in it was first and

**Fig. 2.1, 53** Square 20R – eastern half, general view from north, photo L. Stančo.

foremost to ascertain the extent and verify the course of wall "B." To begin with we removed a surface erosion layer 10 – 15 cm thick. In the eastern section, however, the eroded bricks of wall "B" begin directly

from the surface. The top layer, about 10 cm thick, is so eroded that once again we distinguish it from the wall itself, and it is labelled 20R004. From the analysis of this layer comes the find of a modern coin, as yet not precisely determined (a Soviet coin from the 1920s?). Wall "B" itself, once again composed of 40 × 40 cm mud bricks, is labelled 20R005c, and runs from north to south the whole length of trench 20R. In the rest of the area we found a layer of light brown, fine, loose and dusty soil with considerable admixture of cereal grains, and a medium-count occurrence of cinders to 3 cm. The layer is labelled 20R002, and is between 5 and 20 cm thick. In some places, especially in the western section and in the middle of the trench, the cereal grains form a layer by themselves. We took several samples for analysis. According to Sh. Shaydullaev, this layer was created in an ordinary way during grain winnowing. The Citadel, as the highest place in the whole area, was an ideal place for separating the wheat from the chaff in the way that we ourselves have witnessed in the present day on a small hill in

**Fig. 2.1, 54** Square 20H, general ground plan, drawing by K. Urbanová.

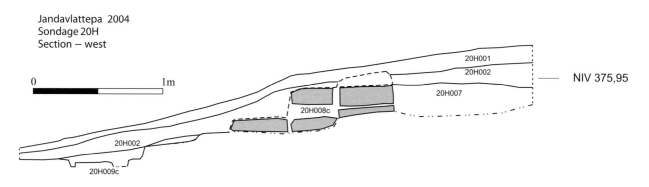

Jandavlattepa 2004
Sondage 20H
Section – west

0                    1m

20H001
20H002
20H007

NIV 375,95

20H008c

20H002

20H009c

**Fig. 2.1, 55** Square 20H, western section (profile), drawing by L. Stančo.

the village of Kalamazar. The grains are thrown up high and the wind blows away the lighter parts, while the grains themselves fall back to the ground, from where they are picked up. Only the bottom layer of dirty grain remains trodden into the dust. It is thus very difficult to date these layers. They might date from ancient times, but it is more likely that they are late mediaeval or early modern, given that they are not very deep under the surface. In these layers we found part of the leather sole of a shoe with holes around its edge left by hobnails. In the southern part of the trench, layer 20R002 mixes with another, similar in character but with more cinders and also ash, labelled 20R003. In the sections the layers are labelled together, because it is very difficult to delineate their course in the space. In the middle of the trench, but not the sections, we found further two shallow pits with children's graves. Once again they were disorderly burials only a little way beneath the surface of the terrain. The filling of the pit is merely layer 20R002 transferred, including its abundant occurrence of cinders. The small pit in the north-eastern corner, which is in fact dug into the crown of Wall "B," is labelled 20R008f, and its filling (20R007) is in places firmly packed, making it difficult to remove the clay from

the bones. The second small pit, approximately in the middle near the western section, is labelled 20R010f, and its filling 20R009. The last layer documented to date is 20R006, which is a medium-brown very firmly-packed soil. It is found mostly in the central and western part, but we also captured it in the western and northern sections.

**Square 20H** (figs. 2.1, 54, 55 and 56)

After our findings in 20R and 20G we opened another square labelled 20H to the south of 20G, following on in a row from 20B–20G. The aim was clear – to find the corner of the building from the last phase of construction, in other words the meeting place of Wall "A" and the potential Wall "D." The situation was complicated by the fact that the terrain sloped again in this direction, which meant it was likely that only the very bottom rows of bricks would have been preserved. Compared to the other squares at the head of this eastern row, however, 20H sloped relatively little.

After removing the surface erosion layer 20H001 it was found that most of the area of this trench was taken up by a mass of compact brickwork, damaged to a greater or lesser extent by erosion. After detailed cleaning of the brick construction and the removal of some of the eroded mud bricks and their rubble (20H002), here, too, we found several disturbances of modest extent. Of these, the pit with loose filling in the south-western corner of the square (20H003/20H004f) may be considered a grave. The grave was not excavated right to the bottom, though, so our assumption was not verified.

In the western part of the square, above all in the section, a wall, 20H008c with bricks of 40 × 40 cm was documented in general terms. It was highly likely to be connected with construction 20R005c, in other words with Wall "B." In the eastern part of the square, under the previous level, there are extensive remains of wall 20H009c. This appears to be the most southerly extremity, and possibly the corner, of Wall "F," which we traced along the whole eastern edge of the Citadel in the older phase of construction.

**Fig. 2.1, 56** Square 20H, general view from south, photo L. Stančo.

N

Jandavlattepa 2004
Square 20N
Groundplan

0 ———————— 1m

Square 20Y

Square 20C

Square 20O

20N012/013f

20N008c

20N009c

20N003

20N015c

20N010/011f

20N004c

**Fig. 2.1, 57** Square 20N, general ground plan, drawing by K. Urbanová.

## Square 20N (figs. 2.1, 57 and 58)

The first square to be opened on the northern edge of the Citadel was 20N. On its eastern side it adjoins square 20C, and so we looked for the northern outer wall of the monumental building, perpendicular to Wall "A." First of all we removed the surface erosion layer, 20N001, over the whole surface. The whole southern half of the square is taken by an almost compact mass of mud bricks. Only after a very careful cleaning of their individual parts could specific fragments of walls be separated. Over much of the area we removed a layer of mud brick rubble with fragments of mud bricks (20N002). Down the eastern part, from north to south, runs the pronounced body of a wall of 40 × 40 cm bricks (20N004c, fig. 2.1, *11*). This is clear-

**Fig. 2.1, 58** Imprint of an unusual building mark, structure 20N004c, Square 20N, photo L. Stančo.

67

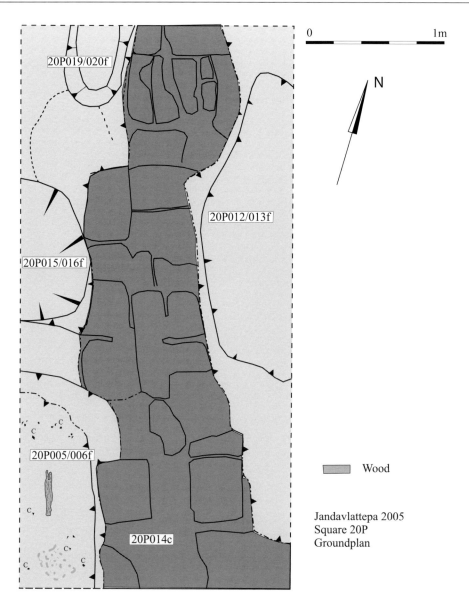

0                                                    1m

N

20P019/020f

20P012/013f

20P015/016f

20P005/006f

20P014c

Wood

Jandavlattepa 2005
Square 20P
Groundplan

**Fig. 2.1, 59** Square 20P, general ground plan, drawing by P. Belaňová.

ly the other end of the phenomenon later observed in square 20R, 25 m further south, in other words Wall "B." Between this wall and the eastern section is a deep pit with the same north-south orientation, which we excavated right to the bottom. It turned out that this was in fact two phenomena: the indeterminate fill of a pit (20N003) and a pit grave lying further to the south with well-preserved bone remains, also filled with loose earth (20N006/20N007f), apparently younger than the previous one. The end of the grave, in the skull area, extends into square 20N. The bottom of this "double pit" comprises a construction of bricks measuring 30 × 30 cm (20N009c, or Wall "I"), which continues in a northerly direction up to the north-eastern corner of the square. Here, in sloping terrain, it is found not far under the surface. The uncovered part measures 3.4 m. Next to the above-mentioned pit, the remains of the architecture are disturbed by several other interventions. The above-mentioned brick

mass in the southern part is disturbed by a shallow pit (20N011f), filled with mud brick rubble (20N010), containing skeletal remains in a slightly haphazard position, clearly caused by erosion. This grave was excavated completely and included a vertically-placed wooden stake. In addition to the above-mentioned Wall "B", in the mass of bricks in the southern part we also distinguished wall 20N015c. The poor condition of this wall made it difficult to describe, however, and it may be only a ruined part of a wall that is standing elsewhere. An important fragment of the construction was documented in the middle of the northern half (unfortunately at this height it is not contained in any section). This wall was constructed of mud bricks measuring 40 × 40 cm, and forms part of Wall "C" (here 20N008c), which ran, at an acute angle, to Walls "A" and "B." In the mortar joining the bricks we found, after the removal of the surface eroded bricks, the imprint of an unusual building mark (fig. 2.1, *58*).

Jandavlattepa  2005
Sondage 20P
Section – axis  south-north (center of square)

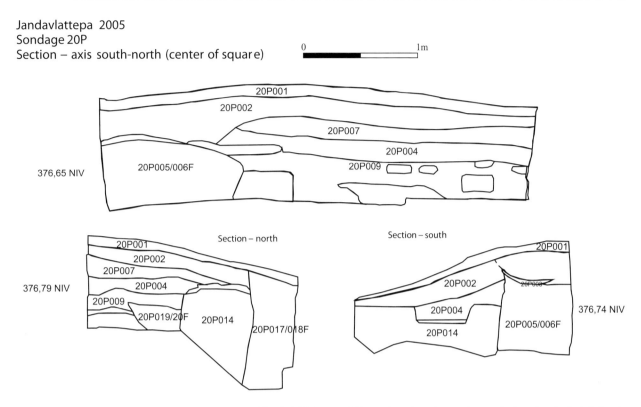

Fig. 2.1, 60 Square 20P, sections (south, north, west), drawing by P. Belaňová.

The wall was considerably disturbed close to the western section (south-western corner) by pit 20N012/20N013f, which we excavated only partially, up to a depth of about 60 cm from the surface. In the north-eastern corner opposite we found a large vessel (clearly connected with the older construction phase, not with the monumental building (which it lay outside), fig. 2.1, 27.

## Season 2005

In the 2005 season we continued our previous plans and tried to follow further the basic ground plan of the monumental building in the eastern part of the Citadel. The row of squares between the earlier-opened 20R and 20N was connected, and squares

Fig. 2.1, 61 Square 20P, general view from west, photo L. Stančo.

were also opened in the third row. First of all the eastern halves of squares 20Q and 20P were opened, and then the whole square 20O. Supervision of the different areas of the excavations was carried out by Ladislav Stančo, Jan Kysela and Kristýna Urbanová, while documentation was carried out by the above-mentioned people plus Petra Belaňová.

## Square 20P – eastern half (figs. 59, 60 and 61)

In this part of the Citadel only the eastern half of the square was opened, in order to preserve the highest point of the whole hillock, partly because of its specific character (see introduction) and partly as a point for later topographic surveys. The situation in this square was, after the removal of the surface erosion layer 20P001, largely clear and simple. In the centre of the rectangle, which measured 2 × 4 m, a wall runs from north to south, taking up almost the whole width of the trench. From the orientation and size of the mud bricks (40 × 40 cm) it is clear that this is part of wall "B" (here 20P014c). As well as cleaning the crown of this wall, we noted that the original situation had been disturbed by several pits. The central part had been preserved in good condition, but the edges were bitten into by these pits on both the east and west sides. In all there are five pits here, of which the most pronounced in area – 2.2 cm long and 0.7 m wide – we documented on the eastern side of the wall (20P012/20P013f), closer to the north-eastern corner of the trench.

In the opposite corner (SW) we uncovered another grave pit (20P005/20P006f, tab. 2.1, 1:4), which after

69

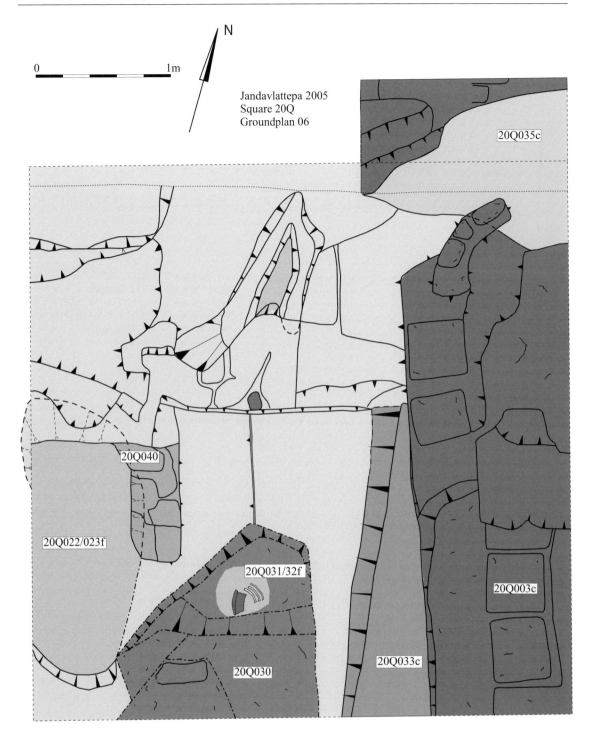

Jandavlattepa 2005
Square 20Q
Groundplan 06

0      1m

**Fig. 2.1,62** Square 20Q, general ground plan, drawing by P. Belaňová.

the body was placed in it was clearly covered with wooden sticks (alternatively, this might be the remains of some sort of wooden bier). Further excavation in square 20P was halted, since it was clear that without removing wall "B" we would have difficulty gaining any further information in this small area. For the sake of completeness we should add that the further probable grave pits are 20P010/20P011f (this continues into neighbouring square 20Q as 20Q012/20Q013f, which allows us to reconstruct its total length as 1.7 m) and also 20P015/20P016f and 20P019/20P020f.

**Square 20Q** (figs. 2.1, 62–68)

As we were uncovering the above-mentioned situation in 20P, we were also working in square 20Q, to begin with only in the eastern half for the same reasons as with 20P. In this narrow strip, after removing the surface erosion layer 20Q001 we once again found, close to the surface near the eastern edge of the trench, a wall with mud bricks measuring 40 × 40 cm. It was labelled 20O003c, and was part of Wall "B." In the south-eastern corner the crown of the wall reached almost to the surface. The actual wall here

70

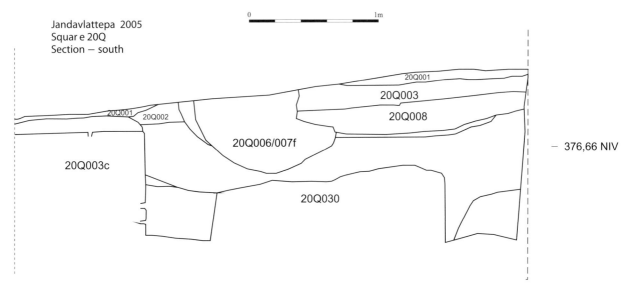

Fig. 2.1, 63 Square 20Q, southern section (profile), drawing by P. Belaňová.

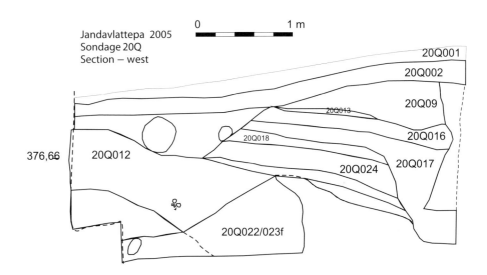

Fig. 2.1, 64 Square 20Q, western section (profile), drawing by P. Belaňová.

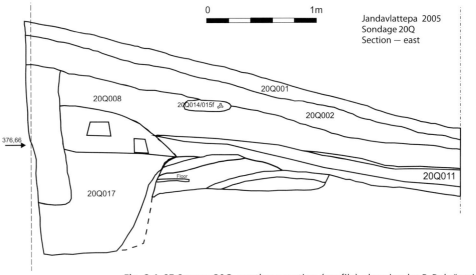

Fig. 2.1, 65 Square 20Q, northern section (profile), drawing by P. Belaňová.

71

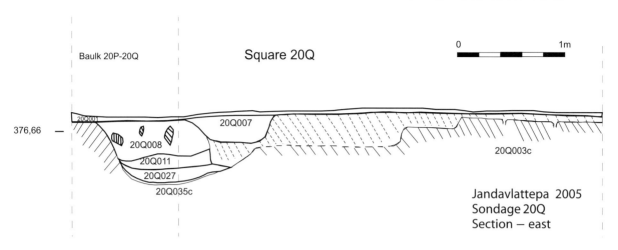

**Fig. 2.1, 66** Square 20Q, eastern section (profile), drawing by P. Belaňová.

was not disturbed by any grave pits, and so its over-all state of preservation was much better than that of the neighbouring part in 20P. A small, secondary type of grave was uncovered in the southern section (20Q004/20Q005f). The shallow pit had dimensions of 0.6 × 0.7 m and contained haphazardly-arranged bones. To the west of the wall, at not a great depth, we excavated and documented a shallow grave pit (20Q009/20Q010f) with bone remains that were, on the contrary, very well preserved (fig. 2.1, *67*) and with a typical orientation from the south-southeast to the north-northwest and with the face turned to the west.

After excavating this pit we analysed the layers that formed the greater part of the area to the west of wall "B," with a very marked admixture of organic particles. They were, by degrees, 20Q002, 20Q008 (this one might have been in reality the filling from the outer grave pit of the above-mentioned grave, which we did not manage to trace in time in the limited space) and above all 20Q011, 12 and 27. The second grave pit then lay in the SW corner of this half of the square (20Q006/20Q007f) and was filled with loose, moderately well-packed soil, with preserved organic frag-

**Fig. 2.1, 68** Square 20Q, general view from north, photo L. Stančo.

ments indicating that it was also covered with some sort of cane mat. Overall it appears that when the pits were being dug, the locations of the walls were fairly clear to the diggers, and that they avoided them because they made it hard to dig graves. When excavating the grave pits we also worked our way down to the foundation trench of Wall "B." It became apparent that another, older construction (20Q033c) served as the foundation for the building of the wall. This older construction was differently orientated and, above all, seems to have been built of *pisé*, or rammed earth blocks. We then turned our attention to analysing the western half of square 20Q, with the aim of casting light on the inner arrangement of the building. The layers were removed in the way that they were designated during the excavation of the eastern half of the square. In the south-western corner of the square we excavated an extensive grave pit that also turned out to be deep (1 m) – 20Q022/023f (fig. 2.1, *14* – bricks above pit). This grave is one of the few from which the bone remains were taken and analysed by anthropologist Z. Shodiev. A peculiarity of this context was that from the eastern side to the grave pit there was a narrow pit, filled with river stones. Ethnographic parallels indicate that it may have been a shaft through which

**Fig. 2.1, 67** Grave pit of the type P1 (simple), context no. 20Q009/20Q010f, view from east photo L. Stančo.

the whole grave pit was dug, and thus the body was also lowered into the grave through it. The actual pit was closed with stones from above.[44] The whole grave pit is also markedly undercut in a direction running north under the older layers, quite clear in the western section. (fig. 2.1, *64*). This distinctive feature also disturbs this group of layers in the north-western corner. It is a deep pit with an almost vertical wall, cut into the older layers practically from the surface. Because the pit continues in a north-westerly direction, just like the above-mentioned group of layers, it is clear that it is connected with the highest point of the Citadel, and that it may be related to the traditional burial place of some local imam. The pit was excavated as deep as possible given the limited space, and the individual layers of the group of layers were further analysed, as far as the level of a very compact brick eroded mass which took up the whole north-western quarter of square 20Q. We stopped work on it and removed only the loose-to-medium-packed layer with fragments of mud bricks which surrounds grave 20Q022/023f in the south-west quarter of the square. Here we stopped work in the moment we reached the compact level with the remains of the brick construction. At the level where digging stopped, a clear line of lime plaster was apparent in the earlier (more deeply situated) context.

## Square 20O (figs. 2.1, 69, 70)

Kristýna Urbanová supervised the work in this square. The square was intended to add to our knowledge of the course of the inner wall of the monumental building (Wall "B") and was also the first that would be able to bring us information on the interior of the building. After removing the surface erosion layer, 20O001, we came across the crown of the wall (20O009c) in the eastern half of the square, as expected. As in the neighbouring square, 20P, its body had suffered considerable damage from grave pits, especially from the outer (eastern) side. Once again it seems that the wall was respected by the grave diggers to a certain extent, and the pits are set apart, only encroaching on the wall from the side. The situation on the eastern side of the wall is quite clear: in the narrow strip between the wall 20O009c and the eastern section were found two grave pits with loose filling, labelled as 20O004/20O005f (SE corner of the square) and 20O006/20O007f (NE corner). Both of them were excavated only partially, just to verify their specific burial character. We intentionally did not reach the level of the skeletal remains here. Small area in the center of this part shows the level of the original layer (no. 20O008) in which both the pits were dug in. The situation on the other side of the wall was considerably different and turned to be much more complicated from the stratigraphical point of view. Much of the surface, after removal of the subsurface layer 20O001, was created by a homogenous layer 20O003 of loose medium brown soil with many organic particles. Among the small finds three fragments of one glass vessel appeared (20O003.II). Below this layer the situation started to differ in southern and central part on one hand and in the northwestern corner on the other. As a main feature in the NW corner we uncovered very cohesive and solid layer of compacted mud bricks 20O020 (60 cm thick) either being part of a construction, labelled Wall "E" in general description, or destruction of it. We decided to remove upper part of this context to check out both eventualities. It was here, where one of only two examples of *in situ* preserved *pithoi* in whole Sector 20 was unearthed (fig. 2.1, *28*). It was labelled 20O022f (hole in the ground) and 20O023c (lime plaster fixture of the *pithos'* bottom).[45] In the SW corner and central part of the square 20O we brought to light a range of cultural layers of diverse nature. Uppermost of these layers was 20O010 contained many organic particles and small cinders and also several small finds (bead, spindle whorl, bronze objects). Below this context – in the central part – first of the levels of compacted clay resembling a floor was uncovered (20O013c), with fragmentary preserved animal figurine made of clay. Most of the lower layers in the SW corner had one common feature: they were burned by heavy fire at some stage of the settlement development. It concerns particularly contexts 20O013c, 20O014, 20O015, 20O018 and 20O019. Sample of the cinders from the 20O014 was taken up but not yet analysed. Special attention deserves context 20O021c, placed just next to the Wall "B" westwards. It is deffinitely earlier than the cultural layers 20O010 and 20O014 and originally probably formed part of inner disposition of the room and may have served as substructure for the fireplace / oven 20O017f, in construction of which a daub was used. It is indicated by numerous finds of burned daub in margins of the given feature. The final context we reached in this square was the floor labelled 20O024c (Floor no. 2), stretching from the Wall "B" to the western section and continuing in the Square 20Z (fig. 2.1, *70*). Its upper (later) and lower (earlier) layers of this floor consist in the SW corner of the layers 20O019 and 20O037 respectively. While cleaning the floor 20O024c group of postholes, disrupting the surface of the floor, was distinguished (fig. 2.1, *26*).[46]

## Square 20R – continued (figs. 2.1, 71–74)

In order to link the picture gained from excavating square 20Q, we continued to excavate square 20R,

---

44  This is one of the methods described by local villagers as an established burial rite.
45  See also subhead 2.3.3.1 *Storage & pithoi* in this chapter.
46  For details see "Wooden structures" in subhead 2.3.2.5 *Architecture* in this Chapter.

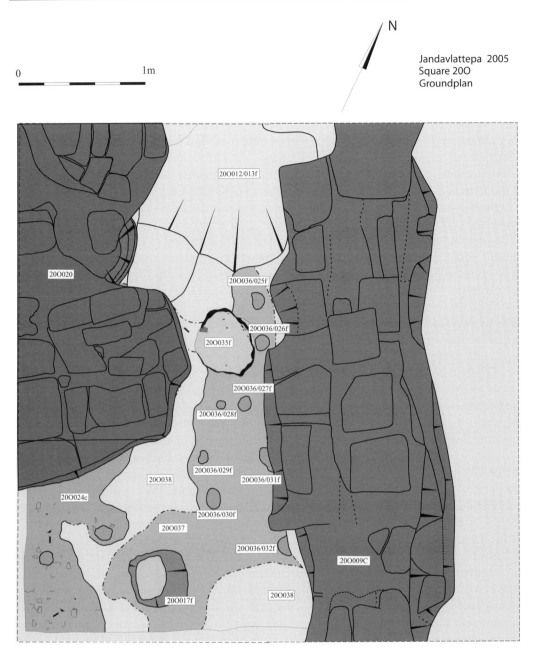

N

Jandavlattepa 2005
Square 20O
Groundplan

0　　　　　　　　1m

**Fig. 2.1, 69** Square 20O, general ground plan, drawing by K. Urbanová.

**Fig. 2.1, 70** Square 20O, general view from south, photo K. Urbanová.

an area that had also been the subject of our interest the previous season. First we removed a layer of loose soil that we had used last season to conserve the level of excavation reached. We then continued to uncover the whole area, during which it was discovered that the uncertain relationship between layers 20R002 and 20R003 in the southern part of the trench last season was the result of the existence of an extensive grave pit, which we had failed to recognise last season. It was labelled 20R013f and its filling 20R012. The filling and bone remains were gradually removed. As with some other graves, in the upper part of the filling, clearly at the level of the former surface, a large lump of compact material was found, reminiscent of a shapeless mud brick of bluish-grey matter.

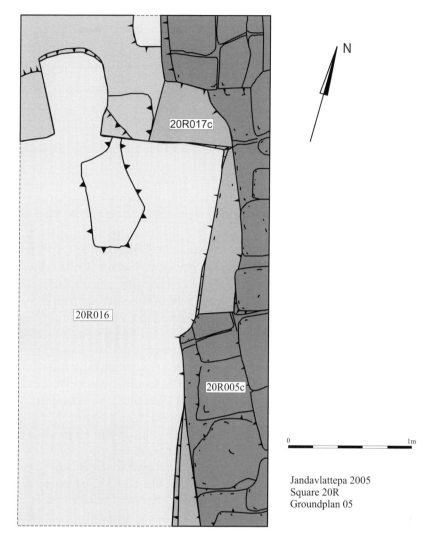

Jandavlattepa 2005
Square 20R
Groundplan 05

**Fig. 2.1,71** Square 20R, general ground plan, drawing by P. Belaňová.

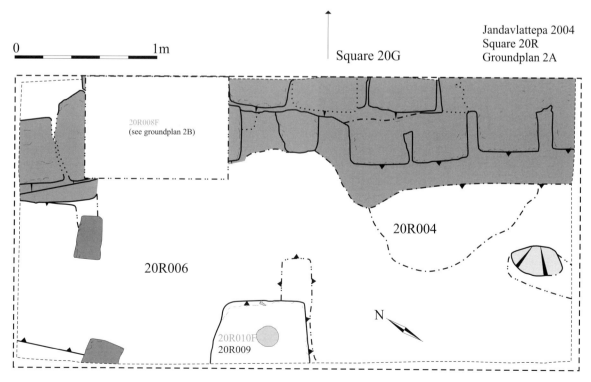

Jandavlattepa 2004
Square 20R
Groundplan 2A

**Fig. 2.1,72** Square 20R, ground plan 2A (upper layers), drawing by K. Urbanová.

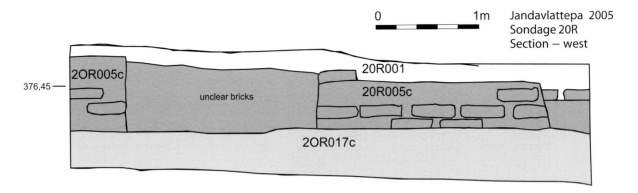

**Fig. 2.1, 73** Square 20R, imaginary eastern section (profile), side view of the wall, drawing by P. Belaňová.

In the remaining part of the area a moderately-to-medium-packed layer of dark brown soil was separated, with an admixture of small burnt grains. It was labelled 20R016, but it is possible that it is identical with 20R006. The dividing element of the two deposits appears to be a heavily-packed clay layer, ochre in colour, with a notable admixture of lime, 20R011. On the horizontal plane it was fairly marked, but in later documentation of the dried-out sections it could only be distinguished with difficulty. An interesting situation arose when we researched wall 20R005c, the foundation seam of which we found at a fairly shallow depth (376.00–376.14 above sea level). The preserved part of this wall was thus only 3–4 mud bricks high at this point. In the middle part it is also very much destroyed, partly by a small grave pit and partly as the result of insufficient support by the underpinning in this part. Under it we discovered a compact wall of rammed earth with a slightly different orientation, clearly belonging to the earlier phase of construction and used as underpinning / foundation during the construction of Wall "B." It was labelled 20R017c, and in the overall plan appears as Wall "G." Work in this square ended with the removal of layer 20R016 on a heavily-packed compact level with an unequal surface.

**Square 20S** (figs. 2.1, 75 and 76)

The area of square 20S was investigated very briefly and quickly. Once again, we excavated only the eastern half of the square, because further to the west are the eroded remains of the exploration carried out by the German-Uzbek team in 1993 (fig. 2.1, 76). For this (western) side we do not have a section, and similarly from the south only a minimum can be observed from the section because of the decline of the terrain in this direction. We wanted to verify how far Wall "B" extended in a southerly direction. After removing the surface erosion layer, 20S001, we also removed a loose medium-brown soil in the north-eastern corner. We found four coins here (see the Chapter 3.5, cat. nos 112 and 115). Loose soil of a similar nature was also removed in other parts of the trench. Pieces of mud brick of various sizes were also discovered in it, as well as grain deposits similar to layers 20R002 and 20R006. Small finds in 20S003 include a bone pin. In the western part, near the irregular border with the old German trench, we ended work at the level of the upper edge of a heavily-packed fine clay, which looked like a surface that had been washed by water for a long time.

This is certainly a level that was for a long time exposed on the surface of the tepa before being covered

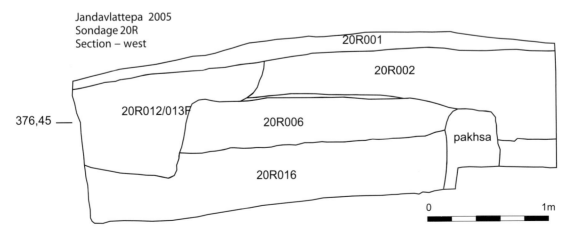

**Fig. 2.1, 74** Square 20R, western section (profile), drawing by P. Belaňová.

by further deposits of eroded material. The remains of the architecture were captured in the north-eastern corner and in the eastern section. They consisted of a brick construction, 20S004c (Wall "H") of 32 × 32 cm bricks, which may be related to the distinctive Wall/fortification "F." In the eastern section the bricks of the edge of construction "B" can be seen. We may also observe here the last two layers, sometimes the last layer, of mud bricks. This is an extreme case in which all that is left of the whole massive wall of a building is the bottom row of bricks, the others having succumbed to destruction. Merely a metre away there are no longer any traces of the monumental building.

Removal of the baulks (control blocks) between squares 20S, 20R, 20H and 20G.

As a result of the situation ascertained during research into the above-mentioned squares, we decided to remove the 1 m wide control blocks between them. From experience we knew that by the follow-

ing season they would be considerably damaged by seasonal rains, and we wanted to preserve at least the most basic information. We were not planning to dig to the level reached in the surrounding squares, only to clean the crown of Wall "B." The erosion of the damaged Wall "B" may therefore be observed over this whole area (fig. 2.1, 77). The only place where the situation was different was in the baulk between squares 20R and 20S. The whole western part of this block is formed by the southern part of a double grave pit, documented in Square 20R (context 20R012/20R013f), which was excavated in its entirety (fig. 2.1, 78).

**Square 20Z** (figs. 2.1, 79, 80)

In connection with the interesting situation in square 20O (see above), square 20Z was opened to the west of it. Work in this square was supervised mostly by Kristýna Urbanová, occasionally by L. Stančo. The

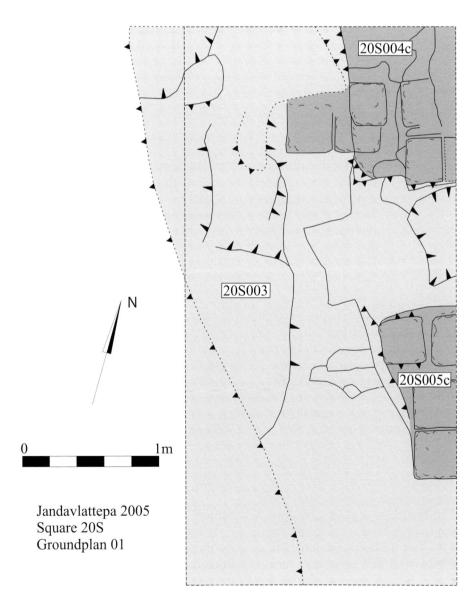

**Fig. 2.1, 75** Square 20S, general ground plan, drawing by P. Belaňová.

**Fig. 2.1, 76** Square 20S, general view from south-west, traces of old German-Uzbek trench in foreground, photo L. Stančo.

aim of the excavation was to provide information about the internal arrangement of the monumental building, and a greater amount of better-stratified ceramic material. The surface sloped down gently from south to north. At the southern side we reached a depth of 1.5 m from the surface, but on the northern side only 0.3 – 0.5 m. We started with removal of the surface erosion layer 20Z001. The upper strata were considerably disturbed by several modern era grave pits 20Z004/005f (tab. 2.1, 1:5), 20Z008/009f, 20Z011/012f, 20Z013/014f, 20Z015/016f. As we sought any traces of inner disposition of the monumental building in this square, we paid special attention to badly preserved segments of walls (20Z007c, labelled as Wall "D" in general description, and 20Z017c, i.e. Wall "E" together with 20O020). In upper part of the construction of the Wall "D" and close to the southern section was uncovered a quern stone (small find no. 20Z002.I) in very good state of preservation (fig. 2.1, *30, 31*), but apparently in secondary position. The same goes for other similar find (no. 20Z002.II). The Wall D was gradually cleaned and partly also taken apart. We searched for relationship with the Wall "C," but the north-western part of the square was not preserved well enough to answer this issue. Under the remains of the walls we uncovered large part of a floor constructed of two layers: compacted pottery fragments in the lower part and

fine clay layer in the upper part, the whole construction was labelled 20Z018c (or Floor no. 2, see fig. 2.1, *18*). All the surface of the floor was carefully cleaned and documented. This level became the bottom of this trench in the same time, while the floor was not removed. The important fact, however, is that these walls were built on the floor no. 2, i.e. they were constructed later than the floor itself. Specific nature of layer with context no. 20Z021 (burned soil preserved in large area, cf. identical context 20O019) leads us to interpret it as a part of an extensive destruction caused by heavy fire. Square 20Z ranks among the few parts of the excavations, where the good preserved examples of burnt bricks were preserved (fig. 2.1, *12*). They were not part of any construction; they were placed simply on the surface of the floor 20Z018c. Substantial part of the floor was disturbed by cluster of nine postholes – context nos. 20Z022 – 20Z030. For interpretation of this situation see description of Square 20O above.

**Square 20Y** (figs. 81–85)

Work in this square was led by Jan Kysela. At the northern edge of the Citadel, it was in a key position, because it might cast light on the relationship between the late-ancient period monumental building and constructions from earlier periods. This was because the slope is very steep in this area, and over an

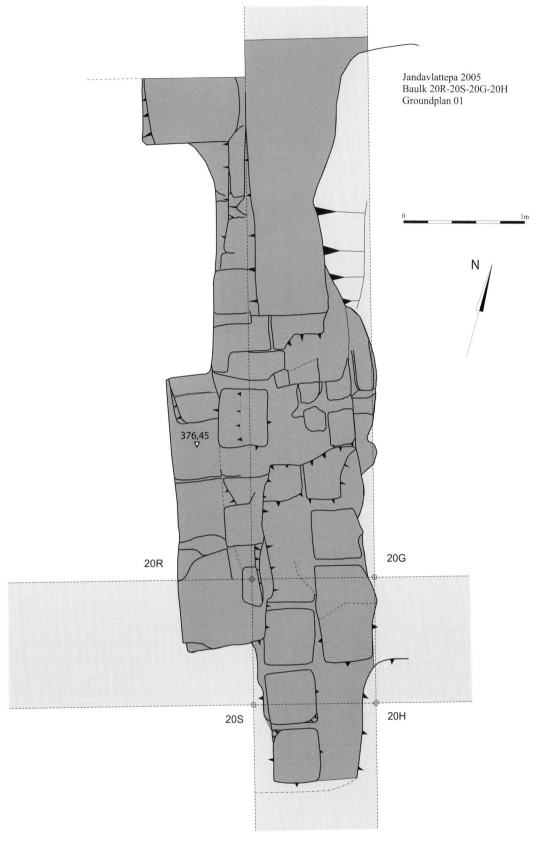

Jandavlattepa 2005
Baulk 20R-20S-20G-20H
Groundplan 01

0          1m

N

376,45

20R                    20G

20S                    20H

**Fig. 2.1,77** Baulk between Squares 20R, 20S, 20G and 20H, a ground plan, drawing by P. Belaňová.

area of 4 × 4 m a height difference of up to 1.3 m can be observed on the surface alone. First the relatively thin surface erosion layer, 20Y001, was removed. Over part of the area, especially in the northern half, we then removed a fine dusty layer, 20Y002, also clearly of erosion origin. This layer yielded a remarkable number of small finds (13 items!) and ceramics. At the corresponding level in the southern part

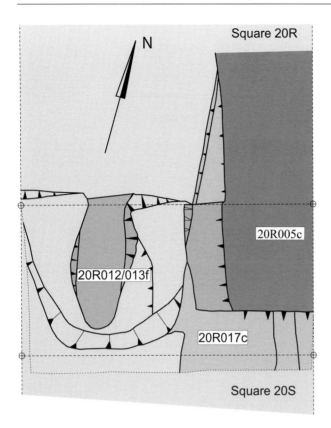

Jandavlattepa 2005
Square 20R/20S (Baulk)   0 ▬▬▬▬▬▬ 1m
Groundplan 01

**Fig. 2.1, 78** Ground plan of the baulk between Squares 20R and 20S, drawing by P. Belaňová.

was a layer of erosion-damaged mud bricks, 20Y010, which once formed the crown of wall 20Y003c. This wall was the dominant phenomenon in the whole square, and its orientation, the dimension of its mud bricks and their poor quality all clearly indicated that it formed part of the monumental building, or more precisely of its perimeter Wall, "C." In the south-eastern corner there remained a small area bordered by this wall and the sections, and this area formed part of the interior of the large building. However, the small size of the area prevented further investigation in more detail. We removed layer 20Y034 here, only discernible retrospectively from the section. We finished the work here by removing layer 20Y009, approximately 50 cm under the surface at a level where there were some largish stones (the largest being 20 × 30 cm, others 20 × 10 and 20 × 11 cm). The above-mentioned body of Wall "C" was disturbed along its northern edge by a long, narrow grave pit with well-preserved remains of a buried child (context 20Y023/20Y024f) (tab. 2.1, 1:2). In contrast to the stratigraphically-clear situation in the southern half of the square, its northern half proved, as we uncovered it further, to be one of the most complicated in the whole sector from the point of view of layer

succession i.e. relative stratigrpahy. Once again this was the result of relatively recent damage in the form of several grave pits. The north-western part of the square was, in its late ancient-period contexts, almost totally devalued. Here we found an extensive double grave pit (outer pit 20Y007/20Y008f; inner pit 20Y017/20Y018f). A further, smaller grave was then found by the eastern section (20Y011/20Y012f) (tab. 2.1, 1:1, fig. 2.1, 7). Its lengthwise axis copied the axis of the edge of wall 20Y003c. Here, too, as in squares 20O, 20P and 20Q, this grave pit respects the course of the wall. The same is true of grave 20Y006f with filling 20Y005, of which only the eastern edge encroaches on square 20Y. After excavation of the grave pits, the northern half of the square was dominated by an extensive deposit across the area, represented by the two layers 20Y013 and 20Y022 (the two are difficult to distinguish from each other in some places). The latter layer was characterised by a large number of fragments of mud bricks, clearly connected to the destruction of the higher-positioned construction 20Y003c. Interesting finds from this group of layers include parts of grindstone and quernstone, (20Y022.I and 20Y022.III).

In the western and eastern sections the thickness of this group of layers can be seen to reach 45 cm. In the whole central part of the square, its bottom edge consisted of a grey-green clayey crust, 20Y020, which may be considered the level of the floor. On top of it a thin layer of lime could be discerned in some places (20Y031c), continuing uninterrupted as the plaster on the remains of walls 20Y025c and 20Y028c (fig. 2.1, 23). These constructions are the most interesting building remains in this square. After the removal of most of the above-mentioned contexts, it could be seen that here, too, wall 20Y003c (or Wall "C" of the monumental construction) is built on foundations created from the walls of the earlier phase of construction. Pictures (fig. 2.1, 23 and 2.1, 82) clearly show that the earlier wall did not originally form a compact wall here, but those two passages around 90 cm wide were cut in it. This situation is described in more detail above in chapter "Constructions earlier than the monumental building." Both the plaster-covered passages were filled with bricks and rubble before construction started on the younger wall. Very careful investigation was also carried out in the north-western corner of square 20Y, where, as we said earlier, the situation was disturbed by two pits, 20Y008f and 20Y018f. Their excavation revealed a construction labelled 20Y021c (Wall "L"), which is clearly connected to the construction activity that preceded the "monumental" building. Because its foundations are at a lower level than the fragments of walls described above, 20Y025c, 28c and 30c (fig. 2.1, 23), Jan Kysela believed that it was not connected to these constructions but preceded them. The fact that its orientation

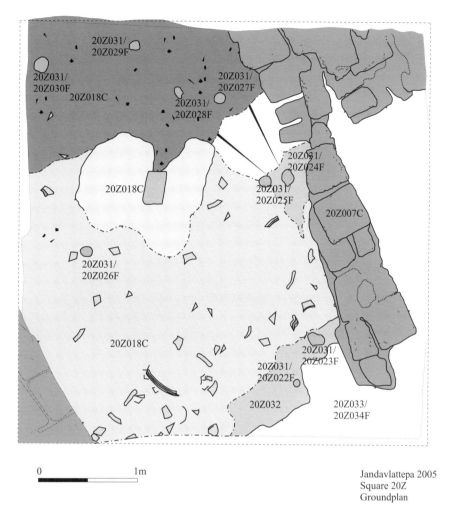

0          1m

Jandavlattepa 2005
Square 20Z
Groundplan

**Fig. 2.1,79** Square 20Z, general ground plan, drawing by K. Urbanová.

**Fig. 2.1,80** Square 20Z, general view from south-west, photo K. Urbanová.

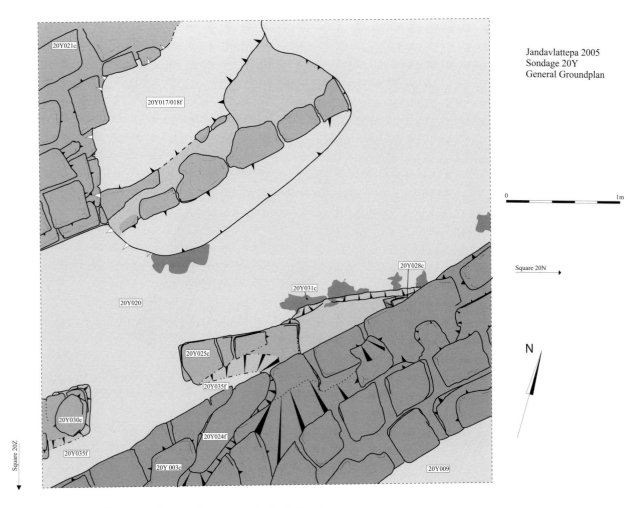

**Fig. 2.1, 81** Square 20Y, general ground plan, drawing by J. Kysela.

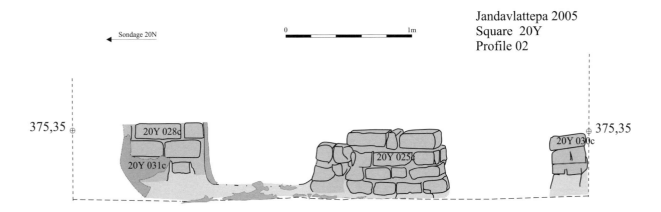

Fig. 2.1, 82 Square 20Y, side view of the Wall "J" (20Y025c and 20Y028c), drawing by J. Kysela.

is the same and the quality of brickwork is identical, however, justifies me in the opinion that it is a wall running parallel to wall "J," equipped with two passages, and that together they enclose some sort of corridor. The lower level of its foundations appears to result from the fact that at that time, too, the terrain was also sloping, no matter how differently it was shaped compared to today. For a detailed description

of this interpretation see again "Constructions earlier than the monumental building."

## Season 2006

During the third excavation season (2006) we focused in the Citadel on the area at the north-west edge of the Citadel, with five newly-opened squares

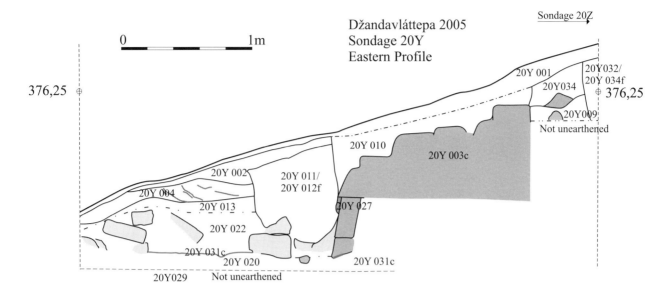

**Fig. 2.1, 83** Square 20Y, eastern section (profile), drawing by J. Kysela.

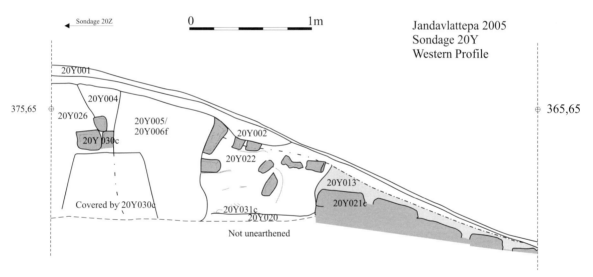

**Fig. 2.1, 84** Square 20Y, western section (profile), drawing by J. Kysela.

following on in space terms from squares 20Y and 20Z. Their excavation was intended to cast as much light as possible on the external ground plan of the monumental building, as well as to bring further information as to how the building was divided up internally. Work on the Citadel in the 2006 season was led by Ladislav Stančo and Jan Kysela, while Petra Belaňová was involved in the documentation. We had to select a provisory point as the basic point for measuring heights, given that no original geodetic measuring point existed. The provisory point chosen was one of the earlier measured points in square 20Q (height above sea level 376.76 m). Texts to this season were written by Jan Kysela and Ladislav Stančo.

**Square 21D** (figs. 2.1, 86–89)

A square on the level, with a location following on from the row formed by 20D, 20O and 20Z. Work here was led by Jan Kysela. Also this square was very extensively affected with posterior funerary activities which damaged most of the topmost anthropic levels. Beneath the superficial erosive layer 21D001 we encountered three very extensive grave pits 21D020/021f, 21D002/003f and 21D025/026f (fig. 2.1, *89*) running diagonally across the whole of the sondage's length. A child burial had been deposited in the superior levels of fillings of the former, the very bottom of the grave pit was not reached. The latter two were characterised with large pits (ca. 3×1.5 m). The actual burial (reached and excav-

**Fig. 2.1,85** Square 20Y, general view from north-east, photo J. Kysela.

N

Jandavlattepa 2006
Square 21D
Groundplan

0                    1m

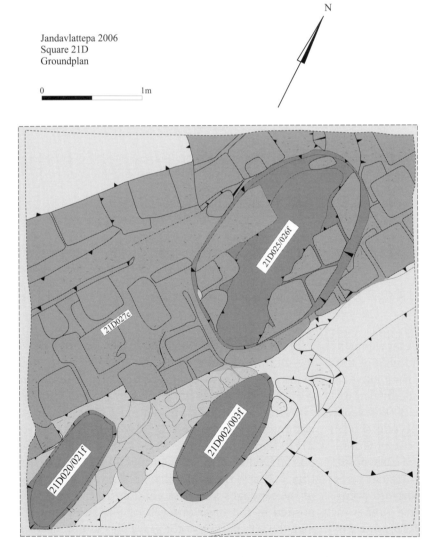

**Fig. 2.1,86** Square 21D, general ground plan, drawing by J. Kysela.

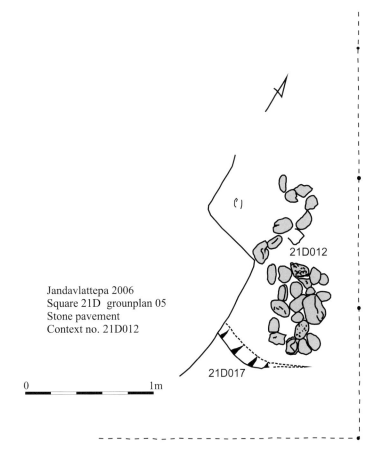

Jandavlattepa 2006
Square 21D  grounplan 05
Stone pavement
Context no. 21D012

21D012

21D017

0                              1m

**Fig. 2.1,87** Square 21D, ground plan no. 5, context no. 21D012 – pavement? drawing by J. Kysela.

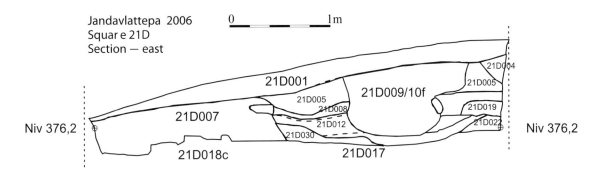

Jandavlattepa 2006
Squar e 21D
Section — east

0                    1m

21D001        21D009/10f        21D004        21D005

21D005        21D019

21D008

Niv 376,2        21D007        21D012        21D022        Niv 376,2

21D030

21D018c        21D017

**Fig. 2.1,88** Square 21D, eastern section (profile), drawing by J. Kysela.

ated only in 21D002/003f) was deposited in additional narrow trenches cut into the pit's bottom. The sondage's eastern edge, too, is partially intersected with an end of a probable grave pit 21D009/010f and the layer 21D004 encountered in the very SE corner may be very possibly interpreted as fill of a gravepit as well. Finally another burial was identified at the very end of the works in the middle of the architectural remains (see below). Overall, the gravepits cover more than a half of the sondage's surface leaving little architecture few stratigraphical relations intact.

These recent interferences intersected the ancient abandon levels: highly erosive 21D006 in the NW corner and 21D005 in the SE corner both overly a strip of eroded architectural remains (21D007) stretching diagonally over the rest of the sondage. A fair stratigraphical sequence was preserved in the SE corner where the layer 21D005 composed of eroded mudbrick with very numerous white admixtures overlaid a much finer 21D008 and it, on its turn, a thin hard-burnt layer 21D011. The 21D012 beneath the latter was very hard beaten greyish clay

**Fig. 2.1, 89** Grave pit of the type P2 (double), context no. 21D025/026f, photo J. Kysela.

forming a pronounced depression. Two postholes (21D013/014f and 21D015/016f) were planted in it and inside it a level of very close packed river pebbles was unearthed (fig. 2.1, *19*). The layer 21D030, a miserable fragment of the original stratigraphy spared by the two grave pits in the southern profile, may be considered as a continuation of 21D012 towards W. The horizon may be interpreted as floor level contemporary with the several mudbrick fragments (21D019c) close to the S profile. The whole phase not only is deposited on the wall remains preserved in the rest of the sondage but also leans very clearly against the walls' eroded superior part and must be therefore interpreted as an occupation phase posterior to that of the monumental building. The architectural remains under 21D007 were labelled 21D018c east of the grave pits and 21D027c and 21D028c West of them. The latter distinction was due to the seeming difference between the bricks used in both constructions (caused in reality by a burial sunken inconspicuously into the wall's surface, masked by its mudbrick fill and only signalled at the very end of our works by a human skull which popped out from the section of the grave pit 21D026f). In fact, all the three stretches of brickwork belong to the same construction, corresponding by their crumbly mudbricks 42–38 × 42–38 × 12 cm to the Wall "C." Studying the masonry in the section

of the grave pits, however, a more significant distinction could be made between the latter constructions and a previous phase on the top of which these were laid. In this construction phase smaller and neater mudbricks were used, identical with those of the Wall J in Square 20Y.

*J. Kysela*

**Square 21E** (fig. 2.1, 90–93)

The area of this square is the closest to the highest point of the Citadel and of the whole site of Jandavlattepa, and follows on in a row from squares 20E and 20P. It slopes gently from east to west and from south to north. At the eastern side we reached a depth of 1.5 m from the surface (fig. 2.1, *92*), but on the western side only 0.3 – 0.5 m. This square was characterised by a minimum yield of architectural remains, and in its eastern half had a marked layering of loose soils with a considerable share of organic admixtures, alternating with layers of cinders and ash. After removing the surface erosion layer, 21E001 (c. 15 cm) we were able to distinguish on the surface the outlines of several pits, which on excavation turned out to be grave pits. Two of them were small graves, either children's graves or graves with incomplete and haphazardly-placed remains (child's grave 21E002/21E003f in the eastern section and secondary burial 21E021/21E022f (fig. 2.1, *93*) about half a metre away in the middle of the square).

The earlier contexts were, however, more markedly disturbed by the "ordinary" grave pits, above all 21E004/21E005f in the north-eastern corner of the square (not excavated to the bottom) and, immediately next to it, 21E010/21E011f and 21E019/21E020f (tab. 2.1, 1:3) in the southern section, with only its northern half (from the pelvis of the bone remains upward) encroaching on square 21E. The other grave pits encroached only in a very minor way on this square (21E031/21E032f and 21E007/21E008f). Even so, however, the occurrence of grave pits in this pit is the highest of all, with only neighbouring square 21F and 20Q having the same number. The reason may have

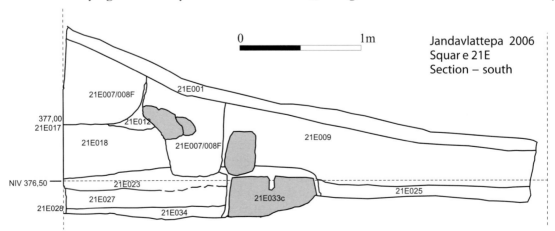

**Fig. 2.1, 90** Square 21E, southern section (profile), drawing by P. Belaňová.

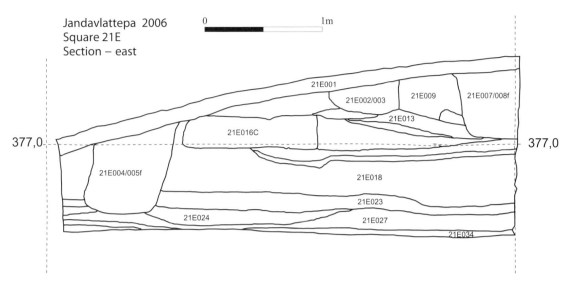

Jandavlattepa 2006
Square 21E
Section – east

been an attempt to bury the dead as close as possible to the grave of the local *Imam*, in the middle of the elevation. In the drawings of the eastern, northern and western section there is a clearly-visible group of layers composed of thickish layers of loose soil with a large number of white (organic) admixtures. (21E018, 21E023, 21E027 and 21E034) and thinner layers

Fig. 2.1, 92 Square 21E, eastern section (profile), photo J. Kysela.

Fig. 2.1, 93 Square 21E, grave pit of the type S (secondary), context no. 21E021/022f, photo L. Stančo.

with ash and cinders (21E015, 21E017, 21E024 and 21E028, some even thinner ones were not recorded), which were gradually investigated after the grave pits were excavated. In the eastern section (fig. 2.1, *91*) it is clear that, as well as being disturbed by grave pits, the group of layers was also disturbed by a single notable fragment of architecture, 21E016c, which appears to be part of a wall destroyed by water erosion, or a collapsed wall. After thorough cleaning, we were only able to distinguish one complete brick here, measuring 40 × 40 cm. This phenomenon only impinges on the edge of square 21E. The layers with ash and loose soil in the eastern section end about 1.2 – 1.4 m from the section, while in a westerly direction we mostly took away layers of an erosion nature. We finished work in this trench at the level of more compact, medium-packed soil (context no. 21E029) after the partial removal of layers 21E025 in the south west and 21E026 in the northwest corner. At approximately the same level, in the southern section a more coherent (1.1 m long) fragment of architecture was found in this square, in other words part of wall 21E033c (wall "V"), built of rectangular bricks 48 × 28 cm (fig. 2.1, 90).[47]

*L. Stančo*

## Square 21F (figs. 94–95)

The southernmost trench in this part of the Citadel was located in line with 21D and 21E. It was opened contemporarily with them with the intention to trace the inner dispositions of the monumental building, hopefully better preserved here where the erosion was supposed to have lesser impact than in the perimetral zones. Also here, however, these questions were destined to remain without answer. In this case, it was so due to the too good preservation of recent or in any case post-abandoned horizons.

---

[47]  For the relationships to other architectural remains in this part see: Overview of all building constructions in Sector 20.

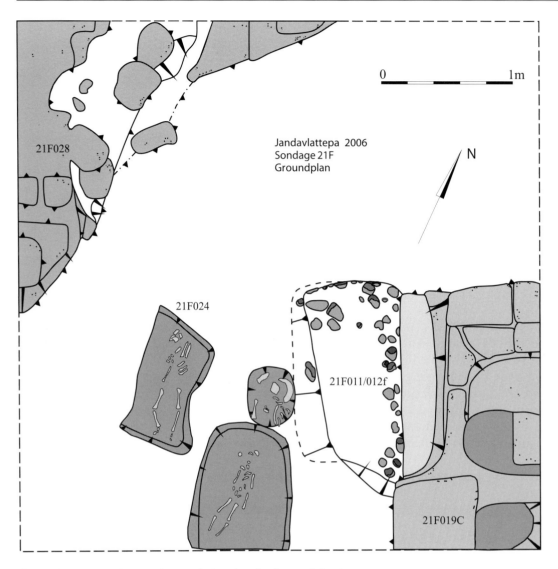

Jandavlattepa 2006
Sondage 21F
Groundplan

0          1m

N

21F028

21F024

21F011/012f

21F019C

**Fig. 2.1, 94** Square 21F, general ground plan, drawing by P. Belaňová.

As in other trenches, a number of recent grave-pits cut through the stratigraphy. Only some of these, however, appeared just below the superior erosion layer 21F001: 21F010/011f, 21F008/009f and 21F006/007f (tab. 2.1, 1:6; fig. 2.1, 9). In the latter case, the human remains lay heaped and completely disarticulated on the bottom of an irregular pit. This situation evidently results from an intervention posterior to the primary deposition of the body. The nature of this intervention is, however, not clear: no traces of a posterior burial were ascertained in the upper levels of the pit. The stratigraphy of the trench's N/ NE corner, closest to the Citadel's peak, differed throughout the excavation from that of the rest of the trench, obviously due to accumulation of strata here, washed or eroded from the higher points. In the uppermost levels, a narrow stripe of very compact greyish layer 21F003 stretching along the trench's E section appeared immediately below 21F001, covering on its turn 21F 004 (a thick pack of light grey dust, at first moment considered a filling of an – in-

existent – pit 21F005f) and black carbonaceous layer with yellow stains of burn earth 21F002 occupying the whole of the trench's NE corner and extending over a third of the trench's surface. Further to the south, the abovementioned grave pits cut through the layer 21F012 consisting mainly of degraded mudbrick (preserved as debris, lumps and even as almost whole pieces). Its outlines are not clear, mainly in the N where it is covered by 21F002 and where it covers 21F013. Both of these black carbonaceous dusty layers got mixed with it and their mutual limits were practically indistinguishable. Below this mudbrick level, the layer 21F014 covering practically the whole of the trench's surface was ascertained: this little consistent brownish earth with concentrations of white spots contained three children burials deposited apparently (on different elevations!) directly "inside" the layer without a grave pit. Two of them were conventionally labelled 21F016/017f and 21F030/31f the search for limits of the grave pit gave, however, no results. After removing 21F014, a mottled layer 21F020

**Fig. 2.1, 95** Square 21F, general view from east, photo J. Kysela.

was discovered in the NE corner and another children burial (21F021/022f this time in a regular pit) in the southern section. The 21F020, burnt and thus highly variegated in terms of both colour (black – grey – orange – ochre) and consistence, copied basically the extension of 21F002 (quite similar to it in both colour and consistence) and can be considered another element linked with the particular situation close to the Citadel's peak. The burial 21F021/022f proved that at least up to this level we remained in modern or sub-recent levels. The layers 21F023 and 21F024 below this level were in their general character very much akin to those so far investigated. This convinced us that, with the time at our disposal, we would be unable to reach and document properly the horizons linked with the destruction, even with the abbandon of the monumental buildingSeveral structures were nonetheless documented. Covered with the most recent levels and substantially differing with their poor construction techniques from those of the perimeter wall, these constructions can be most probably considered as evidence for frequentation of the site after the abandon of the monumental building. The badly preserved narrow wall of poor quality brickwork 21F028c can be very convincingly linked with similar structures in the trenches 21E and 21P (see above) with which it creates a single structure. Also 21F019c building (fig. 2.1, *25*) from which a NW corner is preserved in the SW corner of the trench was evindetly anterior to the activities documented by the excav-

ated layers: the layers in the E section obviously rise against the wall and the "layer" 21F018 filling in the structure consisted of a sequence of burnt layers very similar (identical?) to that observed in the N half of the trench. The construction could be examined more closely thanks to the fact, that its W wall was fully exposed by the grave pit 21F011f which cut through the layers down to the construction's foundations. It was built from rather quality mudbricks 36–38 × 36–38 × × 9 cm lain on a *pakhsa* block which on its turn reposes on a coherent layer of river pebbles. This (rather deep) layer could perhaps originally have made part of a floor of the monumental building and be used subsequently as a substructure for this posterior building.

*J. Kysela*

**Square 21O** (fig. 2.1, 96, 97)

This trench is located on sloping ground, in the place where the perimeter of the Citadel turns southwards. Its position in a direct line of continuity with the course of Wall "C" in squares 20N, 20Y and 21D justified us in our opinion that here, too, we would trace the body of this perimeter wall. The situation here was in this respect similar to that in square 20N, where only a very little of this wall was preserved in the sloping terrain. After removal of the surface erosion layer, the thickness of which varied considerably in the different parts of the square, we cleaned a few mud bricks of wall 21O005c (Wall "C") which had

**Fig. 2.1,96** Square 210, general ground plan, drawing by P. Belaňová.

here resisted erosion. It was by now traditional to find that this construction was built on foundations made up of earlier walls. In this case it was the large, well-built construction 210006c, made of mud bricks measuring c. 30 × 30 cm, which has here been preserved with a length of 5.6 m and a width of at least

**Fig. 2.1,97** Square 210, general view from east, photo J. Kysela.

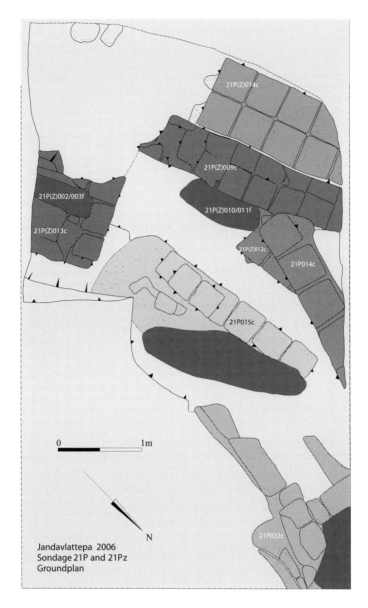

**Fig. 2.1, 98** Square 21P and P(z), general ground plan, drawing by P. Belaňová.

2.2 m (the whole width was not uncovered). In the overall plan it is labelled Wall "U."

*L. Stančo*

### Square 21P + 21P west (figs. 98–100)

This trench was opened to the south of the sondage 21O and to the west of 21E with the intention to follow further the stratigraphy and mainly the perimeter walls observed in the neighbouring trenches. Since only minor portions of the walls were encountered in the square 4 × 4 m, we decided soon to extend the trench westwards without, however, keeping the traditional reserved block which would be extremely difficult to maintain in the sloping terrain covering at the same time the most interesting part of the structures to be studied. This western extension of the trench was called 21Pz ("z" means "západ" = west in Czech, i.e. 21Pz = western part of 21P) and the stratigraph-

ical units ascertained there were labelled with a numerical sequence of their own.

The works stared with stripping the superior erosive layer 21P 001 under which we ascertained a very consistent light layer 21P002 in the eastern part of the trench and a large grave pit 21P003/004f in the center of the western part (tab. 2.1, 1:4; fig. 2.1, *8*). More gravepits were identified along the southern edge of the trench: 21P020/021f in the SE corner, 21P009/010f west of it and 21P011/012f in the SW corner on the border with 21Pz. All these grave pits cut through the very loose cloggy layer 21P005 covering most of the trench's surface and marking generally the abandon of the ancient horizons while 21P002 resulted most probably form erosion of mudbrick structures uphill. Activities dating after the site's abandonment are attested by remains of a small fireplace 21P007/008f documented in the southern pro-

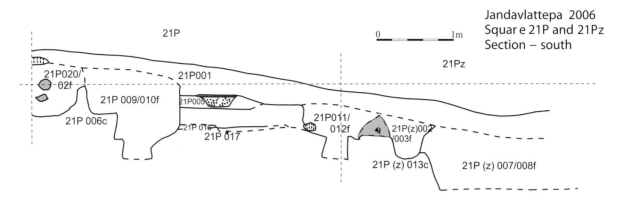

Fig. 2.1, 99 Square 21P, southern section (profile), drawing by J. Kysela.

file. Two constructions were covered by 21P005 in the eastern part of the trench: 21P006c in the south and 21P022c in the north. Both these flimsy narrow structures consist of a single row of very low quality mudbricks of irregular dimensions and varying width of fissures between them while in other cases single bricks even cannot be discerned in the compact brickwork block. This technological correspondence between them together with their mutually perpendicular position suggests very convincingly that they made part of a single structure (see above). The very compact uniform layer 21P023 detected between 21P022c and the N section can be considered the washed remains of the latter construction (see its sloping upper contour in the N section). The construction 21P006c reposes on the top of hard crust 21P016 scattered with concentrations of white particles and traces of vegetal remains ("hay"). This layer as well as the 21P017 and 21P018 below belong already to a horizon preceding

that of the provisory building delimited by the walls 21P006c and 21P022c.

Further to the west, all situation is complicated by virtual absence of stratified layers as all the western part of 21P and the whole of 21Pz consists of stretches of walls while most of the space between them is destroyed by recent pits: minor graves 21Pz 002/003f, 21Pz 010/011f but mainly by a huge pit 21Pz007/008f which destroyed most of the southern profile of the trench 21Pz. A stretch of wall 21P014c = 21Pz005c (and its eroded superior level 21P013) constitute the last preserved portion of the perimeter wall of the later phase of the monumental building. Here a single row of the characteristic 39–42 × 39–42 × 12 cm crumbly mudbricks is preserved. It reposes on an earlier construction 21Pz012c made of similar mudbricks but deviating by several degrees from its orientation (21Pz005 azimuth 48°; 21Pz012 azimuth 20°). 50 cm east of 21Pz012c lies another stretch of brickwork 21P015c

Fig. 2.1, 100 Square 21P and 21Pz, general view from north-east, photo J. Kysela.

which has exactly the same orientation but this time is made of smaller and more compact mudbricks usually associated with constructions of the earlier building phase elsewhere in the Citadel. Only 120 cm long this alineation of mudbricks does not seem to have any connection to any other construction in its surroundings. The space between 21Pz012c and 21P015 is filled in with 21Pz004, a layer consisting mainly of fragments of mudbricks, which seem to come from 21P 015c rather than from 21Pz012c. This deposit is cut by the gravepit 21Pz010/011f. The last preserved mudbrick of 21P014=21Pz 005c partially overlies the structure 21Pz 009c. It consists of two lines of clear ochre mubricks 34–35 × 34–35 × 10 cm made of very well washed dough and separated from one another by regular narrow fissures. Stretching in almost perfect N-S direction, its southern termination was truncated by the posterior pit 21Pz008f. Since the northern face of a mutilated block of brickwork 21Pz013c located to south-east of 21Pz009c is precisely perpendicular to the latter and since the building technique of both structure is basically identical they may be considered as two elements of the same building whose connection was destroyed by the pit. On its western side, the wall 21Pz009c is "doubled" by 21Pz014c. Both walls have the same orientation and remain in direct physical contact on the whole of their course. They are, however, not linked architectonically and they differ in their technology, 21Pz014c being built of brown-grey crumbly mudbricks ca 40 × 40 × ? cm (the mudbricks' thickness could never be studied sice the structure was only uncovered in surface). Perhaps, this last wall could be envisaged as a posterior structure added at an indeterminate later date to 21Pz009c to consolidate its foundations against the steep slope.

*J. Kysela*

## 2.1.8 Bibliography

Azimov, I. (2000): K vostonovleniyu arkhitekturnogo oblika kushanskoy kreposti Kampyrtepa, in: *Materialy tokharistanskoy ekspeditsii*, eds. Rtveladze, E. V. – Iljasov, D., vol. I. Tashkent, pp. 33–38.

Baimatova, N. S. (2008): *5000 Jahre Architektur in Mittelasien: Lehmziegelgewölbe vom 4./3. Jt. v. Chr. bis zum Ende des 8. Jhs. n. Chr.* Archäologie in Iran und Turan 7. Mainz.

Held, W. (2002): Die Reisidenzstädte der Seleukiden. *JdI* 117, pp. 217–249.

Huff, D. (1997): Deutsch-Uzbek Ausgrabungen auf dem Džandaulattepe und in Džarkutan, Süduzbekistan, 1993–1995. *Mitteilungen der Berliner Gesellschaft für Anthropologie, Ethnologie und Urgeschichte*, 18, pp. 83–95.

Huff. D. – Pidaev, Sh. – Chaydullaev, Sh. (2001): Uzbek-German archaeological researches in the Surkhan Darya region, in: *La Bactriane au carrefour des routes et des civilisations de l'Asie centrale*. Actes du colloque de Termez, 1997. Paris, pp. 219–233.

Khmelnitskiy, S. (2001): K vaprosu klassifikacii rannesrednevekovych zamkov Sredney Azii. *IMKU,* 32, pp. 120–132.

Kaim, B. (2002): *Architektura starożytnej Baktrii w okresie kuszańskim*. Warszawa.

Kaim, B. (2000): Znaki na cegłach w architekturze środkowoazjatyckiej, in: *Swiatowit*, Tom II (XLIII), Fasc. A. Warszawa, pp. 70–73.

Lecuyot, G. – Rapin, C. (2000): Samarkand et Aï Khanoum. Les briques marquées en Asie Central, in: *La brique antique et médiévale. Production et commercialisation d'un matériau*, eds. Boucheron, P. – Broise, H. – Thébert, Y., École Française de Rome, pp. 31–52.

Leriche, P. – Pidaev, Sh. (2007): Termez in Antiquity, in: *After Alexander. Central Asia before Islam*, eds.: Cribb, J. – Herrmann, G. London, pp. 179–212.

Pidaev, Sh. (1978): *Poseleniya kushanskogo vremeni severnoy Baktrii.* Tashkent.

Pilipko, V. N. (1985): *Poseleniya severo-zapadnoy Baktrii.* Ashkhabad – Ylym.

Pugachenkova G. A. (1978): Ukrepleniya nizhnogo goroda, in: *Dal'verzintepa. Kushanskiy gorod na yuge Uzbekistana*, eds.: Pugachenkova, G. A. – Rtveladze, E. V. Tashkent, pp. 21–32.

Pugachenkova G. A. (1979): Jiga-tepe (raskopki 1974 g.), in: *Drevnyaya Baktriya. Materialy Sovetsko-Afghanskoy eksepedicii Vyp. 2*, ed. Kruglikova I. T., Moskva, pp. 63–94.

Pugachenkova G. A. – Turgunov, B. A. (1974): Issledovanie Dal'verzin-tepe v 1972 g, in: *Drevnyaya Baktriya*, ed. Masson, V. M., Leningrad: Nauka, pp. 58–73.

Rtveladze, E. V. (1978): Tsitadel' Nizhnego Goroda, in: *Dal'verzintepe. Kushanskiy gorod na yuge Uzbekistana*, eds.: Pugachenkova, G. A. – Rtveladze, E. V. Tashkent, pp. 12–20.

Rtveladze, E. V. (1982): Ob areale i khronologii sasanidskikh zavoevaniy v Severnoy Baktrii – Tokharistane (po danym numizmatiki). *Obshchestvennye nauki v Uzbekistane* (ONU) 1/1982, pp. 47–54.

Rtveladze, E. V. (1974): Razvedochnoe izuchenie Baktriyskych pamyatnikov na yuge Uzbekistana, in: *Drevnyaya Baktriya*, ed.: Masson, V. M., Leningrad: Nauka, pp. 74–85.

Rtveladze, E. V. (1976): Noviye drevnyebaktriyskie pamyatniki na yuge Uzbekistana, in: Masson, V. M., ed., *Baktriyskie drevnosti*, Leningrad: Nauka, pp. 93–103.

Rtveladze, E. V. – Khakimov, Z. E. (1973): Marshrutnyye issledovaniya pamyatnikov severnoy Baktrii, in: Pugachenkova, G. A., ed., *Iz istorii antichnoy kul'tury Uzbekistana*, Tashkent, pp. 10–34.

Rusanov, d. (2000): Gradostraitel'naya kul'tura Kampyrtepa epokhy Kushan, in: *Materialy tocharistanskoy ekspedicii*, eds. Rtveladze, E. V. – Iljasov, d. Vyp. I. Tashkent, pp. 19–32.

Sedov, A. V. (1987): *Kobadian na paroge rannego srednevekov'ya.* Moskva: Nauka.

Schachner, A. (1995/1996): A Special Kind of Pattern Burnished Decoration on the Late Kushan Pottery in Bactria and Afghanistan. *Silk Road Art and Archaelogy* 4, pp. 151–159.

Schachner, A. (2003–2004): Die Keramik der Grabungen 1993 am Džandavlattepe, Süd-Uzbekistan. *Archäologische Mitteilungen aus Iran und Turan* 35–36, pp. 335–372.

Stančo, L. 2006a: Pozdně antická severní Baktrie, in: *Orientalia Antiqua Nova* VI, pp. 73–78 (in Czech).

Stančo, L. 2006b: Antropomorfně zdobený džbánek z Džandavláttepa. *Studia Hercynia* X, pp. 106–110 (in Czech).

Stronach, d. (SD): On the Antiquity of the Yurt. Evidence from Arjan and Elsewhere. *The silkroad Foundation Newsletter*, from URl. <http://www.silk-road.com/newsletter/2004vol2num1/yurt.htm> (available 05/02/2008).

Zav'yalov V. A. (2008): *Kushanshakhr pri sasanidakh. Po materialam raskopok na gorodishche Zar-tepa*, Saint Peterburg.

# 2.2 Excavations in Sector 04 – preliminary report

*Shapulat Shaydullaev*

Sector 04 is situated in the south western corner of the Shakhristan (see general plan in the introductory chapter, fig. 1). Excavation of this area began back in 1993, when the author worked there as a member of a German-Uzbek team. At the time he suggested that the structure formed part of the fortifications, including the city gate. Work was then renewed in 2002 as part of the Czech-Uzbekistani expedition. From the start, therefore, the situation here was opposite to that in other sectors, since it was clear what sort of structure was being excavated. In addition to the author, archaeologists V. Ruzanov and L. Boháč took part in the excavation of this area, while A. Shaydullaev documented it.

The following goals were established for the excavation of Sector 04:

1. To ascertain the overall plan of the gate and the area in front of it.
2. To work out a precise timeline for the fortifications and their stratigraphy.

Even before the start of excavation work, in 1993, it was clear from an analysis of the morphology of the terrain that this was the only part of the site where the mound slopes were not as steep, but rose much more gradually. It was even possible to distinguish some sort of ramp, rising from the west to the east in parallel with the city wall and then turning in a direction

**Fig. 2.2, 1** View of the eastern part of Sector 04 from southwest with the gate and bastion no. 1, photo L. Stančo.

perpendicular to it (figs. 1.2, 7 and 2.2, 1). In 1993 only a small part of the wall was uncovered, together with part of the defences in front of it.[1] As part of the Czech-Uzbekistani excavations, the top erosion layer was gradually removed over a larger area.

A section of the city wall 52 m long and 4.30–4.40 m wide was gradually uncovered. We recorded the use of unfired bricks of various dimensions, 30–32 × 14 cm and 36 × 36 × 16 cm. In places where the wall had been repaired, there were large bricks of 42 × 42 × 16 cm.

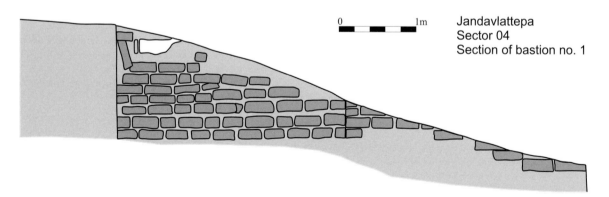

0      1m     Jandavlattepa
Sector 04
Section of bastion no. 1

**Fig. 2.2, 2** Bastion no. 1, Sector 04, section, drawing by Sh. Shaydullaev.

---

1   Huff 1997, p. 86, Huff – Pidaev – Shaydullaev 2001, p. 220.

Jandavlattepa
Sector 04
Section of the citywall with doorway
from inside the bastion no. 1

0 ▬▬▬ 1m

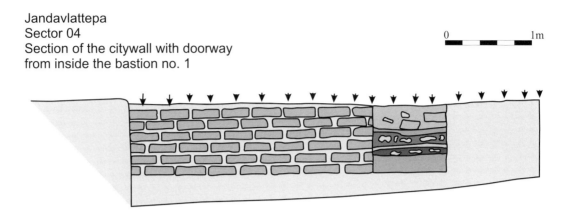

**Fig. 2.2, 3** Section of the city wall with doorway inside the bastion no. 1, drawing by Sh. Shaydullaev.

Gaps of 2–3 cm had been left between the bricks. Various markings were found on the bricks: circles, semicircles, parallel lines and zigzag lines. At the eastern end of Sector 04 next to the wall, a square bastion (bastion no. 1) was recorded on the ground plan, projecting 3.4 m in front of the outer edge of the wall. Only a few rows of bricks have been preserved; indeed, on the southern side (down the slope) there is only one layer of bricks (fig. 2.2, 2).

The height of the preserved wall thus varies from 0.2 to 0.6 m. The inner space of the bastion measures 3 × 4 m, which indicates that the inner room was flush with the body of the wall. This is something we also find with other fortifications, such as those at Zartepa and Surkh Kotal.[2] An entrance to the corridor of the fortifications had also been made at this point at floor level, 0.9 m wide. This passageway can be compared with the slightly eccentrically-situated passage (on the left, looking from the town) found near bastion no. 3 at Kampyrtepa, which has an inside width of 1 m.[3] The inner space itself was filled partly with soft and loose layers with coatings of ash, and partly with regularly-stacked unfired bricks in six rows (fig. 2.2, 3). This suggests that the bastion was deliberately bricked in shortly after it ceased to be used. At floor level a number of large stones were found, clearly for use as ammunition.

Close to the bastion (about 0.8 m to the west of it) a loophole in the shape of an arrow (fig. 2.2, 4) was found in the wall, growing narrower towards the top. At its widest point it was 22 cm wide.[4] Although only one loophole was found in situ, we assume they were situated at regular intervals, including in the bastion, where they could not be found because of the poor state of preservation of the walls.

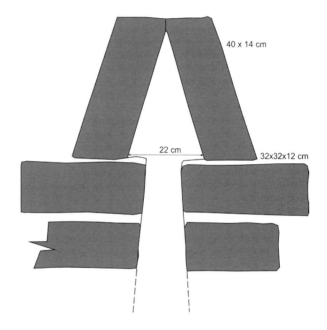

40 x 14 cm

22 cm

32x32x12 cm

**Fig. 2.2, 4** Loophole close to the bastion no. 1, drawing by Sh. Shaydullaev.

In addition to the bastion, a right-angled reinforcement was found on the outer side of the wall between the bastion and the gate, made of a single block of paksha (rammed earth). The preserved part sticks out 1.1 m in front of the wall and is 2.3 m long. There are similar reinforcements in the fortifications at Dilberjin, but they are situated on the inner side of the wall.

On the inner side, the walls of a building that has yet to be explored, 0.6 m wide, join the fortifications at right angles (fig. 2.2, 5). In the middle of the room an oval pit was discovered, 2.8 m long, 1.5 m wide and with its length along a north-south axis.

---

2  Sabirov 1976, p. 48, ris. 2, but the bastion here is curved, not square; Fussman 1983, p. 16, Plan 2 and 3, at Surkh Kotal the bastions project 3.9 m in front of the body of the wall.
3  Sverchkov 2001, p. 49, p. 61 ris. 8.
4  At Kampyrtepa the width of the loopholes varies from 15 to 30 cm, Sverchkov 2001, p. 49; note the 20 cm wide loopholes documented at Bactria in the walls of the upper city, which are equally wide throughout the wall. This means they are of almost no practical use; in the fortifications at Zartepa loopholes 25–30 cm wide have been documented, Sabirov 1976, p. 48, ris. 2; the walls of the Citadel at Dilberjin had loopholes 15–20 cm wide, for their forms see Dolgorukov 1984, p. 62 ris. 4.

Jandavlattepa
Sector 04
Section of the citywall
and adjacent room
close to the gate

**Fig. 2.2,5** Section of the city wall and adjacent room close to the gate, drawing by Sh. Shaydullaev.

Although it was not marked, it is likely that it was a Muslim grave of the same type as the many that were discovered in Sector 07. A pit of the same type was also found outside the same walls, four meters from the first one.

**Projecting fortification elements in the gate area**

On the southern-outer-side the wall is joined by a structure made of unfired bricks of the same dimensions as those used in the wall itself. It goes down the slope, and appears to lie alongside the entrance ramp. At the wall – in the gate area, therefore – the structure is 9 m wide, but as it goes out it gradually narrows, and at its southernmost extremity is about 1.5 m wide. The overall length is 34 m. The first level, connected to the body of the wall, is in the shape of an irregular trapezium with sides measuring 7 × 6 × 9 × 6 m. The second level, connected to the first, is also irregular in shape, with dimensions of 9 × 3 × 9 × 1.5 m. The third part is rectangular, with dimensions of 4 × 1.5 m. All three parts were created at the same time, and in fact form a protective flank on the left of the gate. The structure was covered in a plaster of clay mixed with straw, 2–4 cm wide. In the upper part of the gate area, to the west of the side protective wall and thus right at the point of the presumed passage through the fortifications, a wall running parallel to the main body of the fortifications (and probably connected to it in its construction) was discovered. Its preserved length is 5.3 m, and width a mere 0.9 m. Atypical unfired bricks were used here, with dimensions of 40 × 19 × 15 cm. In the narrow corridor, about 1 m wide, between the main wall and this wall, a pavement of unfired bricks was discovered.[5] This space contained a considerable number of large stones and boulders, between 20 and 40 cm in size, which no doubt served as ammunition for the defenders of the

walls and gates against potential besiegers (figs. 2.2, 6 and 7).[6] The thin wall mentioned above could be taken to be some sort of parapet protecting the defenders as they moved around the fortifications. The paving of unfired bricks, however, suggests that the area was roofed, either with a vault of unfired bricks or with a roof of wood and rushes. It cannot be by chance that so much ammunition was stored in the area over the gate. It lay ready here for the defence of this weak point in the fortifications. Further excavations showed that the corridor and the parapet were built on a foundation of tightly rammed earth, some sort of pisé. It therefore seems that this whole structure was not created at the same time as the main fortifications, but was a later addition.

In 2004 further excavations revealed an earlier stage of the fortifications. About 60 m of this older wall was found, including a sudden break in the wall in a north-westerly direction in the area west of the gate. It was 4.2 m wide, and built of unfired bricks of

**Fig. 2.2,6** Corridor above the gate with ammunition consisting of large stones, view from west, photo L. Stančo.

---

5   It is fairly usual for fortification corridors to be about 1 m wide – at Dilberjin, for example, the corridors or galleries are 0.75 – 1.15 m wide (Kaim 2002, p. 47).
6   Cf. stock of ammunition stored close to the south gate of Dilberjin, consisting of large numbers of small shots (8–12 cm, some of them smaller: 3–4 cm) made of unbaked clay, Pugachenkova 1984, p.105, ris. 19. 7.

**Fig. 2.2, 7** Corridor above the gate with ammunition consisting of large stones, view from north, photo L. Stančo.

30–32 × 30–32 × 14 cm and 36 × 36 × 16 cm. Gaps of 2–3 cm were left between the bricks. These bricks are also marked with signs made with finger strokes, in the form of circles, semicircles and parallel lines. At the above-mentioned break in the wall, a corner bastion was uncovered (bastion no. 2), rectangular in shape with internal dimensions of 5.5 × 1.8 m (fig. 2.2, *8*). The walls of the bastion are 1.85 m thick. In this case, too, the walls have been very badly preserved, with a height of around 0.4 m, and once again several large stones were found here.

From the point of view of stratigraphy, four phases of the fortifications can be distinguished. The first phase is represented by the low fortification wall with a break, and the rectangular bastion no. 2.

The second phase is, of course, the upper fortification wall itself, with a bastion and the projecting left wing of the gate. That the walls and the other parts of the fortifications were built at the same time is clear not only from the dimensions of the unfired bricks, which are the same, but from the connected brickwork that can be seen in the corners.

The third phase consisted of the repair and alteration of the fortifications, seen most clearly in the building of the corridor with parapet, equipped with a large amount of ammunition.

The fourth phase consisted of the secondary covering of the fortifications with a layer of unfired bricks. This lining has been preserved in several places, but not as a continuous layer. In the best-preserved parts, three layers of bricks remain, with dimensions of 30 × 30 × 14 cm. The preserved parts do not permit a full reconstruction of the appearance of this repair or alteration. The brick lining was mostly documented and removed during the uncovering of the surface.

## Ceramics

Although the ceramics that have been found in the upper layers are not significant for the dating of the preserved parts of the fortifications, and the ceramics from the erosion layer were not even systematically collected. The main forms and better-preserved pieces of ceramic vessels will be dealt with in next volume together with the pottery of all Shakhristan. They are mostly large and small storage jars and similar kitchen vessels (*khum, khumcha, tagora* – fig. 2.2, *9*). Most of the vessels were made on a potter's wheel, and most of the forms are characteristic of the Kushan and Kushano-Sasanian period.

## Small finds

Although mostly only the upper layers of the fortification and gate areas have been explored, a representa-

**Fig. 2.2, 8** Bastion no. 2, view from east, photo L. Stančo.

**Fig. 2.2, 9** Group of well preserved ceramic vessels of *tagora* type, photo L. Stančo.

tive cross-section of small finds comes from Sector 04. Given the nature of the contexts in which they were found, however, these finds – which include sensitive objects such as coins – are, with a few exceptions, not used for dating this part of the fortifications.

Five loom weights were found in Sector 04, with holes ranging from 0.3–1.3 cm in size. The height of the preserved fragments varies between 4 and 12 cm, while the width of the bottom part is 1.5–4 cm. In the area of bastion no. 1 a group of three of these loom weights were found together, made of unfired clay. This suggests that the bastion may have had some secondary use for household activities such as weaving material. However, it is possible that the weights found their way here as rubbish when the inside of the bastion was being bricked up. Close to bastion no. 2 an intact loom weight was found, made of fired clay, which is considerably rarer than unfired. Several spindle whorls, hemispherical and discoid in shape, were also found, some made of stone (alabaster?) and some of unfired clay. The majority of whorls had diameters of between 2.3 and 3.0 cm, heights of around 1.6 cm and hole diameters of 0.5 cm on average. Kristýna Urbanová did not include this group in her analysis of objects used in textile production in Chapter 3.1.

Four fragments of bone pins with no heads were also found, with a maximum length of 7–8 cm. From the corridor in the fortifications over the gate comes a bronze ring with a stone (04.000.I), from the area of the wall itself a carnelian bead (04.000.II) and from the area of bastion no. 1 a bronze nail or pin (04.000. III). All these finds are classified and described in more detail by Petra Belaňová in Chapter 3.3 (cat. nos. 32, 73, 90).

The finds from Sector 04 also include an iron knife from bastion no.1 (04.000.XVIII) and three bronze arrow tips, common in the Achaemenid and Greco-Bactrian period, which come from the upper layers and were therefore clearly deposited secondarily in these contexts (04.000.IV–VI). These finds, as well as other fragments of knives, are dealt with by Jan Kysela in Chapter 3.2. (cat. nos. 9–12 and 16–18).

Coin finds in Sector 04 include a well-preserved bronze coin (04.000.XVII), minted under the early Kushan ruler so-called Soter Megas (c. 80–100 AD). It is a tetradrachm, probably minted in Bactria. On the obverse is the bust of a king in profile with rays eman-

ating from him and a diadem, holding a sceptre, while on the reverse is a rider on a horse on the right, holding a whip, and the incomplete inscription EΩTHP.

The Soter Megas coin is not the only one from Jandavlattepa. In their work, Rtveladze and Pidaev mention another, which clearly comes from collections made at the start of the 1970s. There is the bust of a king to the right on the obverse, with traces of a monogram behind his head, while the reverse shows the king on a horse, facing right, and standing on a line. Under it is part of a circular inscription, .... ΛΕΥΩΝ EΩ. It is 21 mm in diameter and 8.4 mm high.

Another relatively well-preserved coin is an AE tetradrachm from the reign of Vima Kadphises (c. 100–127/8 AD) with a portrait of the king standing on the left by an altar on the head, and Shiva and a bull on the tail (04.000.XXII). It is a type relatively commonly found in the sites of northern Bactria.[7] Our find is a significant chronological indicator, since it comes from the area of bastion no. 1 and was found under a layer of stored bricks. It suggests that the bastion, and thus the younger phase of the fortifications, must have been standing by the first quarter of the 2nd century. For the other finds of coins in this sector see chapter 3.5 in this volume, especially cat. nos. 14, 32 and 82.

# Bibliography

Dolgorukov, V. C. (1984): Oboronitel'nye sooruzheniya Dil'berdjina, in: *Drevnyaya Baktriya* Vyp. 3. Materialy sovetsko--afghanskoy arkheologicheskoy ekspedicii, ed. Kruglikova, I. T., Moskva, pp. 58–92.

Fussman, G. (1983): *Surkh Kotal. Tempel der Kuschan-Zeit in Baktrien.* München.

Kaim, B. (2002): *Architektura starożytnej Baktrii w okresie kuszańskim.* Warszawa.

Pugachenkova. G. A. (1984): Raskopki juzhnykh gorodskykh vorot Dilberdzhina, in: *Drevnyaya Baktria, vyp. 3: Materialy sovetsko-afghanskoy arkheologicheskoy ekspedicii,* I. T. Kruglikova (ed.), Moskva, pp. 93–111.

Rtveladze, E. V. – Pidaev, Sh. R. (1981): *Katalog drevnich monet yuzhnogo Uzbekistana.* Tashkent.

Sabirov, K. S. (1976): Kushanskaya fortifikaciya v svete raskopok na gorodishche Zar-tepa, in: *Drevnyaya Baktriya.* Moskva, pp. 49–52.

Sverchkov, L. (2001): Raskopki v severo-vostochnoy chasti Kampyrtepa, in: *Materialy tocharistanskoy ekspedicii,* ed. Rtveladze, E. V., vyp. 2. Tashkent, pp. 47–64.

---

[7]   Rtveladze – Pidaev 1981, pp. 63–65.

# 2.3 Excavations in sector 08[1]

*Ladislav Boháč – Ladislav Stančo*

The excavations of sector 08, conducted by present author, started on 7 October 2002 and lasted until 19 October 2002. Final documentation was completed on 20 and 21 October 2002. Sector 08 was situated approximately in the centre of western part of the tepa, about 30 meters to the east from the sector 06, in order to provide first information for understanding the inner layout of the settlement, respectively of the supposed living quarter. This sector comprises only one square excavation trench (08A) with dimensions 4 × 4 m.

After removing a greyish-brown dusty layer (08A003) that covers the surface of the tepa, two mudbrick walls (Wall "1") of the Kushano-Sasanian period, running at a right angle to one another, were revealed enclosing a small space/room. A "reinforcement" of uncertain purpose projected from the eastern mudbrick wall along the southern profile of the square. Evidently, mudbricks of two different dimensions were used, 32 × 32 cm, resp. 37–38 × 37–38 cm, the larger ones for the crossing of the northern and eastern walls and for the "reinforcement."[2] The mudbrick wall running parallelly to the northern profile of the square had been interrupted in its middle part by a recent grave pit (Pit "1", context no. 08A012), approx. 1.60 m deep. Another pit (Pit "2", context no. 08A002), possibly also intended for a burial, was found in the southeast corner of the square. Inner sides of the walls had been originally covered with a lime plaster (no traces of paint have been discovered yet). A pot of coarser fabric and with sharply articulated belly was found lying in situ on the lime floor of the room. Traces of burning preserved abundantly especially near the pot prove that the building had been destroyed by a fire.

An earlier phase of the room (building?) dating roughly to the Kushan period (1st – 3rd c. AD) showed the same disposition, except for the later added "reinforcement." The mudbrick walls preserved to 0.70–0.80 m of their original height were also in this phase covered with lime plaster. The floor was paved with mudbricks of unusual dimensions (28 × 15 cm) that had been laid upright in regular courses (08A009). The room seems to have been abandoned and immediately filled with debris (08A008) (perhaps to give way for a modernisation?).

On the same place there existed an even earlier predecessor with slightly shifted ground plan. The floor was covered with lime plaster and shows traces of heavy fire. The elevation of this floor varies from 370.92 to 371.12 m. This earliest phase has to be dated, according to the pottery material, to the 1st c. BC – 1st c. Ad. The coins of Soter Megas[3] and Kanishka II[4] were unearthed in the different layers of this square. tab. 2.3, 1 and 2.3, 2

**List of small finds**

08A002.I – spindle-whorl (of limestone) – 07/10/2002 – south: 1.10 m, west: 2.15 m; see Chapter 3.1, *Type 4c, "graded"*, fig. 3.1, *20*.

08A003.I – Æ fragment – 08/10/2002.

08A012.I – Æ coin – filling of a recent grave pit – 10/10/2002. Coin of Kanishka II, see Chapter 3.5, cat. no. 54.

08A007.I – Æ coin – 10/10/2002. Coin of Soter Megas, see Chapter 3.5, cat. no. 16.

08A009.I – whetstone (of greyish-black stone) – 17/10/2002, see Chapter 3.2, cat. no. 33.

08A000.I – bead of cylindrical shape (made of greenish glass paste).

---

1   This chapter is a slightly reworked text, which has been published as a part of preliminary report in 2003, see Abdullaev – Stančo 2003, p. 167–168, actual excavations and documentation were led by L. Boháč.

2   The edges of mudbricks of the eastern wall were rather worn and indistinct giving an impression of a *pisé* rather than a mudbrick wall.

3   See Chapter 3.5 in this volume, cat. nos. 15 and 16.

4   See Chapter 3.5 in this volume, cat. no. 54.

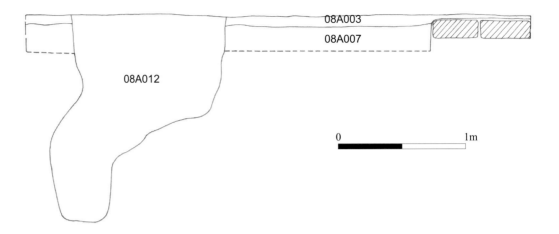

Jandavlattepa 2002, Sector 08, Square 08A, north section

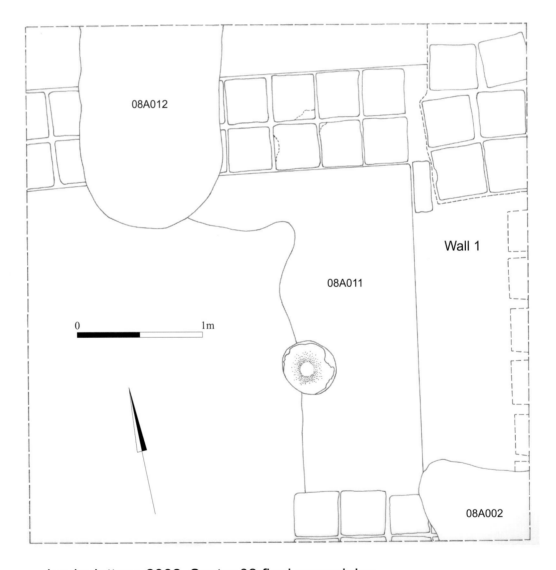

Jandavlattepa 2002, Sector 08,final groundplan

**Tab. 2.3, 1** Sector 08, Square 08A, north section and final ground plan, drawing by L. Boháč.

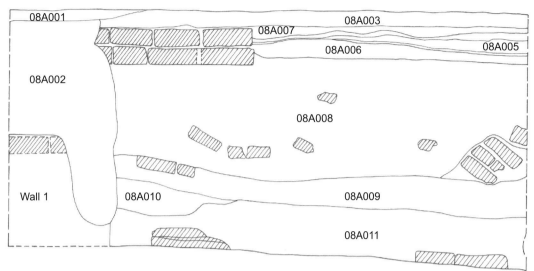

Jandavlattepa 2002, Sector 08, south section

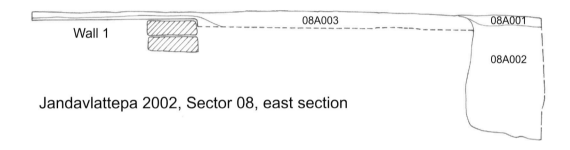

Jandavlattepa 2002, Sector 08, east section

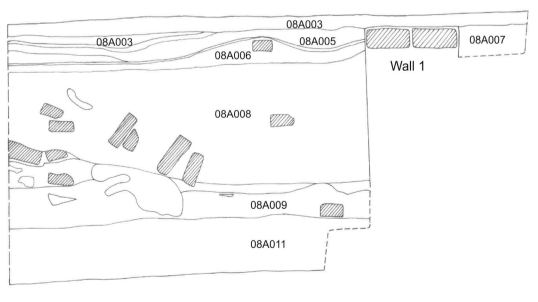

0 _____ 1m

Jandavlattepa 2002, Sector 08, west section

**Tab. 2.3, 2** Sector 08, Square 08A, south, east and west sections, drawing by L. Boháč.

# 2.4 Excavations in Sector 30: preliminary research in the nearby environs of Jandavlattepa

*Kristýna Urbanová*

Sector 30 is a land feature situated just under a kilometre north west of Jandavlattepa (fig. 2.4, *1*). As part of the fourth season of excavations, exploratory work started here on 10 October 2005 and lasted until 20 October 2005. This small hillock was earmarked for exploratory and, indeed, protective research based on land prospection around the *tepa*.

There used to be several similar land features in the immediate surroundings. Gradually, however, all the others were totally razed to the level of the surrounding fields through long-term deep ploughing. The hillock defined as sector 30 (fig. 2.4, *2*) is the only one to have been preserved in its original situation, although even here human activity has had negative consequences. We were told that there had been repeated attempts to plough over the hillock. The remains of the original construction, which according to local inhabitants had been preserved until the middle of the 20th century to the height of a one-storey house, were distributed by tractor over the immediate surroundings. For a band of 25 metres around the hillock, the effect of mixing not-too-fertile brick dust into the soil has been that very bad quality cotton has grown, stunted and crooked. In the immediate surroundings, locals have apparently found small pieces of jewellery, namely earrings.

Before the start of research, the hillock was oval in plan, with gently convex sides of c. 800 × 650 cm, and

**Fig. 2.4, 2** View of the hillock before excavation work started, photo K. Urbanová.

was scantily covered with thorn bushes. On the top, roughly in the middle, there was originally a geodesic measuring point, today badly damaged. On 11 October 2005 the work began on two square trenches with sides of 4 m (fig. 2.4, *3*). Trench 1 was in the north west, mechanical layers were removed to a depth of around 35 cm. Trench 2 was in the south east, also excavated by mechanical layers to a depth of around 220 cm from the top of the hillock. Later, work started on neighbouring trenches 3 (south west) and four (north east), also squares with sides of 4 m. Trench 2 was essentially a section through the hillock, which revealed building construction from unfired bricks, probably the remains of a foundation wall (figs. 2.4, *4* and *5*). It was formed by bricks about 38–42 cm long and 10–14 cm thick (width unknown). The bricks were preserved in three rows on top of each other, with a fourth, topmost row being preserved only in fragments. The brick construction had been considerably damaged, and so the work on uncovering it was lengthy.

A further construction element that had been preserved was a platform of hard-packed earth (pakhsa) on which the wall stood. The platform had an oblong ground plan with curved corners, and had two levels. Its preserved height was around 100 cm (figs. 2.4, *4* and *5*).

**Fig. 2.4, 1** Location of the Sector 30 in the vicinity of Jandavlattepa, IKONOS satellite image in the background.

**Fig. 2.4, 3** Cleaning the surface, first stripping, photo K. Urbanová.

**Fig. 2.4, 4** Section through the hillock. The brick construction can be seen, photo K. Urbanová.

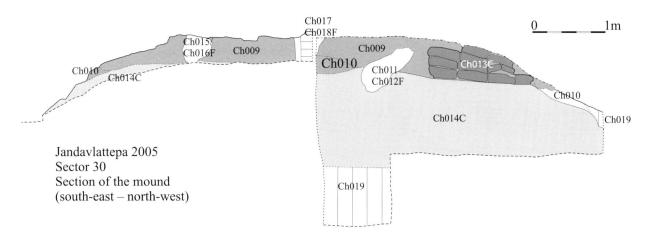

Jandavlattepa 2005
Sector 30
Section of the mound
(south-east – north-west)

**Fig. 2.4, 5** Sections through sector 30, photo K. Urbanová.

If we try to reconstruct the original construction on the basis of the preserved archaeological situation, then it was a smallish, rectangular building with dimensions of approximately 640 by 350–400 cm, built on a split-level platform with the same rectangular ground plan, with the lower level having a maximum length of 850 cm. Each level had a height of approximately 45–50 cm, so the overall height of the construction was around one metre. The building probably had a religious or funerary purpose.

Similar types of construction from the Kushan period have been found at several Central Asian sites, among them that of Dalverzintepa, Tepai Shakh and Yalangtushtepa.[1] In all these cases were these structures interpreted as *nauses*, buildings of a funerary character – mausoleums, where the bones of the dead were kept, together with small gifts. They were situated mostly north-east to a distance of 1 km beyond the

**Fig. 2.4, 6** Ceramics from the uppermost layers of the hillock, late Kushan period (at the right bottom) and from the brick construction, bowls from the Greco-Bactrian period (on the left and up), photo J. Halama.

---

1   Pugachenkova – Dar – Sharma – Joyenda – Siddiga, pp. 331–396; Pugachenkova 1978, p. 203, ris.137).

city walls. The closest parallel comes from the site of Tepai Shakh.[2] In this case, the building's dimensions are 7.6 × 6.3 m, the ground plan is rectangular, and the structure is located less than one km northwards from the main settlement.

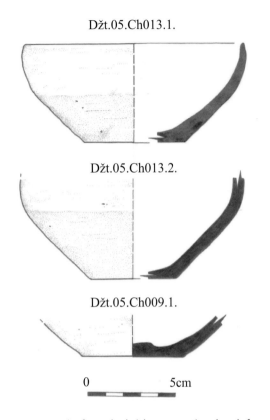

Džt.05.Ch013.1.

Džt.05.Ch013.2.

Džt.05.Ch009.1.

0          5cm

**Fig. 2.4, 7** Ceramics from the brick construction, bowls from the Greco-Bactrian period, drawing K. Urbanová.

A lack of sufficient chronologically-sensitive archaeological material means a more precise dating cannot be attempted. Several ceramic fragments from the uppermost layers, mostly badly damaged, correspond to ceramics of the late Kushan period (fig. 2.4, *6* at the right bottom). However, fragments of bowls that were found when the brick construction was being cleaned off were interpreted as Greco-Bactrian[3] (fig. 2.4, *6* on the left and up and also 2.4, *7*). When the wall was being cleaned off an eroded iron blade was also found[4] (tab. 3.2, *3:1*, fig. 3.2, *12*)*.

It is not possible on the basis of these few pieces of ceramics to date the construction precisely from the Hellenistic period, especially when one takes into account other factors such as the size of the bricks, the shape and dimension of the platform and the location of the building in relation to the Jandavlattepa site, all of which suggest that a date in the Kushan period is more likely.

## Bibliography

Kaim, B. (2002): *Architektura starożytnej Baktrii w okresie kuszańskim.* Warszawa.

Litvinskiy, B. A. – Sedov, A. V. (1983): *Tepai-shakh. Kul'tura i svyazy kushanskoy Baktrii*, Moscow: Nauka.

Pugachenkova, G. A. (1978): K itogam issledovaniy Dal'verzintepa, in: *Dal'verzintepa. Kushanskiy gorod na yuge Uzbekistana*, eds.: Pugachenkova, G. A. – Rtveladze, E. V. Tashkent, pp. 176–221.

Pugachenkova, G. A. – Dar, S. R. – Sharma, R. C. – Joyenda, M. A. – Siddiqi, H. (1994): Kushan Art, in: *History of civilization of Central Asia (vol. II): The development of sedentary and nomadic civilizations: 700 BC to AD 250*, ed.: Harmatta, J., Unesco, pp. 331–396.

---

2   Kaim 2002, p. 112–113. See especialy Litvinskiy – Sedov 1983, chapter 2 (by Litvinskiy), pp. 84–116, for detailed overview of genesis of the Bactrian burial structures.
3   Determined by Kazim Abdullaev, personal communication.
4   See chapter 3.2 below in this volume.

# 3. Special studies

## 3.1 Textile production at Jandavlattepa

*Kristýna Urbanová*

### 3.1.1 Introduction

There is a very long history of textile production on the territory of the Central Asian republics. Of particular note are the textiles produced in the Sogdian workshops of the early Middle Ages, which were imitated both in the west – in Persian, and, later, Byzantine workshops – and, in the east, in China, the cradle of silk-making. The high Middle Ages was another period when demand for cotton cloth rose. It was made famous by the *Zandaniji*, which came from the Bukhara region. Over the last two hundred years, the popularity of *ikats*, with their complex production methods, has confirmed the strong textile-making reputation of these countries. However, this tradition draws on roots that go deep into the past.

The first evidence of textile production on the territory of modern-day Uzbekistan dates from the Neolithic Age, while the first direct textile finds come from the Bronze Age. Finds of actual textiles dating from the heyday of the Kushan Empire are rare – several fragments of kelim carpet and fragments of clothing have been preserved in the locality of Toprak Kala[1], in tumuli in the Namangan region[2], at Kampyrtepa[3], and in a kurgan close to Old Termez.[4] However, there have been many finds of items used for textile production.

During the 2002 to 2006 excavation seasons at Jandavlattepa in southern Uzbekistan a total of 75 items used in textile production were found. They included whorls used for spinning, loom weights, needles and semi-finished versions of these products. However, no preserved textiles or remnants of looms were found.

This article, which is a reworked and shortened version of present author's MA Thesis entitled "*Textile Production in Kushan Central Asia*," defended in 2006 at the Institute of Classical Archaeology at the Faculty of Arts and Philosophy of Charles University in Prague[5], will present a typology of spindle whorls and loom weights, and an overview of other items used to create textiles. Using a spatial analysis, it will then detail the likely centres of production in terms of the residential architectur

### 3.1.2 Spindle whorls

A spindle whorl – a disc-shaped object with a hole punched in the centre – acts as both as a wheel and a weight when raw material is being spun. The whorl is mounted on a shaft, together with which it forms a spindle. Whorls were most often made out of clay, stone, bone or wood. They differ considerably in shape and size, and it is this considerable variation that makes them unsuitable for precise chronological dating. However, they do give an idea of the type of yarn (the size of the wheel allowed the spinner to spin yarn either thicker or thinner) and the material from which it was spun (different weights were used for wool, flax, cotton, silk and so on).

#### Typology of spindle whorls

This typology has been created on the basis of an analysis of body shape, which led to the division of the spindle whorls into five types. These five basic types were then further divided into subtypes, labelled with the small letters a–c. These were created on the basis of the changes in shape of the object's profile – for example, the basic body shape may be compared to a half circle (hemispherical – type 4, see below) but it is then placed in a further subdivision on the basis of its gradated engraved concentric circles, which makes its type hemispherical, and subtype gradated – type 4c.

---

[1]  Nerazik – Rapoport 1984, pp. 230–231, ris. 92,1–9.
[2]  Litvinskiy 1978, pp. 53–59.
[3]  Lyovushkina 1996, pp. 143–150.
[4]  Maytdynova 2001, pp. 81–89.
[5]  Urbanová 2006.

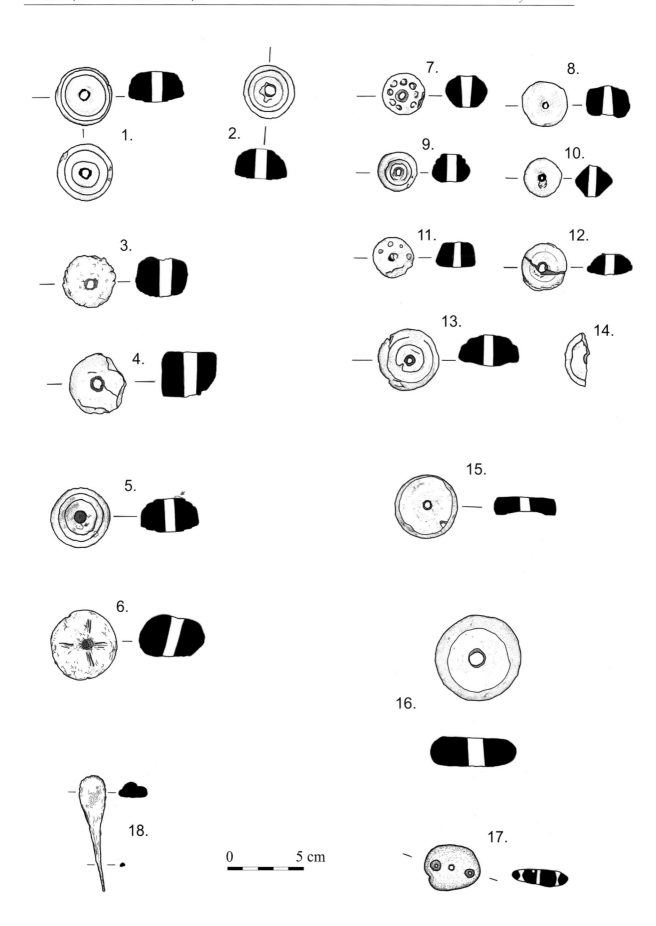

Tab. 3.1, 1

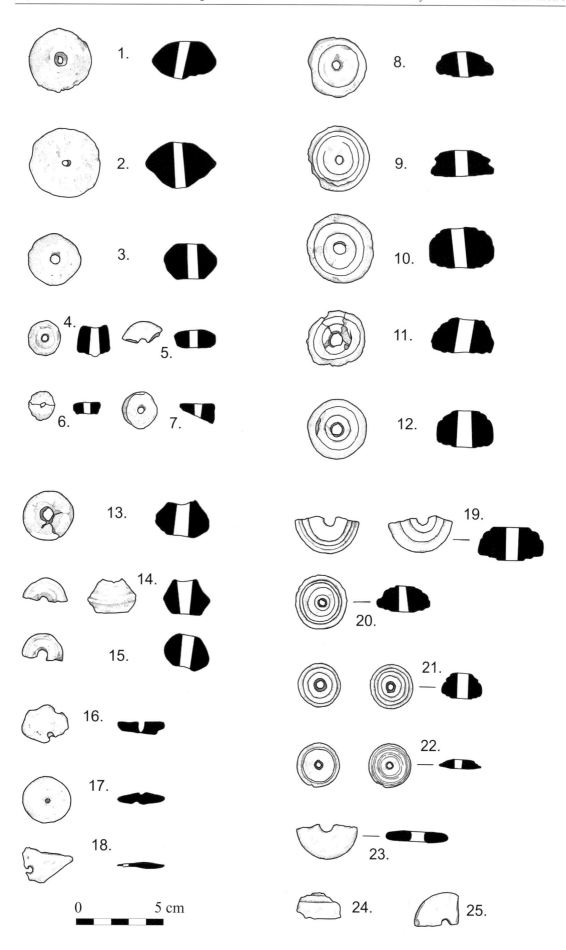

0        5 cm

Tab. 3.1, 2

When describing the different types, I have indicated average measurements and the material from which the objects are made.

The collection includes finds from sectors 07, 08 and 20, in other words from parts of the sites excavated by the Czech team between 2002 and 2006.

## Type 1, conical

This type of whorl is shaped like a cone. It has a hole made in it vertically. There are three items in total: 20Q012.III (fig. 3.1, *1**), 20Y002.V (tab. 3.1, 2:4; fig. 3.1, *2**) and 21E026.I (fig. 3.1, *3**). All the finds come from the site of what is called the "Citadel," from whence 12% of all the types of whorls found come. None have as yet been found in the excavated area of the lower town (Shakhristan). In each case the material is unfired clay.

Object 20Q012.III has no decoration and the surface is merely smoothed. The second find, 20Y002.V, is decorated with a relief band on the upper part, which becomes slightly convex as it approaches the hole in the middle. Whorl inv. no. 21E026.I has one engraved line on the surface.

Measurements: height varies from 1.5 cm to 2.2 cm, diameter from 1.65 cm to 2.35 cm. The diameter of the hole varies from 0.53 cm to 0.65 cm.

## Type 2, biconical

This type of whorl is closest in shape to an ellipsoid. There is a vertical hole in it. Not a single object of this type has been found at Jandavlattepa, but it has been included in the typology for the sake of completeness, since it has frequently been found in sites from the same period in the given area.

## Type 3, spherical

This whorl is spherical and slightly flattened. It has a vertical hole. It is divided into three subtypes, according to the way in which it is further shaped.

*Type 3a, simple spherical*, not shaped or structured in any further way. There are nine objects in total: 10C.001.I (fig. 3.1, *4**), 10C011.I (tab. 3.1, 1:6, fig. 3.1, *5**), 20E007.I (fig. 3.1, *6**), 20G001.I (fig. 3.1, *7**), 20G002.I (fig. 3.1, *8**), 12D008.I (tab. 3.1, 2:13; fig. 3.1, *9**), 12C002.I (tab. 3.1, 1:16; fig. 3.1, *10**), 20O020.I (tab. 3.1, 2:14; fig. 3.1, *11**). This type has been found in both excavated sectors. In sector 07 3a accounts for 22% of all types of whorls, while in sector 20 it accounts for 20%.

In 44% of cases the whorl is undecorated. 22% of whorls of this type are decorated with "stamps" – impressed points, while 22% are decorated with concentric rings in the upper half, 11% have grooves on both the upper and lower surface and 11% are decorated with simple engraving.

In most cases the material is unfired clay (7 items), while one item is stone of an unspecified kind, and there is also a ceramic fragment.

The height ranges from 1.2 cm to 2.6 cm, most frequently being 1.9 cm, while the diameter ranges from 2.4 cm to 5.9 cm, most frequently 2.4 cm. The diameter of the hole ranges from 0.4 cm to 0.9 cm, most frequently being 0.6 cm.

*Type 3b, "lense-shaped,"* with a bi-convex body, 3 items in total. 05.20O010.II (tab. 3.1, 2:1; fig. 3.1, *12**), 05.20O011.I (tab. 3.1, 2:2; fig. 3.1, *13**), 05.20Y003.I (tab. 3.1, 2:3; fig. 3.1, *14**). Found only on the site of sector 20, the "Citadel," where it forms 13.6% of all types.

No decoration. Always made out of unfired clay, sometimes with the surface sometimes smoothed.

The height varies from 2.1 cm to 2.2 cm, the diameter of the body from 3.1 cm to 4.1 cm. The diameters of the holes are the same in all cases – 0.6 cm.

*Type 3c, hexagonal in shape,* 2 items in total: 04.20N002.II (fig. 3.1, *15**), 06.21F005.I (fig. 3.1, *16**). Accounts for 8% of all types of whorls in sector 20. No decoration. Made of unfired clay. Measurements: height 1.7 to 2 cm, diameter 2.4 to 2.6 cm, diameter of the hole 0.5 to 0.55 cm.

## Type 4, hemispherical

This type of whorl is characterised by a hemispherical body with a flattened, slightly convex or concave bottom part. In all, 18 of them have been found in sectors 07 and 20, or 47% of all types. They can also be divided further into three subtypes going by the profile of the body, and named accordingly.

*Type 4a, simple hemispherical.* This has no further shaping or cutting, and is closest to a hemispherical shape. There are two items in all: 02.07A002.I (fig. 3.1, *17**), 05.12D008.II (tab. 3.1, 2:5; fig. 3.1, *18**). They form 11.2% of the whorls found in the Shakhristan. No decoration. One item is made of fired clay, while the other is made out of a ceramic fragment that had previously been used for another purpose and has been adapted. Height 1.1 to 1.6 cm, diameter of whorl 2.3 cm to 4 cm. The diameter of the hole is 0.5 cm to 0.7 cm.

*Type 4b, "cylindrical."* The lower part is elongated into a sort of neck. There is just one example: 03.07D001.II (fig. 3.1, *19**). No decoration. It is made out of an indeterminate black stone. Height 1.5 cm, diameter 2.3 cm. diameter of hole 0.6 cm.

*Type 4c, "gradated."* The body is broken up by an engraved pattern (of concentric circles) gradated in different ways. There are 13 items altogether: 02.08A002.I (fig. 3.1, *20**), 03.07C006.I (tab. 3.1, 2:19; fig. 3.1, *21**), 04.09E012.I (fig. 3.1, *22**), 04.10C005.I (tab. 3.1, 2:10; fig. 3.1, *23**), 04.11C005.I (tab. 3.1, 2:8; fig. 3.1, *24**), 04.12C004.I (tab. 3.1, 2:15; fig. 3.1, *25**), 04.20C000.I (tab. 3.1, 2:9; fig. 3.1, *26**), 04.20C001.II (fig. 3.1, *27**), 04.20N002.I (fig. 3.1, *28**), 20N003.III (fig. 3.1, *29**), 05.12C002.II (tab. 3.1, 2:11; fig. 3.1, *30**), 05.20S001.I (tab. 3.1, 2:12; fig. 3.1, *31**), 05.20Y002.X (fig. 3.1, *32**).

These represent 45% of all the whorls on the site of the Shakhristan. It is thus a very popular type, as is further suggested by the finds of pieces of white stone, the raw material from which these whorls were made, above all in the northern trenches of sector 07. They are also the most typical whorl of the high Kushan phase, found in almost all settlements of the period. In the Citadel they represent 32% of all the whorls that have been found to date.

The decoration consists of concentric circles 0.1 cm wide, with the number varying from one to four on the upper part and two to three on the lower part.

In the great majority of cases they are made of white crystalline stone, probably alabaster. One example is made of fired clay: 05.12D008.II (tab. 3.1, 2:5; fig. 3.1, *18**). The height varies from 1.1 cm to 3.3 cm, with most heights being between 1.9 and 2.1 cm. The diameter of the whorls ranges from 1.2 cm to 3.8 cm – most frequently from 3.4 cm to 3.8 cm. The diameter of the holes ranges from 0.4 cm to 0.75 cm, with the median being 0.6 cm.

*Type 5, "discoid"*. There are 8 of these in total: 03.07C008.I (tab. 3.1, 2:23; fig. 3.1, *33**), 03.07C009. XI (tab. 3.1, 2:24; fig. 3.1, *64**), 03.07D009.III (tab. 3.1, 2:25; fig. 3.1, *66**), 04.20N002.XII (fig. 3.1, *65**), 05.20Q002.II (tab. 3.1, 2:6; fig. 3.1, *34**), 05.20Y002.IV (tab. 3.1. 1:15; fig. 3.1, *35**), 06.21Pz001.I, 06.21F001. III (fig. 3.1, *36**). On the site of the Shakhristan they represent 11.2% of all types, while in the Citadel they form 20%. No decoration (unless the ceramic fragment is decorated, with a glaze for example).

These are made predominantly of fragments of ceramics that were previously used for another purpose[6], or in one case of stone (probably alabaster): 03.07C008.I and also in one case of clay: 06.21Pz001.I.

The height varies from 0.6 cm to 1.2 cm. The diameter of the whorls ranges from 1.6 cm to 4.2 cm, the diameter of the holes from 0.3 cm to 0.8 cm.

Of the total number of 43 whorls found in sectors 07, 08 and 20 during the 2002 to 2006 excavation seasons, approximately 43% are type 4 (hemispherical), 33% type 3 (spherical), 17% type 5 (discoid) and 7% type (conical). Given the variability of the material on the site of the Shakhristan and the Citadel, and given the dating of the settlement of these areas, conclusions need to be drawn separately.

The situations in the sectors covering the Shakhristan and the sector on the site of the Citadel are different. The Shakhristan, excavated in sector 08 (2002 excavation season) and sector 07 (excavation seasons 2002 to 2005) stopped being settled during the third

century Ad. In the Citadel, however, settlement continued, at least partially, until the fifth century. For this reason, excavations of sector 20 produce archaeological material that is different from, or, to be more precise, younger than, that in the lower town, the Shakhristan.

The typological difference between the Shakhristan and the Citadel is clear. Not only are there new forms that were previously less used, but the materials used for production are also different. In sector 07, the most commonly-found types are 4 – hemispherical, 3a – simple spherical and 5 – discoid. The predominant type is 4c, gradated hemispherical, and there are only rare examples of type 4a, simple hemispherical, and 4b, cylindrical hemispherical. These last two types are not found in the Citadel at all. The most frequently-used material for making whorls is stone (which accounts for 65.5%) of which the most frequent type is crystalline stone (50%) and dark, unidentified black stone (12.5%). Stone is followed by reused ceramic fragments (18.75%) and fired clay (12.5%). The fewest whorls in sector 07 are made out of unfired clay (6.25%). Whorls of unfired and fired clay are handmade (moulded or thrown) while the stone ones bear signs of having been worked with a lathe. From analogical finds in other localities, these types can be dated to the end of the 3rd century AD at the latest.

Type 4 – hemispherical is also found in abundance in sector 20, but there are also further types that are not found in the Shakhristan to the same extent, or at all. These are types 1 – conical, 3b – lens-shaped spherical, 3c – hexagonal and 5 – discoid. In the case of these new forms, the material is mostly unfired clay, followed by stone of various kinds, fired clay and ceramics (reused ceramic fragments). Given the stratigraphy of the finds and the considerable typological difference, it appears that the material found in sector 20 is younger, and can be dated roughly to the 4th century.

From the reign of the Kushans, relatively similar types of spindle whorls can be found in all settlements from southern Bactria (modern-day Afghanistan) to the Kushans' northern spheres of influence (Sogdiana, Khorezm, Fergana). Examples are locations such as Khalchayan, Dal'verzintepa, Dilberjin, Tepa-i-shakh, Kampyrtepa, Aultepa, Toprak Kala and so on. The best typological treatment of these is in two essays by V. A. Litvinsky[7] and V. Lunyeva[8]; in other specialist literature spindle whorls are merely included in the lists of finds.

### 3.1.3 Semi-finished products

This group includes stone and ceramic fragments that were designed to become spindle whorls and which

---

6    Cf. for example finds of secondary used cemramic sherds or semi-finished products from Dal'verzintepa.
7    Litvinskiy 1978.
8    Luneva 2002.

show signs of having been worked. A total of nine were found, of which four were stone – 05.10D018.I (fig. 3.1, *37*), 05.20Y002.II (tab. 3.1, 2:38; fig. 3.1, *38*), 05.20Y007.I (tab. 3.1, 2:17; fig. 3.1, *39*), 05.20Y026. II[9] (tab. 3.1, 2:18; fig. 3.2, *30*). They might well have been waste items that were thrown away.

During the 2003 to 2005 excavation seasons a number of white stones (probably alabaster) of various sizes were found. They evidently served as material for making stone whorls. Unfortunately, in most cases they were not documented in any detail, with the exception of 05.20O009C.I (fig. 3.1, *40*). After being cut into approximately the right shape, these very popular whorls made of white semi-transparent stone were then finished on a simple lathe, which allowed the creation of precise concentric circles and gradations.

Further five pieces were semi-finished whorls made out of ceramic fragments – 04.07E028.I (fig. 3.1, *41*), 04.09C018.II (fig. 3.1, *42*), 04.09C021.I (fig. 3.1, *43*), 04.20G002.II (fig. 3.1, *44*), 04.20N003.II (fig. 3.1, *63*). They were made simply by hammering and smoothing fragments of broken vessels to the right size, and then drilling a hole in them. Their size varies from 2.2 cm to 3.7 cm, which corresponds to the dimensions of whorls made out of reused ceramic fragments (e.g. 04.20N002.XII). None of these pieces (except for 20N003.II) has a hole in, and none of them show any signs of drilling, so it is also possible that they served as weights or buttons.

## 3.1.4 Loom weights

Loom weights of various shapes and dimensions were used to keep the warp threads tight on the vertical looms that were used to make both household and decorative textiles.

The vertical loom consists of two vertical posts (side bars) and two transverse ones. They were fixed by being stuck in the ground or by being leant against a wall, or they were equipped with a stand and were free-standing. The warp was kept tight by weights of various shapes (pyramidal, circular etc.). The warp threads were crossed by fastening some to the cross bar and others to weights, which were mostly made of clay (fired and unfired) but also of stone. The weft was drawn through the weaving shed thus formed, and cloth created.

### Typology of loom weights from Jandavlattepa

A shape analysis of the collection was made on the basis of a comparison of two elements: the outline formed by the base, and the shape of the body. In all cases the holes are horizontal. All the weights are undecorated. First the shape of the weight's body was assessed, which gave rise to four types of loom weights. Within these four types, further subtypes were created, designated with the small letters a–z. The descriptions of different types also indicate the average measurements and the material from which the weight was made.

The typology covers finds from sectors 07, 08 and 20. It does not include two finds that are badly damaged fragments of loom weights: nos.: 04.20N002. XIV (tab. 3.1, 4:3; fig. 3.1, *46*), 05.10D018.VII.

### Type 1. "quadrangular"

The weaving weight is quadrangular in form, and of the same width at the top and the bottom. Only the base is of various shapes. There is a horizontal hole. In Jandavlattepa only the type with an **oblong base** has been found. Total one item: 04.10C016.I (tab. 3.1,3: 10; fig. 3.1, *47*). No decoration. Made of unfired clay.

Height 8.1 cm, width 5.3 cm, thickness 3.8 cm. The average size of the hole is 0.6 cm.

### Type 2. "pyramidal"

These weights are shaped like pyramids, narrowing from top to bottom to a greater or lesser degree. There is a horizontal hole. The shape of the base varies, and the type can be divided into three subtypes:

2a. – with a **rectangular base**. 6 items in total: 04.09C022.IV (tab. 3.1, 3:6; fig. 3.1, *48*), 04.09C022.V (tab. 3.1, 4:5; fig. 3.1, *45*), 04.09C022. VI (tab. 3.1, 4:4; fig. 3.1, *50*), 05.09D033.II (fig. 3.1, *51*), 05.10D018.II (fig. 3.1, *52*), 05.11C005.III (tab. 3.1, 4:9; fig. 3.1, *53*)

This type was found only in the Shakhristan, in sector 07, and accounts for 37.5% of all the types found in this sector.

No decoration. All items made out of non-fired clay. The height varies from 8.1 to 9.7 cm, but the median cannot be ascertained, since of the six weights only two are completely preserved. The width varies from 4.3 cm to 5.7 cm, with the median being 5.3 cm. The thickness varies from 3.1 to 4.8 cm, being most frequently between 3.7 and 4 cm. The diameter of the hole varies from 0.5 to 0.7 cm, most usually 0.6 cm.

2b. – with a **square base**. Five items in total: 04.09C022.VII (tab. 3.1, 3:9; fig. 3.1, *54*), 05.09D033.I (fig. 3.1, *55*), 05.10D018.V (fig. 3.1, *56*), 05.11C005.II (tab. 3.1, 4:8; fig. 3.1, *57*). Like type 2a, this type is found almost exclusively in sector 07, where it forms 25% of all the weight types. It has not been found in sector 20.

No decoration. All items made of non-fired clay. The height varies from 5.7 to 8.6 cm, the width from 3.5 to 6.2 cm and the thickness from 3.2 to 6.2 cm. The diameter of the hole varies from 0.4 to 1 cm.

---

9   For other interpreation of this item see cat. no. 31 in Chapter 3.2 below in this volume.

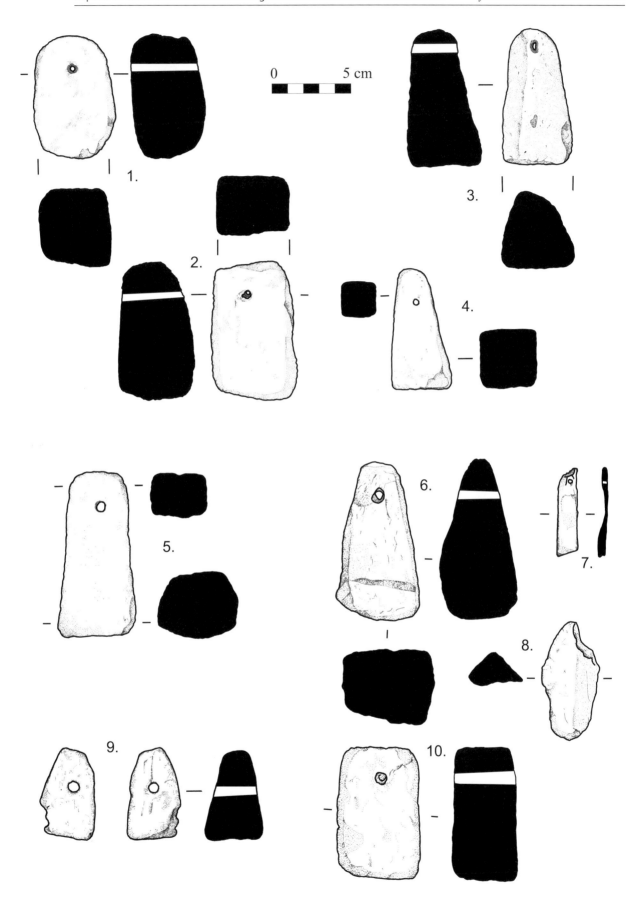

0 ▬▬ 5 cm

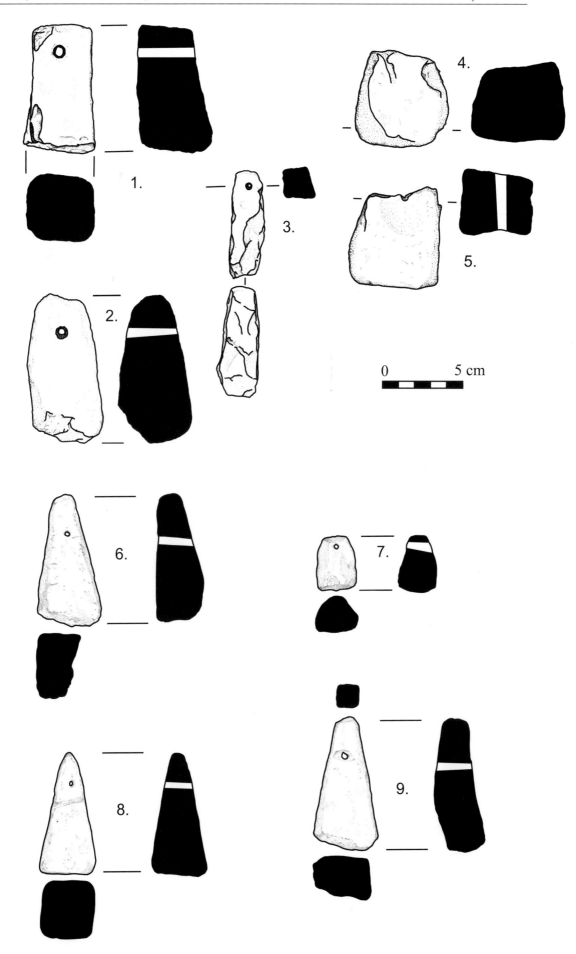

2c. – with a ***triangular base.*** 3 items in total: 04.20H002.IV (fig. 3.1, *58**), 05.20Y026.I (tab. 3.1, 4:7; fig. 3.1, *59**), 05.10D018.IV (fig. 3.1, *60**). Two examples of type 2c were found in the Citadel, where they account for 66.7% of all types. Only one example was found in the Shakhristan. No decoration. All items made of non-fired clay.

Height 3.4 cm to 8.6 cm. Width 2.5 cm to 4 cm, thickness is the same as width. Diameter of hole varies from 0.3 cm to 0.65 cm.

Pyramidal loom weights appear for example among the finds from Khalchayan (Khanakatepa)[10], Dal'verzintepa[11], Kampyrtepa[12], Dilberjin[13], Ak-tepa II (Kobadian)[14], Aultepa and Jangal'tepa (both southern Sogd)[15].

## Type 3. "conical"

These weights have cone-shaped bodies, which become narrower from the base to the upper part to a greater or lesser degree. There is a horizontal hole. The shape of the base may be circular or slightly oval. One item from sector 07: 05.10D018.III. (fig. 3.1, *61**). No decoration. Made of unfired clay. Height 6.1 cm (has not been preserved whole), diameter of base 6.2 cm, diameter of hole 0.5 cm.

Overall, the most common type is Type 2 – pyramidal, with various bases. There are only a few examples of Types 1 and 3.

In sector 07, the settlement, the types most frequently found are 2a (37.5%), 2b (25%) and occasionally types 2c, 1a and 3 (6.25% in each case). In sector 20 the situation is different. The loom weights found here have been almost exclusively of one type, 2c (66.7%) and occasionally 2b (33.3%). Most loom weights were made by hand from unfired clay (89.5%). Only 10.5% were fired.

The finds of loom weights were often one-off (if they were found in one cultural layer they were not found in collections, but were strewn around the area). During the excavation season, two lots of loom weights were found collected together. One was a collection from cultural layer 10D018 (numbering 5 items) and the other was from cultural layer 09C022 (also 5 items). In each case, they are probably the remnants of a single collection for one loom. It is interesting to note that the group from trench 10D contained various types of weight: types 2a and 2b (pyramidal) and 3 (conical). They may have been used at the same time for one loom, but it is also possible that they were waste material that was no longer in use and was

thrown away in one spot. In this case the find would only illustrate the variety of types of loom weights, not their use in combination.

Item 05.10D018.III has a deep groove carved in its body – originally used for the string that tied it to the warp threads. It measures 9 cm and in its deepest place goes 1.6 cm into the body of the weight. Its width varies from 0.6 to 0.8 cm, which was probably the width of the string. The string would have been tied to the weight immediately after it was moulded. It would have been threaded through the hole and tied to the warp (fig. 3.1, 61*). The subsequent weight on the string then created the groove.

Cutting strings and cords, with from three to twelve threads, were commonly used in households. They were used as mentioned above to tie weights to looms, they were used to make nets and were wound round pots that were then hung up and so on. Finds of such cords have been documented in the Namangan region of north-eastern Uzbekistan, for example, where they date from the Bronze Age and the 4th century AD. Loom weights from Jandavlattepa are totally comparable to the types of weights found in other Kushan settlements in the region, such as at Kampyrtepa, Dal'verzintepa, Aultepa and elsewhere.

### 3.1.5 Other items used in textile production and making clothes

**Needles**

Needles were most commonly used for working finished fabric – sewing it up, embroidering and so on – but they were also used to make the decorative elements of clothing (lace and so on). In 2004 two bronze needles were found at Jandavlattepa – 04.09B012.I (tab. 3.3, *6:84*, fig. 3.3, *76**)[16] and 04.09B015.I (tab. 3.3, 6:85, fig. 3.3, *77**). They are circular in cross-section and their diameter ranges from 0.15 cm to 0.2 cm. In the case of item 04.9B015.I a piece of the eye has also been preserved, and at this point the needle becomes flattened. The needle is thin and was probably used for fine embroidery.

Embroidery from the Kushan period is documented in fragments of clothing and decorative fabrics from the Citadel in the Toprak Kala. The embroidery is fine and sewn in wool, sometimes in metal thread. The stitches used were chain stitch and leaf stitch.

In addition to metal needles, there have also been finds of bone needles from this period, but as yet none have been found at Jandavlattepa.

---

[10] Pugachenkova 1966, p. 43, ris. 21; p. 83, ris. 54 and p. 96, ris. 63.
[11] Pugachenkova 1978, p. 203–204, ris. 137.
[12] Shagalina 2002, pp.109–111, nos. 1–31, all of them are of type 2a and 2b, i.e. triangular base is absent.
[13] Pugachenkova 1979, p. 71, ris. 9; "more than ten pieces in two rooms;" ibidem p. 91, ris. 25, 24–28.
[14] Sedov 1987, p. 170, Tabl. VII,15; made of fired clay.
[15] Kabanov 1981, p. 23, ris. 14; cf. especialy find from Aultepa decorated with incised floral ornament.
[16] We deal with this item also in chapter 3.3, cat. no. 84.

## Awls

Awls are simple spike-shaped objects, most commonly made by carving animal bones. They were used to work leather – to make pouches, shoes and so on.

In 2004 an awl with a drop-shaped handle was found in trench 09B – 04.9B010.I (tab. 3.1, 1:18; fig. 3.1, *72*).

## Other items

During the 2006 excavation season an oval flat stone with three drilled holes in a line was found in trench 21P – 21P002.II (tab. 3.1, 1:17; fig. 3.1, *62*). The item may have been used to twist three threads together. Twisted threads from the Kushan period have been found at the Toprak Kala site, for example, where they form both the warp and the weft of simple woven kelim carpets.

## Overview of the finds

| object | type | height (cm) | width / diameter (cm) | diameter of hole (cm) | weight (g) | small find number | material | fig.* | tab. |
|---|---|---|---|---|---|---|---|---|---|
| spindle-whorl or a button | --- | 1.2 | 3.7 | --- | | 07E028.I | pottery | 3.1, 41 | |
| spindle-whorl or a button | --- | --- | 2.2–2.4 | --- | | 09C018.II | pottery | 3.1, 42 | |
| spindle-whorl or a button | --- | 0.7 | 2.3–2.6 | --- | | 09C021.I | pottery | 3.1, 43 | |
| spindle-whorl or a button | | 0.9 | 2.2 | --- | | 20G002.II | pottery | 3.1, 44 | |
| spindle-whorl or a button | 5 | 0.7 | 2.7 | 0.6 | 10.3 | 20N002.XII | pottery | 3.1, 65 | |
| spindle-whorl or a button | --- | 0.35 | 2.7 | 0.4 | 3.1 | 20N003.II | pottery | 3.1, 63 | |
| spindle-whorl or a button | 5 | | | | | 21F001.III | pottery | 3.1, 36 | |
| spindle-whorl | 4a | 1.6 | 4.1 | 0.75 | | 07A002.I | pottery | 3.1, 17 | |
| spindle-whorl | 4c | 1.9 | 3.8 | 0.8 | | 07C006.I | | 3.1, 21 | 3.1, 2:19 |
| spindle-whorl | 5 | 0.6 | 3.6 | 0.8 | | 07C008.I | limestone | 3.1, 33 | 3.1, 2:23 |
| spindle-whorl | 5 | 0.6 | 2.6 | --- | | 07C009.XI | | 3.1, 64 | 3.1, 2:24 |
| spindle-whorl | 4b | 1.4 | 2.2 | 0.6 | | 07D001.II | pottery | 3.1, 19 | |
| spindle-whorl | 4c | 1.5 | 3 | 0.5 | | 08A002.I | limestone | 3.1, 20 | |
| spindle-whorl | 4c | 1.2 | 3.3 | 0.3 | | 09E012.I | alabaster | 3.1, 22 | |
| spindle-whorl | 3a | | | | 14.5 | 10C001.I | stone | 3.1, 4 | |
| spindle-whorl | 4c | 2.1 | 3.7 | 0.8 (0.7) | 33.6 | 10C005.I | alabaster | 3.1, 23 | 3.1, 2:10 |
| spindle-whorl | 3a | 2.6 | 4.2 | 0.6 | 49.3 | 10C011.I | alabaster | 3.1, 5 | 3.1, 1:6 |
| spindle-whorl | --- | 0.4–0.6 | 3.0 | 0.4 × 0.5 | | 10D018.I | stone | 3.1, 37 | |
| spindle-whorl | 4c | 1.5 | 3.4 | --- | 19.6 | 11C005.I | stone | 3.1, 24 | 3.1, 2:8 |
| spindle-whorl | 3a | 1.9 | 5.9 | 0.9 | 79.3 | 12C002.I | pottery | 3.1, 10 | 3.1, 1:16 |
| spindle-whorl | 4c | 1.9 | 3.2 (3.4) | 0.7 | 18.7 | 12C002.II | alabaster | 3.1, 30 | 3.1, 2:11 |
| spindle-whorl | 4c | 1.8 | 2.6 | --- | 6.6 | 12C004.I | pottery | 3.1, 25 | 3.1, 2:15 |
| spindle-whorl | | | | | | 12C008.II | pottery | | |
| spindle-whorl | 3a | 2.1 | 3 (2.9) | 0.75 | 15.2 | 12D008.I | clay | 3.1, 9 | 3.1, 2:13 |
| spindle-whorl | 4a | 1.1 | 2.3 | 0.5 | 2.9 | 12D008.II | pottery | 3.1, 18 | 3.1, 2:5 |
| spindle-whorl | 4c | 1.5 | 3.7 | --- | 22.3 | 20C000.I | alabaster | 3.1, 26 | |
| spindle-whorl | 4c | --- | 3.6 | 0.7 | 28.4 | 20C001.II | alabaster | 3.1, 27 | |
| spindle-whorl | 3a | 1.2 | 2.4 | 0.55 | 9.9 | 20E007.I | clay | 3.1, 6 | |
| spindle-whorl | | 1.7 | 2.4 | 0.5 | 11.1 | 20F002.I | black stone | 3.1, 69 | |
| spindle-whorl | 3a | 1.3 | 2.5 | --- | 15.0 | 20G001.I | clay | 3.1, 7 | |
| spindle-whorl | 3a | 1.6 | 2.4 | 0.6 | 12.8 | 20G002.I | clay | 3.1, 8 | |
| spindle-whorl | 4c | 1.32 | 3.06 | 0.75 | 12.2 | 20N002.I | alabaster | 3.1, 28 | |
| spindle-whorl | 3c | 2 | 2.4 | 0.5 | 8.0 | 20N002.II | clay | 3.1, 15 | |
| spindle-whorl | 4c | 1.5 | 3.25 | 0.6 | 6.8 | 20N003.III | alabaster | 3.1, 29 | |
| spindle-whorl | 3b | 2.2 | 3.6 | 0.6 | 25.5 | 20O010.II | clay | 3.1, 12 | 3.1, 2:1 |

| object | type | height (cm) | width / diameter (cm) | diameter of hole (cm) | weight (g) | small find number | material | fig.* | tab. |
|---|---|---|---|---|---|---|---|---|---|
| spindle-whorl | 3a | 1.9 | 2.8 | --- | | 20O020.I | clay | 3.1, 11 | 3.1, 2:14 |
| spindle-whorl | 1 | 2.2 | 2.35 | 0.53 | 12.4 | 20Q012.III | clay | 3.1, 1 | |
| spindle-whorl | 4c | 2.1 | 3.5 | 0.6 | 28.1 | 20S001.I | alabaster | 3.1, 31 | 3.1, 2:12 |
| spindle-whorl | --- | 2.7 | 2.0 | 0.7 | 5.5 | 20Y002.II | stone | 3.1, 38 | 3.1, 2:38 |
| spindle-whorl | 5 | 1.2 | 4.2 | 0.6 | 24.6 | 20Y002.IV | pottery | 3.1, 35 | 3.1. 1:15 |
| spindle-whorl | 1 | 1.4 | 3.4 | 0.7 | 6.8 | 20Y002.V | clay | 3.1, 2 | 3.1, 2:4 |
| spindle-whorl | 4c | 1.69 | 2.4 (1.82) | 0.65–0.78 | 7.8 | 20Y002.X | alabaster | 3.1, 32 | |
| spindle-whorl | 3b | 2.1 | 3.1 | 0.6 | 21.2 | 20Y003c.I | | 3.1, 14 | |
| spindle-whorl | --- | 0.71 | 2.7 | --- | 8.0 | 20Y007.I | stone | 3.1, 39 | 3.1, 2:17 |
| spindle-whorl | 1 | 3.4 | 2.5 | 0.3 | | 21E026.I | clay | 3.1, 3 | |
| spindle-whorl | 3c | | | | | 21F005.I | clay | 3.1, 16 | |
| spindle-whorl | | | | | | 21O001.I | alabaster | 3.1, 68 | |
| needle? | | | | | | 20O018.I | bone | 3.3, 71 | 3.3, 6:79 |
| needle or pin | | | | | | 09D007.I | bronze | | |
| needle | --- | 2.2 | 0.15 | --- | | 09B.012.I | bronze | 3.3, 76 | 3.3, 6:84 |
| needle | --- | 6.1 | 0.2 (0.45) | --- | | 09B015.I | bronze | 3.3, 77 | 3.3, 6:85 |
| loom-weight | | 10.4 | 5 × 4 | 0.6 | | 07D007.I | clay | | |
| loom-weight | 2a | 9.7 | 5.3 × 4.8 | 0.7 | | 09C022.IV | clay | 3.1, 48 | 3.1, 3:6 |
| loom-weight | 2a | 5.6 | 5.7 × 5.1 | 0.6–0.7 | | 09C022.V | clay | 3.1, 49 | 3.1, 4:5 |
| loom-weight | 2a | 6.0 7.3 | 5.8 × 4.8 3.0 | --- | | 09C022.VI | clay | 3.1, 50 | 3.1, 4:4 and 3.1, 3:8 |
| loom-weight | 2b | 5.7 | 3.5 × 3.2 | 0.5–0.6 | 64.3 | 09C022.VII | clay | 3.1, 54 | 3.1, 3:9 |
| loom-weight | 2b | 6.6 | 3.6 × 3.6 | max. 1.0 | 123.5 | 09D033.I | clay | 3.1, 55 | |
| loom-weight | 2a | 6.8 | 5 × 3.5 | 0.6–0.7 | | 09D033.II | clay | 3.1, 51 | |
| loom-weight | 1 | 8.1 | 5.3 × 3.8 | 0.6–0.7 | | 10C016.I | clay | 3.1, 47 | 3.1, 3:10 |
| loom-weight | 2a | 4.4 | 4.4 × 3.1 | 0.4 | | 10D018.II | clay | 3.1, 52 | |
| loom-weight | 3 | 6 | 6.3 | 0.5 × 0.7 | | 10D018.III | clay | 3.1, 61 | |
| loom-weight | 2c | 8.8 | 4.6 × 4.4 | 0.4 | | 10D018.IV | clay | 3.1, 60 | |
| loom-weight | 2b | 7.1 | 4.15 × 4.2 | 0.4 | | 10D018.V | clay | 3.1, 56 | |
| loom-weight | --- | 7.3 | 3.7 × 2.2 | --- | | 10D018.VII | clay | 3.1, 70 | |
| loom-weight | 2c | 8.6 | 4.5 × 4.75 × 5.5 | 0.5–0.65 | | 20H002.IV | clay | 3.1, 58 | |
| loom-weight | --- | 6.5 | 2 × 2.5 | 0.4 | 42.2 | 20N002.XIV | terracotta | 3.1, 46 | 3.1, 4:3 |
| loom-weight | 2c | | | | 21.8 | 20Y026.I | clay | 3.1, 59 | 3.1, 4:7 |
| loom weight | 2b | 7.6 | 3.5 × 3.4 | --- | | 11C005.II | clay | 3.1, 57 | 3.1, 4:8 |
| loom weight | 2a | 8.2 | 3.9 × -- | --- | 102.1 | 11C005.III | clay | 3.1, 53 | 3.1, 4:9 |
| spindle-whorl/ button | | | | | 4.2 | 07D009.III | clay | 3.1, 66 | 3.1, 2:25 |
| | --- | 4.5 | 2.8 | --- | | 20O009c.I | alabaster | 3.1, 40 | |
| | 3b | 2.6 | 4.1 | 0.6 | 34.0 | 20O011.I | clay | 3.1, 13 | 3.1, 2:2 |
| | | 1.0 | 1.9 | 0.7 | | 20Q002.I | clay | 3.1, 71 | 3.1, 2:7 |
| | 5 | 0.7 | 1.6 | 0.3 | | 20Q002.II | clay | 3.1, 34 | 3.1, 2:6 |
| | --- | --- | 2.8 | 0.3 | | 20Y026.II | stone | 3.2, 30 | 3.1, 2:18 |
| spindle-whorl? | | | | | 1.1 | 21P(z)001.I | clay | 3.1, 67 | |
| loom-weight | | | | | | Gate area | clay | | 3.1, 4:1 |
| loom-weight | | | | | | Gate area, bastion no. 1 | clay | | 3.1, 4:2 |
| object for twisting threads | | | | | | | stone | | 3.1, 1:17 |
| awl | --- | 7.4 | 1.8 | --- | | 9B010.I | bone | 3.1, 72 | 3.1, 1:18 |

115

### 3.1.6 The spatial distribution of textile production items with regard to the architecture of the lower town and the Citadel

Items used for making textiles are frequently found in archaeological excavations. By looking at the way they are grouped with regard to the settlement's architecture, we can determine, at least approximately, where textile production took place.

### Sector 07

In sector 07 we come across two notable groups, in trench 09C (8 items) and 10D (5 items). Other finds are more one-off, from various trenches and stratigraphical layers (see map).

### Trench 10D

This group of loom weights was found in the layer around the *tandür* stove, which was located in a corner between a brick frame and a platform of hard-packed clay. The corner also had vertically-placed bricks, which almost surrounded the stove on three sides. It is not certain whether the stove was situated inside the house, or whether it stood in an open yard for greater safety (to protect against fire, for example). The location of loom weights by the stove in a courtyard may also have been for a reason – looms are relatively large, and were kept outside, where women worked on them. The dryness of the local climate would have aided this.

The situation is similar in trench *09C*, where there is a notable group of items used for textile production (7 items in total): five loom weights and two re-used ceramic fragments, semi-finished spindle whorls. Roughly in the centre of the trench there was a bread oven, on top of which there was a hard-packed floor layer over all the eastern part. This place was designated a part of the house used for domestic work, or a yard. In addition to the finds mentioned above, further remains of bone fragments and a number of pieces of carbon have been found. It is not impossible that it was a waste layer, possibly a waste pit, which could have been created during building alterations or repairs. The fact that some of the weights are badly damaged lends credence to the idea that it was a place used for waste disposal.

The wide dispersal of the items (whorls, needles, semi-finished items) and the number of places where textile production took place is directly connected with the nature of the settlement as one with a large number of dwellings. Each family unit inhabiting a particular dwelling had to be self-sufficient in textile production, at least of practical textiles. Cords, sacks, rough fabrics that were used for household purposes, decorative fabrics used for interior decoration, family clothing – all this required at least a basic supply of

home-produced textiles. The reasons for this full or partial self-sufficiency were, of course, economic – the family could not afford to pay for all the things it used, especially when it could make them itself from raw materials that were available (wool, flax, fur, hair and so on). Members of the family spun or wove in places that were used exclusively for housework, whether in the yard (weaving, spinning) or in rooms inside (spinning, embroidery, sewing etc.).

### Sector 20

Finds of spindle whorls and loom weights were especially concentrated in the area of the neighbouring trenches 20Y, 20N and 20O, with two finds coming from the subsequent trench 20C (see map). One-off finds also come from trenches 21O and 21E, while from trenches 21P and 21F we have two finds each.

In the southern half of trench 20N five items used for textile production were found – three spindle whorls and two weights. In trench 20C, which neighbours it to the west, one spindle whorl was found (layer 20C001) in the south-eastern part, inside the corridor, and one when going through the spoil tip from the trench. In trench 20O a total of four items relating to textile production were found: three whorls and one fragment of white stone, probably used to make a whorl. Trench 20Y was a real treasure trove of finds, with eight objects related to textile production found there: four whorls, three semi-finished whorls and one loom weight.

Further places where there was a concentration of finds of this type are trenches 20Q and 20G. In trench 20Q three whorls were found, and three items in 20G: two whorls and a ceramic fragment worked into a circular shape; it was possibly a semi-finished whorl or loom weight. It is possible that items for producing and working with textiles were concentrated only in one part, in keeping with the architectural map of the monumental building. This concentration would correspond to the internal needs of the residence, whether this was production in the "women's" rooms, known as *gynace*, or as part of the household facilities.

### 3.1.7. Conclusion

A total of 74 items used for textile production and clothes-making were found at Jandavlattepa during the 2002 to 2006 excavation seasons. They consisted of 43 spindle whorls, 19 loom weights, 9 semi-finished spindle whorls, 2 bronze needles, one awl designed for making leather items and one object designed for twisting threads.

There is a clear typological difference between the whorls found in the Shakhristan and in the

Citadel. It is not just a question of newer types that were previously less used, but also that the whorls were made out of different materials. In sector 07 we mostly find type 4 – hemispherical, 3a – simple spherical and 5 – discoid. The predominant type is 4c – gradated hemispherical, with a single find of type 4a – simple hemispherical and 4b – cylindrical hemispherical. These two types are not found at all in the "Citadel." The most frequently used material for making whorls is stone, of which the most common types were white crystallised stone and a dark, unspecified stone. The next most frequent materials are re-used ceramic fragments and fired clay. The most infrequently-found material for whorls in sector 07 is unfired clay. Whorls from unfired and fired clay were handmade (moulded or thrown), while the stone whorls show signs of having been worked with a lathe. Analogical finds from other sites suggest that these types can be dated to the 3rd century AD at the most.

A more frequently-found type in sector 20 is 4c, with a gradated profile (although this often comes from surface finds or from tips). Also found are types 1 – conical, 3b – spherical lens-shaped, 3c – spherical, with six sides, and 5 – discoid. The material is mostly unfired clay, followed by stone of various kinds, fired clay and ceramics. Given the stratigraphy of finds and the considerable typological difference, the material in sector 20 appear to be younger, and can be dated to approximately the 4th–5th centuries AD.

During the high Kushan period the most common type of whorl was one with a complex profile made of white stone (lime or alabaster) that is found from present-day Afghanistan to the Aral Sea. Jandavlattepa is no exception, and these whorls in the Shakhristan represent 45% of all those found. Many places in settlements of the period can be described as production areas, some sort of workshop for making stone objects. Stone was available thanks to a well-established and well-functioning trading system. During the younger period there was a decrease in the population, and with it appears to have come a severing of social and thus also of trade contacts. New types appeared which could be described as being of a local character. This "barbarisation" of spindle whorls is connected with the demise of the settlement workshops and the reduction in size of the settlement to a smaller, more closed complex. The inhabitants of the youngest period of the Citadel had to be self-sufficient in the production of all kinds of fabrics, as well as in the production of objects used for fabric production.

The most frequent type of loom weight found in sector 07 (the Shakhristan) is 2a and 2b, with types 1a, 2c and 3 occasionally being found. In sector 20 the situation is different; here, one type of loom weight is found almost exclusively, type 2c, with occasional finds of type 2b. Most of the loom weights were handmade from unfired clay. Only 10.5% were fired. Weights of this type were used to weigh down a vertical loom.

It is possible to determine the areas that may have been used for textile production by following the concentration of textile-producing objects found. From this analysis, made for the Jandavlattepa site (see map) it appears that textile production may have taken place in open yards, where there was enough room to set up the loom (weaving, spinning, making loom weights etc.) but also in rooms that were inhabited by the family (sewing, embroidery, fine textile techniques).

In sector 07 there are two notable concentrations of various objects used for textile production or textile working, which could designate places where this activity took place. They are the spaces documented in the squares 09C (8 items) and 10D (5 items). The other finds are more one-off, from various trenches and stratigraphical layers.

The dispersal of the material and the number of places where textile crafts took place is directly connected to the fact that the settlement had a large number of dwelling places. Each family unit had to be self-sufficient in textile production, at least for practical use. Cords, sacks, rough material used for domestic purposes or basic pieces of clothing were often made by family members. We cannot yet say with certainty that textile work took place only in some sort of "women's rooms," since the archaeological finds do not bear this out. This is partly because this classification has not been paid sufficient attention by researchers. It is also questionable to what extent work with raw materials or textile crafts were women's work only – they may not have been.

Not all households were forced to be totally self-sufficient, however. Special weaving workshops are presumed to have existed, and they would have supplied the city and its surroundings. Unfortunately, the state of research on this topic is as yet very unsatisfactory. Not even one such workshop has been identified, although a rich collection of loom weights from Dal'verzintepa, which had stamps on them to identify them, could well be an indication of the existence of such a workshop. Pugachenkova believes that this was indeed proof of intense textile production in the settlement.[17] On the site of the lower town at Jandavlattepa, excavated in sectors 07 and 08, no specialised weaving workshop has as yet been distinguished.

---

[17]  Pugachenkova 1978, pp. 203–204.

In sector 20, the Citadel, the finds of objects used for textile production are less dispersed than they are in the Shakhristan. Most of them are concentrated in the area of squares 20Y, 20N and 20O. A comparison of the materials used suggests that they come from a period (the Kushano-Sasanian period) that is younger than the high Kushan period. This, plus the stratigraphy of finds and their concentration inside the complex interior building, allows us to express the hypothesis that objects used for textile production and working were concentrated in only one place in the architectural plan of the monumental building, as part of its domestic facilities. A weaving workshop may also have been part of this. Such a workshop, used purely for the needs of the residence, would have arisen in the younger period of the Citadel's settlement, approximately to the end of the 4th century Ad. Nevertheless, at the present time when the building has not yet been explored to its full extent, this conclusion is more of a preliminary hypothesis that will have to be examined in the future.

Given the insufficient exploration of the older periods of the Citadel's settlement, it is as yet unclear whether the situation was the same during the high Kushan period of settlement. Continuing excavation will bring us more knowledge in this respect.

## Bibliography

Litvinskiy, B. A. (1978): Orudiya truda i utvary iz mogilnikov zapadnoy Fergany, in: *Arkheologicheskie i etnograficheskie materialy po istorii kultury i religii Sredney Asii*, Moskva.

Luneva, V. (2002): Pryaslitsa Kampyrtepa, in: *Materialy tokharistanskoy ekspeditsii*, vyp. 3, Tashkent, pp. 91–100.

Lyovushkina, S. V. (1996): On the history of sericulture in Central Asia, *Silk Road Art and Archaeology* IV, 1995/1996, pp. 143–150.

Maytdynova, G. M. (2001): Znachenie kostyumnogo kompleksa dlya issledovaniya etnogeneza, in: *Drevnyaya i srednevekovaya kultura Surkhandarii*, Taschkent, pp. 81–89.

Nerazik, E. E. – Rapoport, Yu. A. (1984): Toprak-Kala. Dvorets, in: *Trudy Khorezmskoy arkheologo-etnograficheskoy ekspeditsii*, XIV, Moskva.

Pugachenkova, G. A. (1966): *Khalchayan: K probleme khudozhestvennoy kultury severnoy Baktrii*. Tashkent.

Pugachenkova, G. A. (1978): Dal'verzintepe i nekotorie obshchie voprosy istorii i kul'tury Severnoy Baktrii, in: *Dal'verzintepe – kushanskiy gorod na yuge Uzbekistana*. Pugachenkova, G. A. – Rtveladze, E. V. (eds.). Tashkent, 1978, pp. 176–222.

Pugachenkova G. A. (1979): Jiga-tepe (raskopki 1974 g.), in: *Drevnyaya Baktriya. Materialy Sovetsko-Afghanskoy eksepedicii Vyp. 2*, ed. Kruglikova I. T., Moskva, pp. 63–94.

Sedov, A. V. (1987): *Kobadian na poroge rannego srednevekov'ya*. Moskva.

Shagalina, N. (2002): Gruzila s Kampyrtepa i ikh klassifikatsiya, in: *Materialy tokharistanskoy ekspeditsii*, vyp. 3, Tashkent, pp. 109–117.

Urbanová, K. (2006): *Textilní produkce v kušánské Střední Asii*, unpublished MA Thesis, Prague, Charles University.

# 3.2 Metal, stone and bone weapons and implements

*Jan Kysela*

The objects treated in this article are highly varied from both a functional and typological, as well as material, point of view. The materials include various metals, stone and bone, of which, from the functional point of view, there are mostly weapons and tools while a considerable body of the objects is made up of fragments whose original shape is no longer possible to determine.

The objects studied were uncovered at the excavations executed in seasons 2002–2006 at the site of Jandavlattepa, sectors 4 ("Gate"), 7 ("Shakhristan") and 20 ("Citadel") and at a minor excavation of a nearby mound.

The structure of the present paper is that of a catalogue of the single finds (organised by functional classes) followed by short studies of the single classes. The author's main concern is to define the function and, when possible, the type and approximate chronology of the single finds. This chronology is only an extrinsic one, given that the majority of the better definable objects came from evidently secondary deposits, and therefore bring, by themselves, hardly any information, temporal or spatial.

## 3.2.1 Knives

**1.**

11C005.IV – A tanged, one-edged **knife** with a straight, sloping back and a slightly convex edge (forming a "central" point). The transition from the blade to the tang is abrupt and angular on the back side, gradual and rounded on the blade side. Preserved almost integrally in three fragments despite minor breaks on the point and the end of the tang.

Dimensions:  length – 121 mm
l.: (tang) – 29 mm (maximum length on the back side)
w.: (max) – 23 mm
th. 6 mm (blade back) 4.5 mm (tang)

tab. 3.2, *1:1*; fig. 3.2, *1*\*

**2.**

11C005.V – A tanged, one-edged **knife** with a straight back and a more or less straight edge (forming a "central" point). The transition from the blade to the tang is abrupt and angular on the back side, gradual and rounded on the blade side. Preserved integrally in three fragments.

Dimensions:  l.: 140 mm
l.: (tang) 29 mm
w.: (max) 20 mm
th. – 6 mm

tab. 3.2, *1:2*; fig. 3.2, *2*

**3.**

20N002.VII – A one-edged iron **knife blade** with both back and edge being convex, thus forming a central point. The edge seems to be slightly worn due to whetting. The handle part has not been preserved. It seems, however, to have been of the tanged type with the tang passing abruptly to the backside and more gradually towards the edge.

Dimensions:  l.: 88 mm
w.: (max) – 19.7 mm
th. – 15 mm

tab. 3.2, *1:3*; fig. 3.2, *3*\*

**Fig. 3.2, 2** Knife, small find no. 11C005.V.

119

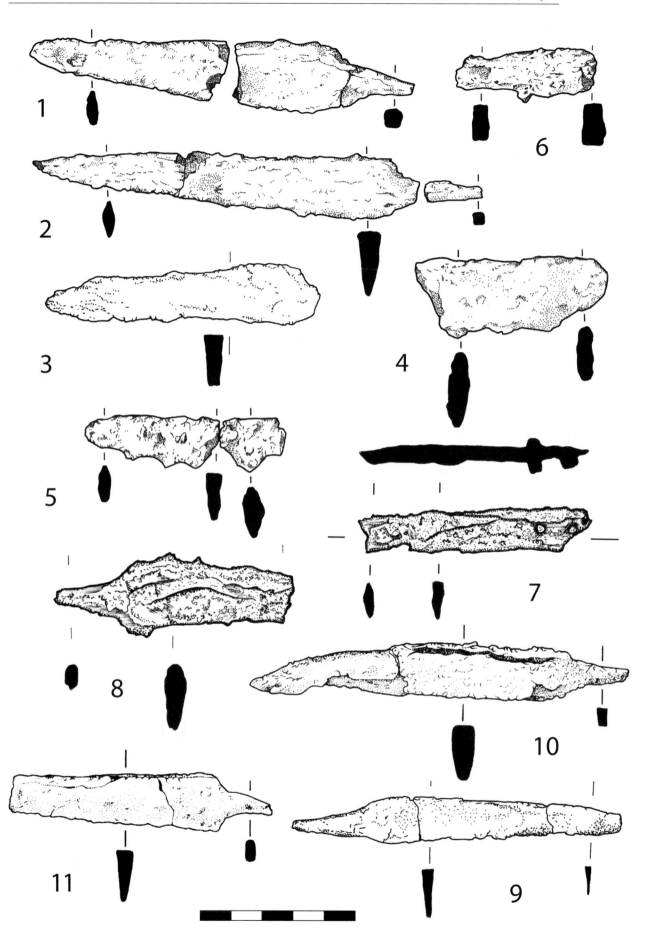

Tab. 3.2,1

**4.**

20O011.II – An iron **knife-blade fragment**. Broken off on both ends and extensively corroded.
Dimensions: l.: 62 mm
w.: 25 mm
th. – 6 mm
tab. 3.2, *1:4*; fig. 3.2, *4*

**5.**

20O003.I – Two fragments of an iron **knife blade**, both fitting together. The resulting blade seems to be slightly convex in both back and edge side with a central tip.
Dimensions: l.: 61 mm (45 + 25 mm)
w.: (max) 20 mm
tab. 3.2, *1:5*; fig. 3.2, *5*

**6.**

20Y002.III – A fragment of an iron **knife**: the tang and the lower part of the blade. On close examination, and as far as may be determined from the extensive rust, the tang seems to be placed closer to the back side rather than to the edge, and the transition seems to be more abrupt on the former, more gradual on the latter side.
Dimensions: l.: 45 mm
w.: 15 mm (blade)
5 mm (tang)
tab. 3.2, *1:6*; fig. 3.2, *6*

**7.**

21P006c.I – A fragment of a one-edged iron **knife** (or other tool?) broken off on both ends. It being a strip of iron tapering in its thickness from the "back" (5 mm) to the "edge" (2 mm), with a slight reduction on the latter (due to whetting?) and with two rivets on one end, tempts one to interpret it as a knife. However, owing to its overall gracility and the unusual use of two rivets very close to each other, the author prefers to leave this interpretation with a question mark.
Dimensions: l.: 72 mm
w.: 14 mm
th. – 5–2 mm
tab. 3.2, *1:7*; fig. 3.2, *7*

**8.**

21P006c.II – A fragment of a one-edged iron **knife**: the tang and the lower part of the blade. The blade (straight on the back and edge in the whole of the preserved part) is visibly worn due to whetting (almost 2 mm difference). The tang is centrally placed with gradual transitions towards both edge and back. Imprints of wood are preserved in the rust on the tang.
Dimensions: l.: 77 mm
w.: (max) – 23.5 mm
th.: 4.3 mm
tab. 3.2, *1:8*; fig. 3.2, *8*

**9.**

04.000.XVIII (Tower No. 1 in Sector 04)
A one-edged iron **knife** with a straight edge and a convex back (forming a "lower" point). A central triangular tang passes gradually to both back and edge side. Preserved in three fragments with the very point missing.
Dimensions: l.: 107.7 mm
w.: 15.7 mm
th.: 3 mm (blade) 4.5 mm (tang)
tab. 3.2, *1:9*; fig. 3.2, *9*

**10.**

Sector 04, 2004 two **knives** not examined personally
04.000.XIX – A tanged, one-edged iron knife with a straight edge and convex back (and thus a "lower" point). The axially placed tang is quadrangular in section, set off abruptly on the backside while passing gradually on the edge side. Preserved in fragments entirely except for the very end of the tang.
Dimensions: l.: 129 mm
w.: 18 mm
tab. 3.2, *1:10*; fig. 3.2, *10*

**11.**

04.000.XX – A fragment of a tanged, one-edged iron knife. The tip-end of the blade is broken off and lost. Both the back- and the edge-side of the preserved portion of the blade are straight without any curvature. The centrally placed tang oval in section is offset abruptly from both sides.
Dimensions: l.: 89.5 mm
w.: 20 mm
tab. 3.2, *1:11*; fig. 3.2, *11*

**12.**

30.013C.I – A group of iron objects originally found together, possibly individual parts of one object:
a) An iron rod oval in section, broken at one end, rounded and mono-laterally widened at the other.
Dimensions: Length: 35 mm, Diameter: 15 mm
b) A fragment of an iron plaque, curved in section with a flat, strip-like part protruding perpendicularly from its straight "upper" edge (as seen in the photograph). The plaque tapers down progressively "from up downwards" in its thickness, suggesting an edge. A rivet seems to be fixed in the plaque (hard to discern due to the rust). Most of the plaque's circumference as well as the "strip-like" part are missing. Dimensions: l. 43 mm, w. 42 mm, th. 1–3 mm
c) A rivet (?) – a minute item, quadrangular in section, widened on one end and broken on the other. Dimensions: l. 10 mm, w. 6 mm
d) An iron "chip" wedge-shaped in section. Dimensions: l. 21 mm, w. 11 mm
tab. 3.2, *3:1*; fig. 3.2, *12*

## 3.2.2 Bronze arrowheads

**13.**

07A010.I – A **three-winged, socketed** bronze arrowhead in a very poor state of preservation. The tip is missing. The badly worn wing blades do not seem to have been reinforced originally. The socket did protrude beyond the wing ends but not enough remains from it to estimate to what extent it did. The portion of the socket, fused to the martial part is well distinguishable from the wings. Found among the debris of a collapsed wall.

Dimensions: l. (max preserved): 14 mm
w. (max preserved): 8 mm
l. of the socket (overall): 5 mm; (only the "free" part): 3.8 mm
depth of the socket: 1.7 mm
th. of the wings: 1.9 mm, 2 mm, 2.3 mm
weight: 1.3 g

tab. 3.2, *2:1*; fig. 3.2, *13**

**14.**

09B009.II – A **socketed, bronze arrowhead, three-sided** in section, badly weathered and so only tentatively classified according to its outline as "leaf-shaped." The tip and the blades are rubbed off and rounded. The socket, protruding well beyond the martial part, is slightly triangular in section and is preserved in its entirety. Found among the debris of a collapsed wall.

Dimensions: l.: 27 mm
w.: 10 mm
l. of the socket (the free part): 8.5 mm
diameter of the socket: 8 mm
weight: 4.5 g

tab. 3.2, *2:2*; fig. 3.2, *14**

**15.**

09C015.I – A **socketed, bronze arrowhead, three-sided in section**, with a triangular outline. The edges are straight and the sides even. The edges terminate on their lower ends with massive barbs of different lengths, the transitions between them (tip-bases of a kind) being arcuate. The socket is completely "hidden" inside the arrowhead. It was found together with a little lump of bronze, originally considered a remnant of a broken-off socket. The arrowhead, however, does not seem to have ever had any exterior socket portion.

Dimensions: l. (without spikes): 21 mm
l. of the spikes: 5.5 mm – 7.8 mm – 7 mm
w.: 10 mm
weight: 3.1 g

tab. 3.2, *2:3*; fig. 3.2, *15**

**16.**

Sector 04, 2004

04.000.IV (surface layer above a mud-brick construction) A **three-winged, socketed** bronze arrowhead with a triangular outline of the wings and "**paws**" **at the socket's mouth**. The tip is not reinforced (i.e. three sided) in a strict sense but still quite substantial. The straight wings – terminating in barbs – lack any reinforcement. The socket measures several millimetres up to the martial part. Its free part is circular in section. The "paws" at its lower end are located in correspondence with the single wings and a "seam" (a result of the casting process) is observable between each wing and the relative "paw."

Dimensions: l.: 36.7 mm
l. of the head (including the thorns – 2 mm): 29 mm
w.: 12 mm

l. of the socket (max): 14 mm; the free part only: 8 mm
diameter of the socket: 7.5 mm
l. of the longest paw: 2.4 mm
th. of wings: 2 mm – 2 mm – 3 mm
weight: 4.3 g

tab. 3.2, *2:4*; fig. 3.2, *16**

**17.**

04.000.V (Tower No. 1)

A **three-winged bronze arrowhead with an ogival outline**. Both the tip and the edges are reinforced. The tip (with a length of 12 mm) is thus triangular in section. The tip-bases are M-shaped (i.e. feature downwardly pointed projections, giving each side the appearance of a "gothic window"). The wings (although it might be damaged) terminate in barb-less bases in obtuse angles to the socket. The socket (circular in section) reaches up to a third of the martial part's length. Outside this it is not preserved to any length.

Dimensions: l.: 36 mm
w. (max): 11 mm
l. of the wings: 32.5 mm
th. of the wings: 2 mm
diameter of the socket (exterior): 7.2 mm; interior: 5 mm
depth of the socket: ca 10 mm
weight: 4.3 g

tab. 3.2, *2:5*; fig. 3.2, *17**

**18.**

04.000.VI (surface layer; oral communication with Dr. Shaydullayev)

A **three-winged bronze arrowhead with an ogival outline**. Both the tip and the wing blades are reinforced with the conformation of the tip-bases analogous to that of the previous item. The wings terminate in acute angles and so form actual barbs. The socket is circular in section and observable to almost a half of the martial part's length. On the exterior it protrudes relatively little. There is an oval aperture in the socket between two of the wing bases.

Dimensions: l.: 37 mm
w.: 11 mm
l. of the wings (incl. the thorns – 2 mm): 33 mm
th. of the wings: 3 mm
diameter of the socket: 7.4 mm
weight: 5.7 g

tab. 3.2, *2:6*; fig. 3.2, *18**

## 3.2.3 Iron Arrowheads

**19.**

07C009.I – A **large, tanged, three-winged iron arrowhead** with a triangular outline of the wings. The single preserved wing-base seems to feature a blunt "barb" aligned with the wing blade. The tang is circular in section. According to Litvinskiy's classification, it appears to be an arrowhead of type 2-1/A-1-7a- – – 1. The very tip is missing, and two of the wings are severely damaged.

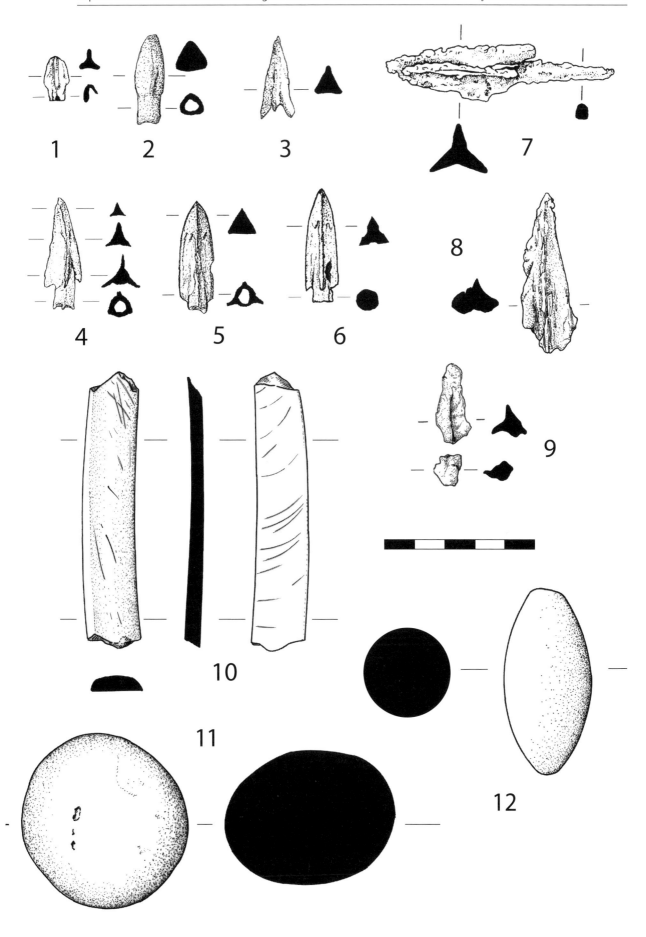

Tab. 3.2, 2

Dimensions: l. (Litvinskiy's h$_1$): 76.4 mm
l. of the head (excluding the "thorn," h$_2$): 46 mm
l. of the thorn (h$_3$): 5 mm
l. of the tang (h$_4$): 34.5 mm
w. (max preserved, l$_1$): 21 mm
w. between the thorns (l$_2$): not preserved
diameter of the thorn: 7–3 mm
tab. 3.2, *2:7*; fig. 3.2, *19*[*]

## 20.

09C016.VII – A fragmentary **large, three-winged iron arrowhead**. The heavily corroded margins suggest slender, straight or slightly S-shaped outlines. The lower part of the wings and the supposed tang are totally absent. A fragment of wood seems to have been preserved in the rust.
Dimensions: l.: 51 mm
w. (max): 18 mm (no other measurements were taken considering the poor state of the item)
weight: 7.1 g
tab. 3.2, *2:8*; fig. 3.2, *20*[*]

## 21.

20Y023.I – A fragmentary **small, three-winged iron arrowhead**. The tip, the outlines, the wing bases and the tang are all absent and so any observation as to the item's original shape is indeterminate. Another shapeless fragment of iron was found with it. Found in a modern grave sunk in a wall.
Dimensions: l.: 26.5 mm
w.: 11 mm
the associated fragment: 12 × 9 mm
tab. 3.2, *2:9*; fig. 3.2, *21*[*]

## 3.2.4 (possible) fragmentary blades

## 22.

20D002.II – Six fragments of an iron object (**a blade**?). The three major ones more or less preserve the object's original lentoid section and smooth surface. All of them feature breaks transverse to the original object's longitudinal axis: The fragment a) visibly tapers from one short end to the other (a fragment of the blade's tip?). The break on the broader side is surprisingly regular (arcuate) and clean. The fragments b) and c) match together. The three minor fragments are mere "crumbs" without any connection to each other or to any of the major ones.
Dimensions: a) w.: 32.8–26.6 mm, l.: 47.5 mm th. (max): 14.1 mm
b) w.(max): 32.5 mm, l.: 39.4 mm th. (max): 12 mm
c) w.(max): 36.7 mm, l.: 48 mm th. (max): 9.5 mm
b+c) l.: 85 mm
d) 31×25×7 mm
e) 36×15×8 mm
f) 27×23×6 mm
tab. 3.2, *3:2*; fig. 3.2, *22*[*]

## 23.

20S003.II – Two matching fragments of a **pointed iron object**. Put together, its section seems to be flat rather than lentoid (a thick layer of rust on the surface makes discerning this quite difficult). The break on the broadest side shows a surprising likeness to that of Fragment a) of Find 20D.002.II (a blade), i.e. concavely rounded with an unusually clean and smooth surface.
Dimensions: frgmt a) l.: 28.5 mm  w. (max): 22 mm
frgmt b) l.: 36 mm  w. (max): 37.6 mm
a+b) l.: 53 mm;  w. (max): 37.6 mm;
Th (max): 10.5 mm
tab. 3.2, *3:3*; fig. 3.2, *23*[*]

## 24.

21E025.I – A **pointed object**, flat to lentil-shaped in section. Its present shape is greatly affected by an extensive rusty involucre. The side opposite the point seems to have resulted from a break.
Dimensions: l.: 54.5 mm
w.: 26 mm
th.: 10 mm
tab. 3.2, *3:4*; fig. 3.2, *24*[*]

## 3.2.5 Sling-shots

## 25.

11C014.I – A light red-brown stone worked into the shape of a flattened ball. **A sling-shot or a pestle**.
Dimensions: diameter: 52–56 mm
th. (max): 45 mm
weight: 174.3 g
tab. 3.2, *2:11*; fig. 3.2, *25*[*]

## 26.

12D003.II – A bi-conical to egg-shaped polished stone, light grey to greenish in color. One of the ends is rounded, the other rather flat. Traces of polishing (diagonal hairline grooves) are observable on the surface. A **sling-shot**.
Dimensions: l.: 58 mm
diameter (max): 29 mm
weight: 63.5 g
tab. 3.2, *2:12*; fig. 3.2, *26*

**Fig. 3.2, 26** Sling-shot, small find no. 12D003.II.

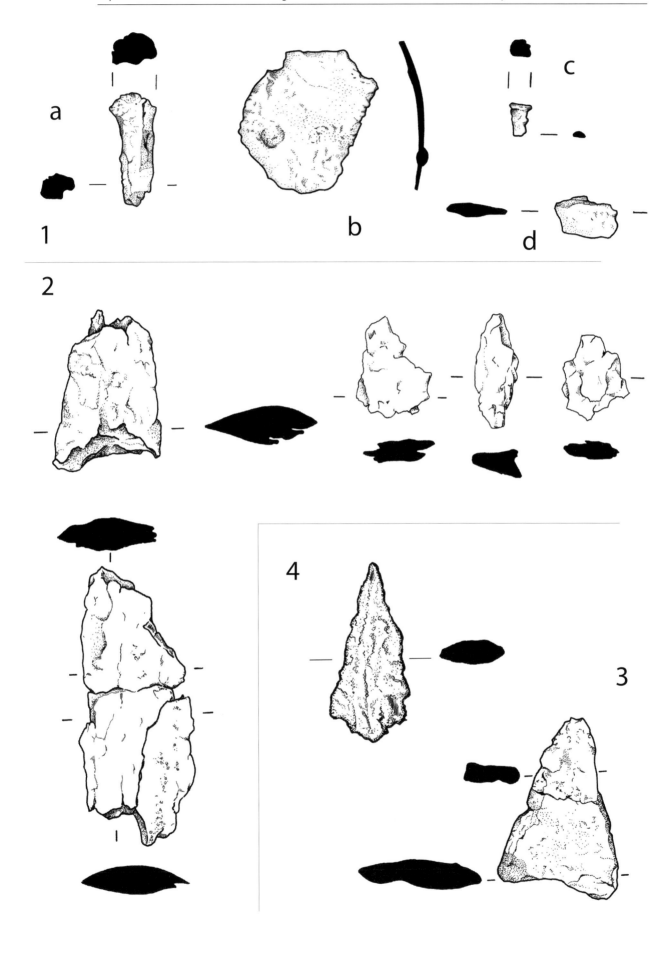

Tab. 3.2, 3

**27.**

09E023.I– A stone in the shape of a flattened ball. Possibly a **sling-shot**. Unfortunately, this find was lost.

Dimensions (approximate):

          diameter (max): 45 mm

          width: 35 mm

          weight: not measured

          No picture.

### 3.2.6 A bone plaque – finial of a bow

**28.**

21F025.I – An oblong, slightly curved bone plaque, progressively diminishing in width and thickness. Plano-convex in section, the edge of the convex side of the plaque being upright, that of the concave one rounded. Both faces are covered with numerous thin, diagonal grooves: those of the convex face are straight and intersect one another quite freely, while those of the plain one are arcuate and never intersect. Both ends of the plaque are broken off.

Dimensions:  l.: 90 mm

          w.: 18.2–16.8 mm

          th.: 5.2–4.4 mm

tab. 3.2, *2:10*; fig. 3.2, *27a** and *27b*

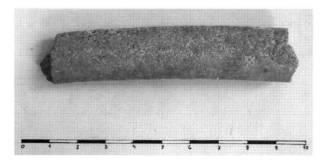

**Fig. 3.2, 27b** Finial of a bow, small find no. 21F025.I.

### 3.2.7 Whetstones

**29.**

10C003.III. – A thin, oblong slab of grey stone (a **whetstone**). There are breaks on both of the short and one of the long sides. A hole is drilled through the slab near one of the short ends with some chipping around its mouth on the "obverse" side. On the "reverse" side, two grooves are cut into the surface: one (21 mm long) passing through the hole, the other skirting the broken long side (a possible reason for the breakage). On the "obverse" side, usage resulted in a considerable reduction of the whetstone's volume, creating a rectangular depression to which the surface gradually sinks. A little cross (4 × 4 mm) is carved in this sloping surface.

Dimensions:  l.: 56 mm

          w. (max): 14 mm

          th.: 3–7 mm

          diameter of the hole: 2.5 mm

tab. 3.1, 3:7; fig. 3.2, *28**

**30.**

20Y002.XIV – A flat, sub-quadrangular slab of smooth, black stone. The surface is rather irregularly formed with a dense "hairline pattern" on both faces of the stone, indicating obvious traces of its use as a **whetstone**.

Dimensions:  l.: 134 mm

          w.: 39–43 mm

          th.: 4–10 mm

tab. 3.2, *4:1*; fig. 3.2, *29*

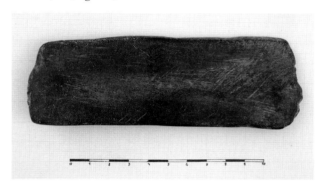

**Fig. 3.2, 29** A whetstone made of black stone, no. 20Y002.XIV

**31.**

20Y026.II – A triangular chip of grey stone. The "obverse" side is slightly convex and smooth, while the "reverse" side is basically plain and coarse. There are remnants of a drilled hole in the middle of one of the sides. This find could possibly have been chipped away from the surface of a **whetstone**.

Dimensions:  l.: 29 mm

          w.: 21 mm

tab. 3.1, 2:18 (!); fig. 3.2, *30**

**32.**

07D009.IV – A cylindrical object oval in section made from dark grey stone. Broken away on both short ends, in one of which, remains of a transversely drilled hole are visible. Possibly a fragment of a **whetstone** with a drilled suspension hole.

Dimensions:  l.: 45 mm

          w.: 17 × 14 mm

fig. 3.2, *31**

**33.**

08A009.I – A little block of grey stone slightly oblong in section with a hole drilled bilaterally in the upper side. Probably a **whetstone**.

Dimensions:  l.: 54 mm

          w.: 26 × 19 mm

tab. 3.2, *4:3*; fig. 3.2, *65**

### 3.2.8 Varia

**34.**

07C002.II – A slightly cylindrical bar of grey stone, circular in section. Possibly a **pestle** or a **whetstone**.

Dimensions:  l.: 153 mm

          diameter: 28–42 mm

tab. 3.2, *4:2*, fig. 3.2, *32**

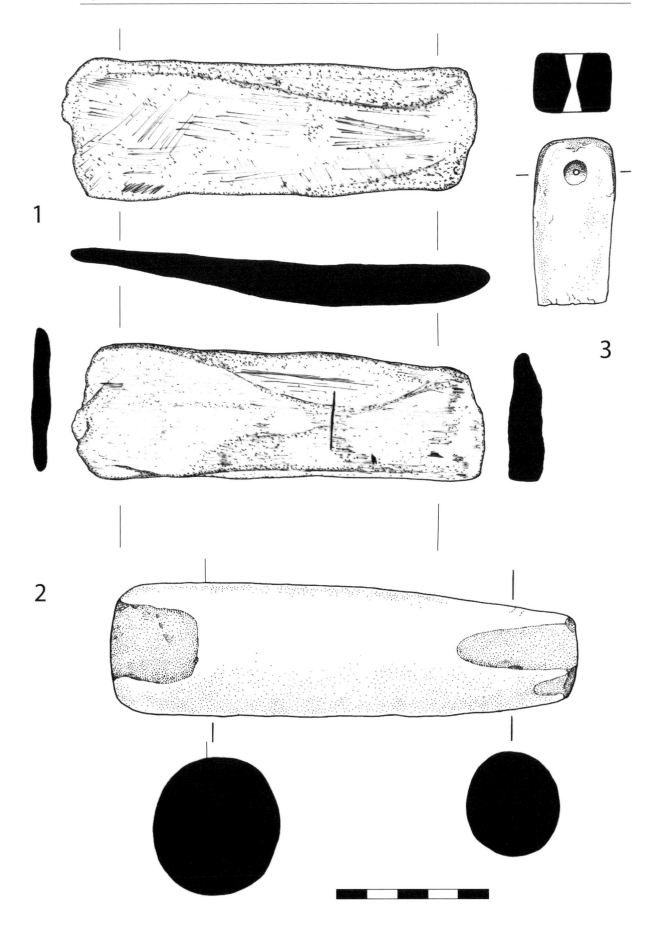

Tab. 3.2, 4

**35.**

09C016.V – A **bronze pin** with a globular head. Probably secondarily bowed. Broken up into two fragments.

Dimensions: l.: 41 mm

diameter: 3–4 mm

fig. 3.2, *33*

**36.**

09D010.I – A **bronze nail** or rivet. The shaft is circular in section with an obtuse tip. The head is semi-globular with the shaft's upper extremity visible on the surface. Longitudinal crevices are present on the shaft's surface.

Dimensions: l.: 31 mm

l. of the head: 5 mm

diameter of the head: 9 mm

diameter of the shaft: 4 mm

tab. 3.2, *5:1*; fig. 3.2, *34*

**37.**

20Q001.I – An **iron hook**. The two arms make up basically a right angel. The whole surface is covered with an exuberant layer of rust. A voluminous accumulation of rust is adhered mono-laterally to the "long" end. Fragments of wood seem to be preserved within the rust.

Dimensions: l.: 63 mm

w.: 28 mm (the L. of the short arm)

diameter 4–16 mm

tab. 3.2, *5:2*; fig. 3.2, *35*

**38.**

20Q012.I – Two fragments of a rectangular **iron hook**. Made from a flat strip by simple bending, it tapers progressively in its width. Probably fragmentary on both ends.

Dimensions: l.: 48 mm

l. of the shorter part: 22 mm

w.: 11–7 mm

th.: 3 mm

tab. 3.2, *5:3*; fig. 3.2, *36*

**39.**

20Y004.I – A **bronze hook.** Made from a rod circular in section with a decreasing diameter. The end opposite of the hook is broken away. There are longitudinal crevices on the surface of the rod.

Dimensions: overall l.: 82 mm

l. of the hooked part: 24 mm

w. of the hooked part: 25 mm

diameter: 8–5 mm

fig. 3.2, *37*

### 3.2.9 Minor metal fragments

**40.**

07C009.III – A heavily corroded iron object, teardrop-shaped in outline. The narrow end slightly projects forward in a kind of a **hook**.

Dimensions: l.: 67 mm

w.: (max) 34 mm; (min) 14 mm

th.: 18 mm; (at the "hooked" end): 23 mm

fig. 3.2, *38*

**41.**

07C010.III – A fragment of an iron band. Trapezoid in section, broken off at both ends.

Dimensions: l.: 104 mm

w. (lower face): 45 mm; w.(upper face): 40 mm

th. (max): 13 mm

fig. 3.2, *39*

**42.**

07C010.IV. – A flat, pointed iron object. A trefoil projection is adhered to one of the ends. Heavily corroded.

Dimensions: l.: 47 mm

w.: 12 mm

th.: 8–12 mm

the projection: 6 × 5 × 1 mm

fig. 3.2, *40*

**43.**

07E033.II – A fragment of an iron strip. Broken off at both short ends. One of the long sides is flat, the other rounded in section.

Dimensions: l.: 37 mm

w.: 22 mm

th.: 9.5 mm

fig. 3.2, *41*

**44.**

09E002.III – A fragment of an iron object. Oblong, quadrangular in section, heavily corroded.

Dimensions: l.: 27 mm

w.: 7 mm

th.: 3–4 mm

fig. 3.2, *42*

**45.**

11C005.VI – An **iron rod** basically quadrangular in section, broken on one end and rounded on the other. A wood fragment seems to be preserved in the rust on the rounded end. Despite the rounding, this is certainly not a broken-off knifepoint because the object is too fragile and has no definite edge. Two fragments were found.

Dimensions: l.: 45 mm

w.: 8 mm

tab. 3.2, *5:6*, fig. 3.2, *43*

**46.**

11C005.IX – A fragment of iron wire.

Dimensions: l. (max): 21 mm

diameter: 3 mm

fig. 3.2, *44*

**47.**

20B.001.I – A fragment of an iron object.

fig. 3.2, *45*

**48.**

20N001.I – A club-shaped bronze rod, thickened at one end and broken off on the other. Circular in section. Broken into three fragments in the course of excavation.

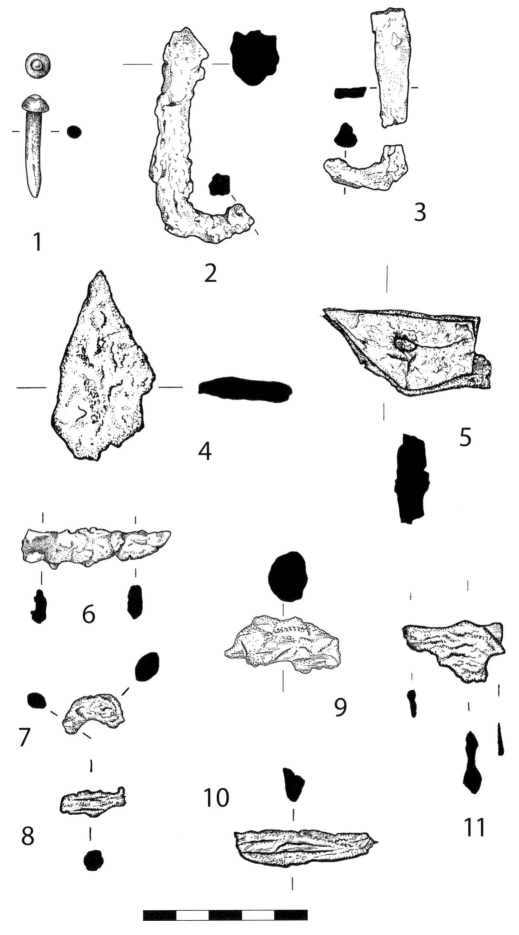

Tab. 3.2, 5

Dimensions:  l.: 70 mm

diameter: 6–10 mm

fig. 3.2, *46*[*]

**49.**

20O010.I – A fragment of a bronze rod, circular in section. Broken off on both ends. There is a wedge-shaped crack along its full length along with several other minor longitudinal crevices.

Dimensions:  l.: 37 mm

diameter: 10 mm

fig. 3.2, *47*[*]

**50.**

20O020.III – A fragment of iron.

Dimensions: 17 × 9 × 5.5 mm

fig. 3.2, *48*[*]

**51.**

20Q001.IV – A fragment of an iron rod, perhaps originally quadrangular in section. Heavily corroded.

Dimensions:  l.: 22 mm

diameter: 6 mm

fig. 3.2, *49*[*]

**52.**

21D025.II, IV, VII–X – Shapeless fragments of iron, all having recent breaks. Found in the fill of a modern grave.

Dimensions:  l.: 12–49 mm

w.: cca 10 mm

tab. 3.2, *5:10* (21D025.II), figs. 3.2, *50–54*[*]

**53.**

21D025.VI – A trapezoidal iron object with a rivet fixed in its centre. The shortest side and the surface without the rivet seem to have been recently broken and chipped off respectively. The object's thickness and quadrangular section disqualify it from being interpreted as a knife fragment. Found in the fill of a modern grave.

Dimensions:  l.: 49 mm

w.: 32 mm

th.: 7–10 mm

tab. 3.2, *5:5*, fig. 3.2, *55*[*]

**54.**

21E006.II – A fragment of thin iron band covered with a thick layer of rust.

Dimensions:  l.: 31 mm

w.: 11 mm

th. (of a projecting part of the band): 1 mm

tab. 3.2, *5:11*, fig. 3.2, *56*[*]

**55.**

21E010.I – A fragment of bronze sheet with irregular outlines.

Dimensions:  32 × 24 × 2 mm

fig. 3.2, *57*[*]

**56.**

21E026.II – A shapeless iron fragment. Conspicuously slaggy rust is present on one of the object's faces.

Dimensions:  cca 45 × 55 × 17–20 mm

fig. 3.2, *58*[*]

**57.**

21F014.I – A fragment of a trapezoidal iron object, flat in section. There are recent breaks on two sides.

Dimensions:  l.: 56.5 mm

w.: 31 mm

th.: 6–4 mm

tab. 3.2, *5:4*, fig. 3.2, *59*[*]

**58.**

21F020.I – A heavily corroded fragment of iron.

Dimensions:  l.: 38 mm

w.: 18 mm

th.: 5 mm

fig. 3.2, *60*[*]

**59.**

21O001.II – A fragment of bronze wire.

Dimensions:  l.: 11 mm

diameter 1.5 m

fig. 3.2, *61*[*]

**60.**

21O002.I – A tiny fragment of bronze sheet.

Dimensions:  l. (max): 10 mm

th.: 1.5 mm

No picture

**61.**

21P002.III – A fragment of iron rod. Semi-circular in section, pointed on one end, broken off on the other.

Dimensions:  l.: 36 mm

w. (max): 10 mm

fig. 3.2, *62*[*]

**62.**

21P005.I – A shapeless fragment of bronze, oval in section.

Dimensions:  l.(max): 35.5 mm

w.: 13 × 10 mm

tab. 3.2, *5:9*, fig. 3.2, *63*[*]

**63.**

21P007.I – A shapeless fragment of iron.

Dimensions:  21×6 mm

tab. 3.2, *5:8*, fig. 3.2, *64*[*]

### 3.2.10 Synthesis

The **knives** (at least those sufficiently preserved to be examined) from the Citadel and from the Shakhristan (sectors 20 and 7 respectively) belong almost all to one type: tanged, one-edged knives with both backs and edges being either straight or only slightly convex; thus, forming basically central tips.

Conspicuously enough, in both of the knives from the Gate zone (Sector 4) where the tips have been preserved, these are not "central" but "lower" (with curved backs curving to the straight edges). This difference might point to a divergence in the knives' functional designation rather than to a chronological difference.[1]

Some minor diversities in the shape of the tang are certainly not to be understood as testimonies of various knife-types, but rather as individual features of single knives[2].

A single knife (if this is a knife at all) features a handle made up of two rivet-fixed grip scales (no. 8, 21P006c.I). This way of fixing the handle is rare in both antique and early medieval central Asian knives, being usually utilized on those with a curved blade (i.e. sickle shaped), none of which were found in the Citadel and the Shakhristan, while in the one from **Sector 02a** – the handle arrangement is not preserved. The straight-bladed knives from other more or less contemporary sites feature almost universally a pointed tang, sometimes with a single rivet between the tang and the blade to secure the slip-on handle[3].

The unusual assembly of iron items from the elevation (sector 30) raises several questions, the first one concerning the fragments' pertinence or not to a single original object. If we limited ourselves to an attempt to interpret each major fragment, the task would be no less troublesome. The object's decreasing thickness might suggest a kind of bladed instrument. Indeed, this suggestion would be further supported by the supposed band of metal (i.e. a handle) projecting from the "lower" (the thickest) half. Tentative interpretations as a razor or a leather knife would probably not be untenable, though doubtless Central Asian parallels are unknown to the present author[4]. Such interpretations are, however, difficult to conciliate with the object's curved profile and the possible nail or rivet head fixed in the surface (if this is not merely a bulge in the rust). This might lead one to consider the fragment part of an iron mounting of a wooden object with a curved profile.

**Bronze arrowheads** went out of use in Central Asia in the 2nd century BC[5]. Their presence in the Great Kushan Shakhristan is, therefore, certainly due to a secondary deposition. This phenomenon is not unusual in Central Asia. Yagodin[6] suggests that arrowheads (and other minor objects) may accidentally intrude into later contexts in mud-bricks made from material taken from earlier constructions and layers of settlements. This is well imaginable even though one might argue that the (at least partial) cleaning of the mud (an unavoidable step in the production of mud-bricks) would probably easily reveal most of these intrusions. Intentional deposition, however, is definitely not to be excluded. Pugachenkova[7] takes this for granted in the case of Khalchayan (the palace of Khanaktepa, Room 4) where five iron arrowheads were sealed in the very finely washed clay of the floor. The author explains this as an apotropaic measure, considering the arrowhead an object of notable magical and protective value.

Little can be said about lacunary Arrowhead 07A010.I (no. 13), as practically none of the typological features can be determined.

Typological determination of Arrowhead 9B009.II (no. 14) is complicated, too. Given the quite compact character of the object, the wear may not have been great. Perhaps the once sharp edges were only rubbed off. In that case, the original shape could have been that of a "purely three-sided" arrowhead with a long socket. Smirnov lists an analogous arrowhead from distant Mechet-chay (Orenburg region, Russia; a Sauromatian burial, 5/6th century BC) and mentions others of the same kind from the Near East

---

1 Knives of both types were found "side-by-side" both in barrow cemeteries in the Kafirnigan valley (the last century/ies BC – early 1st century AD (see Mandel'shtam 1966, pp. 115f, pl. XLVII–XLIX and idem 1975, pp. 50 and 117, pl. XV, XXXVII) and in the late "Pogrebal'naya yama 2" in Ak-tepe II (Sedov: 1987, p. 65, pl. VI). Both types are also known from early medieval Sogd (Raspopova 1980, p. 64, tbls. 9 and 10, fig. 40) to list only some examples. The knives from the Ferghana barrows were studied by B. A. Litvinskiy (1978, pp. 10–25). Here, too, both types appear contemporaneously within the course of the whole of the first half-millennium Ad. The scholar notes a marked prevalence of knives with a central tip over those with a lower one. This impression seems to be confirmed by their relative representation in other contexts, too.

2 This, of course, does not hold for the knives where the tang is placed in line with the blade back, none of which has, however, come to light at our site. This feature seems to prevail in the central Asian knives of antiquity and the early middle ages.

3 A scale-grip is relatively well represented in Hellenistic Ai-Khanoum (Francfort 1984, p. 68, pl. 25: no. 1, XXX: second from the left-hand side; Guillaume – Rougelle 1987, p. 43, nos. 0850–0857, pl. 15: 27–30). In later contexts its representation decreases notably. One straight-bladed knife with two rivets was found in Chaqalaq tepe (Higuchi – Kuwayama 1970, fig. 48: 65–53) and another in Ak-tepe (Sedov 1987, p. 65, pl. VI: 3). The one straight-edged knife with two rivets from early medieval Sogd (Raspopova 1980, fig. 40:40, the provenance is not specified in the text) and another from Chaqalaq tepe (Higuchi – Kuwayama 1970, fig. 48: 67–101) seem to have been reworked in antiquity after the blades were broken and, as well, originally might have been sickle-shaped.

4 Leather knives of a "mushroom" outline were widespread throughout history (e.g. Trubnikova 1947 or Gaitzsch 2005, pp. 98–101, pl. 30). The only possible identification of this object from a central Asian context (the Khwarazmian Iron Age site of Dinghilje – see Borob'eva 1973, pp. 153f, fig. 45: 1) is as insecure as ours.

5 Yagodin 1984, pp. 52f. The same takes place at the same time in the whole of the Eurasian zone. For the development there, see the classic work by Smirnov (1961), which was also the point of departure for the present study.

6 1984, p. 33.

7 Pugachenkova 1966, p. 51f.

(7th century BC), from the "archaic" Scythian burials and "later" from Southern Siberia and Kazakhstan.[8] Similar arrowheads were also found at Olympia in Greece.[9]

Smooth, three-sided, triangular, barbed arrowheads with inner sockets (like no. 15, i.e. 9C015.I) appear rarely in archaeological contexts (unlike their ogival variety[10]). In the Sauromatian area they can be found in the 4th–3rd cent BC with some unique precursors in the 6th century.[11] In the same period, they appear in Scythia, while those from southern Siberia were being made of bone[12]. In Central Asia, pieces perhaps comparable with 9C015.I (no. 15) were found in Erk-Kala in Margiana (obviously secondarily deposited in an early Sassanid construction).[13]

### Sector 04

Three-winged, socketed arrowheads with a triangular outline are common among the finds from both Central Asia and Eurasia in general. Appearing as early as the 6th century BC, they are particularly frequent in the 4th–3rd (and 2nd) centuries BC, both among the Sauromatians[14] and the peoples of Central Asia (both nomad and sedentary)[15]. A small particularity of the piece in question is the presence of three tiny "stalks" at the socket base. There is, indeed, a Central Asian group of arrowheads (of the same type) whose sockets terminate in "paws."[16] In them, however, the protrusions are much more substantial

(making a kind of a "cut-up socket" on their own) while in the piece discussed they leave rather an impression of uselessness. Besides that, "genuine paws" are usually located in the intervals between the wings while the stubs of the Jandavalttepa find are aligned with them (as well as with the casting "seam"!). As a result, this weird feature need not be anything else other than a by-product of a loose, leaking mould, not cleaned after the casting[17].

The other two arrowheads from Sector 4 are basically of the same type[18] (three-winged, ogival, socketed bronze arrowheads with reinforced tips and blades and insignificantly protruding sockets). Once again, direct parallels (all from Khorezm) are not exuberant. Two of these arrowheads, with M-shaped tip-bases, are known to the author from the 5th century site of Dinghildje[19] and another from "slag mounds" in the area of the Syrdaria Estuary near the Aral Sea.[20] Their varieties, with either straight or arcuate tip-bases, are only a little more frequent in our region.[21]

The only determinable **iron arrowhead**[22] found in Jandavlattepa belongs to the most common type of these objects: three-winged, tanged arrowheads with barbs. They appeared in Central Asia in the last centuries BC and were in existence to the middle ages (7th/8th centuries AD). After standardization of their basic forms around the turn of the eras, these objects

---

[8] Smirnov 1961, pp. 51f, fig. 23-A: 26, tabl. IV B-IV "Otdel III, Typ 1, Varianta A" (in the following, Smirnov's types will be abbreviated in the form: III-1-A).

[9] Baitinger 2001, p. 25, mainly nos. 374 and 375, pl. 11. The date is not given.

[10] Cleuziou, in his study (1977, p. 197), reasonably considers both varieties (his H18 and H19) as representative of the same type, making them part of his "recent" (sixth to third century) and Central Asian (as opposed to "Pontic" and "Near-Eastern") groups.

[11] Smirnov 1961, p. 57, type IV-16, tabl. V B-88, Г-13.

[12] For an example from the site of Aimyrlyg (Tuva, 5th–3rd century BC) see Moshkova (ed.) 1992, pl. 75:36.

[13] Usmanova 1963, p. 66, fig. 33a, type IV (but they are called "type V" in the text). Unfortunately, neither the description nor the drawing give undeniable proof of the typological analogy.

[14] Smirnov 1961, pp. 48f, pl. III, (type III-9-A).

[15] For a summary see Yagodin 1984, p. 48f, fig. 5: 11–17, cat. nos. 50–69 (type II-6) and Litvinskiy 2001, pp.72–73 (type II-"ε"). Both authors list the sites where this type came to light: Ai Khanoum (with 15 items being the best represented type in the arsenal: Yagodin 1984, tabl. I: 53–67; 2nd century BC), Afrasiab, Erk-Kala (Usmanova 1963, p. 65, fig. 33a: IIIb), Dinghildje (Borob'eva 1973, p. 199, tabl. A: 37, type VII; 5th century BC), Dilberdjin (Yagodin 1984, tabl. I: 50–52; 2nd/1st century BC and 3rd–4th century AD – a secondary deposition).

[16] While Yagodin (1984, p. 48, fig. 5: 9–10, cat. nos. 48–49) classes them as a type on their own (type II-6), for Litvinskiy (2001, pp. 72–73) they are only varieties of his type II-"ε" (see the previous note). With the finds reported from Koy-krylgan-kala (Tolstov – Vaynberg 1967, pl. 34, fig. 53:3), Ai Khanoum and cemeteries of Fergana, Pamir and Altai (for the references see the works of Yagodin and Litvinskiy), these seem to be endemic to Central Asia.

[17] This is obvious in several arrowheads exhibited in the Tashkent museum. Along with these, however, there are also some in which the "stalks" are located in the intervals and so, seem to have been made on purpose (whatever that was). The provenance of these pieces is not specified and their date is stated as 6th–4th centuries.

[18] It is, however, not certain whether the barbs of these finds from Tower 1 were not preserved or were never present. In a meticulous typology, this might be taken as a typological feature, too.

[19] Borob'eva 1973, p. 200, pl. III-III-5, pl. A: 64–65. Items with absent barbs are present at this site, too (III-I and III-II, nos. 50–52).

[20] Levina 1979, p. 183, fig. 5: 6. Others are reported from the Uygarak barrow-cemetery (ibidem). They are also fairly represented in the Samara-Ural zone of Sauromantia (rare pieces in the 7th and 4th centuries, the highest concentration in the 6th and 5th). See Smirnov 1961, p. 52f, fig. 12: 2,4; 15: A8,14, D 2,6 etc., tabl. IV, Type III-V-G.

[21] Yagodin 1984, p. 47, fig. 5: 1–5, cat. nos. 40–44 (type II-3-a/b), found in Dilberdjin, Djiga tepe and Emshi tepe, dated by the author to 6th–5th centuries. See also Borob'eva 1973, p. 200, pl. A, *otdel* III; Levina 1979, p. 183, fig. 5: 1–3, 8; Yagodin calls them "three-winged" unlike Smirnov and Borobeva for whom they are "three sided in section." In these arguments surrounding terminological subtlties, the author follows Yagodin's way. In Cleuziou's less pedantic (though for this not less efficient) typology (Cleuziou 1977, p. 197) the arrowheads enter well into type F7 and – one more time – are considered by the author to be representants of his "recent" and "central asiatic" groups (see note 10).

[22] For the big theme of the Central Asian iron arroheads see Litvinskiy 2001, pp. 80–119 and also idem 1965; Obel'chenko 1965; Gorbunova 2000.

did not change. It is their size rather than their form that may say something about them. This particular piece, with its 76 mm of total length, belongs among the large-sized ones, which only become widespread from the 3rd century AD onward. However, they were already singularly present in the old era along with the small-sized ones, which on their turn, continued to be used, though in a limited extent, down to the late antiquity and the early middle ages. There is not much sense in searching for precise duplicates of our piece among the countless comparable items. The single varieties of the quite simple type are widespread, and a mere similarity can hardly be taken as a testimony of direct kinship in this case.

**Blade** 20D002.II (no. 22) gives little evidence to indicate the kind of weapon to which it originally belonged, its lentoid section and its breadth being the only possible clues.

Few spearheads are known from Central Asian antiquity, and these rarely present a lentoid section (those flat with a midrib or, conversely, more compact ones, being more common)[23].

In swords and daggers, on the contrary, a lentoid section is the leading and practically only form. This holds true for a long period between the 2nd century BC and 4th century Ad. The change comes in the 4th–5th centuries AD, when single-edged swords appear beside two-edged ones[24]. It is not possible to decide if the blade was that of a sword or of a dagger, let alone to specify its type. The breadth of blades is basically the same in both weapon classes and the maximum measured breadth of our fragment (35–36 mm) is a common value for both. Although sword-blades might tend to be slightly broader than those of daggers, they at the same time often taper

towards the tip, and so even broad blades may reach the breadth of 35 mm at one point in their length (and there is no way to determine from which part of the blade the fragment originates)[25]. As a result, it cannot be stated with any certainty which type of weapon the item is a fragment of, neither a sword, nor a dagger (nor even a spear as mentioned above) can be excluded.

Keeping in mind the above said, the same must be said about **Point** 20S003.II (no. 23). Here, the very fact that the object is a fragment of a weapon may be questioned. Its coat of rust does not allow a secure statement on this, but the section seems more oblong than lentoid (i.e. without marked edges). Besides that, the original thickness of the object is not at all clear (again, due to the rust), and quite probably the object would have been too thin and, thus, too fragile for a sword or a dagger. At the same time it lacks a midrib, which might make it more credibly a spearhead. Again, none of the three interpretations can be excluded, but scepticism is highly advisable here.

The same holds for Fragment 21E025.I (no. 24). Its obviously pointed form and lentoid section might indicate its martial use. Any specific interpretation (the very tip of a spearhead or a dagger, an arrowhead lentoid in section[26], etc.) would, however, be no more than guesswork.

The **Sling** is a weapon of noticeable antiquity and surprising efficiency in both interpersonal violence and venatic activities[27]. Unfortunately, only man-made slingshots (i.e. those of unbaked clay, worked stone or cast lead) are archaeologically vis-

---

[23] The spearheads from Oxos temple (Litvinskiy 2001, pp. 109–200, for the catalogue see pp. 120–139) most commonly feature a midrib. Those purely lentoid (i.e. without a midrib) are often too narrow (cat. nos. 2582, 4072/2, 4100) or too short (cat. nos. 2046, 2075, 2078, 3230) to be comparable with our piece (minimum reconstructed length of our fragments – i.e. not of the original blade – is cca.130 mm). Several Oxos finds, however, make possible the suggestion that the Jandavlattepa fragment is that of a spearhead (cat. nos. 2580, 2583). Except for Oxos temple, finds of spearheads are extremely rare in Central Asia. In Pendjikent (in a considerably later context – 8th century), two flat to lentoid in section, tanged spearheads were found, but these are quite too short, being 9 and not much over 8 cm (Raspopova 1980, pp. 74f, fig. 49: 8, 9). Other spearheads from that site are triangular or square in section (ibidem), as is that from Toprak-kala (Rapoport – Nerazik 1984, p. 222, fig. 89: 10). Another spearhead with such a compact section, circular in this case, comes from Chaqalaq tepe (Higuchi – Kuwayama 1970, figs. 50: 67–27). In the east-European area, the finds of spearheads are more frequent (Khazanov 1971, p. 47f, pl. XXV, XXVI). Despite the lentoid section of some of them, comparison of these broad, leaf-shaped objects with our relatively slender blade is hardly imaginable.

[24] The change is, however, very gradual, and two-edged swords are attested in Pendjikent and other sites as late as the 8th century onward (Obel'chenko 1978, pp. 125f; Raspopova 1980, p. 78).

[25] For finds of swords and daggers in Central Asia see Obel'chenko 1978, (and idem 1961, 1962, 1969, 1972), Litvinskiy 2001, pp. 204ff, mainly 234–238; Gorbunova 2000 (summarizes the various contexts and gives reference to numerous sites); Brykina 1982, p. 83, fig. 36; Kruglikova 1986, fig. 22: 17; Lokhovits – Khazanov 1979, pp. 126–127, pl. I: 1–2; Lokhovits 1979, p. 142, pl. III: 10; Mandel'shtam 1966, pp. 102–111, pl. XXXIX–XL; idem 1975, pp. 135–140, 141–143, pl. XXX; Manylov 1990, p. 52, fig. 1: 18, 19; idem 1992, pp. 67f, fig. 2:1; Maslov – Yagodin 1996, pp. 172nn, fig. 4; Sedov 1987, pp. 58ff, pl. I: 2,4; Francfort 1984, p. 67, tabl. 33. pls. 24: 12, 13; while Khazanov 1971 provides a most useful review of the contemporary East-European material. Unfortunately, in many of these works the documentation is not exemplary and the breadth of the blade is usually not mentioned and has to be estimated from the (sometimes poor, even unfathomable) drawings. Those few more scrupulous works (by Litvinskiy, Khazanov and Raspopova), however, show that a breadth of 30 to 50 mm is shared by both swords and daggers.

[26] Although rare, such arrowheads appear throughout Bactrian antiquity from the Hellenistic period down to the Middle Ages (see Litvinskiy 2001, pp. 88–90, 114).

[27] For the earliest testimonies on the use of the sling, see Korfmann 1972. The use of the sling is studied in detail by Baatz 1990 (the ballistics) and Völling 1990 (the history of its use in the western, mainly Roman, world in antiquity).

ible. A simple, smooth pebble of appropriate shape does the job well enough, but it is, of course, impossible to distinguish between "a simple pebble" and "a pebble slingshot" during excavation. There are two basic shapes of slingshots (or *glandes*) used all over the world: a) globular or a form derived from it, i.e. that of a flattened ball or even slightly cubic and b) elongated which may vary from ovoid to bi-conical or bi-pyramidal with pointed or blunt extremities.

The use of the sling is attested in Central Asia as early as the Mesolithic period. Several stone pieces of both globular and the characteristic elongated shape were found at the Neolithic site of Chagyly-depe in Turkmenistan[28]. Numerous finds of stone slingshots come from the Bactrian Bronze Age site of Sapalitepa[29]. Their use continues uninterruptedly in the Iron Age[30]. From Central Asian sites of the antique period, indisputable slingshots are known from Aï Khanoum[31], Dilberdjin[32] and Surkh Kotal[33] in Bactria, Chopli-depe in the "North-western Bactria"[34], Erk-Kala and Marghiana in general[35], Koy-Krylgan-Kala in Khorezm.[36]

The function of the elongated glandes is unmistakable. In the case of the globular pieces, however, their interpretation as slingshots is not the only possibility, and their use as pestles (as suggested in Tolstov – Vaynberg 1967) is not excluded. It should be also noted that the weight of these objects often exceeds that adequate for slinging: It is almost regu-

larly higher than 150 g while indubitable slingshots known to me from the western world practically never reach this[37].

Bone Plaque 21F025.I (no. 28), though fragmentary and lacking the most essential detail (i.e. the string notch at the top), may be without hesitation proclaimed a **bone finial of a bow**. Countless parallels can be found in both burials and habitations of the Euro-Asian steppes, Central Asia, the Near East and their "neighbouring areas." These implements were glued (hence the hairline grooves on the plain face) in a pair onto each end of a bow in order to make it rigid and resistant to flexing and so to increase the weapon's efficiency. Their origin is sought in Western Siberia in the 3rd/2nd centuries BC, and from the first centuries of the new era they seem to have got firmly rooted in the martial traditions of Central Asia, too. This new type of bow remained then in use until modern times[38]. Within these broad chronological and geographical limits, these simple objects remained practically unchanged. Different conformations of the string-end and more or less arcuate profiles and dimensions are the only possible variables, none of these being of any chronological value probably. Their lengths usually vary around 20 cm (some measure only half of this), their breadth of around 2 cm is average (they usually taper from the "string" end to the "handle" end). The only feature

---

[28] Berdyev 1966, figs. 10: 11–13, 18.

[29] Shirinov 1977; Mirsaatov – Shirinov 1974. All of the shots are basically globular. Their dimensions vary from 44 to 98 mm in diameter and from 100 to over 2000 g in weight.

[30] This documentation comes mainly from the western areas of Central Asia – Dinghildje: Borob'eva 1973, p.148, fig. 56. Unbaked clay, globular shape, dimensions 37 × 40 – 51 × 49 mm. Koy-Krylgan-Kala: Tolstov – Vaynberg 1967, pp. 137–139. They are all globular or sub-globular. Their diameters range from 44 to 78 mm, their weights from 77.5 to 238 g for those made of unbaked clay and from 98 to 507 g for those made of stone. The authors assume that both the clay and the stone shots were used in the first period (4th–3rd centuries BC) while only those from stone remained in use in the posterior phase (till the 4th century AD). In this period, some – if not all – were being used secondarily as pestles. For Margiana, see Usmanova 1963, p. 59.

[31] Leriche 1986, pp. 13 and 114–115, photograph 27–28; twenty stone balls are listed with diameters and weights ranging from 91 to 258 mm and from 70 g to 20.5 kg (apparently, the greater part of them was ammunition for artillery rather than for *funditores*).

[32] Kruglikova 1984, p. 53, fig. 36: Twelve more or less globular pieces from (unbaked?) clay can be counted in the photograph. The diameter indicated by the author is 5–6 cm; Pugachenkova 1984, p. 105, fig. 19. Almost one hundred pieces are mentioned, concentrated near the southern gate. They are said to be made of unbaked clay, globular, with diameters of 8–12 cm, some only 4–5 cm.

[33] Fussman – Guillaume 1990, p. 136, pl. 8 and X, globular: cat. nos. 545–557 unbaked clay, diameter 15–33 mm; elongated: cat. nos. 558, terracotta 46 × 26 mm and 559, limestone 56 × 31 mm.

[34] Pilipko 1985, p. 46, pl. IV: 14: the stone is ovoid with dimensions (estimated according to the scale of the drawing) cca. 55 × 40 mm. According to the author, the find "*sleduet veroyatno, otnosit´ k epokhe rannego zheleza*". No reason is given for this conclusion. The date of the "stratigraphic horizon" in which it was found is well established by coin finds to late antiquity (the earliest of which is that of Vasudeva, followed by those of Kushano-Sassanid rulers).

[35] Usmanova 1963, pp. 59–64. The author briefly summarizes the presence of slingshots in Margiana and Parthia. Though her main interest is given to the more sizable artillery missiles characteristic for the first centuries AD, the constant use of hand-slings in the area from the Iron age to the early Middle Ages is well attested by both globular and bi-conical pieces, often made of terracotta.

[36] See Footnote 15.

[37] Völling 1990, p. 36, fig. 31: The heaviest slingshot known from a Roman context was found in Haltern and weighs 155 g, while the average weight for a Roman *glans* is that of 40–70 g. It is only in late antiquity that there was a tendency to increase the weight, but it still usually remained below 100 g. In the earlier Greek world this value is even lower with 18–36 g at Olynthos (Robinson 1941, pp. 418–443); 30–42 g in Olympia (Baitinger 2001, p. 31), and 21–74 g in Hellenistic southern Thrace (Paunov – Dimitrov 2000: here with four exceptionally heavy, weighing 102, 104, 144 and 150 g). All of these pieces are cast of lead, mostly with an elongated form (no lead slingshot is known to the present author from Central Asia). As such they had different ballistic features than the spherical stones/ "clay lumps" from Central Asia, and it is not simply possible to juxtapose the two groups. In any case, however, the boulders of 300 g and more cannot be seen as ammunition for hand-slings; therefore, another functional designation must be sought for them (e.g. ammunition for staff-slings, yet more sophisticated war machines or a more peaceful use, for instance the mentioned pestles).

[38] For a detailed discussion of the composite type of bow, see Litvinksiy 1966 and idem 2001, pp. 28–58, Plate 7, for exceptional finds of entire bows see Rapoport – Nerazik 1984, pp. 216–220, and Brown 1937.

in which our item slightly differs from other contemporary pieces is the form of the section, which is usually semicircular (i.e. without the squared "back" or "string" side).[39]

## 3.2.11 Bibliography

Baatz, D. (1990): Schleudergeschosse aus Blei – eine waffentechnische Untersuchung. *Saalburg-Jahrbuch* 45, pp. 59–67.

Baitinger, H. (2001): Die Angriffswaffen aus Olympia; *Olympische Forschungen* XXIX. Berlin – New York.

Berdyer, O. K. (1966): Chagyly-depe. Novyy pamyatnik neoliticheskoy dzheytunskoy kultury, in: *Materialna kultura narodov Sredney Azii i Kazakhstana*. Moskva, pp. 3–28.

Bogomolov, P. I. – Gendel'man, P. I. (1990): Metallicheskie izdeliya iz gorodishcha Kanka. *IMKU* 24, pp. 93–106.

Brown, F. E. (1937): A recently discovered compound bow. *Seminarium Kondakovianum* IX, pp. 1–9.

Brykina, G. A. (1982): *Yugo-zapadnaya Fergana v pervoy polovine I tysyachletiya nashey ery*. Moskva.

Cleuziou, S. (1977): Les pointes de flèches «scythiques» au proche et moyen orient, in: *Le plateau iranien et l'Asie centrale des origines à la conquête islamique*. Colloques internationaux du CNRS 567. Paris, pp. 187–199.

Francfort, H.-P. (1984): *Fouilles d'Ai Khanoum III. Le sanctuaire du temple a niches indentées*, vol. 2. Les trouvailles, MDAFA XXVII, Paris.

Fussman, G. – Guillaume, O. (1990): *Surkh Kotal en Bactriane, vol. II., Les monnaies – les petits objets*. MDAFA XXXII, Paris.

Gaitzsch, W. (2005): Eisenfunde aus Pergamon; Geräte, Werkzeuge und Waffen; *Pergamenische Forschungen* Bd. 14. Berlin – New York.

Gorbunova, N. G. (2000): O vooruzhenii sredneaziyaticheskikh skotovodov. *RA* 2, pp. 40–51.

Guillaume, O. – Rougelle, A. (1987): *Fouilles d'Aï Khanoum VII. Les petits objets*. MDAFA XXXI, Paris.

Higuchi, T. – Kuwayama, Sh. (1970): *Chaqalaq tepe; fortified village in North Afghanistan excavated in 1964–1967*. Kyoto.

Itina, M. A. (ed.) (1979): *Kochevniki na granitsakh Khorezma*, TKhAEE XI. Moskva.

Khazanov, A. M. (1971): *Ocherki voennogo dela Sarmatov*. Moskva.

Kolyakov, S. M. (1979): Masterskaya po obrabotke roga i kosti v kreposti Kaparas, in: Vinogradov, A. V. (et. al.eds): *Etnografiya i arkheologiya Sredney Azii*. Moskva, pp. 48–53.

Korfmann, M. (1972): Schleuder und Bogen in Südwestasien von den frühesten Belegen bis zum Beginn der historischen Stadtstaaten. *Antiquitas* 3,13. Bonn.

Kruglikova, I. T. (1974): *Dil'berdzhin (raskopki 1970–1972 gg)*, 1. Moskva.

Kruglikova, I. T. (1986): Dil'berdzhin, khram Dioskurov. *Materialy sovetsko-afganskoy arkheologicheskoy ekcpedicii*. Moskva.

Kruglikova, I. T. (ed.) (1984): Drevnaya Baktriya. *Materialy sovetsko-afganskoy arkheologicheskoy ekspedicii*, 3. Moskva.

Leriche, P. (1986): *Fouilles d'Aï Khanoum V. Les remparts et les monuments associés*. MDAFA XXIV. Paris.

Levina, L. M. (1979): Poseleniya VII–V vv. do n. e. i "shlakovye" kurgany yuzhnykh rayonov syrdarynskoy del'ty, in: *Kochevniki na granitsakh Khorezma*, TKhAEE XI, Itina, M. A. (ed.), Moskva, pp. 178–189.

Litvinskiy, B. A. (1965): Sredneaziyaticheskie zheleznye nakonechniky strel. *SA* 3, pp. 75–91.

Litvinskiy, B. A. (1966): Slozhnosostavnoy luk v drevney Sredney Azii. *SA* 4, pp. 51–69.

Litvinskiy, B. A. (1978): Orudya truda i umvar iz mogilnikov zapadnoy Fergany. *Mogilniki zapadnoy Fergany* IV. Moskva.

Litvinskiy, B. A. (2001): Baktriyskoe vooruzhenie v drevnevostochnom i grecheskom kontekste. *Khram Oksa v Baktrii*, Tom 2. Moskva.

Litvinskiy, B. A. – Sedov, A. V. (1983): *Tepai-Shakh, kultura i svyazi v kushanskoy Baktrii*. Moskva.

Litvinskiy, B. A. – Sedov, A. V. (1984): *Kul'ty i ritualy kushanskoy Baktrii*. Moskva.

Lokhovits, V. A. (1979): *Podboyno-katakombnye i kolektivnye pogrebeniya mogil'nika Tumek-kichidzhik*, in: *Kochevniki na granitsakh Khorezma*, TKhAEE XI, Itina, M. A. (ed.), Moskva, pp. 134–150.

Lokhovits, V. A. – Khazanov, A.M. (1979): Podboyne i katakombnye pogrebeniya mogilnika Tuz-Gyr, in: *Kochevniki na granitsakh Khorezma*, TKhAEE XI, Itina, M. A. (ed.), Moskva, pp. 111–133.

Mandel'shtam, A. M. (1966): *Kochevniki na puti v Indiyu*. MIA 136. Moskva – Leningrad.

Mandel'shtam, A. M. (1975): Pamyatniki kochevnikov kushanskogo vremeni v severnoy Baktrii. *Trudy tadzhikskoy arkheologicheskoy ekspedicii AN SSSR* VIII. Leningrad.

Manylov, Yu. P. (1990): Raskopki kulkudutskoy kurgannoy gruppy v centralnykh Kyzylkumakh. *IMKU* 23, pp. 46–60.

Manylov, Yu. P. (1992): Kurgany Kokpatasa. *IMKU* 26, pp. 59–65.

Maslov, V. E. – Yablonskiy, L.T. (1996): Mogilnik Gyaur-IV v severnoy Turkmenii. *RA* 2, pp. 168–181.

Mirsaatov, T. M. – Shirinov, T. (1974): Funkcional'nyy analiz nekotorykh kamennykh izdeliy iz Sapalitepa. *IMKU* 11, pp. 61–70.

Moshkova, M. G. (*ed.*) (1992): *Stepnaya polosa aziatskoy chasti SSSR v skifo-sarmatskoe vremya*. Moskva.

Obel'chenko, O. V. (1961): Lyavandatskyy mogil'nik. *IMKU* 2, pp. 97–176.

Obel'chenko, O. V. (1962): Mogil'nik Akdzhartepe. *IMKU* 3, pp. 57–70.

Obel'chenko, O. V. (1969): Mirankul'skie kurgany. *IMKU* 8, pp. 80–89.

Obel'chenko, O. V. (1972): Agalysayskie kurgany. *IMKU* 9, pp. 56–72.

Obel'chenko, O. V. (1978): Mechi i kinzhaly iz kurganov Sogda. *SA* 4, pp. 115–127.

Paunov, E. – Dimitrov, D.Y. (2000): New data on the use of war sling in Thrace (4th–1st century BC). *Archaeologia Bulgarica* IV/3, pp. 44–57.

Pilipko, V. N. (1985): *Poseleniya severo-zapadnoy Baktrii*. Ashkhabad.

Pugachenkova, G. A. (1966): *Khalchayan: K probleme khudozhestvennoy kultury severnoy Baktrii*. Tashkent.

Pugachenkova, G. A. (1984): Raskopki yuzhnykh gorodskikh vorot Dil'berdzhina, in: *Dil'berdzhin (raskopki 1970–1972 gg)*, 1, Kruglikova, I. T. (ed.) 1984, pp. 93–110.

Rapoport, Yu. A. – Nerazik, E. E. (1984): *Toprak-Kala, Dvorets*. TKhAEE XIV. Moskva.

---

[39] For other bone plaque finds from Central Asia (especially extensive is the documentation from Khawrezm) see for instance, besides the works mentioned in the previous footnote, Kolyakov 1979 ("Kushan period"); Tolstov – Vaynberg 1967, tabl. XX: 8–10; Lokhovits – Khazanov 1979, p. 127, pl. I: 3–10 (1st–3rd c. AD); Lokhovits 1979, p. 142, pl. III:1); Manylov 1990, p. 53; idem 1992, pp. 64f (dated to 3rd–2nd and 3rd–1, centuries BC respectively according to the author); Maslov – Yablonskiy 1996, pp.174f; for Eastern Europe see Khazanov 1971, pp. 29–35 etc. They are absent from the mound cemeteries in the Kafirnigan Valley (Mandel'shtam 1966 and 1975) dated to the last centuries BC and first century AD.

Raspopova, V. I. (1980): *Metalicheskie izdeliya rannesrednevokogo Sogda*. Leningrad.

Robinson, D. M. (1941): Metal and minor miscelanous objects. *Excavation at Olynthos* X; Baltimore.

Sedov, A. V. (1987): *Kobadian na poroge rannego srednevekov'ya*. Moskva.

Smirnov, K. F. (1961): *Voruzhenie Savromatov*. MIA 101. Moskva – Leningrad.

Tolstov, S. P. – Vaynberg, B. I. (1967): *Koy-Krylgan-Kala*. TKhAEE V. Moskva.

Trubnikova, N. B. (1947): K voprosu o nazhanchnii "kobanskikh sechek," in: *KrSoobsh IIMK* XVIII, pp. 49–53.

Usmanova, Z. I. (1963): Erk-kala (po materialam YuTAKE 1955–1959 gg), in: *Trudy yuzhno-turkmenstanskoy arkheologicheskoy kompleksnoy ekspedicii* Tom XII. Ashkhabad, pp. 20–94.

Shirinov, T. (1977): Kamennye yadra Sapalitepa. *IMKU* 13, pp. 13–21.

Vorob'eva, M. G. (1973): *Dingil'dzhe, usadba serediny I tysyachletiya do n.e. v drevnem Khorezme*. Moskva.

Völling, T. (1990): Funditores im römischen Heer. *Saalburg-Jahrbuch* 45, pp. 24–58.

Yagodin, V. N. (1984): Bronzovye nakonechniki strel iz yuzhnoy Baktrii, in: *Dil'berdzhin (raskopki 1970–1972 gg)*, 1, Kruglikova, I. T. (ed.) 1984, pp. 33–57.

# 3.3 Personal ornaments, jewellery and cosmetic implements

*Petra Belaňová*

This chapter is devoted to small items of a decorative nature that have been found during excavations of Jandavlattepa (in the Citadel, Shakhristan and gate sectors) in the 2002–2006 seasons. It includes descriptions of 116 finds, divided firstly by function, and then by the material from which they were made. For two groups of items (bone pins, beads) the descriptions take the form of a table. In the case of bone pins, this is only partial – a table has been used for small fragments that cannot be specified. Pins with preserved heads, meanwhile, are described in short texts. Beads have been divided into tables according to shape. For other items, text descriptions have been chosen. The last group of finds consists of items that have been incompletely preserved or have suffered considerable damage, and so their purpose is not entirely clear.

- bone pins (1–27)
- finger and other rings (28–33)
- bracelets (34)
- earrings (35–37)
- beads and pendants (38–75)
- metal items (76–77)
- fragments of cosmetic and decorative items – metal, bone (78–93)

## Bone pins

Bone is the predominant material from which pins from Jandavlattepa were made. Of the objects made of metal, most have been only partially preserved, and it is not clear whether they were pins or not. As a result they have been listed elsewhere in the catalogue (`fragments of cosmetic and decorative items). In the Citadel and Shakhristan sectors 27 bone pins have been found, mostly in the form of fragments. Of these, 10 have

heads that have been completely or partially preserved to the extent that the pins can be classified as belonging to one of four basic types by appearance (anthropomorphic, zoomorphic, geometric or plant)[1]. More space is then devoted to a factual description of these pins, and the various fragments are included in the table.

Bone pins are relatively frequent finds at Central Asian sites from the first five centuries AD, which shows that they were a favourite ornament among the general population. In addition to their basic decorative function, they could also serve as cosmetic instruments – small spoons, toothpicks, small palette knives or small sticks for putting on makeup.[2] It is possible to classify these relatively simple objects on the basis of the form taken by their decorative heads.

The anthropomorphic group includes a fragment of a pin from the Shakhristan (cat. no. 14) – a head in the form of a human palm with outstretched fingers. From the position of the fingers it appears to be a representation of the right hand. The object bears clear signs of having been worked, which have not been smoothed. The fingers have hard edges, and are noticeably divided from each other. At the bottom a ring has been preserved. It divided the head from the functional body which is oval in cross-section. Pins of a similar type – showing an outstretched or partially-outstretched palm or a closed fist – come from several different sites. In Jandavlattepa itself another, almost completely preserved pin has been found in sector 2a, with a head in the form of a palm. Several examples of pins like this come from Dalverzintepa[3]. Judging by the illustration in the excavation publication, three pins from the so-called *naus* have heads with outstretched fingers, while the head of item *Дт-6* features a palm with only one finger extended. They are dated to the 1st–2nd century Ad. The

---

[1]  According to: Zav'yalov 1993, p. 31–41, this classification is based on an extensive collection of pins from excavations of Zartepa, complemented by many examples from other sites in Central Asia.

[2]  For more detailed discussion of the function of these items see for example: Skugarova, N. G. 2001, p. 45 or Zav'yalov 1993, p. 38–39, of the older publications, Pugachenkova 1966, p. 96 or Zhukov 1961, p. 186.

[3]  Pugachenkova – Rtveladze 1978, p. 56, ris. 36,8 and pp. 108–112, ris. 78, 79, photographs of four pins from this site in: Drevnosti yuzhnogo Uzbekistana, 1991, ill. 88.

heads with outstretched palms that were found at the Aktepe II site in southern Tajikistan[4] are dated to the mid-4th–5th centuries AD.

Of the other Bactrian sites, bone pins with hands have been found in Zartepa[5] (with one finger extended, believed to date from the 4th–5th century AD), Khalchayan[6] (with two extended fingers and a "cuff" decorated with cross-hatching, replacing the ring that usually acts as a divider, late 1st–3rd century AD). There is an unusual bone pin from Kampyrtepa[7], with a head in the form of a hand holding a small vessel with a narrow neck (1st–2nd century AD). Other sites where pins have been found are Setalak I[8] (head with one extended finger; one of the pins has a cuff decorated with cross-hatching), Ayaz Kala[9] (with one extended finger, Kushan period), Varakhsha[10] (head with extended fingers) and Gyaur Kala[11] (closed fist). From the contexts in which the finds have been made, the occurrence of heads with human hands can be dated relatively widely from the 1st to 5th century Ad. In dating the head from Jandavlattepa – from the context in which it was found – to the 2nd–3rd century AD we are leaning towards an earlier occurrence of this type of pin.The motif is also a favourite one for metal pins, especially ones with heads in the form of a closed fist, as shown by finds from, for example, Kampyrtepa[12], Zartepa[13], Jalangtushtepa[14], and an artistically-interesting pin from Kavad Kala[15], which has a head in the form of a hand holding a small ball (a pomegranate?) and decorated with a "snake" bracelet.

A new find belonging to the relatively small zoomorphic group is a pin from Jandavlattepa, found in the 2005 season in trench 10D in the Shakhristan (cat.no 9). The head, in the shape of a horse, has been completely preserved. The horse is depicted simply and schematically, but at the same time is well-captured and artistically effective. The horse's head is shown from the right, and is meant to be viewed in that way, since the pin is much narrower when viewed side on. The mouth, the transition from the jaw to the neck and the outer edge of the mane are depicted using triangular tooth-shaped incihsions, and the ears are sharp. Both surfaces of the head are decorated with several broad and also long diagonal grooves in two directions – two diagonally from the top, and two from the bottom.

Six similar pins have been found, one of which comes from excavations at Akkurgan[16], while the remaining five have been found at Zartepa[17]. All the pins are essentially similar in style, although there are minor differences in the way they are executed (the overall shape of the head, the distribution of decorative motifs). Common characteristics of the group are the notably oval cross-section of the pin, the two-dimensional nature of the head, elements of its decoration, and two rings dividing the head from the body.

It is interesting to note the location of finds of these pins in the area near Old Termez[18], which is confirmed by the find from Jandavlattepa. In this case it may be assumed that the pins were made in a common workshop, which may have been located at

---

4  Sedov 1987, p. 170, tab. VII, 1–3., description of finds also in: Drevnosti Tadzhikistana 1985, p. 145/405,406.
5  Zav'yalov 1993, p. 34, ris. 1,37, illustrations in: Drevneyshie gosudarstva Kavkaza i Sredney Azii 1985, p. 400, tab. CXII.
6  Pugachenkova 1966, p. 96, ris. 62.
7  Illustration in: Gretsiya – Uzbekistan, 2001, ill. 80. The item is interpreted here as a *stylos*. For more details see: Luneva 2005, p. 62, ris. 6,2. The pin's upper part is oval in cross-section, it is 10.5 cm long, of which the head accounts for 2.8 cm. V. Luneva believes the vessel in the hand is a type of lamp.
8  Cf. Suleymanov 1983, p.107, ris. 39, pin on display in the Bukhara museum, description from the author's own observation.
9  Tolstov 1964, p. 111, tab. 27, 1.
10  Shishkin 1963, p. 119–120, ris. 58.
11  Zhukovskiy 1884, p. 96, ris. 36.
12  Luneva 2005, pp. 55–60, ris. 5 a 6, Four pins come from this site, of which 3 have heads in the shape of a closed fist (right hand), while the last has a hand that is highly stylized, practically an ornament, while the pin is miniature. All are dated to the 1st–2nd century Ad. Leaving out the miniature pin, there are horizontal lines under the heads, which might be imitating a ring. However, there are quite a few of them, often 7 to 10. The cross-section of the pin body is circular, but the part under the head at the level of the above-mentioned lines changes to rectangular. The miniature pin differs from the other three not only in its dimensions, but in its artistic style. The head is 2.5 cm long, and the transition from the body of the pin and the almost square hand with its finely-indicated fingers creates an ornament that gives the impression of being created from different parts. This part is made up of simple geometric shapes placed on top of each other: a diamond, a trapezium, and narrow bands.
13  Zav'yalov 1993, p. 36, ris. 2, 2. This pin with a head in the shape of a closed fist is approximately 7 cm long, and there are three progressively broader rings between the head and the body of the pin. The body of the pin is circular in cross-section, while the part where the rings are is rectangular.
14  Rtveladze 1983, p. 125–143. This Kushan burial place dating from the 2nd–early part of the 3rd century AD has provided several metal pins, in addition to a large amount of ceramics and other jewellery. From the first room of the *naus* III come 6 bronze pins. One of them has a head in the form of a closed fist, and is the longest of all the pins, measuring approximately 12 cm. It is narrower in the middle part of its body, and from that point grows slightly broader in both directions. At one end it finishes in a sharp point and at the other end in a head.
15  Kul'tura i iskusstvo drevnego Uzbekistana – vol. 1, 1991, p. 195. The head is in the form of a hand holding a small ball in three extended fingers, while two fingers are tucked into the palm. The head is divided from the body by a spiral bracelet in the form of a snake, which on one side has a head pointing upwards towards the palm, and at the other ends in a tail in the opposite direction. The whole object is very finely stylised and aesthetically-pleasing, and is considerably different from the other metal pins mentioned above. It is 12.6 cm long and dates from the 1st–2nd century AD.
16  Pidaev 1978, p. 80, ris. 27,7.
17  Zav'yalov 1993, p. 35; illustration in: Drevneyshie gosudarstva Kavkaza i Sredney Azii 1985, p. 400, tab. CXII, Zav'yalov 1986, ris. 9; according to Zav'yalov, the pin from Akkurgan is identical to a pin from Zartepa (more precisely, to type 2).
18  Zav'yalov 1993, p. 35.

any of the above-mentioned three sites, or at another centre close by. This cannot be said with certainty, of course. The dating for all the finds is the same, approximately from the mid-3rd to the 5th century AD, and in the case of the Jandavlattepa pin, most probably 3rd century AD.

A further pin from Jandavlattepa (cat. no. 7) has only part of its head preserved, but the style of its decoration is similar to the pin with the horse's head. The body is divided from the head by a flattish square shape, decorated with four wide parallel grooves. Above this shape the object has been broken, and only two pointed protuberances have been preserved. On one there are several fine parallel grooves, which are fairly likely to have been meant to imitate a mane. Even if the pin did not in fact have the head of a horse or other animal, the decoration is very close to this type.

Bone pins with anthromorphic and zoomorphic heads tend to have oval cross-sections at the body, and so we presume that the fragments from Jandavlattepa (cat. nos. 10, 18, 19, 20, 27) may belong to other pins from these two groups.

Seven pins from Jandavlattepa clearly belong to the geometric group. The number of examples found makes it the most numerous group of bone pins, and many types can be distinguished within it. The reason is that the patterns are relatively simple and modest compared to the previous two groups. A frequent motif in pin decoration is rings, which alternate on the heads of pins with other geometric motifs (balls, biconical shapes, quadrilaterals, even miniature stylised amphorae and daggers) or points, and the decoration is sometimes complemented by grooves, indentations, slots or even polychrome. The cross-section of the body is usually circular. Pins from the geometric group are generally dated to between the 1st and 5th centuries AD, depending on the locality.

A type of pin with a head in the shape of a miniature spoon is represented at Jandavlattepa by three finds from trench 21F (the Citadel) (cat. nos 1, 2, 3). This simple spoon, which could also represent a schematised human hand, is a polyfunctional instrument that in addition to being a pin also served as a cosmetic implement. The head is divided from the body by varying numbers of rings – one of the pins has six, while the other two each have four. The pin dates from the 4th century AD according to the context.

At Zartepa[19], 17 examples of a similar type have been found (4th – mid 5th century), while others have been found at Khairabadtepa[20] (1st century AD), Chakalaq Tepe[21], Aktepa[22] and Dilberdjin[23]. A head in the form of a spoon is also found on metal pins[24].

A further two pins from the Shakhristan, trench 07D (cat. nos. 23, 24) have heads created by joining two rings on to the body. Above them is a biconical shape, with a further ring on its surface. They date from the 2nd – 3rd century AD according to the context. Similar items have been found at Zartepa[25], Begram III[26], Durman Tepe[27] and Khairabadtepa[28].

Two pins from Jandavlattepa have a very simple head with two points, which was created merely by sharpening the end of the pin and probably fulfilled a further function (cat. no. 15). Three further examples are known from Zartepa[29], and one from the layers of Begram[30]. These are similar in type to a probably older pin with two points from Ay-Khanum[31], although the decoration of the latter is slightly more complex.

In the case of the remaining 12 fragments we are unable to reconstruct the head, but given the circular cross-section of the body they could well be from the geometric group. None of the finds from Jandavlattepa come from the plant group.

## Pins with completely or partially-preserved heads

### 1. 06.21F001.I

Fragment of bone pin – geometric head – in the shape of a little spoon (a schematic fist?) divided from the body by six rings, body cross-section is circular, point broken off. Preserved length: 20 mm, size of head: 20 mm, max. diameter: 5 mm, weight: 0.5 g
(Citadel, sector 20/square 21F, tab. 3.3, *1:1*, fig. 3.3, *1*)

### 2. 06.21F010.I

Fragment of bone pin with completely preserved head – in the shape of a small spoon (a schematic fist?), head is divided from the body by four rings, body cross-section is circular, point broken off.

19  Zav'yalov 1993, p. 35. In this case, according to Zav'yalov, further classification depends on the number of rings dividing the spoon from the body of the pin. Their number varies from three to six. At Zartepa there is also a variant with 5 rings.
20  Zhukov 1961. pp. 185–186, ris. 5.
21  Chaqalaq Tepe, 1970, fig. 60, pl. 56.3.
22  Pidaev 1978. p. 78, ris. 27.
23  Kruglikova 1974. p. 92, ris. 64.
24  For example the metal pins from Tup – Khona (Litvinskiy – Sedov 1984, p. 58) or the Babashov necropolis (Mandel'shtam 1975, p. 118, tab. XXXIX, 2–3).
25  Zav'yalov 1993, p. 35; 8 examples come from Zartepa.
26  Ghirshman 1946, P. 77, pl. XLVII.
27  Durman Tepe and Lalma, 1968. pl. 12.15.
28  Zhukov 1961, pp. 185–186, ris. 5.
29  Zav'yalov 1993, p. 36.; illustration in: Drevneyshie gosudarstva Kavkaza i Sredney Azii 1985, p. 400, tab. CXII.
30  Ghirshman 1946, p. 48, pl. XXVII.
31  Guillaume – Rougeulle 1987. pl. 27,3 et XXIV,11.

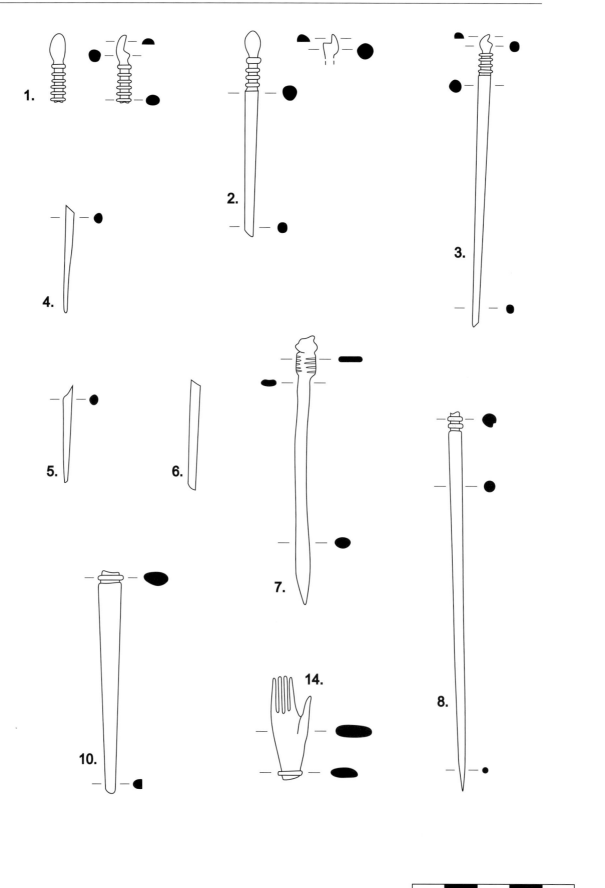

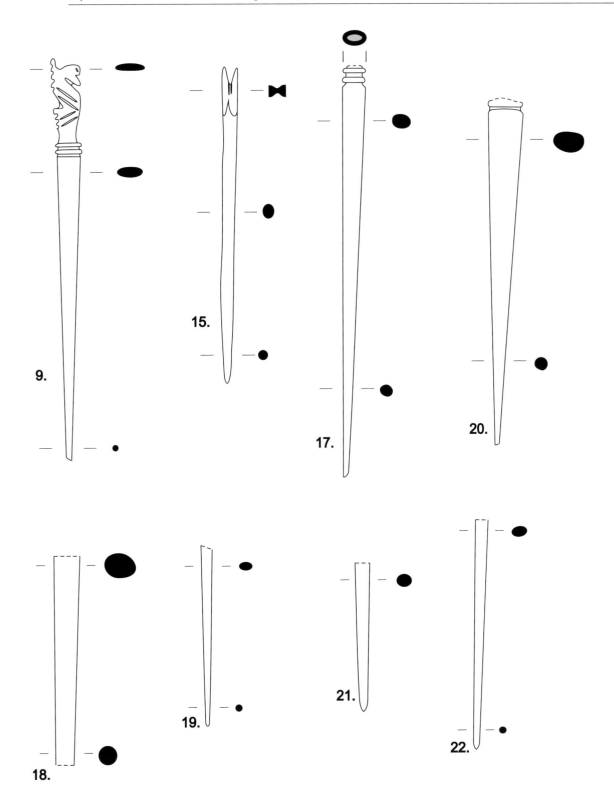

0                    5 cm

Tab. 3.3, 2

Preserved length: 58 mm, size of head: 20 mm, max. diameter: 4 mm, weight: 1.6 g
(Citadel, sector 20/square 21F, tab. 3.3, *1:2*, fig. 3.3, *2\**)

### 3. 06.21F024.I

Bone pin with completely preserved geometric head in the shape of a little spoon (schematic fist?), the head is divided from the body by four rings, body cross-section is circular, point broken off.
Preserved length: 84 mm, size of head: 12 mm, max. diameter: 4 mm, weight: 2.5 g
(Citadel, sector 20/square 21F, tab. 3.3, *1:3*, fig. 3.3, *3\**)

### 7. 05.20S003.I

Bone pin with part of head, transitional element between body and main, the probably figural (zoomorphic) decoration is a rectangular shape with four deepish horizontal flutes, the bottom part of the figural decoration has been preserved, with shallow grooves on one side (perhaps in imitation of a mane?) body cross-section is oval.
Preserved length: 78 mm, preserved size of head: 12 mm, max. diameter: 4 mm, weight: 1.6 g
(Citadel, sector 20/square 20S, tab. 3.3, *1:7*, fig. 3.3, *4\**)

### 9. 05.10D001.II

Bone pin with completely preserved zoomorphic head, broken in two (the break is at the point where the head joins on), point broken off, body divided from head by two rings, head in the form of a schematic horse, anatomical details achieved with deep diagonal grooves, body cross-section is oval.
Dimensions: preserved length: 118 mm, size of head: 22 mm, diameter of body: 8 mm, weight: 0.5 g
(Shakhristan, sector 07/square 10D, tab. 3.3, *2:9*, fig. 3.3, *5a\** and *5b*)

**Fig. 3.3, 5b** Bone pin with head in the form of a schematic horse, no. 05.10D001.II.

### 14. 04.09C007.I

Fragment of the body of a bone pin from the anthropomorphic group – head in the form of a human hand with extended fingers, clearly divided from each other, one ring dividing the pin from the head has been preserved (may be meant to imitate a bracelet), hand bears clear signs of having been worked, oval body cross-section.

Size of head: 35 mm, max. diameter of body: 7 mm, weight: 2.2 g
(Shakhristan, sector 07/square 09C, tab. 3.3, *1:14*, fig. 3.3, *6a* and *6b\**)

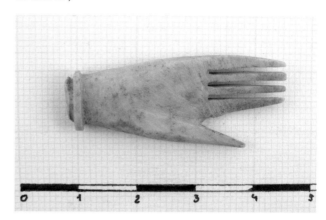

**Fig. 3.3, 6a** Fragment of a bone pin with head in the form of a human hand, no. 04.09C007.I.

### 15. 04.09C022.II

Completely preserved bone pin with a simple head of the geometric type – created by two points in a "V" shape, body of the pin has a circular cross-section.[32]
Preserved length: 96 mm, max. diameter 4 mm, weight: 1.9 g
(Shakhristan, sector 07/square 09C, tab. 3.3, *2:15*, fig. 3.3, *7\**)

### 23. 03.07D000.I

Completely preserved bone pin, geometric head is biconical in shape, divided from the body of the pin by two rings, one ring above the head, which is reminiscent of a vessel, body of the pin is circular in cross-section.
Length: 106 mm, size of head: 10 mm, max. diameter of body: 6 mm, weight: not known
(Shakhristan, sector 07/square 07D, tab. 3.3, *3:23*, fig. 3.3, *8:1\**)

### 24. 03.07D000.II

Almost completely preserved bone pin, geometrical head is biconical in shape, divided from the body of the pin by two rings, one ring above the head, which is reminiscent of a vessel, body circular in cross-section.
Preserved length: 71 mm, size of head: 10 mm, max. diameter of body: 7 mm, weight: not known
(Shakhristan, sector 07/square 07D, tab. 3.3, *3:24*, fig. 3.3, *8:2\**)

### 25. 03.07D009.II

Fragment of the central part of the body of a bone pin, no point, and partially preserved geometrical head originally had two sharp points in the shape of a "V," body circular in cross-section.
Preserved length: 51 mm, max. diameter: 5 mm, weight: unknown
(Shakhristan, sector 07/square 07D, tab. 3.3, *3:25*, fig. 3.3, *9:2\**)

---

[32]  Other function of this item – tool for making a thread – has been proposed by K. Urbanová, cf. Urbanová 2006, p. 119.

## Pins with heads that are unpreserved or whose shape cannot be ascertain

| cat. no. | inv. no. | degree of preservation | length in mm | max. diameter of body in mm | cross-section | place found, square no. | tab. / fig. |
|---|---|---|---|---|---|---|---|
| 4. | 06.21P023.I | point | 33 | 3 | circular | Citadel, 21P | tab. 3.3, *1:4*, fig. 3.3, *10*\* |
| 5. | 06.21P(Z)004.I | point | 29 | 4 | circular | Citadel, 21P(Z) | tab. 3.3, *1:5*, fig. 3.3, *11*\* |
| 6. | 06.07.000.I | central part of body | 32 | 4 | circular | Shakhristan, | tab. 3.3, *1:6*, fig. 3.3, *89*\* |
| 8. | 05.10D001.I | body with point, 2 rings | 112 | 4 | circular | Shakhristan, 10D | tab. 3.3, *1:7*, fig. 3.3, *12*\* |
| 10. | 05.10D018.VIII | central part of body, 1 ring | 68 | 8 | oval | Shakhristan, 10D | tab. 3.3, *1:10*, fig. 3.3, *13*\* |
| 11. | 04.20N002.XI | point | 48 | 4 | circular | Citadel, 20N | fig. 3.3, *14*\* |
| 12. | 04.07C014. I | point | 44 | 5 | circular | Shakhristan, 07C | fig. 3.3, *15*\* |
| 13. | 04.07D017.I | central part of body | 42 | 5 | circular | Shakhristan, 07D | fig. 3.3, *16*\* |
| 16. | 04.10C003.II | central part of body | 28 | 4 | circular | Shakhristan, 10C | fig. 3.3, *17*\* |
| 17. | 03.07B000.IV | whole body 2 rings | 123 | 7 | circular | Shakhristan, 07B | tab. 3.3, *2:17*, fig. 3.3, *18*\* |
| 18. | 03.07C000.I | central part of body | 67 | 10 | oval | Shakhristan, 07C | tab. 3.3, *2:18*, figs. 3.3, *19:3*\* and 3.3, *88*\* |
| 19. | 03.07C002.I | point | 54 | 4 | oval | Shakhristan, 07C | tab. 3.3, *2:19*, fig. 3.3, *19:1*\* |
| 20. | 03.07C008.II | body, 1 ring | 103 | 11 | oval | Shakhristan, 07C | tab. 3.3, *2:20*, fig. 3.3, *20*\* |
| 21. | 03.07C008b.I | point | 44 | 4 | circular | Shakhristan, 07C | tab. 3.3, *2:21*, fig. 3.3, *19:4*\* |
| 22. | 03.07C012.II | part of body, point | 69 | 4 | circular | Shakhristan, 07C | tab. 3.3, *2:22*, fig. 3.3, *19:2*\* |
| 26. | 03.07D011.II | central part | 22 | 4 | circular | Shakhristan, 07D | tab. 3.3, *3:26*, fig. 3.3, *9:3*\* |
| 27. | 03.07D013.I | point | 70 | 5 | oval | Shakhristan, 07D | tab. 3.3, *3:27*, fig. 3.3, *9:1*\* |

## Finger and other rings

This group consists of 6 items – two metal finger rings, three bone rings and one stone ring. Going by their dimensions, the bone rings could either be finger rings or circular pendants. They are circular in form, with an inner diameter usually 1.3–3.0 cm, and decorated on the surface with flutes or fine grooves. The band is wider than is usual for metal rings, with a cross-section that is roughly oblong and gently curved on the outer edge. On the inner edge of the band, at least in the case of the finds from Jandavlattepa, both edges are sharp. If the object is to be interpreted as a finger ring, however, the inner side would have to show signs of wear, and this would manifest itself in a rounding of the edges. Three in-

complete bone rings come from the Citadel/sector 20 (cat. nos 28, 29, 30). Other similar items have been found at the Dalverzintepa, Yalangtushtepa, Tepai Shakh, Surkh Kotal and Taxila sites.

At Dalverzintepa[33] two bone rings have been found, judging by the illustrations in the excavation publication. The simpler of the two, decorated with several circles in relief around the band, divided by grooves, appears to be part of a bracelet made out of threaded beads. The second ring, pictured separately, has a series of straight grooves in various directions on its surface, leading towards the outer edge. Going by the second period during which the burial site was used, they date from the 1st–2nd century AD. Both objects have diameters of up to 2 cm, and have rounded edges on the outer side. The inner edges are sharp.

---

[33] Pugachenkova – Rtveladze 1978, pp. 110–111, ris. 79.

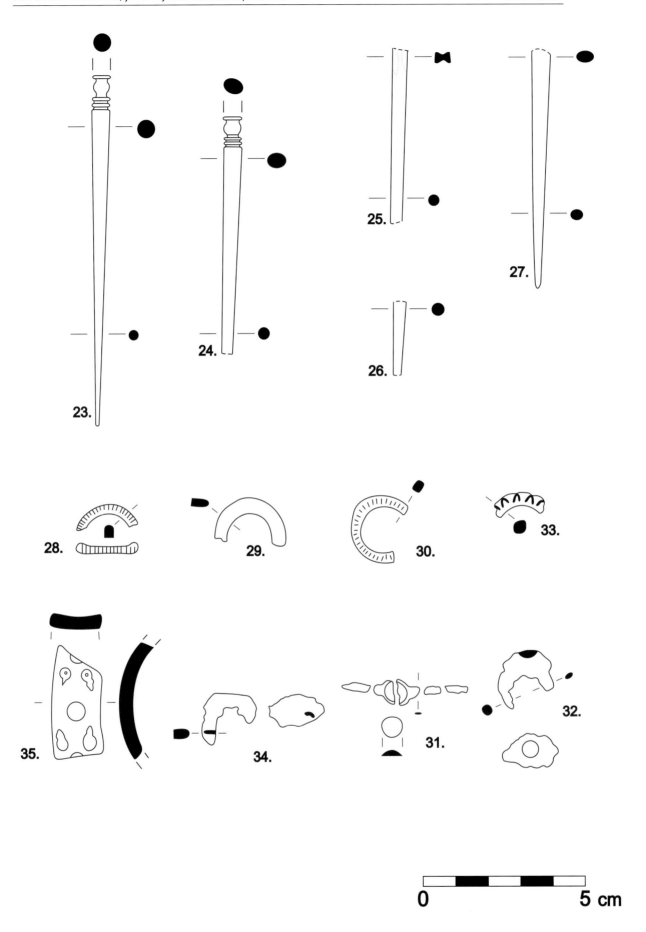

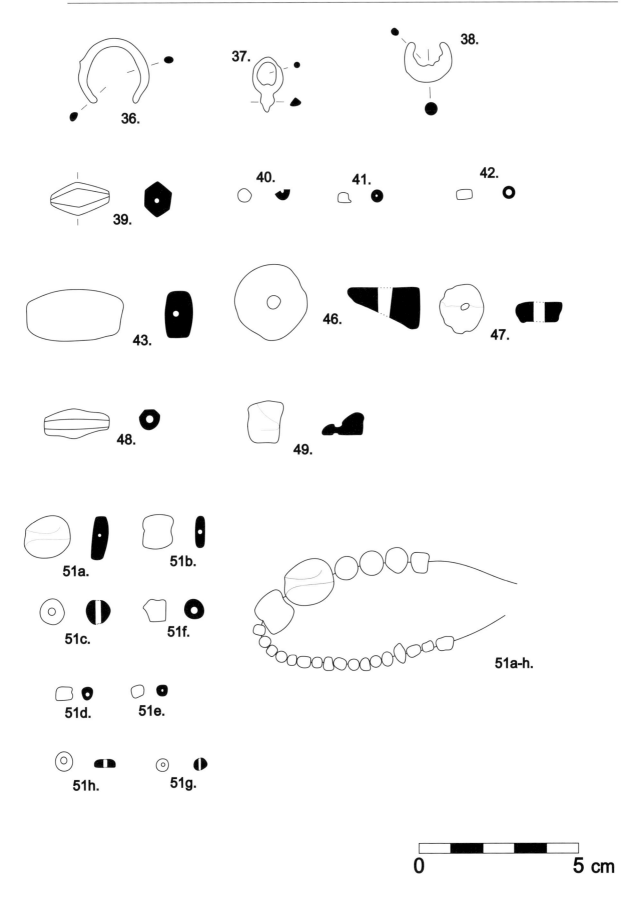

Two bone rings have been found in the necropolis at Yalangtushtepa[34], and are indicated in the text as rings. Both were found in the *naus* II. The first ring is gently flattened in one part, creating a level surface with two outlined edges, reminiscent of the scutcheon of a ring. The surface of the ring is decorated by two long grooves that go from each edge to the centre of the ring. The rest of the surface is densely decorated around the outer edge with short grooves, almost dots. The cross-section of the ring's body is the shape of an irregular quadrilateral. The second ring is similar to the first, with part of its band flatter and wider, but with no edges. It is decorated with several increasing grooves around the outer edge. The remaining, narrower part of the band is decorated with short grooves. Both are dated in accordance with the necropolis, to the 2nd – early 3rd century AD.

Among the finds from Tepai-Shakh[35] is one bone ring, with a diameter varying from 2.6–2.8 cm, slightly larger than the other rings. The body is flat, oblong in cross-section, and has gentle scallops around the outer edge. Part of the band has been formed into a bed, with two deeper grooves around its edges. The bed suggests the ring was used as an aid when drawing a bow.

From the Surkh Kotal[36] site come one whole ring and part of another. Unlike the above-mentioned rings, both are made from mother of pearl. The fragment belonged to a ring with a diameter of 1.7 cm, oval in cross-section, with an undecorated surface. The other, completely preserved one is 1.3 cm in diameter. It is oblong in cross-section, and the surface is decorated with deepish grooves the whole way round. They go from the outer to the inner edge.

Similar rings have been found at Taxila[37].

A fragment of a stone ring found in the Shakhristan of Jandavlattepa bears a certain resemblance to the bone rings, (cat. no. 33), and may thus have served a similar purpose to the above-mentioned objects.

In the gate area of Jandavlattepa a bronze ring has been found (cat. no. 32), damaged by corrosion but with a preserved stone inset, originally semi-transparent and yellow-brown. The ring is solid, and grows gradually higher and broader towards the round bed. It is considerably corroded, however, and so it is impossible to reconstruct its shape and to find close parallels. Another ring (cat. no. 31), preserved in a badly damaged state and made out of clearly low-quality metal, seems to be a modern-era item, but late antique origin cannot be excluded.[38]

### 28. 05.20Y002.I

Fragment of bone ring (finger ring or pendant), nearly half has been preserved, cross-section is trapezoid with the inside of the band slanting, edges relatively sharp, surface undamaged, clearly polished, outer edge of the band and its surface decorated with regular flutes all the way round.

Width of ring: 4 mm, internal diameter: 16 mm, weight: 0.8 g
(Citadel, sector 20/square 20Y, tab. 3.3, *3:28*, fig. 3.3, *21*)

### 29. 05.20Y022.II

Fragment of bone ring (finger ring or pendant), more than half of the circumference preserved, cross-section is oblong with a straight inner side and a more rounded outer side, inner edges relatively sharp, surface undamaged, clearly polished, the top side of the ring is decorated with delicate engraved lines around its circumference.

Width of ring: 35 mm, inner diameter: 13 mm, weight: 0.7 g
(Citadel, sector 20/square 20Y, tab. 3.3, *3:29*, fig. 3.3, *22*)

### 30. 04.20C004.I

Fragment of bone ring (finger ring or pendant), almost three quarters of circumference preserved, cross-section trapezoid with inner side flat, edges relatively sharp, surface undamaged, polished, surface of the ring decorated with regular grooves all the way round.

Width of ring: 35 mm, inner diameter: 14 mm, weight: 0.8 g
(Citadel, sector 20/square 20C, tab. 3.3, *3:30*, fig. 3.3, *23*)

### 31. 04.20D001.I

Small ring of lightweight, low-quality metal (5 fragments). A round scutcheon has been fixed to the thin band, and is edged with little balls. A purple crystal has been mounted in it. Probably a recent object?

Diameter of ring: unknown, diameter of crystal: 7 mm, weight: 1.4 g
(Citadel, sector 20/square 20D, tab. 3.3, *3:31*, fig. 3.3, *24*)

### 32. 04.04.000.I

Bronze finger ring with round semi-transparent yellow-brown stone, object has been considerably damaged by corrosion, part of the band is missing, precise form cannot be ascertained, band grows gradually wider to the relatively large bed, into which a round, slightly concave stone with no surface decoration has been inset.

Preserved length: 42 mm, diameter: approximately 12 mm, weight: unknown
(Gate, sector 04, tab. 3.3, *3:32*, figs. 3.3, *25* and *26*)

### 33. 05.10C000.II

Fragment of stone ring, dark grey in colour (pendant or finger ring), almost half of the circumference preserved, diameter of the ring almost square, edges smoothed, almost rounded, surface undamaged and polished, top surface decorated with grooves forming "V"s all the way round, with the points touching the outer edge and the arms pointing towards the inner edge.

34  Rtveladze 1983, p. 125–143, ris. 4 and 6.
35  Litvinskiy – Sedov 1983, p. 56 and 151, tab. XXXIII, 26.
36  Fussman – Guillaume 1990, p. 5 et VIII.
37  Marshall 1961, p. 649, pl. 209/ 64, 65.
38  See Kabanov p. 75, ris. 38,4 for glass-made inlay for a copper ring from Aultepa, southern Sogd, dated to 5th–6th c. AD.

Edge of ring: 45 mm, inside diameter: approximately 1.7–1.8 cm, weight: 0.8 g
(Shakhristan, sector 07/square 10C, tab. 3.3, *3:33*, fig. 3.3, *27*)

## 34. 03.07D008.II

Largish fragment of bronze finger ring, part of the band missing, object damaged by corrosion, precise shape cannot be ascertained, band, probably circular in cross-section, broadens up to the flat oval bed, likely decoration of the bronze bed cannot be reconstructed.
Preserved length: 4 cm, diameter: approximately 1.3 cm, weight: unknown
(Shakhristan, sector 07/square 07D, tab. 3.3, *3:34*, fig. 3.3, *28*)

## Bracelets

A small number of finds from several Bactrian (Surkh Kotal, Dalverzintepa, a new find from Jandavlattepa) and Gandharan sites (Taxila, Saidu Sharif) belong to a group of bracelets sometimes made of ivory but more often of mother of pearl. Unlike metal ones, mother of pearl bracelets are made out of two or three parts, connected to each other by ties threaded through holes made at the end of each part.[39] The number of parts depends on the size of the shell from which the bracelet was made. The shape of the bracelet is also dependent on the shape of the shell, and is irregularly oval or egg-shaped. The cross-section of the bracelet is approximately rectangular, and convex. The outer edge is usually decorated with simple geometric or floral designs, created by arrangements of carved-out holes and teardrops of various sizes. The finds from Surkh-Kotal can be divided into 6 subgroups on the basis of their decoration, and fundamentally similar decorative motifs are found on bracelets from other sites. Dating the items is problematic in the case of the above-mentioned sites, but we could probably say 2nd (mid-3rd) – mid-5th century Ad. The material from which they are made – ivory or mother-of-pearl – may point to the southern jewellery-making tradition.

A fragment of bracelet made of mother of pearl was found at Jandavlattepa in square 20Q (cat. no. 35). It is well-made, with a smooth surface. The decoration consists of a fairly large, dividing indentation, around which two slanting "crowns" on each side from the preceding and following motif have been preserved. Each of the slanting shapes is created by three connecting indentations, which grow smaller towards the

edge. The fragment is mildly convex. The bracelet is dated to the 4th century AD according to its context. Another related find, which comes from a stratigraphic section (sector 02a) is a bone (or ivory?) fragment of a bracelet with a preserved perforated end, simpler and thinner, with decoration in the form of several miniature indentations.

Finds of related bracelets from Surkh Kotal[40] are dated to the 2nd – mid-3rd century Ad. There are 16 of them; one is made of ivory, while the rest are made of mother of pearl. The mother of pearl is worked fairly roughly in some cases, with badly-cut pieces that have not been smoothed. Some of them are smooth, without further decoration. In the case of the decorated bracelets, as mentioned above, there are 6 types of decoration made of indentations. It is highly likely that the indentations contained inlays, and traces of lapis lazuli have even been found in some of the bracelets from the site. A similar bracelet appears in the description of objects from the Shaikhan Dheri[41] site in Pakistan.

About 7 examples of bracelets of this type, made of other of pearl, come from excavations at Dalverzintepa[42] in 1989–1993. One of them is incompletely worked. The decorative patterns are similar to those familiar from Surkh Kotal, and in one case the whole bracelet is edged on both sides with miniature engraved dots. There is an unusual example of a bracelet with a relief decoration of lengthwise stripes.

From the Saidu Sharif I[43] site come 16 fragments of undecorated bracelets made of mother of pearl, with an estimated internal diameter of 4.8–6.5 cm. The bracelets were found all together in one place, together with a similar article made of glass paste.

A bracelet was found at Taxila[44] with a design similar to the first pattern from Surkh Kotal, with a central indentation surrounded by two teardrops. Two small discs made of mother of pearl seem to have been decorated in the same style. The finds are not dated. From the material used, the bracelets could even be classed as grand jewellery, especially when we imagine the contrast between the shining mother of pearl and the blue inlaid lapis lazuli, or other stones. There is a relevant iconographic parallel in the form of two depictions of jewellery from a sculpture at Dalverzintepa[45], decorated with indentations that form a floral pattern.

---

[39]  Fussman – Guillaume 1990, p. 122.
[40]  Ibidem. The first, simpler in design, has a basic pattern of a circular indentation surrounded by a teardrop on each side with its rounded end pointing towards the indentation. This pattern is repeated all round the bracelet. The second pattern is a floral one, with a repeated rosette made out of one central and six surrounding indentation. A further pattern also has a larger indentation between the rosettes. The fourth and fifth floral patterns are similar to each other, consisting of alternating larger and smaller indentations around the bracelet, with the smaller ones also having four "crowns" pointing diagonally away from the indentation. Each of the crowns is made of a sequence of indentations – two or three – growing smaller as they go outwards. The last pattern is a rosette design with seven indentations around a central one.
[41]  Dani 1966, p. 131/ 1–9.
[42]  Dal'verzintepa schakhristoni: qadimshunoslik tadqiqotlari yaqunlari 1996, pp. 52, 63.
[43]  Callieri 1989, p. 171, figs. 133, 134.
[44]  Marshall 1961, p. 673, pl. 201/ 41.
[45]  Luneva 2005, ris. 10/7, 8.

### 35. 05.20Q002.III
Fragment of rounded bone or mother of pearl scutcheon – part of a bracelet, with a cross-section that is almost oblong with gently convex sides, edges gently smoothed, decoration on the outer side consists of a simple pattern of hollowed-out circles (a larger circle in the centre, with four groups of smaller circles nearby or close to the edge).
Length: 31 mm, width: 14 mm, thickness: 4 mm, weight: 3.5 g
(Citadel, sector 20/square 20Q, tab. 3.3, *3:35*, fig. 3.3, *29*)

**Fig. 3.3, 29** Part of a bracelet, no. 05.20Q002.III.

## Earrings

Three items from the finds can be interpreted as earrings. The first, from square 9D (cat. no. 36) is cast in bronze and takes the form of a circle with open ends. The diameter grows smaller towards the end. The internal diameter of the circle is approximately 15 mm.

Objects similar to this simple type of earring appear very frequently in finds from the central Asian sites.

Of more interest is the other bronze earring, which is grape-shaped (cat. no. 37). Its original form has been partially obscured by corrosion damage, but it is an oval earring with originally separate ends in the upper part, with a fixed pendant made out of four little balls. It was found in square 20H and has been dated to the 4th century AD according to its context.

It is similar to an earring from Kampyrtepa[46] which has been dated to the 1st–2nd century AD. Two identical grape-shaped earrings of a more complex type were found at Yalangtushtepa[47]. They are made of two parts, resembling the shape of a horseshoe, joined flexibly with circular wires. A pendant of three larger balls was fixed to the bottom, wider part of the earring, and then three smaller balls were fixed to that, thus resembling a bunch of grapes. A further three grape-shaped earrings with open ends have a pendant made out of four little balls. One is made out of gold. Going by the necropolis, they can be dated to the 2nd – mid-3rd century AD.

Grape-shaped earrings also come from Tepai-Shakh[48], and there is an example from the Syrdarya region in the form of a find from the Jety-Asar site[49].

The last bronze fragment (cat. no. 38) found at Jandavlattepa is probably the bottom, broad part of a circular-shaped earring, reminiscent of a find from Dalverzintepa.

### 36. 05.9D033.III
A bronze earring probably made by casting, in the shape of an open circle, narrowing on one side while on the other a small part has broken off.
Max. diameter of wire: 3 mm, min. diameter of wire: 1.5 mm, diameter of earring: 19 mm, weight: 0.9 g
(Shakhristan, sector 07/square 09D, tab. 3.3, *4:36*, fig. 3.3, *30*)

### 37. 04.20H002.I
Bronze earring made by casting, oval in shape, at the bottom it has a firmly fixed pendant (pyramidal or grape-shaped), corrosion damage means the precise shape cannot be established. The oval body of the earring is now continuous, since corrosion has probably caused the two ends to connect.
Max. length: 16 mm, max. width: 8 mm, weight: 0.5 g
(Citadel, sector 20/square 20H, tab. 3.3, *4:37*, fig. 3.3, *31*)

### 38. 03.9B002.II
Fragment of the bottom part of an oval, maybe from a small bronze earring, circular cross-section, becoming gradually wider in the middle, resembles a "moon-shaped" earring
Max. width: 15 mm, max. diameter: 4 mm, min. diameter: 2 mm, weight: unknown
(Shakhristan, sector 07/square 09B, tab. 3.3, *4:38*)

## Beads and pendants

During excavations of the site, 58 beads were found in sectors 20, 7 and 8. The predominant shapes are simple, spherical (sometimes with flattened ends) and cylindrical, followed by discoid, prismoid and bipyramidal beads. A similar classification is used in the following tables. Most of the beads are made of glass (40) followed by stone (12), bone (3) and coral (3). The glass beads are varied in colour, with green, blue and grey shades, together with some transparent ones with a subtle hint of colour, which are more complex in form (bipyramidal with cut ends). Some beads have been damaged, and the original colour cannot be ascertained. The glass beads also include an example of a polychromatic bead with several coloured stripes. The 12 stone beads are a good-quality collection. Four of them are made of cornelian, and their surface is in three cases undamaged and highly polished. Small flaws can be seen in the structure of the semi-transparent stone. Three of the beads belong to the bipyramidical group, with the edges between each surface

46   Ibidem, p. 65–68.
47   Rvelatze 1983, pp. 125–143.
48   Litvinskiy – Sedov 1983, p. 155, tab XXX.
49   Rapoport – Nerazik 2000, ill. 54.

being clearer in some cases and less clear in others. The last bead is solid and heavy, and its surface has been slightly damaged by scratches (cat. no. 43). It is roughly barrel-shaped, in cut form. Given its size, the bead might have been the central amulet in a necklace.

Of the three bone beads, one has been badly damaged, while the remaining two are roughly discoid in shape, with lengthwise holes. The three examples of red coral beads are of ordinary cylindrical shape.

A group of beads (cat. no. 51), which are highly likely to have formed part of an armlet or necklace, were found in layer 20Y001. The armlet would have consisted of 24 beads, of which one is stone, one bone and one coral, with the others made of glass of various colours (fig. 3.3, 33). In all, 7 types of bead can be distinguished. There is a stone bead, light brown in colour in the shape of a disc with a lengthwise hole, which might have been made of chalcedony. The bone bead is disc-shaped with rounded edges and an undamaged surface. Of the remaining glass beads, most are small, roughly cylindrical and dark blue in colour. It is difficult to date the group, but given the relatively

high-quality working of the stone and bone beads and the use of coral that is almost unaltered on the surface, the find may date from the older period. From the same layer in square 20Y (002) comes a bone ring with a carved decoration on the surface, which may have belonged to the armlet, judging from a parallel from Dalverzintepa.[50] In that case the armlet might date from the Kushan period.

*Cockle and conch shells* regularly formed part of necklaces and armlets, in combination with other beads, and in addition to their aesthetic function they also had a protective one. They were sometimes the central pendant in a necklace. Conch shells of the genus *Cypraea Moneta* frequently form parts of groups of finds. They are white, usually 1.8–2.5 cm in size, with decorative grooves around the opening. They are oval or egg-shaped, with the curve being wider on one side. The hole is usually made at the end of their narrower part. In the case of finds from central Asia, it should be noted that these objects were almost definitely brought from the nearby coast around the Indian Ocean. Two finds come from Jandavlattepa (cat. no. 75, 76).

## 1. Spherical and moderately flattened spherical beads

| cat. no. | inv. no. | material | length[51] in mm | diameter in mm | place found, square | ill./tab. |
|---|---|---|---|---|---|---|
| 49. | 05.20R012.I | white glass opaque | 4.5 | 5 | Citadel, square 20R | tab. 3.3, *4:49*, fig. 3.3, *32** |
| 51. | 05.20Y002.XVI | dark blue glass opaque | 7 | 8 | Citadel, square 20Y | tab. 3.3, *4:51*, fig. 3.3, *33* |
| 51. | 05.20Y002.XVII | dark blue glass opaque | 7 | 8 | Citadel, square 20Y | tab. 3.3, *4:51*, fig. 3.3, *33** |
| 51. | 05.20Y002.XVIII | dark blue glass opaque | 7 | 8 | Citadel, square 20Y | tab. 3.3, *4:51*, fig. 3.3, *33** |
| 51. | 05.20Y002.XX | light green glass opaque | 4 | 4 | Citadel, square 20Y | tab. 3.3, *4:51*, fig. 3.3, *33** |
| 51. | 05.20Y002.XXI | light green glass opaque | 4 | 4 | Citadel, square 20Y | tab. 3.3, *4:51*, fig. 3.3, *33** |
| 53. | 05.20Y005.I | dark glass opaque | 7 | 7 | Citadel, square 20Y | tab. 3.3, *5:53*, fig. 3.3, *34** |
| 61. | 05.11C005.VII | white stone opaque | 4 | 5 | Shakhristan, square 11C | tab. 3.3, *5:61*, fig. 3.3, *35** |
| 62. | 05.11C008.I | glass – 2 layers top white, opaque inner colourless, transparent | 10 | 14 | Shakhristan, square 11C | tab. 3.3, *5:62*, fig. 3.3, *36** |
| 63. | 05.12D003.I | Cornelian orange-red, semi-transparent | 13 | 14 | Shakhristan, square 12D | tab. 3.3, *5:63*, fig. 3.3, *37** |
| 66. | 04.07E002.I | glass, white with bluish tones, opaque | 5 | – | Shakhristan, square 07E | tab. 3.3, *5:66*, fig. 3.3, *38** |
| 68. | 04.07E004.II | dark blue glass | 8 | – | Shakhristan, square 07E | tab. 3.3, *5:68*, fig. 3.3, *39** |
| 71. | 03.07D011.I | black glass opaque | 8 | 6 | Shakhristan, square 07E | tab. 3.3, *5:71*, fig. 3.3, *40** |

---

[50]  Pugachenkova – Rtveladze 1978, pp. 110–111, ris. 79.
[51]  This value indicates dimension of the head in the direction of the threading hole. In the case of beads from Jandavlattepa it is also the maximum lenght.

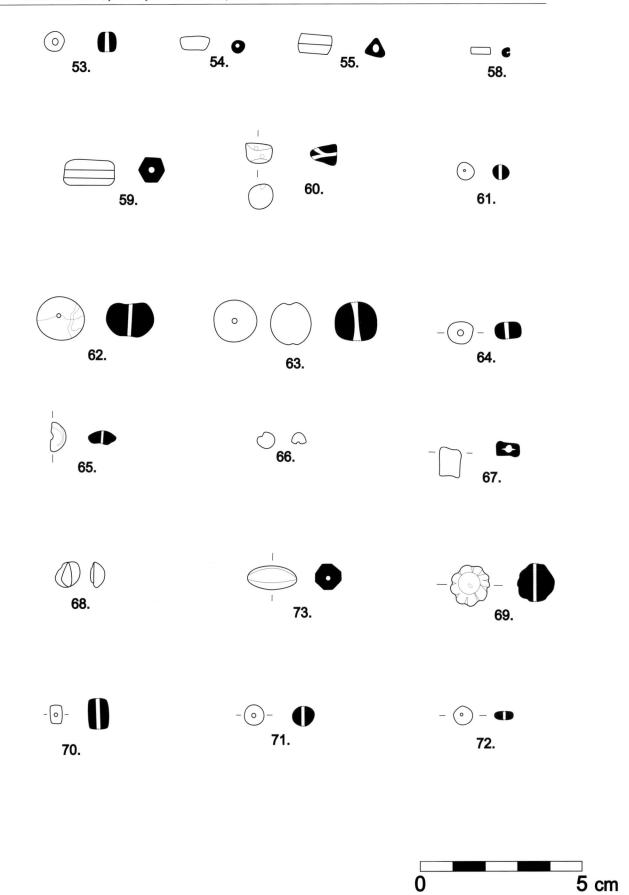

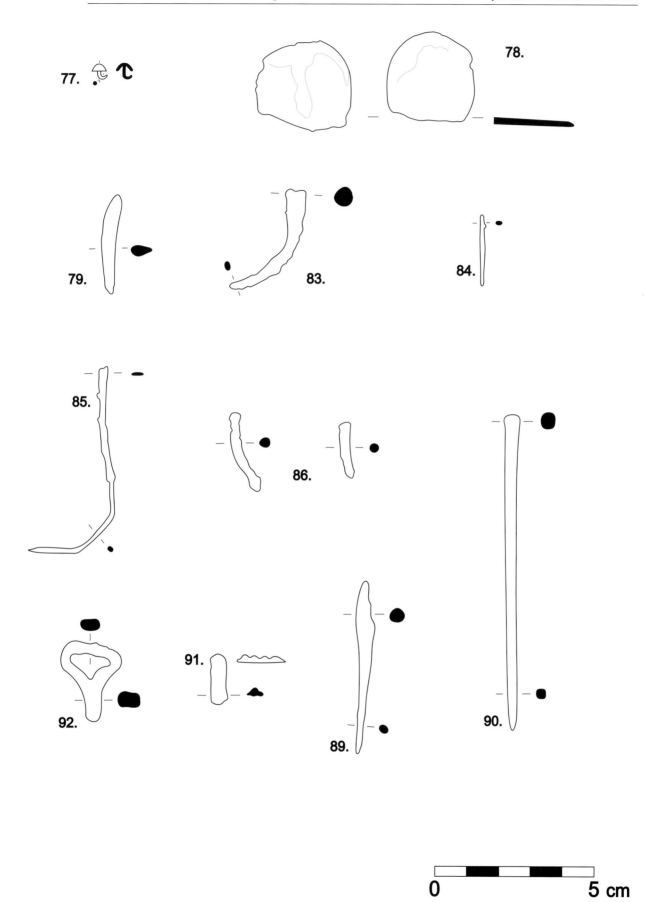

Tab. 3.3, 6

## 2. Cylindrical beads (cylindrical and tubular[52])

| cat. no. | inv. no. | Material | length in mm | diameter in mm | place found, square | ill./tab. |
|---|---|---|---|---|---|---|
| 41. | 06.21F024.II | yellow glass opaque | 4.5 | 3.5 | Citadel, square 21F | tab. 3.3, *4:41*, fig. 3.3, *41** |
| 42. | 06.21P001.I | green glass opaque | 5 | 3.5 | Citadel, square 21P | tab. 3.3, *4:42*, fig. 3.3, *42** |
| 51. | 05.20Y002.XIX | sea coral red | 6 | 4 | Citadel, square 20Y | tab. 3.3, *4:51*, fig. 3.3, *33** |
| 51. | 05.20Y002.XXII | brown glass opaque | – | – | Citadel, square 20Y | tab. 3.3, *4:51*, fig. 3.3, *33** |
| 51. | 05.20Y002.XXIII | blue glass semi-transparent | 4 | 4 | Citadel, square 20Y | tab. 3.3, *4:51*, fig. 3.3, *33** |
| 51. | 05.20Y002.XXIV | blue glass semi-transparent | 4 | 4 | Citadel, square 20Y | tab. 3.3, *4:51*, fig. 3.3, *33** |
| 51. | 05.20Y002.XXV | blue glass semi-transparent | 4 | 4 | Citadel, square 20Y | tab. 3.3, *4:51*, fig. 3.3, *33* |
| 51. | 05.20Y002.XXVI | blue glass semi-transparent | 4 | 4 | Citadel, square 20Y | tab. 3.3, *4:51*, fig. 3.3, *33* |
| 51. | 05.20Y002.XXVII | blue glass semi-trans parent | 4 | 4 | Citadel, square 20Y | tab. 3.3, *4:51*, fig. 3.3, *33* |
| 51. | 05.20Y002.XXVIII | blue glass semi-transparent | 4 | 4 | Citadel, square 20Y | tab. 3.3, *4:51*, fig. 3.3, *33* |
| 51. | 05.20Y002.XXIX | blue glass semi-transparent | 4 | 4 | Citadel, square 20Y | tab. 3.3, *4:51*, fig. 3.3, *33* |
| 51. | 05.20Y002.XXX | blue glass semi-transparent | 4 | 4 | Citadel, square 20Y | tab. 3.3, *4:51*, fig. 3.3, *33* |
| 51. | 05.20Y002.XXXI | blue glass semi-transparent | 4 | 4 | Citadel, square 20Y | tab. 3.3, *4:51*, fig. 3.3, *33* |
| 51. | 05.20Y002.XXXII | blue glass semi-transparent | 4 | 4 | Citadel, square 20Y | tab. 3.3, *4:51*, fig. 3.3, *33* |
| 51. | 05.20Y002.XXXIII | blue glass semi-transparent | 4 | 4 | Citadel, square 20Y | tab. 3.3, *4:51*, fig. 3.3, *33* |
| 51. | 05.20Y002.XXXIV | blue glass semi-transparent | 4 | 4 | Citadel, square 20Y | tab. 3.3, *4:51*, fig. 3.3, *33* |
| 51. | 05.20Y002.XXXV | blue glass semi-transparent | 4 | 4 | Citadel, square 20Y | tab. 3.3, *4:51*, fig. 3.3, *33* |
| 51. | 05.20Y002.XXVI | blue glass semi-transparent | 4 | 4 | Citadel, square 20Y | tab. 3.3, *4:51*, fig. 3.3, *33* |
| 51. | 05.20Y002.XXXVII | blue glass semi-transparent | 4 | 4 | Citadel, square 20Y | tab. 3.3, *4:51*, fig. 3.3, *33* |
| 54. | 05.20Z006.I | sea coral red | 9 | 5 | Citadel, square 20Z | tab. 3.3, *4:54*, fig. 3.3, *43** |
| 58. | 05.10D025.I | sea coral red | 6.5 | 3.5 | Shakhristan, square 10D | tab. 3.3, *4:58*, fig. 3.3, *44** |
| 64. | 04.20H002.III | dark grey glass opaque | 7 | 7 | Citadel, square 20H | tab. 3.3, *5:64*, fig. 3.3, *45** |

---

[52] According to the simple classification in: Sklenář 1998.

## 3. "Disc-shaped" beads (ring-shaped, puck-shaped[53])

| cat. no. | inv. no. | material | height in mm | diameter v mm | hole[54] | place found, square | ill./tab. |
|---|---|---|---|---|---|---|---|
| 45. | 05.20Q001.V | black glass opaque, 4 white dots round circumference | 5 | 9 | perpendicular | Citadel, square 20Q | fig. 3.3, *46** |
| 46. | 05.20Q002.I | brownish-white stone, crumbly, opaque | 2–11 | 24.5 | perpendicular | Citadel, square 20Q | tab. 3.3, *4:46*, fig. 3.3, *47** |
| 47. | 05.20Q002.II | brownish-white stone, crumbly, opaque | 7 | 12.5 | perpendicular | Citadel, square 20Q | tab. 3.3, *4:47*, fig. 3.3, *48** |
| 51. | 05.20Y002.VII | brown chalcedony semi-transparent | 6 | 15–17 | parallel | Citadel, square 20Y | tab. 3.3, *4:51*, fig. 3.3, *33** |
| 51. | 05.20Y002.XV | bone | 3 | 10–12 | parallel | Citadel, square 20Y | tab. 3.3, *4:51*, fig. 3.3, *33** |
| 56. | 05.10D002.III | bone | 3–5.5 | 14 | parallel | Shakhristan, square 10D | fig. 3.3, *49** |
| 60. | 05.11C004.II | black stone opaque divider | 3–6 | 7 | parallel two holes from one side | Shakhristan, square 11C | tab. 3.3, *5:60*, fig. 3.3, *50** |
| 72. | 03.07D012.II | orange-red glass opaque | 3 | 8 | perpendicular | Shakhristan, square 07D | tab. 3.3, *5:72*, fig. 3.3, *87** |

## 4. Prismoid beads (with hole lengthwise)

| Cat. no. | inv. no. | material and characteristics | height in mm | diameter/ dimensions of base in mm | place found, square | ill./tab. |
|---|---|---|---|---|---|---|
| 55. | 05.09D003.I | colourless glass transparent three-sided prism | 7 | edge = 4 | Shakhristan, square 09D | tab. 3.3, *5:55*, fig. 3.3, *51** |
| 59. | 05.11C004.I | colourless glass transparent six-sided prism | 16 | diameter = 7 | Shakhristan, square 11C | tab. 3.3, *5:59*, fig. 3.3, *52** |
| 67. | 04.07E004.I | stone brownish-red opaque cube-shaped | 8 | 6.5 × 4.5 | Shakhristan, square 07E | tab. 3.3, *5:67*, fig. 3.3, *53** |
| 70. | 03.07C003.VII | grey stone opaque cube-shaped | 9 | 6 × 4 | Shakhristan, square 07C | tab. 3.3, *5:70*, fig. 3.3, *54** |

## 5. Bipyramidical beads (with hole lengthwise)

| cat. no. | inv. no. | material and characteristics | length in mm | diameter in mm | place found, square | ill./tab. |
|---|---|---|---|---|---|---|
| 39. | 06.21D001.I | colourless glass opaque six-sided cross-section | 19 | 10 | Citadel, square 21D | tab. 3.3, *4:39*, fig. 3.3, *55** |
| 48. | 05.20Q020.I | cornelian orange-red semi-transparent | 21 | 9 | Citadel, square 20Q | tab. 3.3, *4:48*, fig. 3.3, *56** |
| 73. | 04.04.000.II | Cornelian orange-red semi-transparent | 16 | 8 | Gate | tab. 3.3, *5:73*, fig. 3.3, *57** |

## 6. Bead fragments where the shape cannot be ascertained

| cat. no. | inv. no. | material and characteristics | approx. dimensions in mm | place found, square | ill./tab. |
|---|---|---|---|---|---|
| 40. | 06.21F023.I | turquoise glass opaque | 4 | Citadel, square 21F | tab. 3.3, *4:40*, fig. 3.3, *58* |
| 44. | 05.20O019.I | glass, coloured stripes, opaque | – | Citadel, square 20O | fig. 3.3, *59** |
| 50. | 05.20Y002.VI | dark glass, fire-damaged | 12 × 5 | Citadel, square 20Y | fig. 3.3, *60** |
| 52. | 05.20Y002.XII | bone, wood? fire-damaged | 12 × 19 | Citadel, square 20Y | fig. 3.3, *61** |
| 57. | 05.10D003.I | turquoise glass opaque | 8.5 | Shakhristan, square 11C | fig. 3.3, *62** |

---

[53] According to Sklenář, K. 1998: Archeologický slovník 3., Praha.
[54] In relation to the circular surfaces of the "disc" – diameter – perpendicular or parallel.

## 7. Less common bead shapes

| cat. no. | inv. no. | material and characteristics | length in mm | diameter in mm | place found, square | ill./tab. |
|---|---|---|---|---|---|---|
| 43. | 05.20O010.III | cornelian, orange-red semi-transparent barrel shaped | 31 | 12 | Citadel, square 20O | tab. 3.3, *4:43*, fig. 3.3, 63* |
| 65. | 04.07A000.I | light blue glass transparent biconical shape | 5 | 8 | Shakhristan, square 07A | tab. 3.3, *5:43*, fig. 3.3, 64* |
| 69. | 03.07B007.I | white stone, opaque, spherical, segmented lengthwise | 11 | 11 | Shakhristan, square 07B | tab. 3.3, *5:69*, fig. 3.3, *65** |

**Fig. 3.3, 33** Necklace or armlet made of glass, stone, coral and bone beads, no. 05.20Y002.XVI–XXXVII.

## 8. Shells

### 74. 05.20O019.II
Fragment of cockle shell, sand-coloured.
Max. length: 26 mm, max. width: 21 mm, weight: unknown
(Citadel, sector 20/square 20O, fig. 3.3, *66**)

### 75. 04.20F007.I
Small conch shell, genus *Cypraea Moneta*, white, hole at the narrower end.
Max. length: 17 mm, max. width: 12 mm, weight: unknown
(Citadel, sector 20/square 20O, fig. 3.3, *67**)

### 76. 04.09E013.I
Small conch shell, genus *Cypraea Moneta*, hole at narrower end.
Max. length: 17 mm, max. width: 13 mm, weight: unknown
(Shakhristan, sector 07/square 09E, fig. 3.3, *68**)

## Metal items

The modest group of metal items with a more or less clear purpose includes two finds made of bronze. The first is a small decorative nail, with a smooth round head (cat. no. 77). A smaller, slightly convex metal clasp with a pin in its bottom part might have acted as a buckle (cat. no. 78) – its top side was probably decorated in relief. The nature of the picture cannot be ascertained due to considerable damage. The preserved part of the pin goes from the edge of the object to its centre.

### 77. 06.21F001.II
Small bronze nail, smooth convex head from the bottom part of the pin, the latter is bent half way along and is circular in cross-section.
Length of pin: 7 mm, diameter of head: 5.5 mm, weight: >0.1 g
(Citadel, sector 20/square 21F, tab. 3.3, *6:77*, fig. 3.3, *69**)

### 78. 04.20N003.I
Round bronze disc, served as a buckle or brooch, part of the edge now broken, slightly convex, originally had relief decoration, badly corroded; part of a pin has been preserved in the bottom part.
Diameter: 26 mm, length of pin: 17.5 mm, weight: 3.9 g
(Citadel, sector 20/square 20N, tab. 3.3, *6:78*, fig. 3.3, *70**)

## Fragments of cosmetic and decorative items – metal, bone

### 79. 05.20O018.I
Badly damaged fragment of a bone object, originally may have been in the form of a stick, today narrowed at both ends, the object may have been used as a pin or awl.
Preserved length: 32 mm, diameter: 4–5 mm, weight: unknown
(Citadel, sector 20/square 20O, tab. 3.3, *6:79*, fig. 3.3, *71**)

### 80. 04.09C022.III a, b
Two animal teeth, used as ivory implements, in the shape of sticks narrowing at both ends, oval cross-section, surface smooth with only fine grooves.
Preserved length: 40 mm, diameter: 3–5 mm, weight: unknown
(Shakhristan, sector 07/square 09C, fig. 3.3, *72**)

### 81. 04.09E008.I
Badly damaged fragment of a bone object in the form of a stick, seven-sided cross-section, original form cannot be ascertained, traces of having been worked.
Preserved length: 42 mm, diameter: 6 mm, weight: unknown
(Shakhristan, sector 07/square 09E, fig. 3.3, *73**)

### 82. 04.07C009.XXII
Partially damaged bronze object – pin – with head in the shape of a flat beaten oval surface – a small spoon or spatula, possibly a cosmetic instrument, body is circular in

cross-section, part of head missing, during retrieval the pin was broken in two, badly corroded.

Length: 97 mm, diameter: 4 mm, weight: 4.8 g
(Shakhristan, sector 07/square 07C, fig. 3.3, *74*)

## 83. 04.07C/09C005.I

Small bronze item, damaged by corrosion, probably a peg or small pin, bent into an arc and broken in two, widens on one side into a simple flat head, body is circular in cross-section.

Length: 38 mm, diameter of head: 6 mm, weight: 2.3 g
(Shakhristan, sector 07/square 07C/09C, tab. 3.3, *6:83*, fig. 3.3, *75*)

## 84. 04.09B012.I

Part of the tip of a bronze item, probably a pin or a peg, circular cross-section.

Length: 22 mm, max. diameter: 1.5 mm, weight: unknown
(Shakhristan, sector 07/square 09B, tab. 3.3, *6:84*, fig. 3.3, *76*)

## 85. 04.09B015.I

Part of an item made out of bronze rod, bent into an arc, probably a hook or a pin, body is circular in cross-section, rod flattens towards the top, object is corroded.

Length: approximately 80 mm, diameter: 2 mm, weight: unknown
(Shakhristan, sector 07/square 09B, tab. 3.3, *6:85*, fig. 3.3, *77*)

## 86. 04.09C016.V

Part of a bronze item (pin) damaged by corrosion, formed of a rod bent into an S shape with a rounded end on one side, object is broken in two, rod is circular in cross-section.

Length: 41 mm,\ diameter: 3 – 4 mm, weight: 1.7 g
(Shakhristan, sector 07/square 09C, tab. 3.3, *6:86*, fig. 3.3, *78*)

## 87. 04.09E018.I

Part of a bronze object, head and part of the body, probably a peg or a pin, body grows gradually wider towards the flat head, corroded.

Length: 8 mm, diameter of head: 6 mm, diameter of pin: 2 mm, weight: 0.5 g
(Shakhristan, sector 07/square 09E, fig. 3.3, *79*)

## 88. 04.10C003.I

Top part of damaged bronze item, consisting of angular handle with fragment of body, probably the top of a bell, clothing ornament or part of a piece of jewellery.

diameter: 8 mm, weight: unknown
(Shakhristan, sector 07/square 10C, fig. 3.3, *80*)

## 89. 04.10C009.I

Fragment of a small metal item of grey metal, probably lead, elongated screw-shaped form with broken point, surface damaged by cuts, may have been a cosmetic or surgical implement, palette knife.

Length: 50 mm, max. diameter: 5 mm, weight: unknown
(Shakhristan, sector 07/square 10C, tab. 3.3, *6:89*, fig. 3.3, *81*)

## 90. 04.04.000.III

Bronze pointed item, slightly corroded, probably a simple pin with a flat head or a large peg, quadrilateral cross-section with clear edges.

Length: 96 mm, max. diameter: 5,5 mm, weight: unknown
(Gate, sector 04, tab. 3.3, *6:90*, fig. 3.3, *82*)

## 91. 04.07E001.I

Fragment of bronze item with relief decoration (hammered decoration?), thin band/stick of metal with four pyramidical protuberances along its central axis, corroded.

Length: unknown, diameter: unknown, weight: unknown
(Shakhristan, sector 07/square 07E, tab. 3.3, *6:91*, fig. 3.3, *83*)

## 92. 04.09C001.I

Part of a bronze key-shaped implement with a triangular eye (the handle of an implement?) body circular in cross-section.

Length: unknown, diameter: unknown, weight: unknown
(Shakhristan, sector 07/square 09C, tab. 3.3, *6:92*, fig. 3.3, *84*)

## 93. 04.20E004c.I

Thin band/rod of bronze, object is twisted into a spiral, corroded

Length: unknown, diameter: unknown, weight: unknown.
(Citadel, sector 20/square 20E, fig. 3.3, *85*)

## 94. 04.20N002.X

Fragment of a metal item, part of rod bent into an arc, circular cross-section, badly corroded.

Length: unknown, diameter: unknown, weight: unknown
(Citadel, sector 20/square 20N, fig. 3.3, *86*)

## Bibliography

Callieri, P. (1989): *Saidu Sharif I (The Buddhist sacred area, The monastery)*. Rome.

*Dal'verzintepa schakhristoni: qadimshunoslik tadqiqotlari yaqunlari*. Tokyo, Soka Universiteti, 1996.

*Dal'verzintepe – kushanskiy gorod na yuge Uzbekistana*. Pugachenkova, G. A. – Rtveladze, E. V. (eds.). Tashkent, 1978.

Dani, A. H. (1966): Shaikhan Dheri Excavation (1963 and 1964 seasons), *Ancient Pakistan* II, 1965–66, pp. 17–120.

*Drevneyshie gosudarstva Kavkaza i Sredney Azii*. Koshelenko, G. A. (ed.). Moscow, 1985.

*Drevnosti Tadzhikistana* – Katalog vystavki. Dushanbe, 1985.

*Durman Tepe and Lalma: Buddhist sites in Afghanistan surveyed in 1963 – 1965*. Mizuno, S. (ed.). Kyoto University, 1968.

Fussman, G. – Guillaume, O. (1990): Surkh Kotal en Bactriane. *Mémoires de la Délégation Archéologique Française en Afghanistan* XXXII, Tome II. Paris.

Ghirshman, R. (1946): Begram. Le Caire, *Mémoires de la Délégation Archéologique Française en Afghanistan* XII. Paris.

Guillaume, O. – Rougeulle, A. (1987): Fouilles d' Aï- Khanoum VII, Les petits objets. *Mémoires de la Délégation Archéologique Française en Afghanistan* XXXI, Paris.

Higuchi, T. – Kuwayama, Sh. (1970): *Chaqalaq tepe; fortified village in North Afghanistan excavated in 1964–1967*. Kyoto.

Kabanov, S. K. (1981): *Kul'tura sel'skikh poseleniy yuzhnogo Sogda III–IV vv*. Tashkent.

Khakimov, A. – Gyul, E. – Yangos, D. (2001): *Greciya – Uzbekistan*. Katalog vystavki. Tashkent.

Kruglikova, I. T. (1974): *Dil'berdzhin, vol. 1 (raskopki 1970–1972 gg)*. Moskva.

*Kultura i iskusstvo drevnego Uzbekistana* – katalog vystavki, vol. 1. Moskva, 1991.

Litvinskiy, V. A. – Sedov, A. V. (1983): *Tepai–Shakh, kultura i svyazi v kushanskoy Baktrii*. Moskva.

Litvinskiy, V. A. – Sedov, A. V. (1984): *Kul'ty i ritualy kushanskoy Baktrii*. Moskva.

Luneva, V. (2005): *Yuvelirnoye iskusstvo Severnoy Baktrii*. Tashkent.

Mandel'shtam, A. M. (1975): Pamyatniki kochevnikov kushanskogo vremeni v severnoy Baktrii. *Trudy tadzhikskoy arkheologicheskoy ekspedicii AN SSSR* VIII. Leningrad.

Marshall, J. (1951): *Taxila III*. Cambridge.

Pidaev, Sch. R. (1978): *Akkurgan*. Tashkent.

Pugachenkova, G. A. (1966): *Khalchayan: K probleme khudozhestvennoy kultury severnoy Baktrii*. Tashkent.

Pugachenkova, G. A (ed.) (1991): *Drevnosti yuzhnogo Uzbekistana*. Tokio.

Rapoport, Yu. A. – Nerazik, E. E. (1984): Toprak-Kala, Dvorets. *Trudy Khorezmiyskoy arkheologo-etnograficheskoy ekspeditsii* vol. XIV. Moskva.

Rtveladze, E. V. (1983): Mogil'nik kushanskogo vremeni u Yalangtusch-Tepe. *Sovetskaya arkheologiya* 2, pp. 125–143.

Schischkin, V. A. (1963): *Varakhsha*. Moskva.

Sedov, A. V. (1987): *Kobadian na paroge rannego srednevekov'ya*. Moskva, Nauka.

Sklenář, K. (1998): *Archeologický slovník 3. Keramika a sklo*. Praha, NM.

Skugarova, N. G. (2001): Kostyanye zakolki Kampyrtepa, in: *Drevnyaya i srednevekovaya kultura Surkhandarii*, Taschkent, pp. 44–51.

Suleymanov, R. Ch. (1983): *Arkheologicheskie nakhodki kompleksa Setalak I*. Taschkent.

Tolstov, S. P. (1964): *Drevniy Khoresm*. Moskva.

Urbanová, K. (2006): *Textilní produkce v kušánské Střední Asii*, unpublished MA Thesis, Prague, Charles University.

Zav'yalov V. A. (1993): Kostyanye predmety tualeta iz pamyatnikov Sredney Azii kushanskogo vremeni, in: *KrSoobsh IIMK*, vol. 209, Moskva, pp. 31–40.

Zav'yalov V. A. (1986): Raskop 6 na gorodishche Zartepa, in: *Arkheologicheskie otkrytiya*, Moskva, pp. 458–459.

Zhukov, V. d. (1961): Arkheologicheskaya razvedka v Shakhristane Khairabadtepe. *IMKU* 2, pp. 177–191.

Zhukovskiy, V. A. 1883: *Gyaurkala*.

# 3.4 Terracotta figurines, appliques and gem imprints

*Kazim Abdullaev*

Archaeological work on the Jandavlattepa site has produced a collection of terracotta figurines. They were found in the cultural layers, mostly those from the Kushan period. Some of them were found on the surface of the settlement. All the terracotta material belongs chronologically to the Kushan and post-Kushan periods.

Based on what they depict, the figures can be classified as anthropomorphic – male and female, and zoomorphic. In order to gain a more coherent picture of the world-view of the ancient inhabitants and their most popular cults, we also include in this overview two terracotta images that were found here by the previous Uzbek-German expedition that worked on Jandavlattepa in 1993.

The first terracotta figurine from Jandavlattepa provokes special interest. The terracotta is executed in high relief and is relatively large (h. 14.2 cm, w. 6.2 cm; the proportion of head to body is 1:4). It is painted a dark red-brown colour. The figure was imprinted in a deep mould on a thick clay slab, which was later cut from the figure (fig. 3.4, *1\**). The figure is seen frontally. The left hand is bent and is resting on the hip; the right is lowered along the body with its palm turned toward the viewer. Apparently the figure does not hold an attribute. The right leg is slightly set aside and back. Barely visible on top of the head is a strip indicating the *ushnisha*. The hairline corresponds to the lower part of the headdress, decorated above the ears by reliefs of rosettes, which one can barely make out. The hair is shown as curls in relief. Rectangular pendants with pearls adorn the lobes of the ears. The eyes are shown in the form of round reliefs with a horizontally pressed line for the heavy eyelids – a sign characteristic of many terracottas of Buddhist type. The mouth with depressions at the corners simulates a smile. The slightly increased relief of the upper lips with a barely inclined depression hints at a moustache.

The wide shoulders are adorned with bracelets. On the breast there is a double embellishment of a necklace in the form of a wide strip and a pectoral, dangling on the stomach with a quadrangular pendant. On the wrists are more bracelets. The dress of the figure represents the *uttariya* and *paridhana*. The *uttariya* is shown as two large folds running obliquely from the bottom upward (from right to the left) and covering the wrist of the left hand. The end of the fold of the *uttarya* freely hangs down at the left to the level of the knees of the figure. Folds indicated by more frequent slanting lines pass at the left from the top downward. The hem of the dress (*paridhana*) is emphasized by parallel lines forming something like a border.

The identification of the Jandavlattepa image is difficult because its details are rather vague.[1] The headdress in flat relief at the base and with two sockets on either side is reminiscent of that of a Bodhisattva[2], but is less ornate. The *ushnisha*, though, would speak in favour of a Bodhisattva. The ear-pendants, in the form of threaded pearls, are also close to the adornment of Bodhisattvas.[3] Further supporting our reading of the image is the ornamentation and the form of the dress with its schematic *paridhana* and *uttariya*. The pose of the hands also follows the traditional iconography of the Bodhisattva. If we take into consideration the fact that the palm of the right hand with the fingers lowered downwards is turned toward the viewer, this pose signifies *varada-mudra*, symbolizing grace or boon.[4] However, this hand-pose occurs relatively seldom in Buddhist figurative art. An example is the statue of an upright Buddha of the Gupta period at the Sarnath Archaeological Museum (inv. no. 5512), which has been dated to the 6th century AD.[5]

---

1   D. Huff characterizes this figurine as "unusual." See Huff 1995, pp. 269–274. In other publications this figurine was determined simply as "Bactrian deity," cf. Mkrtychev 2002, p. 178.
2   Tissot 1987, pl. XXIX, 1a, 2a.
3   Ibid, pl. XXXII, 10.
4   Gupte, pp. 4, 9.
5   *The Route of Buddhist Art* 1988, n17, p. 164.

There is a terracotta figurine without a head, depicting a male figure in a long caftan that to all appearances seems to belong to the Kushan artistic complex.[6] The character and the form of dress are worthy of special attention. The upper layer of clothing, going over the shoulders, is an ankle-length caftan. Its edges have stripes in relief, with oblique grooves, giving the impression of a fur trim (fig. 3.4, 2*). In the upper part, at chest level, the relief is in the form of two flaps – fastenings that join the edges of the caftan. The relief around the neck clearly represents a pectoral or other type of neck cloth. The undergarment consists of a knee-long blouse gathered at the waist. The feet protrude from underneath the clothes and are shod in soft (?) shoes. The figure stands on a lowish pedestal, with a horizontal relief.

Judging by the relief that indicates arms, and by the way in which the arms are held, it seems that the left arm, hanging along the side of the body and bent at the elbow, clearly held some sort of horizontal attribute. The right arm, also bent at the shoulder, was raised and pressed to the chest, and probably also held some sort of attribute.

A type that is iconographically close to this depiction comes from finds from the Airtam settlement. In the early phase of excavation of this site a terracotta statuette (10.6 cm × 7.5 cm)[7] was found with its head knocked off, but with a highly distinctive signature. Dressed in a long caftan, it held a round vessel in its left hand (fig. 3.4, 3*), while in its right hand it pressed to its chest an object depicted with notches, most probably representing a branch of a plant.[8] During the subsequent excavation of Airtam in the mid-1960s[9] a totally analogous fragment of terracotta was found (6.5 × 7.5 cm). It may have come from the same mould (fig. 3.4, 4*).[10]

Our example from Jandavlattepa suggests associations with the image of a donor, something that features fairly often in compositions that represent scenes of worship in the art of Gandhara and the neighbouring historical and cultural regions in the Kushan period.[11] It is interesting to note one characteristic of the clothing of the above-mentioned figures, and that is above all the way in which the long caftan is worn. Its shape is in many ways reminiscent of the Persian *kandis*. This does not need to be described here in detail, but it is worth noting that depictions of male figures, for example those on the gold tablets of the Amu Darya Treasure, show a long caftan thrown over the shoulder. A characteristic feature of these caftans is a long, narrow, non-functional sleeve. The caftan of the Kushan grandees is looser, judging by the depictions, and the arms are always in the sleeves. It is possible that in our case it is a type of clothing that is thrown over the shoulder, similar to a kandis but differing in a number of ways in addition to the above-mentioned characteristic of the kandis – that it was worn without the arms in the sleeves. A number of gold tablets with carved pictures of princes and donors (the Oxus Treasure) show the kandis with narrow, probably false sleeves.[12] If we are to judge by the depictions from the Oxus Treasure, then there is one further detail that distinguishes these two groups from each other. This is a fastener in the shape of two connected flaps that is found in all the terracotta statues surveyed from northern Bactria, and is totally missing from the clothing of the figures in the Oxus group, including silver statuettes, depicting princes. The form of the fastening changed, as can be seen on reliefs depicting Kushan grandees, and its main function was to join the edges of the caftan at approximately chest height, below which the edges hung loose.[13] There is no doubt that this type of clothing was worn mostly by the nobility. An excellent example of this sort of over-the-shoulder clothing is provided by coin iconography, specifically coins minted by Vima Kadphises and Kanishka, which on the head side show the ruler in a long caftan in front of an altar. The depiction clearly shows the edges clasped at the chest with round pins.[14]

Another subject of the terracotta statues from Jandavlattepa is represented by a fragment of the upper part of what is clearly a depiction of a woman's body. The figurine was found in sector 2A (stratigraphic section) in layer no. 18, which means at a depth of about 340–360 cm under the present-day surface of the mound, in a complex from the Yuezhi period and the early Kushan period. The terracotta is made of fine-consistency clay, with a large number of fine white particles (chalk). A similar clay composition can be seen in a ceramic from Jandavlattepa (4.1 × 5.0 × 1.9 cm). The surface of the figurine is scratched and uneven. Unfortunately it is so battered from the chin downwards that we cannot gain a full idea of what this figure looked like. However, the preserved part still gives us a lot of interesting information. The long narrow face stands out in relief against a background of long, straight hair, falling to the shoulders (tab. 3.4, 1:6; fig. 3.4, 5). The narrow eye openings, sloping diagonally towards the temples,

6 Huff – Pidaev – Chaydoullaev 2001, p. 220, fig. 2.
7 In giving dimensions, the first figure is the maximum height, the second the width and the third the depth.
8 Masson 1940, fig. 51; Vyaz'mitina 1945, p. 51, fig. 11; Pugachenkova 1973, p. 117, fig. 33.
9 Turgunov 1973, pp. 52–77.
10 Pugachenkova 1973, p. 117; *Antiquities of Southern Uzbekistan* 1991, no. 24.
11 Rosenfield 1967; Schlumberger 1952, p. 443, pl. VI; Meunie 1942, pl. XXIX; Dajens 1964, pl. VIII, X.
12 Dalton 1964, pl. XV, 69; pl. XIII, 2, 2a; *Forgotten Empire* 2005, nos. 228, 235, 258, 259.
13 Rosenfield 1967, figs. 23, 94, 98a, 108, 121.
14 Göbl 1984, taf. 1, type 4; Rosenfield 1967, pl. II, fig. 29.

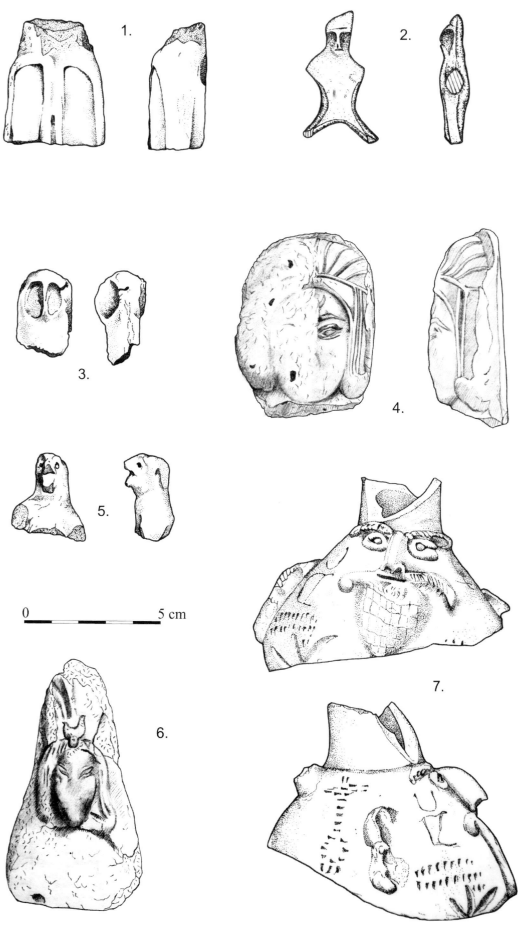

Table 3,4, 1

Fig. 3.4,5 Goddess Nana, fragment of a terracotta figurine, Sector 2°, layer no. 18.

indicate a Mongoloid ingredient in the figure's anthropological type. The narrow forehead, slightly sloping in profile, is framed by straight hair, with a short fringe over the forehead and then falling to the shoulders. The ends are curved, like a scroll. In the middle, on the forehead against the background of the hair, is a circular relief, on top of which is a crescent moon with its horns turned upwards. Still higher on the head there are lines radiating outwards.

From the iconographic point of view, the closest analogy to this example comes from a group of terracotta images found in northern Bactria. Judging by finds from dated layers, they come from the first century AD. It is interesting to note that one and the same layer (dated by Kanishka-era coins) provided terracotta images representing different anthropological types. Some of them show clear Mongoloid signs. All this gives us reason to assume that the settlement of northern Bactria in the Kushan period was ethnically mixed. It should also be noted that the depiction of a seated female figure is found more frequently on objects to the north of the Oxus up to the slopes of the southern Hissar. In any case, during excavations of Payonkurgan a large number of images of

the same type showing a female goddess on a throne were found. An iconographic analysis of the group of terracottas allows us to identify them as an image of the goddess Nana.[15] Nana was one of the most popular and most-worshipped divinities in the Kushan pantheon, as shown not only by artworks from the Kushan period, but also an inscription by Kanishka from Rabatak (Afghanistan) in which he declares this goddess to be the most worshipped.[16]

Our example from Jandavlattepa shows one of the early types of depiction. Note once again the Mongoloid features in the face of the figure, which we interpret as the figure of Nana. This is suggested by important symbols such as the round relief – a solar symbol – and the crescent moon on the forehead, well-documented in the coin iconography of the Great Kushans.

Another female image is a small terracotta head, of which the right side of the face is battered (5.1 × 3.9 × 2.1 cm). The back of the head is flat, and has been smoothed by an instrument during rough preparations for firing. It was found in sector 2A (stratigraphic section) at a depth of 290–300 cm, in a layer with ceramics from the period of the Great Kushans. The oval face is framed by straight hair, falling in vertical direct lines from the horizontal relief line (tab. 3.4, 1:4; fig. 3.4, 6). The hair is curled at the bottom. The relief line passes across the forehead and creates an arch between it and the horizontal line, above which there is a smooth area, with no hair marks, that may have represented part of a head covering. In the upper part, above the horizontal line, regular relief lines radiate outwards. The face is full, with eyes wide open and long, arched, eyebrows, and

Fig. 3.4,6 A female head, fragment of a terracotta figurine, Sector 2A.

[15] Abdullaev 2003, pp. 15–38.
[16] Sims-Williams – Cribb 1995/96, pp. 77–79.

**Fig. 3.4, 7** Upper part of a female torso, fragment of a terracotta figurine, Sector 2A.

a small mouth with hollows around it, giving the face the hint of a smile. From the centre of the forehead a relief emerges, becoming sharper in an upwards direction, showing a veil in the form of a crescent moon with horns turned upwards.

This subject is also well known in the terracotta of northern Bactria. It is interesting that analogous hairstyles and head decorations, together with a veil in the form of a crescent moon, are characteristic of the depiction of female musicians. In any case, a very close analogy comes from the settlement of Dalverzintepa, in the form of a mould for the depiction of a female figure with a stringed instrument of the lute type, and also a separately-found terracotta statue (made from the above-mentioned mould?). The figure has the same hairstyle and decoration in the shape of a crescent moon on the forehead. The find is dated to the 1st–2nd century AD.[17] Also from the same period is a find of a similar statue, but in this case seated, from the settlement of Payonkurgan (Baysun district).[18]

One item that is not completely clear is a terracotta fragment of what seems to be a statuette (?) or more precisely its middle part. It was found in sector 2A, in the surface layer during the first removal of soil – 10–15 cm under the present-day surface. As long as the terracotta did not come to the surface from the lower layers, it might be possible to classify it as from the late Kushan period. The fragment has a compact structure and is made of good-quality clay. The reverse side has been smoothed with an instrument. Both ends have been broken off, but one end, which is narrower than the other, seems to be a neck. The figure is decorated with relief bands, issuing from the centre in the upper part and going out to the hips, while in the centre

there is a sort of moulding in the shape of two parallel relief lines (tab. 3.4, 1:1; fig. 3.4, 7). Between the side strips and the central moulding there are symmetrical zig-zag relief strips. The schematic nature of the depiction, and above all the fact that it is a fragment, make it difficult to identify in any way. It can only be assumed that it is a depiction of a figure with a cloak thrown over the shoulder. A terracotta figure that is schematic in a broadly similar way is a statuette from Mirzabekkala (Turkmenistan), a settlement by the central course of the river Amu Darya.[19]

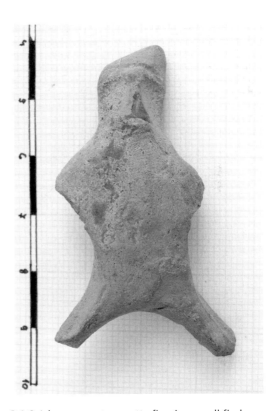

**Fig. 3.4, 8** A horseman, terracotta figurine, small find no. 21D012.I.

An interesting category in the terracottas of Jandavlattepa is that of figurines modelled by hand. All these figures are characterised by a fairly primitive three-dimensional modelling. Still, some of them are distinctive, and they include some very small-sized depictions of horsemen. The figure of the rider was usually modelled separately and then attached to the horse's back. In the layers they are often found separately, either a figure of a rider with legs apart, if found whole, or only the upper part with roughly-modelled arms and a head. There are frequent finds of little horses that would have once carried riders that have now been lost. All that remains of them is a trace on the horse's back or the remains of the reliefs of the broken-off "hands" of the rider on the horse's mane.

---

[17] *Dalverzintepe* 1978, pp. 165, 167, fig. 2; Pugachenkova 1978; *Antiquities of Southern Uzbekistan* nos 66, 68.
[18] Abdullaev 2005, p. 39, fig. 18.
[19] *Drevneyshie gosudarstva Kavkaza i Sredney Azii* 1985, tab. CVI, 10.

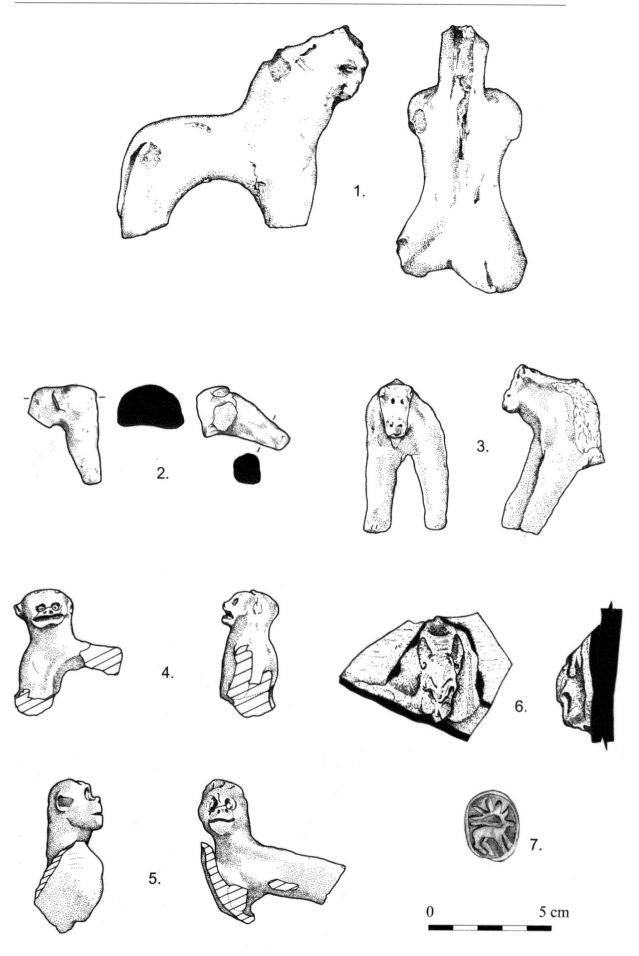

Table 3,4, 1

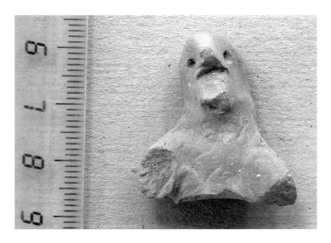

**Fig. 3.4, 9a** A horseman, fragment of a terracotta figurine.

This category includes a miniature figure (5.0 × × 3.1 × 1.3 cm), found in square 21D (in the Citadel) in layers from the late Kushan or Kushano-Sasanian period. The figure is modelled from a single, compact piece of clay, and its legs are spread in a sort of arch (for fastening to the horse's back). The head has been modelled with maximum simplicity, by squeezing clay between the index finger and thumb (the terracotta retains traces of finger prints) (tab. 3.4, 1:2; fig. 3.4, 8). This method creates several elements of the face: the eyebrows, eye sockets and prominent nose. Another detail is the dent made under the squeezed nose, as if to divide the nose from the bottom part of the face, depicting a mouth opening. The artist has also created a head covering in conical form, with a pointed upper part.

The second figurine, found in sector 2A in a layer that comes from the early Kushan period, is broken off at the waist (3.0 × 2.9 × 1.5 cm) and depicts only the upper part of a rider with fragmentary stumps instead of arms. Unlike the previous example, it is made of good-quality clay and has been evenly fired to a reddish-orange colour. The methods used for the three-dimensional modelling are approximately the same, but the figure of the rider looks a little different. First, the way in which the head has been pinched is the same, but the bent nose gives a more grotesque impression through having been more markedly extended forwards (tab. 3.4, 1:5; fig. 3.4, 9a). Secondly, the pinching is deeper, which gives the impression, especially from sideways on, of a beard (fig. 3.4, 9b*). The eyes are indicated with deep drilled holes. The head covering has not been preserved, but in its place is a transverse impression, probably from the detail of a head covering or diadem (?).

This category of figures may include a smallish fragment (3.2 × 2.1 × 1.6 cm) of a larger image. The break is at the neck and on the reverse side. On this example only the pinched part can be seen – the artist's finger prints can be clearly seen (tab. 3.4, 1:3;

fig. 3.4, 10). No other three-dimensional modelling has been observed, and the head is not even divided from the neck.

At this point, it is appropriate to say something about the depiction of riders in the terracotta sculpture of Bactria. These depictions became the most popular subject of the small-format art in the Yuezhi and Kushan periods. It is hard to say whether these small figures were used in worship, or whether they were toys. Either way, they reflected the image of what was this people's most popular figure, and also reflected a characteristic of the society, inasmuch as it was a nomadic one. This does not by a long way mean that the figure was less popular in an urban environment, however. When the image pressed into the terracotta statuettes is compared with the depictions of a monumental and official nature such as wall paintings, coin dies, seals and other works of art, it is logically fully possible that the rider figure also had a religious significance. The dominance of the theme in the Saka, Yuezhi and Kushan period (2nd century BC – 2nd–3rd century AD) shows that the rider figure is, more than others, connected with the culture of nomadic nations.[20]

Together with riders, figures of horses are one of the most popular subjects in the terracottas of Bactria, and seemingly the whole of Central Asia. They are mostly modelled in the hand, and together with primitive examples we come across some highly distinctive specimens. If we analyse the theme, we

**Fig. 3.4, 10** A horseman (?), fragment of a terracotta figurine.

---

[20]  Abdullaev – Pidaev 1989, pp. 51–57.

**Fig. 3.4, 11** Horse head, fragment of a terracotta figurine, accidental find.

encounter the same question – what role did these statuettes fulfil? To consider them toys would certainly provoke no particular objections, but the cult of the horse and its role in the religious and mythological world view of the nations of Central Asia in the past is a consideration of no small importance. The phenomenon is clearly reflected both in the written sources and in art works and ethnography.[21]

Two fragments of terracotta depictions of horses have been found at Jandavlattepa. One of them was brought to us by a local inhabitant, who found it on the surface of the settlement. The preserved part of the figurine shows a horse's head with a bent neck (5.5 × 5.3 × 2.3 cm). The pinched and sharpened edge creates a high mane. The head has shortened proportions, and the lower jaw is extended downwards (fig. 3.4, *11*). The eyes, nose and mouth holes are depicted by indentations in the form of a semicircle (eyes), vertical grooves (nostrils) and a horizontal line (mouth). The upper part of the head is depicted in high relief, showing a plume and ears.

**Fig. 3.4, 12** Horse, fragment of a terracotta figurine, Sector 04.

The second figurine was found in sector 04 (the gate). It is a light, greyish-yellow colour, and made of finely-washed clay. The ends of the legs and the head have been broken off (8.1 × 7.5 × 5.1 cm). The horse's mane has been created in a way similar to that described above (tab. 3.4, 2:1; fig. 3.4, *12*a). The example in question also allows us to see how the tail was created. It takes the form of a squeezed cylinder, and is stuck to the right leg (fig. 3.4, *12*b*). The mane is smooth, without any trace of a rider.

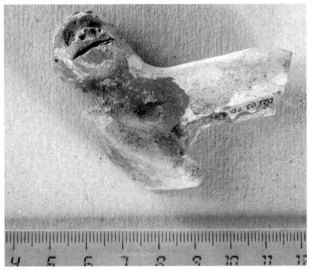

**Fig. 3.4, 13** Monkey's head, fragment of a vessel's handle, Sector 07.

Also connected with the Kushan period are depictions of monkeys, which often form part of the handles of vessels. There are two fragments of such handles from the Jandavlattepa site, from two different vessels. The first fragment, which also has part of the neck of the vessel (5.7 × 6.3 × 2.3 cm), was found in square 07D (the Shakhristan). The fragment is covered by a brownish-red slip, which has come off in parts. The monkey's head is turned sideways, to the left. The hair is indicated by a number of deep grooves (tab. 3.4, 2:5; fig. 3.4, *13*). The mouth openings are indicated by deep indentations. The lower part of the face juts out significantly in front of the eye part, and the nostrils are also indicated by means of deep holes, although the eye holes are larger in diameter than the nostrils. The mouth is indicated by a deep horizontal line on the prominent area of the lower part of the face.

The second fragment with a similar theme is also a vessel handle, brought by a local inhabitant who found it at the bottom of a gulley not far from sector 02A. The surface of the vessel is covered in reddish-orange slip (6.4 × 4.1 × 2.2 cm). The figure, which has slightly shortened proportions, was probably fixed to a smallish vessel. The head is turned to the left. There is also a difference in the way some of

---

[21] Belenickiy 1978, pp. 31–39; Belenickiy 1948, pp. 162–168; Vyatkina 1968, pp. 117–122; Toktabay 2004.

**Fig. 3.4, 14** Monkey's head, fragment of a vessel's handle, accidental find.

the details are depicted. The hair on the head, for example, is indicated by indentations made with a small hollow tube. The eyes are also made from the imprint of a hollow tube, with a hole for a pupil drilled in the middle (tab. 3.4, 2:4; fig. 3.4, *14*). The ears on this example are shown as triangular shapes projecting from the head, with a groove in the middle. In my opinion, these details would hardly represent another kind of animal. The differences arise from the working methods and style of each artist in reproducing the same subject. In this case, the more significant thing is that monkeys are specifically depicted with their heads turned sideways to the left (or right).[22]

With the penetration of the Indo-Buddhist cultural complex into the terracotta art of Bactria, as well as making anthropomorphic depictions of the Buddhist pantheon[23] it also became very popular to depict animals (elephants, monkeys, zebus and so on) that were connected in any way with Buddhist mythology and legends (the "Jataka"). These depictions are reflected fairly clearly in works of monumental art, the compositions of wall reliefs, wall paintings, and architectural ornament etc. The fact that they were so widespread in decorative art shows that Buddhist art

traditions had penetrated a broad area to the north of the river Oxus. Monkeys have been found at a number of archaeological sites, including Zartepa, Khayrabadtepa[24], Old Termez[25], Karatepa[26], Shortepa, Ayrtam and Baratepa.[27]

G. A. Pugachenkova believes that monkey images penetrated the Bactrian area from Indo-Kushan areas, where they were significantly widespread in the plastic arts. Large numbers of monkey figurines have been found in Taxila[28], Charsada[29] and Sheikhan Deri.[30]

It is more difficult to identify a fragment of a terracotta statuette found on the slopes of a gulley close to the 02A object. The fragment depicts the front part of an animal, clearly not a predator, with large front legs and chest (6.2 × 4.7 × 3.3 cm). A remarkable characteristic of the animal's anatomy is the disproportionately small head compared to the body (or, more precisely, to its preserved part) and the hanging fold

**Fig. 3.4, 15** A domestic animal, fragment of a terracotta figurine, Sector 02A.

---

22  In such a case I cannot agree with the identification of the zoomorphic handle from Shortepa as "a vessel handle in the shape of an animal, similar to a lion," Pugachenkova 1973, ill. 42. It is probably the same subject of a monkey carried out in a slightly different style.
23  Abdullaev 1998.
24  Al'baum 1960, p. 27, fig. 12; Zav'yalov – Osipov 1976, p. 57, ill. 3,3.
25  Kozlovskiy – Nekrasova 1976, p. 32, ill. 2, 6; however, the authors interpret the figure of the monkey as a depiction of a polecat, ibid. p. 32.
26  Staviskiy 1974, pp. 110–112, ill. 85.
27  Pugachenkova 1973, p. 121.

Fig. 3.4, 16 A rear part of an animal, fragment of a terracotta figurine, small find no. 20O013c.I.

of the short neck from the cheeks to the chest (tab. 3.4, 2:3; fig. 3.4, 15). The last detail is more characteristic of large domestic animals such as bulls and cows. Small traces of broken-off parts have been preserved on the head, possibly ears or horns, but nothing can be said about these for certain. The nostrils and eyes are indicated by deep drilled holes. The mouth is indicated by a broad, deep opening. Hypothetically it may be assumed that a ceramic artist has tried to create an image of some sort of domestic animal (a bull?).

Another piece that can clearly be classified as a zoomorphic depiction is a not very distinctive fragment of terracotta, representing the rear part of an animal (4.4 × 2.9 × 2.1 cm). It was found in layer 20O013c in sector 20. In almost all these depictions of animals, the limbs are modelled in a generalised way. With this fragment, a break can be observed where the tail would be, and a short distance away, another on the left leg (tab. 3.4, 2:2; fig. 3.4, 16). The terracotta is made of good-quality clay, as shown by the thick shard, light brown in colour and evenly fired.

The next fragment is hard to identify as any kind of depiction. It is a terracotta item, longish in shape

and light in tone, flat on one side and convex on the other (semicircular in cross-section) and smooth on one side. The end of the item is rounded into a circle on the upper side (4.9 × 2.9 × 2.3 cm). The fragment was found in sector 20.

Ceramics complexes of the late Kushan and Kushano-Sasanian period of northern Bactria characteristically include finds of smallish cups with the edges lightly curved inwards. The cups are frequently covered in slip ranging from cream to bright reddish-orange tones. The inner surfaces are also covered in slip. Very often the slip is coming off the vessels, and in Russian-language archaeological literature these ceramics have acquired a special term, "ceramics with flaking slip." Another characteristic of this type of cup is the existence of a three-dimensional ornament in the form of a lion's mask (fig. 3.4, 17). These ornaments are usually found around the upper part of the vessel, under the edge of the rim. They were decorated in various ways, depending on the habits and experiences of the artist. In some examples there are squeezed places on the inner surface of the vessel at the point at which the ornament was fixed on the outside. This may mean that when the ornament was fixed on the other side, the artist used strong pressure in the opposite direction. In all likelihood the imprint of a lion's face in a mould was made separately on a piece of clay, which was then stuck to the unfired semi-finished vessel and smoothed. On some examples the layer of the ornament, or more precisely its inner surface, can be seen fixed to the outer surface of the cup.

Of the five fragments of cups with lion's head ornaments found at Jandavlattepa, three come from the

Fig. 3.4, 17 Lion's mask, clay applique of a cup.

28  Marshall 1951, p. 458, pl. 135, m, n.
29  Wheeler 1962, p. 111.
30  Dani 1965/66, p. 94, pl. XXXVIII.

**Fig. 3.4, 18** Head of an animal, clay applique of a vessel, Sector 20.

same place and layer, while two others come from various parts of the settlement (chance finds). They can be divided into two different types of lion's head (dimension of whole ornament from 2.5. to 3.0 cm; dimension of actual lion's head 2.0 cm). This indicates that either they were made in various workshops or that the craftsman used various moulds. Overall, finds of similar ornaments in various places, sometimes quite far apart, indicates that this type of cup ornament was fairly popular in the late Kushan and the Kushano-Sasanian period. It may be assumed that a mould for printing the relief in question was part of the equipment of ceramics makers in northern Bactria.

The actual cups, with ornaments placed symmetrically around the edge, were to all appearances created in imitation of luxurious metal cups. It is not impossible that they were also meant to imitate glass vessels, a frequent luxury vessel in the Sasanian and Roman world. In any case, the decoration of this type of cup is one of the characteristics of the decoration of ceramic vessels in the Kushano-Sasanian period.[31]

Even closer to the imitation of metal vessels is a fragment of a ceramic vessel found in the upper layers of the settlement's Citadel (sector 20).[32] The ornament is stuck to the outer surface of the vessel. Where it has been damaged, and is no longer covered by slip, traces of having been turned on a potter's wheel can be seen. Dark brown slip has been preserved in the hollows of the relief and also on the edges of the ornament. The relief, a longish shape, depicts a zoomorphic head of an animal, but of what kind it is

hard to determine (tab. 3.4, 2:6; fig. 3.4, 18). The long relief bands receding back with elongated bulbs at the base are more reminiscent of horns than ears. The first thing that comes to mind is that this is a depiction of some sort of horned animal like an *arkhar* (steppe sheep, *ovis orientalis vignei* Blyth, 1841) as the publication cited also states. However, there are several features that suggest it may be a fantastic beast of prey of the griffin type – the exaggerated details of the way in which the head is shaped, such as the markedly protuberant and bent eyebrows, connected by a semicircle in relief in the entre, the hollow eyes, two almost imperceptible reliefs above the eyebrows, meeting with rounded and pointed ends that stick upwards (these reliefs are faintly reminiscent of the comma or animal-style). One further detail of this depiction attracts attention, and that is the relief line bent into a semicircle, projecting from the animal's mouth. It can be seen easily from the left, but is hard to see from the right. It gives the impression that the creature is biting a circle or that a bit has been put on it.[33]

Finally, there is one more ornament in the shape of an anthropomorphic face that was found in the surroundings of Jandavlattepa and brought by a local inhabitant.[34] The terracotta is a greyish-yellow colour, almost circular in shape (diameter 2.9 × 3.2 cm,

**Fig. 3.4, 19** Human face, fragment of a terracotta figurine, accidental find.

---

31  Al'baum 1960, fig. 5; Zav'yalov 2008, p. 105, fig. 45, tab. 6, 3, 4.
32  A drawing and short description has been published in the preliminary excavation report, cf. Stančo 2006b, p. 168, fig. 4.
33  I have seen a similar ornament, but with a clearer imprint, among photographs of the material from the ancient city of Balkh (Baktra), which Bertille Lyonnet kindly showed me. In the photo a semicircular part of a circle could be clearly seen in the creature's mouth. The material has not been published.
34  According to the local inhabitant who brought the ornament, it was found in Kurgantepa, which is spread along the bank of the river Sherabad Darya, about a kilometre east of Jandavlattepa. An inspection of this site, which has been half flooded by the river, yielded material that can be classified as coming from the early Middle Ages.

**Fig. 3.4, 20** An old man face, applique on the neck of a small juf, Sector 20.

height of relief 2.2 cm). On the rear side the surface is concave, and white particles can be seen in the structure. There are eyes, created schematically with a wide horizontal shape, a nose broad at the base, and a slightly pointed chin (fig. 3.4, *19*). The ornament in all likelihood decorated a ceramic vessel or other item.

Of especial interest is a find from the Citadel (sector 20). It is the neck of a small jug (8 × 9.4 cm) in the shape of a bearded head (tab. 3.4, 1:7; fig. 3.4, *20*). We shall not spend time here in a detailed description of the find and the search for an analogy – a separate article has been devoted to the object.[35] It is worth adding that anthropomorphic vessels are sometimes found in metalwork, and it is not impossible that the clay examples may have been copying metal vessels. A small jug from Count Orlov's collection in the Hermitage collections (inv. S 60) is of interest in this respect.[36]

## Imprints of gems and seals on ceramics

During the process of cleaning the eastern slope of the gulley that adjoins the site at its eastern to north-eastern edge, two fragments were found that bear the imprints of gems and small seals. The first of them is the shoulder of a ceramic vessel of fairly large proportions (an amphora?) made on a potter's wheel, with light slip on its outer surface. The fragment was found in a complex with ceramics from the Kushan

period and coins from Vima Kadphises. The imprint has been made on an area that projects slightly, in the place where the shoulder meets the base of the neck. Under the imprint are two deep parallel lines engraved on the body of the vessel, 0.6 cm apart. The lines themselves are 0.2 cm wide. The thickness of the wall of the vessel is 1.3 cm in the lower part and 0.6 cm in the upper part, at the level of the neck. The fragment is pinkish with a compact shard and high-quality, even firing.

The actual imprint is oval in shape and deep, and the depiction was on the convex side of the stone (cobochone?). On the other side the raw clay has sagged and cracked in this area. There were grain imprints around the circumference of the gem, in the form of numerous round shallow indentations. The height is 1.35 cm and the width 1.13 cm. The depiction is on a vertical axis. There is a figure of a naked Eros, stepping to the right, with a helmet on his head. Judging by the shallow reliefs on the upper and rear side of the helmet, it was decorated with a feather (fig. 3.4, *21*). A small wing projects horizontally from the line of the shoulders, and then falls downward. Eros' right hand is stretched out in front of him, and holds the handle of a kantharos-type vessel on a plinth.

The stylistic characteristics of the depiction indicate that the gem belonged to the Greco-Roman world. Portrayals of a walking Eros, holding various objects (attributes) in his hand, are fairly popular

**Fig. 3.4, 21** Standing figure of Eros, imprint of a gem on a ceramic vessel.

35 Stančo 2006a, pp. 106–109, tab. IV–V.
36 Orbeli – Trever 1935, pl. 42–43; Trever – Lukonin 1987, no. 28, p. 93, 94, 115, 116, pl. 84–87; *Les Perses sassanides* 2006, no. 46.

in Greco-Roman glyptic, and mostly date from the 1st – 2nd century AD.[37] There is a close analogy to this image in a red chalcedony gem from the Masson collection (BM, 1880-3552). The naked figure of Eros stepping to the left (on a stone) is depicted on an oval shield shape. In his outstretched left hand he has an item which in profile is close to the kantharos on the Jandavlattepa example, and in his right hand he has the branch of a plant.[38] A similar composition can be found on two gems from the John Marshall collection, one of which features a winged figure (Eros) and the other a figure with no wings.[39]

The image of Eros reached the territory of Bactria during the Hellenistic period, but continued to gain broad popularity during the subsequent periods. Depictions of Eros can be seen both in terracotta, as is shown by these two fragments with reliefs on the subject of Eros' banquets,[40] and in metalwork.[41]

The second object with an imprint is a fragment of terracotta that is flat on both sides, greyish-yellow in colour, with a rough structure. It may be a fragment of fired brick, 4.5 cm thick. It has a fairly smooth surface, on which an imprint has been created with sharp, straight edges, possibly using a metal stamp. The imprint is oval and 2.2 cm by 2 cm. In the centre is the figure of a horned animal stepping to the right (an arkhar? see above) with large horns bent behind into a semicircle (fig. 3.4, 22). One of its front legs is raised, the tail is short, and there is a curved relief to the left over the animal's hindquarters – a depiction of a crescent moon with horns pointing upwards. Between the animal's legs there is a small shrub, in the form of a little pine tree.

The image of a stepping goat has been one of the most widespread on Central Asian seals since ancient times. The subject enjoyed considerable popularity during the Kushan era. We shall not include all the analogies here, since there are so many of them, but note only that the closest composition can be seen on a stone pendant from a burial ground in the Stalinabad uplands.[42] The goat holds a significant place in the religious ideologies of the ancient societies of the Central Asian cultural region.[43] Cults connected with the goat can be found as far back as the Mousterian, as is shown

**Fig. 3.4, 22** A horned animal, imprint of a gem or other object on a ceramic vessel.

by materials from the Teshik-Tash cave.[44] It would also be possible to list many Stone Age sites (the paintings in Zarautsay), the ancient painted ceramics of Iran (Sialk 2),[45] metalwork objects and glyptics from sites in the Oxus valley, early ancient works and those from the Kushan period and early Middle Ages. The goat figured in religion and ritual until recent times, which provides us with an ethnographical comparison.[46]

The composition on the Jandavlattepa terracotta, which includes depictions of a lunar symbol and a tree, associated the image of a goat with the tree of life, which is one of the most widespread themes in the ancient metalwork of Central Asia. In Bactria this composition has an analogy from many years earlier in a cylindrical seal from Jarkutan, made from lime and dated to the last phase of the Sapalli culture (11th–10th century BC).[47] In the composition from Jandavlattepa the lunar system is complemented by a shape consisting of horns bent into a semicircle, which to the same extent symbolises Luna and the lunar cult.[48]

The last example of gem imprint was found in the Sector 07, square 07B, as part of a large storage jar.

[37] Furtwangler 1900, pl. XXVIII, 21, 22; Walters 1926, pl. XX, 1478; Fossing 1929, pl. X, 761, 763.
[38] Callieri 1997, pp. 50–51, pl. 2, cat. no. 1.20. The author believes that the figure is holding the same helmet (true, there is a question mark here), and we assume that the position of the hand is the same, and that he is holding it in the same way, i.e. by the hand, turned upside down.
[39] Ibid. pl. 2, cat. no. 1.22, cat. no. 1.23.
[40] Abdullaev 2005, pp. 238–239, fig. 35, 36.
[41] Litvinskiy – Pichikyan 1979, no. 2
[42] Litvinskiy 1958, pp. 38–43, fig. 3, 5.
[43] Andreev 1958.
[44] Okladnikov 1949, pp. 78–79; Bader 1978, pp. 40–46.
[45] Ghirshman 1954, pp. 30–33.
[46] Litvinskiy 1981, p. 110.
[47] Meytarchiyan 1984, pp. 41–45, fig. 1; For zoomorphic depictions on Bronze Age ceramics in southern Uzbekistan see Rakhmanov 1981, pp. 27–30.
[48] Fox 1928; Hentze 1932; Derchain et alii 1962; Ceren 1976.

The imprint was placed close to rim. It depicts a deer facing right (tab. 3.4, 2:7).

Concluding this brief overview of terracotta depictions from Jandavlattepa, it is worth adding that the terracotta art in the region in question is represented by totally traditional examples of the art of the Kushan and late Kushan periods. As we have shown, many examples of terracotta figurines, as well as applied ornaments on vessels, have close analogies in the surrounding archaeological sites of northern Bactria. In many ways they reflect the general trends in the development of the artistic figurative traditions of the region.

## Bibliography

Abdullaev, K. (1998): Buddhist Terracotta plastic Art in Northern Bactria, *Silk Road Art and Arhaeology*, vol. 5.

Abdullaev, K. (2003): Nana in Bactrian Art, *Silk Road Art and Archaeology*, vol. 9, pp. 15–38.

Abdullaev, K. (2005): New Finds of Pre-Kushan and Early Kushan Plastic Art in Northern Bactria and the Khalchayan Reliefs, *Parthica* 6, 2004, Pisa – Roma.

Abdullaev, K. (2005a): Les motifs dionysiaques dans l'art de la Bactriane et la Sogdiane, in: *Afghanistan ancien carrefour entre l'est et l'ouest*, ed. Bopearachchi, O. – Boussac M.-F., Turnhout, pp. 227–257.

Abdullaev, K. – Pidaev, Sh. (1989): Rannekushanskaya terrakovaya plastika iz Mirzakultepa, *Obshchestvennye nauky v Uzbekistane* 9/1989, pp. 51–57.

Al'baum, L. I. (1960): *Balalyk-tepe*. Tashkent.

Andreev. M. S. (1978): Tadzhiki doliny Khuf (verkhov'ya Amudar'i), Stalinabad.

*Antiquities of Southern Uzbekistan*, Catalogue, The Khamza Fine Art Research Centre – Soka University, 1991.

Bader. O. N. (1978): Elementy kul'ta svetil v paleolite, in: *Drevnyaya Rus' i slavyane*, Moscow, pp. 40–46.

Belenickiy, A. M. (1978): Kon' v kultakh i ideologicheskykh predstavleniyakh narodov Sredney Azii i evropeyskykh stepey v drevnosti i rannem srednevekov'e, *Kratkie soobshcheniya Instituta arkheologii*, vol. 154, Moscow, pp. 31–39.

Belenickiy, A. M. (1948): Khuttal'skaya loshad' v legende i v istoricheskom predanii, Sovetskaya etnografiya 4, pp. 162–168.

Callieri, P.-F. (1997): *Seals and Sealings from the North-West of the Indian Subcontinent and Afghanistan (4th century BC – 11th century AD)*. Naples.

Ceren, E. (1976): *Lunniy bog*, Moscow.

Dajens, B. (1964): *Fragments de sculpture inedits*, MDAFA, vol. XIX, Paris.

Dalton, O. M. (1964): *The Treasure of the Oxus. With Other Examples of Early Oriental Metal Work*, London.

*Dal'verzintepa. Kushanskiy gorod na yuge Uzbekistana*. Pugachenkova, G. A. – Rtveladze, E. V. (eds.).Tashkent, 1978.

Dani, A. H. (1966): Shaikhan Dheri Excavation (1963 and 1964 seasons), *Ancient Pakistan* II, 1965–66, pp. 17–120.

*Drevneyshie gosudarstva Kavkaza i Sredney Azii*. Koshelenko, G. A. (ed.). Moscow, 1985.

Fox, H. M. (1928): *Selene: or Sex and the moon*, London.

*Forgotten Empire. The World of Ancient Persia*. Curtis, J. – Tallis, N. (eds.). University of Calfornia Press, Berkeley – Los Angeles, 2005.

Fossing, P. (1929): *Catalogue of the Antique Engraved Gems and Cameos*. The Thorvaldsen Museum, Copenhagen.

Furtwängler, A. (1900): *Die antiken Gemmen. Geschichte der Steine im klassischen Altertum*, Leipzig – Berlin.

Ghirshman, R. (1954): *Iran from the earliest times to the Islamic conquest*. Harmondsworth.

Göbl, R. (1984): *System und Chronologie der Munzpragung des Kusanreiches*, Wien.

Gupte R.S. (SD): *Iconography of the Hindu, Buddhist and Jains.*

Hentze, C. 2006 (1932): *Mythes et symbols lunaires*, Anvers.

Derchain, Ph. et alii (1962): *La lune. Mythes et rites*, Paris.

Huff, D. (1995): An unusual type of terra-cotta figurine from north Bactria, in: *In the Land of the Griphons*. A. Invernizzi, A. (ed.). Florence.

Huff, D. – Pidaev, Ch. – Chaydoullaev, Ch. (2001): Uzbek-German archaeological researches in the Surkhan Darya region, in: *La Bactriane au Carrefour des routes et des civilizations de l'Asie central*, Leriche, P. et al. (eds.), Paris, pp. 219–233.

Kozlovskiy, V. A. – Nekrasova, Ye. G. (1976): Stratigraficheskiy shurf na Citadeli Drevnego Termeza, in: *Baktriyskie drevnosti*, Leningrad, pp. 30–39.

*Les Perses sassanides. Fastes d'un empire oublie (224–642)*, catalogue, Paris musees, Edition Findakly, 2006, no. 46.

Litvinskiy, B. A. (1958): Predmety iz pogrebeniya na Stalinabadskikh kholmakh, in: *Soobshcheniya Respublikanskogo istoriko-kraevednogo muzeya Tadzhitskoy SSR*, Stalinabad, pp. 38–43.

Litvinskiy, B. A. (1981): Semantika drevnikh verovaniy i obrayadov pamirtsev, in: *Srednyaya Aziya i eyo sosedi v drevnosti i srednevekov'e*, Moscow.

Litvinskiy, B. A. – Pichikyan, I. R. (1979): Kushanskie eroty, *Vestnik drvney istorii* 148/2, pp. 89–109.

Marshall, J. (1951): *Taxila*, (3. vols), Cambridge.

Masson, M. E. (1940): Gorodishche Starogo Termeza i ikh izuchenie, in: *Termezskaya arheologicheskaya kompleksnaya ekspeditsiya (TAKE)*, ser.I, Istoriya, arheologiya. Tashkent.

Meunie, J. (1942): *Shotorak*, MDAFA, vol. X, Paris.

Meytarchiyan, M. (1984): Amulet epokhy bronzy s poseleniya Jarkutan, *Istoriya materialnoy kultury Uzbekistana* 19, pp. 41–45.

Mkrtychev, T. (2002): *Buddiyskoe iskusstvo Sredney Azii*. Moskva.

Okladnikov, A. P. (1949): Issledovanie must'erskoy stoyanki i pogrebeniye neandertal'tsa v grote Teshik-Tash, Yuzhnyy Uzbekistan", in: *Teshik-Tash, paleoliticheskij chelovek*, pp. 7–85.

Orbeli, J. – Trever, C. (1935): *Orfererie sasanide: objets en or, argent et bronze*, Moscow-Leningrad.

Pugachenkova, G. A. (1973): Novye dannye o khudozhestvennoy kul'ture Baktrii, in: *Iz istorii antichnoy kul'tury Uzbekistana*, Tashkent.

Pugachenkova, G. A. (1978): *Les Trsors de Dalverzintepe*, Leningrad, 1978.

Pugachenkova, G. A. (1991): Novye dannye o khudozhestvennoy kul'ture Baktrii", in: *Iz istorii antichnoy kul'tury Uzbekistana*, pp. 78–133.

Rakhmanov, U. (1981): Zoomorfnye izobrazheniya na keramike poseleniya epokhy bronzy Bustan 4, *Istoriya materialnoy kultury Uzbekistana* 16, pp. 27–30.

Rosenfield, J. (1967): *The Dynastic Art of the Kushans*, Los-Angeles – Berkley, 1967.

Schlumberger, D. (1952): *Le temple de Surkh Kotal en Bactriane*, JA.

Sims-Williams, N. – Cribb, J. (1996): A New Bactrian Inscription of Kanishka of the Great, *Silk Road Art and Archaeology*, vol. 4, 1995/96, pp. 77–79.

Stančo, L. (2006a): Jug with a human face from Jandavlattepa, *Studia Hercynia* X, pp. 106–109, tab. IV-V.

Stančo, L. (2006b): Jandavlattepa 2005. Preliminary excavation report, *Studia Hercynia* X, pp. 167–172.

Staviskiy, B. Ya. (1974): *Iskusstvo Sredney Azii*. Moscow.

Tissot F. (1987): *Gandhara*. Paris.

*The Route of Buddhist Art. The Great Exhibition of Silk Road Civilizations*. Nara, 1988.

Toktabay, A. (2004): *Kul't konya u Kazakhov*, Almaty.

Trever, K. V. – Lukonin, V.G. (1987): Sasanidskoe serebro, in: *Sobranie Gosudarstvennogo Ermitazha: khudozhestvennaya kul'tura Irana III–VIII vekov*, Moscow.

Burgunov, B. (1973): K izucheniyu Ayrtama, in: *Iz istorii antichnoy kul'tury Uzbekistana*, Tashkent, pp. 52–77.

Vyatkina, K. V. (1968): Kul't konya u mongol'skikh narodov, *Sovetskaya etnografiya* 6, pp. 117–122.

Vyaz'mitina, M. I. (1945): Keramika Ayrtama vremeni Kushanov, in: *TAKE II*, pp. 35–64.

Walters, H. B. (1926): *Catalogue of Engraved Gems, Greek, Etruscan and Roman in the British Museum*, London.

Wheeler, M. (1962): *Charsada. A Metropolis of the North-West Frontier*, Oxford.

Zav'yalov V. A. – Osipov, V. I. (1976): Raskopki zhilogo kompleksa na gorodishche Zar-tepe v 1973 g., *Baktriyskie drevnosti*, Leningrad, pp. 51–58.

Zav'yalov V. A. (2008): *Kushanshakhr pri sasanidakh. Po materialam raskopok na gorodishche Zar-tepa*, Saint Peterburg.

# 3.5 Numismatic finds (2002–2006)

*Kazim Abdullaev*

The basis of this published collection consists of coins found in archaeological layers and on the surface of the site of the ancient settlement of Jandavlattepa, as well as at nearby monuments in the Sherabad oasis. In order to provide a complete representation of the archaeological context of the numismatic finds, we give a brief description of the objects of the excavations.

The object, Sector 2A, is a stratification trench in the north-east part of site, near the old trench executed by the German-Uzbek Expedition in 1993.[1] The trench was begun in 2003 and completed in 2006. During works on Sector 2? all the layers of cultural accumulations were investigated, beginning from the Kushano-Sassanian layers of the upper level down to the subsoil, i.e. prior to the beginning of the first layers of the lower level of habitation. It was discovered that the settlement was created and functioned not in the Achaemenid period as was assumed on the basis of preliminary research[2], but since the late Bronze and early Iron age. The numismatic finds in this sector can be divided into two categories: coins from layers, and those from the bottom of the gulley. Given that seasonal waters washed away the top layers, carrying with them coins, fragments of pottery and other objects, we cannot consider these finds to have come from authentic "untouched" layers. If we wish to ascertain the origin of such coins we must take into account the approximate course of the seasonal waters. As a rule, the description of such coin finds state that they come from deposited layers. Such an origin is, suggested by, for example, the fact, that a cultural level belonging to the early Hellenistic period, in a channel (at the bottom of a gulley) provided coins from the Kushan period. The second category, which we presume to be the more authentic, comprises layers untouched by earth flows, running horizontally across up to the surface of the slope.

Sector 07 (Shakhristan) was found on excavation to contain a monumental construction in mud bricks from the late Kushan period. The disposition of the layers in certain sections has been disturbed by 19th and early 20th century burials. Finds of Hellenistic coins in these layers can be considered to have been removed from earlier layers.

Sector 20 (Citadel): archaeological excavations of this object have provided plentiful material, essentially from the Kushano-Sassanian period. The architectural remains of the most recent period of inhabitation of this part of Jandavlattepa, mostly mud brick constructions, are featureless and consist of dwelling rooms, as well as structures where handicraft (weaving) was possibly carried out. This area has yielded numerous copper coins of low face value / denomination but mostly in bad condition, and belonging in the main to the Kushano-Sassanian period.

Several coins have been found on the surface of archaeological sites during occasional surveys. In particular, three copper coins of a satisfactory condition have been found on the site Talashkan 2 (Sherabad district). One copper coin, presumably of Samanid mint has been picked up on the surface of Khaita-badtepa (Jarkurgan District).

## Catalogue

### Bactria: Greco-Bactrian Kings

**Euthydemus I (c. 230–200 BC)**
1. Euthydemus
AE khalk
obverse: Bearded head of Heracles to the right
reverse: A horse prancing to the right; the legend is legible only in the bottom horizontal line: [EY]ΘΔYHMOY
d. 11.5 mm; th. 5.0 mm; weight 9.5 g; die axes: 45 degrees

---

[1]  Huff – Pidaev – Shaydullaev 2001, pp. 219–233.
[2]  Rtveladze – Khakimov 1973, p. 14; Pidaev 1974, p. 33.

Jandavlattepa 2005, 04. X, small find no. 20Y002.VIII.[3]

figs. 3.5, *1** (obverse) and 3.5, *2** (reverse)

## Demetrius (200–190 BC)

2. Demetrius, bronze

obverse: A diademed bust of the king to the right, wearing an elephant's scalp

reverse: A frontally standing figure of Artemis (?), indistinct; to the left a vertical line, not clear

d. 29.7 mm; th. 5.4 mm, weight 21.5 g

Jandavlattepa 2002, 21.X; small find no. 07B000.I

figs. 3.5, *3** (obverse) and 3.5, *4** (reverse)

## Eucratides (170–145 BC)

3. Eucratides, a square bronze coin

obverse: Bust of the king to the right, diademed and helmeted; an indiscernible legend in Greek along the square's sides

reverse: Mounted Dioscuri to the right (?), indiscernible legend in Kharoshti script

21.5 × 20.0 mm, th. 0.5 mm, weight 7.4 g

Jandavlattepa 2003, Sector 2a, a secondarily deposited layer

figs. 3.5, *5** (obverse) and 3.5, *6** (reverse)

## Graeco-Bactria, general

4. Graeco-Bactria, general, bronze

obverse: Head of the king to the right

reverse: Illegible due to strong wear

d. 20.0 mm, th. 3.5 mm, weight 3.1 g

Jandavlattepa 2005, an accidental surface find

figs. 3.5, *7** (obverse) and 3.5, *8** (reverse)

## Heliocles – Imitation of tetradrachms
## (so called "barbarous Heliocles")

5. Heliocles, An imitation of a tetradrachm (so called "barbarous Heliocles")

obverse: A bust of the king (advanced age), diademed and clad in himation, to the right

reverse: A figure of Zeus standing frontally, clad in himation; in his right hand he holds a winged thunderbolt, resting his left hand on a long sceptre; a legend in three lines: to the right vertically: ΒΑΣΙΛΕΩΣ; to the left vertically ΗΛΙΟΚΛΕΟΥ; below transversely ΔΙΚΑΙΟΥ; The diagonal beams of "kappa" are truncated and almost perpendicular to the vertical beam; under the thunderbolt there is a monogram in the form of a "Λ," inscribed inside a "Π"; sigma in the form of an angular "C."

d. 31.5–32.1 mm, th. 5.0 mm, weight 15.3 g

Jandavlattepa 2003, 13.X; Sector 2A, a layer of 360 cm from the fixed points

figs. 3.5, *9** (obverse) and 3.5, *10** (reverse)

6. Heliocles, An imitation of a tetradrachm (so called "barbarous Heliocles")

obverse: A bust of the king (young age) to the right

reverse: A monogram in the form of a Π with an alpha (A) inscribed inside; sigma in the legend has the normative form

d. 28.5–29.5 mm, th. 4.8 mm, weight 15.2 g

Jandavlattepa 2003, 11.X; Sector 2A, a layer of 350 cm from the original surface

figs. 3.5, *11** (obverse) and 3.5, *12** (reverse)

7. Heliocles, An imitation of a tetradrachm (so called "barbarous Heliocles")

"Sigma" in the legend is transformed in a square "C," "kappa" is represented in the form of a vertical stick with two short shoots departing perpendicularly

d. 31.2–29.0 mm, th. 3.3 mm, weight 11.0 g

Jandavlattepa 2005, the western slope of a ravine, under the monumental wall, in a layer with ceramics of early Kushan period

figs. 3.5, *13** (obverse) and 3.5, *14** (reverse)

8. Heliocles, An imitation of a tetradrachm (so called "barbarous Heliocles")

Bad state of preservation, only some details of the image of a figure of Zeus with a thunderbolt are visible on the obverse; the legend is indiscernible, a monogram under the thunderbolt has the form of an overturned Russian letter «Ш»

d. 32.5 mm, th. 7.5 mm, weight 16.2 g

Jandavlattepa 2005, accidental find, a bottom of a ravine, in a deposited layer

figs. 3.5, *15** (obverse) and 3.5, *16** (reverse)

9. Heliocles, An imitation of a tetradrachm (so called "barbarous Heliocles")

Bad state of preservation

obverse: The only visible elements are the lower part of a face in profile to the right with a pointed chin and the outline of a himation on the shoulder

reverse: Some letters of a legend are preserved: to the left vertically ...ΛΙΙΛ... to the right ...ΛΕ...; bellow there are only two letters preserved (...ΙΥ) with an "omicron" as a relief point between them

d. 31.1 mm, th. 1.8 mm, weight 8.9 g

Jandavlattepa 2003, an accidental find, north-eastern part of the site (ravine)

figs. 3.5, *17** (obverse) and 3.5, *18** (reverse)

10. Heliocles, an imitation of a tetradrachm (so called "barbarous Heliocles")

A bad state of preservation, strongly corroded, the images and the legend are not distinguishable

d. 30.0–30.5 mm, th. 7.0 mm, weight 18.7 g

Jandavlattepa 2005, an accidental find, the bottom of the ravine – a secondarily deposited layer

---

3   The abbreviations employed in the catalogue are the following ones: d. = diameter; th. = thickness. The last line after the description refers to the find circumstances: the site and the year of the respective excavation season. If the find comes from a layer, we record the trench number and the date of the find (the day in the Arabic numbers and the month in the roman ones). All the published coins are minted in a copper alloy (bronze) with the exception of the 83 minted in silver. A question mark following the coin's number means that it could not be defined due to the bad state of preservation or that the definition remains uncertain.

## Heliocles – imitation of a drachma

11. An Imitation of a Heliocles drachma
obverse: A bust of the king in a diadem to the right, the upper part of the hairdo above the diadem is rendered in the form of rounded reliefs
reverse: A horse prancing to the left; the image is hardly discernible, the legend is not legible
d. 18.3 mm, th. 3.0 mm, weight 4.4 g
Jandavlattepa 2003, small find no. 07C009.VI
figs. 3.5, *19*\* (obverse) and 3.5, *20*\* (reverse)

## Soter Megas (80–105)

12. Soter Megas
obverse: A bust of the king to the right, diademed and radiated, the right hand is lifted upwards with a gesture of power, treatment of hairdo is not clear
reverse: The mounted king to the right, the long ribbons of the diadem behind his head; in a hand held out above the horse's mane he holds an attribute (an axe?); a hardly discernible tamga below in the right field; the circular legend is indiscernible
d. 20.5 mm, th. 4.2 mm, weight 8.2 g
Jandavlattepa 2005, 06.10, Sector 02A, a bottom of the ravine, a secondarily deposited layer

13. Soter Megas
obverse: A bust of the diademed king to the right
reverse: The king on horseback to the right, the image is poorly discernible
d. 20.6 mm, th. 4.1 mm, weight 8.4 g
Jandavlattepa 2003, 01.X; Sector 02A, 90 cm from the original surface
figs. 3.5, *21*\* (obverse) and 3.5, *22*\* (reverse)

14. Soter Megas
obverse: A bust of the king to the right, holding an attribute in his held-out hand.
reverse: The mounted king to the right, bad state of preservation
d. 21.3 mm, th. 4.5 mm, weight 8.5 g
Jandavlattepa 2002, Sector 04 (Gate), east part, the upper layer
figs. 3.5, *23*\* (obverse) and 3.5, *24*\* (reverse)

15. Soter Megas
obverse: Poor state of preservation, only the contours of the image are distinguishable
d. 21.3 mm, th. 4.6 mm, weight 8.8 g
Jandavlattepa 2002, Sector 08

16. Soter Megas
Bad state of preservation; only the contours of the image are distinguishable
obverse: bust of the king to the right with the right hand extended forward
reverse: The mounted king to the right, long ribbons of a diadem behind his head
d. 20.7 mm, th. 4.0 mm, weight 8.3 g
Jandavlattepa 2002, 10.X; Sector 08, small find no. 08A007.I, depth 78 cm
figs. 3.5, *25*\* (obverse) and 3.5, *26*\* (reverse)

17. Soter Megas
Bad preservation, only scarce traces of images visible
d. 19.0–20.0 mm, thick. 5.6 mm, weight 6.0 g
Jandavlattepa 2005, 06.X., Sector 02A, bottom of the ravine, secondarily deposited layer (caused by seasonal rain)

18. Soter Megas
obverse: A bust of the king, curls of hair are intercepted by a diadem
d. 21.4 mm, th. 6.0 mm, weight 9.0 g
Jandavlattepa 2005, an accidental surface find
figs. 3.5, *27*\* (obverse) and 3.5, *28*\* (reverse)

19. Soter Megas
obverse: A bust of the king to the right, diademed.
reverse: The mounted king to the right, diademed, one arm held out forward; he holds an attribute (an axe?)
The legend around the coin's circumference and a tamga are not distinguishable
d. 20.0 mm, th. 4.0 m, weight 8.2 g
Jandavlattepa 2005, an accidental surface find
figs. 3.5, *29*\* (obverse) and 3.5, *30*\* (reverse)

20. Soter Megas
obverse: A bust of the diademed king to the right
reverse: The mounted king to the right, long fluttering ribbons of a diadem behind his back, a tamga in the right bottom field; a horizontal line; only some letters of a circular legend are legible: ...OTEP ... ΛΕΩΣ
d. 20.2–21.2, th. 4.1 mm, weight 6.9 g
Jandavlattepa 2005, an accidental surface find
figs. 3.5, *31*\* (obverse) and 3.5, *32*\* (reverse)

21. Soter Megas
d. 23.3 mm, 5.9 mm, weight 9.1 g
Jandavlattepa 2006, Sector 2a, 1, layer no. 16
figs. 3.5, *33*\* (obverse) and 3.5, *34*\* (reverse)

22. Soter Megas, a coin of fine face value
obverse: A bust of the king to the right; the image is barely visible
reverse: The king on the horseback to the right, the hand extends forward, holds an attribute (axe?); a tamga in the left bottom field
d. 13.0 mm, th. 1.4 mm, weight 1.4 g
Jandavlattepa 2003, an accidental surface find
figs. 3.5, *35*\* (obverse) and 3.5, *36*\* (reverse)

## Vima Kadphises (105–127 AD)

23. Vima Kadphises
obverse: The king, standing frontally with his head turned to the left and wearing a diadem and a high headdress, is sacrifying at an altar. To the left there is a trident combined with an axe (tresula), to the right a club. The legend around is indiscernible.
reverse: Shiva facing frontally; wears headdress and a draped cloak over his shoulder; holds a trident in the right hand; a bull (Nandi) to the right, behind him
d. 30.3 mm, th. 5.0 mm, weight 16.3 g

Jandavlattepa 2005, 05.X; in the western slope of the ravine, in a construction of mud bricks of a monumental structure
figs. 3.5, *37** (obverse) and 3.5, *38** (reverse)

24. Vima Kadphises
d. 27.6–29.1 mm, th. 3.7 mm, weight 15.2 g
Jandavlattepa 2005, 29.IX; Square 09D; small find no.09D001.II
figs. 3.5, *39** (obverse) and 3.5, *40** (reverse)

## Kanishka I (127/8–147 AD)
25. Kanishka I
obverse: The king standing frontally with his head turned to the left, sacrificing at an altar, he wears a diadem and is clad in a coat, trousers and a cloak
reverse: Wind-god (Oado) running to the left, in both hands holds the ends of his garment (cloak) which flutter around him
d. 24.0–25.2 mm, th. 4.7 mm, weight 15.8 g
Jandavlattepa 2005, 03.X, Sector 02A, 1, layer no. 16
figs. 3.5, *41** (obverse) and 3.5, *42** (reverse)

26. Kanishka I
d. 24.1–26.5 mm, th. 5.4 mm, weight 16.2 g
Jandavlattepa 2003, 13.X, Sector 02A, a layer of 360 cm from the original surface
figs. 3.5, *43** (obverse) and 3.5, *44** (reverse)

27. Kanishka I
reverse: A standing figure of a deity (Mao?) to the left with a hand extended forward
d. 24.7 mm, th. 4.8 mm, weight 15.5 g
Jandavlattepa 2005, an accidental surface find
figs. 3.5, *45** (obverse) and 3.5, *46** (reverse)

28. Kanishka I
obverse: A standing figure of the king to the left, the upper part of the image is lost
reverse: A standing figure of a deity to the left; behind him an inscription MAO; not integrally preserved: the right upper part is lost
d. 23.5, thick. 2.4 mm, weight 5.9 g
Jandavlattepa 2003, Square 09A, small find no. 09A015.I
figs. 3.5, *47** (obverse) and 3.5, *48** (reverse)

29. Kanishka I
reverse: A standing figure to the left (?)
d. 25.1 mm, th. 4.3 mm, weight 10.9 g
Jandavlattepa 2005, an accidental surface find
figs. 3.5, *49** (obverse) and 3.5, *50** (reverse)

## Huvishka (circa 152–192 AD)
30. Huvishka
obverse: The king, frontally, half reclining on the throne
reverse: A standing figure of a deity, clad in a coat (Mao?), in the held-out right hand holds a wreath or diadem; below is a tamga with four vertical dents in the top part
d. 22.4–23.4 mm, thick. 3.2 mm, weight 11.4 g
Jandavlattepa 2005, an accidental surface find
figs. 3.5, *51** (obverse) and 3.5, *52 ** (reverse)

31. Huvishka
obverse: The image is not clear
reverse: A standing figure of a deity to the left (Mao?), in the held-out right hand holds a wreath, a tamga below
d. 23.1–22.5 mm, th. 5.0 mm, weight 12.2 g
Jandavlattepa 2005, 03.X, sector 2a, 1, layer no. 15
figs. 3.5, *53** (obverse) and 3.5, *54** (reverse)

32. Huvishka
obverse: The king riding an elephant to the right
reverse: A figure of a standing deity to the left
d. 24.9 mm, th. 5.7 mm, weight 15.8 g
Jandavlattepa 2002, Sector 04, surface layer of the Gate area (on the ramp)
figs. 3.5, *55** (obverse) and 3.5, *56** (reverse)

## Vasudeva I (192–225)
33. Vasudeva I
obverse: The king offering at an altar to the left, helmeted and diademed, the right arm extended over the altar while holding a spear in the left hand
reverse: Shiva facing frontally, bull Nandi behind him, a tamga in the right field
d. 22.4 mm, th. 3.3 mm, weight 9.1 g
Jandavlattepa 2005, 14.X, Sector 02a, an accidental find in the ravine, deposited layer
figs. 3.5, *57** (obverse) and 3.5, *58** (reverse)

34. Vasudeva I
d. 20.0–21.0 mm, th. 2.2 mm, weight 6.2 g
Jandavlattepa 2003, Square 07D, small find no. 07D008.I
figs. 3.5, *59** (obverse) and 3.5, *60** (reverse)

35. Vasudeva I
d. 22.5 mm, th. 3.0, weight 7.9 g
Jandavlattepa 2005, 14.X, 2a, an accidental find in the ravine, deposited layer
figs. 3.5, *61** (obverse) and 3.5, *62** (reverse)

36. Vasudeva I
d. 20.5–22.4 mm, th. 4.2 mm, weight 7.7 g
Jandavlattepa 2005, 11.X, a bottom of the ravine, deposited layer
figs. 3.5, *63** (obverse) and 3.5, *64** (reverse)

37. Vasudeva I
d. 18.5, th. 4.4 mm, weight 5.9 g
Jandavlattepa 2003, Sector 7C, small find no. 07C010.II
figs. 3.5, *65** (obverse) and 3.5, *66** (reverse)

38. Vasudeva I
d. 21.5, th. 4.2 mm, weight 9.4 g
Jandavlattepa 2005, an accidental surface find
figs. 3.5, *67** (obverse) and 3.5, *68** (reverse)

39. Vasudeva I
d. 21.0 mm, th. 5.1 mm, weight 8.6 g
Jandavlattepa 2003, 20.X; small find no. 7C009.VII
figs. 3.5, *69** (obverse) and 3.5, *70** (reverse)

40. Vasudeva I
obverse: The diademed and helmeted king standing to the right in front of an altar in the form of a plinth in the top and the bottom part; the king's holds his right arm out over the altar; the left hand is lifted upwards resting on a spear with ends of a ribbon below
reverse: Shiva holding a trisula sceptre in his left hand in front of the bull Nandi; separate letters of a circular legend
d. 22.6–24.5 mm, th. 3.5 mm, weight 9.8 g
Jandavlattepa 2005, an accidental surface find
figs. 3.5, *71** (obverse) and 3.5, *72** (reverse)

41. Vasudeva I
obverse: The king holds right hand over altar to the left
reverse: Shiva in front of bull Nandi, barely visible
d. 19.0, th. 3.9 mm, weight 5.5 g
Jandavlattepa 2003, an accidental surface find
figs. 3.5, *73** (obverse) and 3.5, *74** (reverse)

42. Vasudeva I
d. 20.3–21.4 mm, th. 3.5 mm, weight 8.1 g
Jandavlattepa 2003, 24.X; Sector 02a, secondarily deposited layer
figs. 3.5, *75** (obverse) and 3.5, *76** (reverse)

43. Vasudeva I
d. 20.0–21.0 mm, th. 4.0 mm, weight 7.8 g
Jandavlattepa 2003, small find no. 7C002.III

44. Vasudeva I
Coin has an irregular form
d. 21.5–18.0 mm, th. 3.0 mm, weight 6.2 g
Jandavlattepa 2005, 3.X; Sector 02A, 1, layer no. 15
figs. 3.5, *77** (obverse) and 3.5, *78** (reverse)

45. Vasudeva I
d. 20.3 mm, th. 3.1 mm, weight 5.7 g
Accidental find on the surface of the site of Talashkan-2, Sherabad district

46. Vasudeva I
d. 22.5–24.0 mm, th. 3.4 mm, weight 8.1 g
Jandavlattepa 2005, small find no. 11C009.I
figs. 3.5, *79** (obverse) and 3.5, *80** (reverse)

47. Vasudeva I (?)
obverse: The king to the left (not clear)
reverse: Shiva with bull Nandi (?)
d. 21.9 mm, th. 9.8 mm, weight 8.9 g
Jandavlattepa 2005, an accidental surface find

## Vasudeva II (circa 290–310 AD)
48. Vasudeva II
d. 19.5–20.5 mm, th. 3.8 mm, weight 5.9 g
Coin has an irregular form
Jandavlattepa 2005, an accidental surface find
figs. 3.5, *81** (obverse) and 3.5, *82** (reverse)

49. Vasudeva II
obverse: A standing figure to the left in front of an altar, not clear

reverse: Shiva and bull Nandi behind him; dots around
d. 21.5–23.1 mm, th. 3.6 mm, weight 8.1 g
Jandavlattepa 2006, small find no. 21P003.I
figs. 3.5, *83** (obverse) and 3.5, *84** (reverse)

50. Vasudeva II
d. 22.2–21.0 mm, th. 1.8–4.1 mm, weight 8.5 g
Jandavlattepa 2006, small find no. 12C0018.I
fig. 3.5, *85** (obverse)

51. Vasudeva II
The coin has almost a square form
d. 17.0–17.1 mm, th. 3.4–4.1 mm, weight 4.7 g
Jandavlattepa 2003, an accidental surface find

52. Vasudeva II
obverse: The king to the left in front of an altar; schematic rendering
reverse: Shiva with bull Nandi behind him
d. 17.0–19.1 mm, th. 2.5 mm, weight 2.9 g
Jandavlattepa 2003, 24.X; Sector 02A, layer of 310–325 cm from the original surface

53. Vasudeva II
The coin has almost a square form with rounded corners
Only contours of the images are visible, bad preservation
d. 19.8–19.2 mm, th. 3.9 mm, weight 8.0 g
Jandavlattepa 2003, 30.10; Sector 02A, 45 cm from the surface
figs. 3.5, *86** (obverse) and 3.5, *87** (reverse)

## Kanishka II (circa 225–240)
54. Kanishka II
obverse: illegible due to the bad state of presevation
reverse: Ardokhsho on the throne facing frontally, holding an attribute (cornucopia) in his left hand; the head is surrounded by a nimbus
d. 19.0–20.0 mm, th. 2.0 mm, weight 3.2 g
Jandavlattepa 2002, Sector 08, small find no. 08A012.I
fig. 3.5, *88** (reverse)

55. Kanishka II
obverse: The king to the left in front of an altar, schematic rendering
reverse: Ardokhsho on the throne facing, dots around
A. 18.0–17.4 mm, th. 4.4 mm, weight 6.1 g
Jandavlattepa 2003, small find no. 7D012.I
figs. 3.5, *89** (obverse) and 3.5, *90** (reverse)

56. Kanishka II
d. 19.9–21.6 mm, th. 4.0 mm, weight 8.0 g
Jandavlattepa 2005, small find no. 11C007.I

57. Kanishka II
A coin of an irregular shape
obverse: figure to the left, schematic rendering
reverse: Ardokhsho on the throne frontally, dots around
d. 18.0–20.5 mm, th. 4.0 mm, weight 6.1 g
Jandavlattepa 2003, small find no. 7C010.I
figs. 3.5, *91** (obverse) and 3.5, *92** (reverse)

**58. Kanishka II**
Shape of the coin is irregular; the upper part seems to be cut off
d. 16.7–18.8 mm, th. 3.8 mm, weight 6.5 g
Jandavlattepa 2005, accidental surface find
figs. 3.5, *93** (obverse) and 3.5, *94** (reverse)

**59. Vasudeva II or Kanishka II (?)**
obverse: A standing figure to the left in front of an altar, depicted very schematically
reverse: indiscernible
d. 20.2–19.9 mm, th. 3.0 mm, weight 5.9 g
Jandavlattepa 2006, 05.X; small find no. 21Pz004.II
fig. 3.5, *95** (obverse)

**60. Kanishka II**
obverse: The king standing to the left, holding a spear in his left hand; an altar is depicted to the left of his lowered right arm
reverse: Ardokhsho on the throne frontally
d. 18.5–22.0 mm, th. 3.8 mm, weight 6.9 g
Jandavlattepa 2006, 23.IX; small find no. 21E006.I
figs. 3.5, *96** (obverse) and 3.5, *97** (reverse)

**61. Kanishka II**
The left part of the coin is missing
obverse: Very worn only the contours of the images are discernible: a standing figure to the left in front of an altar
reverse: Ardokhsho on the throne frontally
d. 22.2–19.0 mm, th. 3.5 mm, weight 7.1 g
Jandavlattepa 2005, 13.X; small find no. 20S002.III
figs. 3.5, *98** (obverse) and 3.5, *99** (reverse)

**62. Kanishka II**
Coin of an irregular shape
reverse: Ardokhsho on the throne, frontally; there are two letters visible in the left field … ΔO…
d. 21.1 mm, th. 4.1 mm, weight 7.5 g
Jandavlattepa 2005, 13.X; Sector 02A, found during cleaning of the ravine

**63. Kanishka II**
Coin of an irregular shape
obverse: A standing figure to the left, depicted schematically
reverse: A sitting figure, the image is fragmentary, the left part cut off by die
d. 17.0–18.8 mm, th. 4.0 mm, weight 5.9 g
Jandavlattepa 2003, small find no. 9B002.IV

**64. Kanishka II**
obverse: A standing figure to the left in front of an altar, holding a spear in his left hand, the right arm is lowered.
reverse: a figure sitting on a throne, indistinct
d. 19.8 mm, th. 3.8 mm, weight 7.1 g
Jandavlattepa 2005, 14.X; sector 02A, found during clearing the ravine
figs. 3.5, *100** (obverse) and 3.5, *101** (reverse)

**65. Kanishka II**
obverse: A standing figure to the left, schematically depicted
reverse: Ardokhsho on the throne frontally, indistinct
d. 18.5–20.0 mm, th. 4.0 mm, weight 8.4 g
Jandavlattepa 2005, an accidental find on the surface of the site
figs. 3.5, *102** (obverse) and 3.5, *103** (reverse)

**66. Kanishka II (?)**
obverse: A standing figure
reverse: not clear
d. 19.1 mm, th. 4.6 mm, weight 6.9 g
Jandavlattepa 2005, an accidental find on the surface of the site

**67. Kanishka II**
A coin of an irregular form
obverse: A standing figure to the left in front of an altar, with his right arm extended over the altar and the left arm lifted
reverse: Ardokhsho on the throne frontally
Jandavlattepa 2005, 05.X; small find no. 9D010.III
figs. 3.5, *104** (obverse) and 3.5, *105** (reverse)

**68. Kanishka II**
reverse: Ardokhsho on the throne frontally, holds an attribute in the lifted left hand while the right arm is lowered
d. 20.1 mm, th. 4.5 mm, weight 8.1 g
Jandavlattepa 2005, an accidental surface find
figs. 3.5, *106** (obverse) and 3.5, *107** (reverse)

**69. Kanishka II**
obverse: A standing figure, indistinct
reverse: Ardokhsho on the throne frontally; dots around
d. 21.5 mm, th. 3.2 mm, weight 7.3 g
Jandavlattepa 2005, an accidental find
figs. 3.5, *108** (obverse) and 3.5, *109** (reverse)

**70. Kanishka II**
obverse: A standing figure, schematically depicted
reverse: A sitting figure (?), the circle not equal, a segment of the left top part is absent, only contours of the images are visible
d. 17.5–20.2 mm, th. 4.2 mm, weight 7.2 g
Jandavlattepa 2004, 21.IX; small find no. 20C004.I

**71. Kanishka II**
d. 19.0–22.0 mm, th. 2.2–4.3 mm, weight 6.4 g
Jandavlattepa 2005, 15.X; small find no. 10D018.VI
figs. 3.5, *110** (obverse) and 3.5, *111** (reverse)

**72. Kanishka II**
obverse: king standing to the left, clad in trousers and high boots; the right hand extended over altar, holds a spear in the left hand
reverse: Ardokhsho on the throne, facing frontally, the left top of coin's edge cut off
d. 19.8, th. 2.7 mm, weight 5.9 g
Jandavlattepa 2005; found on the site by a local resident
figs. 3.5, *112** (obverse) and 3.5, *113** (reverse)

**73. Kanishka II**
d. 20.9–21.1 mm, th. 3.5 mm, weight 7.2 g
Jandavlattepa 2005, 03.X; Sector 02A, 1, layer no. 15
figs. 3.5, *114*ˣ (obverse) and 3.5, *115*ˣ (reverse)

**74. Kanishka II**
Coin of an irregular form
obverse: The king standing to the left in a long shirt, the right hand is extended over an altar; the letters of the legend around the coin's circumference are not clear
reverse: Ardokhsho sitting on the throne, facing frontally
d. 19.5–22.0 mm, th. 4.0 mm, weight 7.5 g
Jandavlattepa 2003, 23.X; Sector 02A, a layer 310–325 cm from the original surface
figs. 3.5, *116*ˣ (obverse) and 3.5, *117*ˣ (reverse)

**75. Kanishka II**
obverse: The king standing to the left in front of an altar, wearing a garment with pointed corners on each side, narrow trousers and an upward tapering headdress, his head is surrounded with a nimbus and in the raised left hand he holds a trident (?)
reverse: Ardokhsho on the throne with a high backrest, holding a cornucopia in his left hand, in the left field vertically: …PΔOXPO; dots around in the right field
d. 19.5–21.0 mm, th. 3.5 mm, weight 8.1 g
Talashkan 2, 2005, an accidental surface find
figs. 3.5, *118*ˣ (obverse) and 3.5, *119*ˣ (reverse)

**76. Kanishka II**
obverse: A standing figure to the left, schematically depicted; the left part of the image is cut off by the die
reverse: Ardokhsho sitting on the throne, facing frontally; dots in the right field
d. 20.9–23.0 mm, th. 4.0 mm, weight 8.9 g
Talashkan 2, 2005, an accidental surface find
figs. 3.5, *120*ˣ (obverse) and 3.5, *121*ˣ (reverse)

**77. Kanishka II**
reverse: Ardokhsho sitting on the throne, facing frontally, holding cornucopia in the right hand
d. 31.0–33.0 mm, th. 3.0 mm, weight 7.1 g
Jandavlattepa 2005, 06.X; Sector 02A, deposited layer no. 28

**78. Kanishka II**
Bad state of preservation
d. 17.0–18.0 mm, th. 3.2 mm, weight 4.2 g
Jandavlattepa 2005, 06.X; Sector 02A, deposited layer no. 28

**79. Kanishka II**
Bad state of preservation: only the outlines of the images are traceable
obverse: A figure standing to the left
reverse: a sitting figure (?)
d. 17.4–20.1 mm, th. 2.1, weight 4.2 g
Jandavlattepa, an accidental find on the site, brought by a local resident

**80. Kanishka II**
Bad state of preservation, coin of an irregular, oval form
reverse: A sitting figure, dots around
d. 19.5–23.9 mm, th. 3.1 mm, weight 6.1 g
Jandavlattepa 2004, 17.IX; small find no. 20D002.III

**81. Kanishka II (?)**
Bad state of preservation
obverse: A standing figure
reverse: not clear, a figure on a throne (?)
Weight 2.8 g
Jandavlattepa 2003, an accidental surface find

**82. Kanishka II**
obverse: A figure to the left, schematically depicted
reverse: The image is not clear
d. 17.0 mm, th. 2.3 mm, weight 3.3 g
Jandavlattepa 2003, Sector 04, (Gate area), 68 cm from the surface

## Mint of Southern Sogdia

**83. Silver coin**
obverse: Zeus sitting on the throne to the left, schematically, the image is difficult to distinct because of strong oxidation
reverse: standing figure of Heracles to the right, facing, the left hand holds a club and the right hand holds a wreath with long falling ends, to the left of the figure is legend of Aramaic letters
d. 13 mm, th. 4 mm, weight 0.4 g
Jandavlattepa 2006, 26.IX; small find no. 21E012.I
figs. 3.5, *122*ˣ (obverse) and 3.5, *123*ˣ (reverse)

## Kushano-Sassanians

**84. Peroz (?)**
obverse: A standing figure of the king to the left, holding an attribute (wreath ?) in his left hand, a crown (corona muralis?) on his head
reverse: Deity sitting on the throne, frontally (?)
d. 24.7–26.2 mm, th. 4.4 mm, weight 9.1 g
Jandavlattepa 2003, 18.X; small find no. 07D013.II
figs. 3.5, *124*ˣ (obverse) and 3.5, *125*ˣ (reverse)

**85. Peroz**
obverse: A bust of the king in a crown to the right, the top part of the crown in the form of moon and solar signs, dots around
reverse: The image is not distinctive, a bust over an altar (?)
d. 19.5 mm, th. 2.2 mm, weight 1.6 g
Jandavlattepa 2005, small find no. 12D003.III

**86. Peroz (?)**
obverse: Bust of the king in a crown to the right
reverse: Indistinct: an altar (?)
d. 13.6 mm, th. 2.2 mm, weight 1.5 g
Jandavlattepa 2005, small find no. 12D003.IV

**87. Peroz (?)**
d. 13.0 mm, th. 2.2 mm, weight 1.2 g
Jandavlattepa 2005, small find no. 10D005.I

88. (?)
Bad state of preservation; images are not distinct
d. 10.5 mm, th. 1.1 mm, weight 0.3 g
Jandavlattepa 2002, Sector 06, square no. 2

89. Kavad (?)
obverse: A bust of the king to the right
reverse: An altar
d. 11.6 mm, th. 3.1 mm, weight 1.7 g
Jandavlattepa 2003, small find no. 9B002.I

90. (?)
Bad state of preservation. Fragmentary
d. 13.0 (?), th. 1.0 mm, weight 0.8 g
Jandavlattepa 2002, an accidental surface find

91. Peroz (?)
obverse: Bust of the king to the right with a crown on his head
reverse: A bust on an altar facing frontally
d. 17.0 mm, th. 2.8 mm, weight 3.7 g
Jandavlattepa 2002, an accidental surface find

92. Peroz
obverse: A standing figure of the king in front of an altar to the left
reverse: Shiva with a bull behind him, facing frontally
d. 16.6–14.0 mm, th. 2.5 mm, weight 2.2 g
Jandavlattepa 2003, an accidental surface find

93. (?)
Bad state of preservation, not clear
d. 14.0 mm, th. 2.0 mm, weight 2.2 g
Jandavlattepa 2006, 26.IX; small find no. 21P001.II

94. (?)
d. 11.1 mm, th. 1.0 mm, weight 0.6 g
Jandavlattepa 2006, 27.IX; small find no. 21D019.I

95. (?)
d. 10.1 mm, th. 1.5 mm, weight 0.9 g
Jandavlattepa 2006, 22.IX; small find no. 21F001.IV

96. (?)
d. 11.0 mm, th. 0.8 mm, weight 0.4 g
Jandavlattepa 2005, small find no. 20Q001.II

97. (?)
d. 8.8–10.0 mm, th. 0.8 mm, weight 0.5 g
Jandavlattepa 2004, 25.IX; small find no. 20N002.VI

98. (?)
reverse: altar of fire
d. 11.0–12.0 mm, th. 1.1 mm, weight 1.2 g
Jandavlattepa 2006, an accidental find on the surface of the site

99. (?)
d. 12.2 mm, th. 1.4 mm, weight 1.4 g
Jandavlattepa 2005, 25.X; small find no. 20Q038.I

100. (?)
d. 13 mm, th. 1.6 mm, weight 0.9 g
Jandavlattepa 2005, small find no. 12D003.V

101. Peroz (?)
obverse: A bust of the king to the right
reverse: Shiva with the bull behind him
d. 12.0 mm, th. 0.5 mm, weight 0.5 g
Jandavlattepa 2006, 05.X; small find no. 21F010.II
figs. 3.5, *126** (obverse) and 3.5, *127** (reverse)

102. (?)
d. 13.6 mm, th. 2.2 mm, weight 2.3 g
Jandavlattepa 2005, small find no. 10D002.II
figs. 3.5, *128** (obverse) and 3.5, *129** (reverse)

103. (?)
d. 12.7 mm, th. 1.6 mm, weight 1.0 g
Jandavlattepa 2006, 28.IX; small find no. 21D017.I

104. (?)
d. 12.3 mm, th. 2.2 mm, weight 1.3 g
Jandavlattepa 2005, small find no. 12C016.II

105. (?)
d. 10.0–13.1 mm, th. 1.7 mm, weight 1.0 g
Jandavlattepa 2006, 22.IX; small find no. 21D001.II

106. (?)
d. 14.0 mm, th. 2.4 mm, weight 1.8 g
Jandavlattepa 2003, 29.IX; small find no. 07C002.IV

107. (?)
Fragment
d. 13.0 mm, th. 2.0 mm, weight 0.7 g
Jandavlattepa 2005, 13.1X; small find no. 20Q018.I

108. (?)
d. 11.0 mm, th. 0.5 mm, weight 0.4 g
Jandavlattepa 2005, small find no. 20P002.I

109. (?)
d. 13.5 mm, th. 2.2 mm, weight 1.6 g
Jandavlattepa 2003, 04.X; small find no. 07C003.V

110. (?)
d. 13.1 mm, th. 2.4 mm, weight 1.2 g
Jandavlattepa 2006, 26.IX; small find no. 21E012.I

111. (?)
d. 12.5 mm, th. 1.5 m, weight 1.0 g
Jandavlattepa 2005, 20.X; small find no. 20Q001.VII

112. (?)
d. 13.5–15.0 mm, th. 4.1 mm, weight 4.1 g
Jandavlattepa 2005, 13.X; small find no. 20S002.I

113. (?)
d. 16.0 mm, th. 3.1 mm, weight 2.5 g
Jandavlattepa 2005, 30.IX; Sector 02A, layer 4

114. (?)
d. 13.5–15.0 mm, th. 2.5 mm, weight 1.9 g
Jandavlattepa 2005, accidental find on the surface of the site

115. Shapur II (?)
obverse: A bust of the king to the right
reverse: An altar of fire
d. 14.0–16.1 mm, th. 3.5 mm, weight 3.9 g
Jandavlattepa 2005, 13.X; small find no. 20S002.II

116. (?)
reverse: Shiva with the bull (?)
d. 15.0 mm, th. 2.7 mm, weight 2.2 g
Jandavlattepa 2005, 15.X; small find no. 10D013c.II

117. (?)
d. 15.5 mm, th. 2.7 mm, weight 2.3 g
Jandavlattepa 2005, 14.X; small find no. 10D013c.I

118. Vasudeva II
obverse: A standing figure of the king to the left, schematically depicted
reverse: Shiva with bull Nandi behind him, facing frontally
d. 16.3 mm, th. 3.9 mm, weight 2.7 g
Jandavlattepa 2005, small find no. 12C005.I
figs. 3.5, *130** (obverse) and 3.5, *131** (reverse)

119. Vasudeva II (?)
obverse: A standing figure to the left
reverse: Shiva (?)
d. 17.1–19.0 mm, th. 4.0 mm, weight 7.5 g
Jandavlattepa 2005, 04.1X; small find no. 09D010.II

120. Vasudeva II (?)
obverse: A standing figure to the left
reverse: Shiva with bull Nandi
d. 17.5–19.0 mm, th. 3.0 mm, weight 4.3 g
Jandavlattepa 2005, 04.X; small find no. 20Y002.IX
figs. 3.5, *132** (obverse) and 3.5, *133** (reverse)

121. (?)
d. 14.0–16.1 mm, th. 3.5 mm, weight 2.7 g
Jandavlattepa 2006, 03.IX; small find no. 21P016.I

122. Fragment of a coin (Vasudeva II?)
reverse: A figure with bull Nandi
d. 16.3–18.5 mm, th. 3.8 mm, weight 4.5 g
Jandavlattepa 2003, accidental find on the surface of the site
figs. 3.5, *134** (obverse) and 3.5, *135** (reverse)

123. (?)
A fragment (a semicircle part of a coin)
obverse: Indistinct: a standing figure to the left (?)
reverse: A figure sitting frontally (Ardokhsho on a throne?)
d. 13.5 mm, th. 1.5 mm, weight 0.7 g
Jandavlattepa 2003, 03.X; small find no. 07B007.II
figs. 3.5, *136** (obverse) and 3.5, *137** (reverse)

124. Vasudeva II (?)
obverse: A standing figure to the left
reverse: A figure with a bull; depicted schematically
d. 15.5 mm, th. 3.2 mm, weight 1.4 g
Jandavlattepa 2003, 24.X; Sector 02A, a layer on depth of 310–325 cm from the original surface
figs. 3.5, *138** (obverse) and 3.5, *139** (reverse)

125. Vasudeva II (?)
obverse: A standing figure to the left, not clear
reverse: A standing figure facing frontally (Shiva with Nandi?)
d. 16.1 mm, th. 2.7 mm, weight 2.3 g
Jandavlattepa 2005, an accidental surface find
figs. 3.5, *140** (obverse) and 3.5, *141** (reverse)

126. Vasudeva II (?)
obverse: A standing figure to the left in front of an altar
reverse: A figure (Shiva with bull Nandi?)
d. 14.2–16.1 mm, th. 2.3 mm, weight 1.6 g
Jandavlattepa 2005, an accidental surface find
figs. 3.5, *142** (obverse) and 3.5, *143** (reverse)

127. Vasudeva I (?)
Coin of an irregular form
obverse: A standing figure to the left (?)
reverse: A figure, to the right outlines of an animal (Shiva with bull?)
d. 22.0 mm, th. 4.0 mm, weight 7.1 g
Jandavlattepa 2005, an accidental surface find
figs. 3.5, *144** (obverse) and 3.5, *145** (reverse)

128. Kushano-Sassanians (?)
d. 14.3–15.4 mm, th. 3.3 mm, weight 2.3 g
Jandavlattepa 2005, an accidental surface find

129. (?)
d. 21.6–22.0 mm, th. 4.0 mm, weight 8.5 g
Jandavlattepa 2005, an accidental surface find

## Early Middle Ages

130. (?)
obverse: A bust of the king, head facing to the right, dots around; two reliefs showing the breast of the personage, to the right at the level of shoulders a V-shaped sign (a hand?)
reverse: an animal to the right (a lion?)
d. 13.0 mm, th. 2.2 mm, weight 1.9 g
Jandavlattepa 2002, an accidental surface find
figs. 3.5, *146** (obverse) and 3.5, *147** (reverse)

131. The Middle Ages (?)
obverse: An animal to the right; a big head with small pointed ears and long vertical horns; a relief line running from the muzzle downwards (a beard ?); a long tail curled up onto the animal's back
reverse: Arabic letters (?)
d. 13.9 mm, th. 2.8 mm, weight 2.9 g
Jandavlattepa area, 2003; brought by a local resident
figs. 3.5, *148** (obverse) and 3.5, *149** (reverse)

132.
obverse: letters of Arabic alphabet poorly distinct
reverse: letters, not clear
d. 16.5–17.8 mm, th. 1.8 mm, weight 3.6 g
Jandavlattepa area, 2003, an accidental find
figs. 3.5, *150** (obverse) and 3.5, *151** (reverse)

## Middle Ages

133. Samanids (?)
obverse: A legend around the coin's perimeter and an Arabic letter in the centre
reverse: not clear
d. 22.0 mm, th. 1.0 mm, weight 2.3 g
2006, Khaitabad site, Jarkurgan District
figs. 3.5, *152** (obverse) and 3.5, *153** (reverse)

## Late Middle Ages

134.
Coin has an oval elongated form
obverse: elements of Arabic letters
reverse: Arabic inscription, poorly legible
d. 17.0–22.7 mm, th. 1.0 mm, weight 3.6 g
Jandavlattepa 2005, 05.X; small find no. 20Y007.II
figs. 3.5, *154** (obverse) and 3.5, *155** (reverse)

135.
Coin has an oval elongated form
Length 27.0 mm, th. 1.0 mm, weight 3.0 g
Jandavlattepa 2005, small find no. 20Y014.I
figs. 3.5, *156** (obverse) and 3.5, *157** (reverse)

136. (?)
d. 23.5 mm, th. 6.6 mm, weight 10.1 g
Jandavlattepa 2005, an accidental surface find

## Commentary

A separate article by the present author will be devoted to recent finds and localisation of Hellenistic coins to the north of the river of Amu Darya/Oxus. Here it is desirable to note some remarkable peculiarities among the finds of coins from the site of Janadvlattepa. One of the earliest coins from Jandavlat is a Bronze (*khalkos*) coin of the Bactrian king Euthydemus (No. 1). This coin is quite well known in the numismatic finds to the north of Amu Darya.[4] It should be noted that another coin of this king was found during excavation of the gulley closer to its southern part. Unfortunately, the authors of the find do not indicate which type of coin from Euthydemus was found.[5] All that can be noted is that together with the

coin published in the present catalogue, their number in Jandavlattepa makes two.

Of great interest is a copper coin of Demetrius of considerable size and weight (tetrakhalk?). Unfortunately, the image is hardly visible though a head of an elephant scalp is rather clear (No. 2). The reverse of the coin showing the head of a blowing elephant (?) was less precisely kept. It is worth noting that a find from Old Termez with a standing figure of Artemis taking an arrow from a quiver belongs approximately to the same face value.[6]

The next example is perhaps a first find of a square copper coin of Eucratides in archaeological conditions to the north of Amu Darya/Oxus. The layer in which the coin was found is situated at the bottom of a gulley; here, during seasonal rains, pa channel forms of the water which flows down from all the surfaces of the site. It was found together with other Kushan coins. There are two possible assumptions: either the coin was in circulation with all of these coins, or it has been washed off from an earlier layer of the site.

There are numerous finds of, what are known as "Barbarous Heliocles" coins. It is no exaggeration to say that this is the most frequent category of numismatic material in the territory of Surkhan Darya from the Saka/Yuezhi period. Since the last report of these coins in E. V. Zeymal's (1983) generalising work, the number of finds has increased considerably. Certainly, the Kushan archaeological sites of Northern Bactria have yielded the greatest quantity from regular archaeological excavations. A recently-published work by V.A. Zavyalov devoted to excavations on the Zartepa includes, among other coins, brings nine imitations of tetradrachms and one of a drachma of king Heliocles.[7] Another site that has yielded a significant amount of "Barbarous Heliocles" is Kampyrtepa. On this site (for the period 1979–1992) 13 coins have been found, of which four coins are imitation of drachmas of Heliocles and the other 13 of tetradrachmas of the same king.[8] Of six coins found in Jandavlattepa, the best–preserved coins (nos. 5, 6) represent an early imitating mint. One of the six coins (no. 11) with the image of a horse on the reverse provides an association with the imitations of Heliocles' drachmas.

These coins have a special place in the numismatics of Bactria. Although they have been studied for a long time, many questions remain unresolved. Numerous materials have allowed us to resolve questions of the metric system, localisation and typology to a certain degree. However, certain aspects of the iconography, and in particular the attribution of the coins, remain unclear. The basic difficulty in unravelling the phe-

---

4    For the recent finds of bronze coins of Euthydemus to the north of Amudarya/Oxus cf. Abdullaev 2006, no. 113.
5    Huff – Pidaev – Shaydullaev 2001, p. 220.
6    Abdullaev 2006, p. 109.
7    Zavyalov 2008, p. 256, 257, 270.
8    Ayupova 2001, p. 129; Rtveladze 2002, pp. 117–131.

nomenon of the "barbarous Heliocles" coins is the duration of the currency and typological diversity. The chronological frame of their functioning suggest a period more than a century long. Geographically, the coins are concentrated mainly on the territory of the modern Surkhan Darya area of Uzbekistan. The opinion has been expressed that the earliest types of imitations might have been be minted not by the Yuezhi, but by the Sakas (Sakarauloi), who historically preceded the Yuezhi invasion of the territory of Sogdia and Bactria in the second half of the 2nd century BC. Moreover, the image of these Sakas appears sure enough on fine art items monuments from the 2nd century BC to the 1st century AD.[9]

Another category of disputable coins in Bactrian numismatics are the coins of the "anonymous king" Soter Megas, which the archaeological layers would suggest are chronologically adjacent, to the previous coins – imitations of Heliocles. Works in Jandavlattepa have yielded eight coins of Soter Megas (nos. 13–22). It has yet to be reliably established who minted these coins, so numerous in the archaeological monuments of Bactria, and much more widespread than "barbarous Heliocles" coins. With the discovery of the Bactrian inscriptions of Kanishka the Great from Rabatak (Afghanistan) on the historical arena the little-known figure of Vima Takto from the Kushan dynasty appeared. The tempting idea which has been put forward by Joe Cribb,[10] identifying Vima Takto with Soter Megas has not been accepted unanimously. In particular, Gerard Fussman's detailed article has made the case against such identification.[11]

Anyway, the question of the historical interpretation and ethnic attribution of the anonymous king Soter Megas remains current. It would be desirable to say something about the some remarkable iconographic features on the reverse of Soter Megas coins. This concerns first of all the general composition, including the image of the central figure – a horseman on a horse, and the manner of transfer of the legend and the positioning of the monogram. The image of the horseman to the right with his hand spread forward holding a symbol of authority (an axe or a whip) is similar to the images of Indo-Scythian kings of the Azes dynasty. On the coins of Azes himself the horseman is represented in knightly armour with his spear lowered downwards.[12] The image of a spear is absent on the coins of Soter Megas. Another difference in

these coins lies in the position of the hands, although on one type of Azes I' coins where he is siting on an animal reminiscent of a camel, his pose is similar to a pose on coins of Soter Megas i.e. his hand is extended forward and holds an axe.[13] The position of the arm extended forward with a symbol of authority (in this case a whip) is characteristic of the images on the coins of another Indo-Scythian king, Azilises. However the horseman on these coins is represented without armour.[14] Moreover, these coins share a number of other details – for example, the legend running around the composition and the positioning of a monogram sign in the bottom part under the head of the horse. All this suggests that there is some connection between the coins of Soter Megas and the coins of the Indo-Scythian kings, which probably had common ethnic roots. However, to decide this question requires a more thorough argument and all-round analysis. In connection with the coins of Soter Megas it is interesting to note a fine coin (no 130) which we have classified as coming from the early Middle Ages, although it is possible that it comes from an earlier period. On the obverse is a bust to the right with a hand lifted at shoulder level (holding a sign). On the reverse of the coin is the image of a horseman on a horse to the right with a hand of the horse lifted above the mane. True, is hard to distinguish, but the general scheme of the image is highly reminiscent of the image on the coins of Soter Megas. We cannot exclude the possibility that it might be an imitation of the coins of the anonymous king Soter Megas.

Another remarkable find in the numismatic collection of Jandavlattepa is the find of silver coins with images of Zeus and Heracles. These coins are essentially localised in Southern Sogdia. This may be the first find of this coin in an archaeological layer in Northern Bactria. E. V. Zeymal wrote about the coins with images of Zeus and Heracles from the museum collections.[15] The question of the localisation of these coins remains unsolved, but in the course of archaeological research in the region of Southern Sogdia it was found out that they are essentially concentrated in this area.[16] Most likely, they were minted by local governors. The most numerous in the top layers of the site of the ancient settlement are the coins from the Kushano-Sassanian epoch; however, the great majority of these coins are in bad condition, and in most cases their attribution can only be tentative.

---

[9] Abdullaev 1999, pp. 368–377.
[10] Sims-Williams – Cribb 1996, pp. 75–142.
[11] Fussman 1998, pp. 571–651.
[12] Mitchiner 1976, types 743–760.
[13] Mitchiner 1976, types 761–762.
[14] Mitchiner 1976, types 776–786.
[15] Zeymal 1972, pp. 70–75.
[16] Kabanov 1961, pp. 137–141; Kabanov 1965, pp. 71–86; Abdullaev 2000, pp. 147–152.

# Bibliography

Abdullaev, K. (1999): Eshcho raz o podrazhaniyakh monetam Geliokla (k voprosu o politicheskoy istorii Baktrii vo vtoroy polovine 2 v. do n.e., in: *Problemy istorii, filologii, kul'tury* VIII, Moskva – Magnitogorsk, pp. 368–377.

Abdullaev, K. (2000): A Coin from the Kashkadarya valley with representation of Zeus and Hercules, *Parthica*, 2, pp. 147–152.

Abdullaev, K. (2006): Nekhodki ellinisticheskikh monet k severu ot Amudar'i – Oksa, *Rossiyskaya arkheologiya* 2006/3, p. 112ff.

Ayupova, F. – Gorin, A. (2001): Podrazheniya monetam Geliokla i monety Soter Megasa iz Kampyrtepa, in: *Materialy Tokharistanskoy ekspeditsii*, vyp. 2, Tashkent, pp. 129–133.

Fussman, G. (1998): L'inscription de Rabatak et l'origine de l'ere saka, *Journal Asiatique* 286/2, pp. 571–6Huff, D. – Pidaev, Ch. – Chaydoullaev, Ch. (2001): Uzbek-German archaeological researches in the Surkhan Darya region, in: *La Bactriane au Carrefour des routes et des civilizations de l'Asie central*, ed. P. Leriche et al., Paris, pp. 219–233.

Kabanov, S. K. (1961): Nakhshebskie monety V–VI vv., *Vestnik drevney istorii* (VDI) 1961/ pp. 137–141.

Kabanov, S. K. (1965): Ruiny poseleniya III–IV vv. V doline Kashkadar'i, *Istoriya materialnoy kultury Uzbekistana* (IMKU) 6, pp. 71–86.

Mitchiner, M. (1976): *Indo-Greek and Indo-Scythian coinage*. London.

Rtveladze, E. V. (2002): *Drevnie i rannesrednevekovye monety istoriko-kulturnykh oblastey Uzbekistana*, Tashkent.

Rtveladze, E. V. – Khakimov, Z. E. (1973): Marshrutnye issledovaniya pamyatnikov severnoy Baktrii, in: *Iz istorii antichnoy kul'tury Uzbekistana*. Tashkent, pp. 10–34.

Pidaev, Sh. (1974): Materialy k izucheniyu drevnikh pamyatnikov Severnoy Baktrii, in: *Drevnyaya Baktria*, pp. 32–42.

Sims-Williams, N. – Cribb, J. (1996): A New Bactrian Inscription of Kanishka of the Great, *Silk Road Art and Archaeology*, vol. 4, 1995/96, pp. 77–79.

Zav'yalov V. A. (1972): Rannesogdiyskye monety s izobrazheniyem Gerakla i Zevsa, *Soobshcheniya Gosudarstvennogo Ermitazha*, XXXIV.

Zav'yalov V. A. (2008): *Kushanshakhr pri sasanidakh. Po materialam raskopok na gorodishche Zar-tepa*, Saint Peterburg.

# 4. Concluding remarks

*Kazim Abdullaev – Ladislav Stančo*

From 2002 to 2006 the site of Jandavlattepa was investigated by the Czech-Uzbekistani archaeological expedition organised in cooperation between the Institute of Archaeology of the Academy of Sciences of Uzbekistan and Charles University in Prague. The archaeological excavations of Jandavlattepa have shown that this site was inhabited over many centuries, from the late Bronze Age to the late Kushan (Kushano-Sasanian) period.

The cultural accumulations, many metres thick, documented in the stratigraphic trench (sector 02a) permit us to distinguish a clearly-outlined Kushano-Sasanid horizon in the upper levels followed by Kushan layers represented by a massive volume of accumulations. The Hellenistic period is also clearly present. One of the longest periods in the existence of Jandavlattepa is that of the early Iron Age, as is well illustrated by the many metres of thickness of the relevant cultural layers. The lowermost layers of the site, resting directly on the sub-soil (a loess-sandy conglomerate: tertiary sandstone), produced a find complex (basically pottery) including several painted sherds.[1] Space will be dedicated in the future to a detailed study of the archaeological complexes of the stratigraphic trench (sector 02a). As the present volume presents the results of the investigation of the upper horizons of Jandavlattepa, which essentially concern the Kushan, the Late Kushan and Kushano-Sasanian periods, the next volume should be devoted primarily to the stratigraphic trench and its rich archaeological finds. The archaeological material gained from the investigations in Sectors 07 and 20 proves clearly by many analogies a resemblance with the other sites in the area, especially that of Zartepa. Thus the site of Jandavlattepa represents not only one of the largest sites in the Sherabad oasis but also one of those with longest sequence of occupation.

Many interesting questions arise in the matter of setting of Jandavlattepa in the landscape and especially of function of various archaeological features surrounding the site, such as small platform / structure to the northwest (see chapter 2.4), ruins of medieval house within one of the Saitabad orchards, small settlement up on the right bank of Sherabad Darya (so-called Kurgan) or a no more distinguishable site of Pachmaktepa.[2] The landscape, once densely populated and scattered with many archaeological sites of different functions, shows, due primarily to the intensive farming and rapid population growth of late, just a tiny fragment of its former glory. These issues, among the others, connected with the historical landscape, land use and settlement dynamics, we would like to resolve in our current project.

[1]  Abdullaev, K. – Stančo, L. 2007: Jandavlattepa 2006. Preliminary excavation report. Studia Hercynia XI, pp. 157, 158, fig. 1–3 (see also online: http://arcis.ff.cuni.cz/jandavlattepa-2006-preliminary-excavation-report).

[2]  Cf. Pidaev, Sh. P. (1973): Otkrytiye novogo pamyatnika serediny I tysyacheletiya do nashey ery. *Obshchestvennyye nauki v Uzbekistane* 11/1973, pp. 77–82.

# 5. List of small finds from Sectors 04, 07, 20 and 31

| small find number | material | object | description | p. | tab. / fig. |
|---|---|---|---|---|---|
| 04_000.I | bronze | finger ring | | 98, 146 | 3.3, 3:32 / 3.3, 25* and 26* |
| 04_000.II | carnelian | bead | | 98, 153 | 3.3, 5:73 / 3.3, 57* |
| 04_000.III | bronze | pin | | 98, 155 | 3.3, 6:90 / 3.3, 82* |
| 04_000.IV | bronze | arrowhead | a three-winged, socketed bronze arrowhead | 98, 122 | 3.2, 2:4 / 3.2, 16* |
| 04_000.IX | | | | 98 | |
| 04_000.V | bronze | arrowhead | a three-winged bronze arrowhead with an ogival outline | 98, 122 | 3.2, 2:5 / 3.2, 17* |
| 04_000.VI | bronze | arrowhead | a three-winged bronze arrowhead with an ogival outline | 98 | 3.2, 2:6 / 3.2, 18* |
| 04_000.VII | | | | --- | --- |
| 04_000.VIII | | | | --- | --- |
| 04_000.X | | | | --- | --- |
| 04_000.XI | | | | --- | --- |
| 04_000.XII | | | | --- | --- |
| 04_000.XIII | | | | --- | --- |
| 04_000.XIV | | | | --- | --- |
| 04_000.XIX | iron | knife | a tanged, one-edged iron knife with a straight edge and convex back | 121 | 3.2, 1:10 / 3.2, 10* |
| 04_000.XV | | | | --- | --- |
| 04_000.XVI | | | | --- | --- |
| 04_000.XVII | bronze | coin | bronze tetradrachm of Soter Megas, minted probably in Bactra | 98, 174 | --- / 3.5, 23* and 24* |
| 04_000.XVIII | iron | knife | one-edged iron knife with a straight edge and a convex back | 98, 121 | 3.2, 1:9 / 3.2, 9* |
| 04_000.XX | iron | knife | fragment of a tanged, one-edged iron knife | 121 | 3.2, 1:11 / 3.2, 11* |
| 04_000.XXI | bronze | coin | Kushan period coin | --- | --- |
| 04_000.XXII | bronze | coin | bronze tetradrachm of Vima Kadphises (cca 100–127/8 AD); obverse: king standing left; reverse: Shiva and bull | 98 | --- |
| 07A000.I | glass | bead | fragment of a bluish glass paste bead (half), diameter 0,8 cm. | 154 | 3.3, 5:43 / 3.3, 64* |
| 07A000.II | bronze | sheet | bronze sheet | --- | --- |
| 07A000.III | bronze | | fragment of bronze object | --- | --- |
| 07A002.I | pottery | spindle-whorl | spindle-whorl (pottery), reshaped and reused pottery fragment | 108 | --- / 3.1, 17 |
| 07A010.I | bronze | arrow-head | bronze three-winged socketed arrowhead in a very poor state of preservation | 121, 131 | 3.2, 2:1 / 3.2, 13* |
| 07B000.I | bronze | coin | Demetrius | 173 | --- / 3.5, 3* and 3.5, 4* |
| 07B002.I | bronze | fibula | Roman fibula, type "Lunula," bronze; 1.70 m west, 0.66 m north, 0.80 m surface | --- | --- |

| small find number | material | object | description | p. | tab. / fig. |
|---|---|---|---|---|---|
| 07B007.1 | stone | bead | white stone | 154 | 3.3, 5:69 / 3.3, 65* |
| 07B007.2 | bronze | coin | fragment of Æ coin | 180 | --- / 3.5, 136* and 137* |
| 07B012.I | bone | pin | | --- | --- |
| 07C/09C005.I | bronze | | bronze object, bent (pin?), 3.8 cm long | 155 | 3.3, 6:83 / 3.3, 75* |
| 07C000.I | bone | pin | fragment of bone pin | 143 | 3.3, 2:18 / 3.3, 19:3* and 3.3, 88* |
| 07C002.I | bone | pin | | 143 | 3.3, 2:19 / 3.3, 19:1* |
| 07C002.II | stone | whetstone | | 126 | 3.2, 4:2 / 3.2, 32* |
| 07C002.III | bronze | coin | Vasudeva I | 176 | --- |
| 07C002.IV | bronze | coin | small bronze coin | 179 | cat. no. 106 |
| 07C003.I | bronze | | fragment of bronze object | --- | --- |
| 07C003.II | bronze | | fragment of bronze object | --- | --- |
| 07C003.III | plaster | | fragment of plaster object | --- | --- |
| 07C003.IV | glass paste | | fragments of glass paste object | --- | --- |
| 07C003.IX | shell | shell | small shell | --- | --- |
| 07C003.V | bronze | coin | | 179 | cat. no. 109 |
| 07C003.VI | bronze | | fragment of bronze object | --- | --- |
| 07C003.VII | iron | slag | | 153 | 3.3, 5:70 / 3.3, 54* |
| 07C003.VIII | tooth | tooth | polished animal tooth | --- | --- |
| 07C003.X | | bead | | --- | --- |
| 07C004.I | bronze | strip | | --- | --- |
| 07C004.II | bone | astragal | | --- | --- |
| 07C006.I | | spindle-whorl | fragment of spindle-whorl | 108, 114 | 3.1, 2:19 / 3.1, 21* |
| 07C008.I | limestone | spindle-whorl | fragment of spindle-whorl or a button | 109, 114 | 3.1, 2:23 / 3.1, 33* |
| 07C008.II | bone | pin | | 143 | 3.3, 2:20 / 3.3, 20* |
| 07C008.III | iron | slag | | --- | --- |
| 07C008b.I | bone | pin | fragment of bone pin | 143 | 3.3, 2:21 / 3.3, 19:4* |
| 07C008b.II | bronze | | fragment of bronze object | --- | --- |
| 07C008b.III | iron | | fragment of iron object | --- | --- |
| 07C009.I | iron | arrowhead | | 122 | 3.2, 2:7 / 3.2, 19* |
| 07C009.II | bronze | bead | | --- | --- |
| 07C009.III | iron | | fragment of iron object | 128 | --- / 3.2, 38* |
| 07C009.IV | eggshells | | | --- | --- |
| 07C009.IX | iron | slag | | --- | --- |
| 07C009.V | ? | | fragment of red dye | --- | --- |
| 07C009.VI | bronze | coin | imitation of Heliocles | 173 | --- / 3.5, 19* and 20* |
| 07C009.VII | bronze | coin | Vasudeva I | 175 | 3.5, 69* and 70* |
| 07C009.VIII | bronze | | fragment of bronze object | --- | --- |
| 07C009.X | bone | astragal | 3x | --- | --- |
| 07C009.XI | | spindle-whorl | fragment of spindle-whorl | 109 | 3.1, 2:24 / 3.1, 33* |
| 07C009.XII | bronze | pin | bronze pin, 9.7 cm long | 154 | 3.3, 74* |
| 07C010.I | bronze | coin | Kanishka II | 176 | 3.5, 91* and 92* |
| 07C010.II | bronze | coin | Vasudeva I | 175 | 3.5, 63* and 66* |
| 07C010.III | iron | strip | small iron strip | 128 | --- / 3.2, 39* |
| 07C010.IV | bronze | arrowhead | | 128 | --- / 3.2, 40* |
| 07C012.I | eggshell | eggshell | | --- | --- / --- |
| 07C012.II | bone | pin | fragment of bone pin | 143 | 3.3, 2:22 / 3.3, 19:2* |
| 07C014.I | bone | pin | fragment of bone pin, 4.5 cm long | 143 | --- / 3.3, 15* |

| small find number | material | object | description | p. | tab. / fig. |
|---|---|---|---|---|---|
| 07C014.II | bronze | sheet | fragment of bronze sheet in two pieces | --- | --- |
| 07D000.I | bone | pin | | 142 | 3.3, 3:23 / 3.3, 8:1* |
| 07D000.II | bone | pin | | | 3.3, 3:24 / 3.3, 8:2* |
| 07D001.I | clay | pottery application | pottery handle with applied zoomorphic head, a monkey | 164 | 3.4, 2:5 / 3.4, 13 |
| 07D001.II | pottery | spindle-whorl | small spindle-whorl? (pottery), reshaped and reused pottery fragment, north: 0.50 m, east: 2.00 m | 108, 114 | --- / 3.1, 19* |
| 07D003.I | iron | | unidentified iron object, west: 0.50 m, south: 1.30 m, depth: 0.45 m | --- | --- / --- |
| 07D005.I | iorn | | unidentified iron object, west: 0.90 m, south: 1.30 m, depth: 0.75–0.80 m | --- | --- / --- |
| 07D007.I | clay | loom-weight | | --- | --- / --- |
| 07D008.I | bronze | coin | Vasudeva I | 175 | 3.5, 59* and 60* |
| 07D008.II | iron | finger ring | fragment of iron finger ring, west: 0.80 m, south: 1.60 m, depth: 1.15 | 147 | 3.3, 3:34 / 3.3, 28* |
| 07D009.I | leaded bronze | tool | leaded bronze tool (medical?, cosmetic?), north: 0:60 m, east: 1.60 m, depth: 1.20 m | --- | --- / --- |
| 07D009.II | bone | pin | hairpin, bone, north: 2.20 m, east: 0.22 m, depth: 1.44 m | 142 | 3.3, 3:25 / 3.3, 9:2* |
| 07D009.III | clay | button | | 109, 115 | 3.1, 2:25 / 3.1, 66* |
| 07D009.III | stone | whetstone | | 126 | --- / 3.2, 31* |
| 07D011.I | glass paste | bead | bead, black glass paste | 149 | 3.3, 5:71 / 3.3, 40* |
| 07D011.II | bone | pin | hairpin, bone, south: 0.60 m, east: 0 m, depth: 1.10 m | 143 | 3.3, 3:26 / 3.3, 9:3* |
| 07D012.I | bronze | coin | Kanishka II | 176 | --- / 3.5, 89* and 90* |
| 07D012.II | stone | bead | bead made of red stone, north: 1.20 m, east: 0.66 m, depth: NIV 374.16 m | 3.3, 5:72 / 3.3, 87* | 3.3, 5:72 / 3.3, 87* |
| 07D013.I | bone | pin | hairpin, bone, south: 2.25 m, west: 0.05 m, depth: 2.00 m | 3.3, 3:27 / 3.3, 9:1* | 3.3, 3:27 / 3.3, 9:1* |
| 07D013.II | bronze | coin | Peroz (?) | 178 | --- / 3.5, 124* and 125* |
| 07D015.I | crystal | | fragment of worked crystal, east: 0.50 m, north: 0 m, depth: 2.05 m | --- | --- / --- |
| 07D017.I | bone | pin | | 143 | --- / 3.3, 16* |
| 07E001.I | bronze | | fragment of bronze object | 155 | 3.3, 6:91 / 3.3, 83* |
| 07E002.I | glass paste | bead | fragment of light blue bead of glass paste, diameter 0.5 cm | 149 | 3.3, 5:66 / 3.3, 38* |
| 07E004.I | clay | bead | block orange bead of fired clay, perforated, 0.8 × 0.6 × 0.45 cm | 153 | 3.3, 5:67 / 3.3, 53* |
| 07E004.II | glass paste | bead | fragment of bead of dark blue glass paste, diameter 0.8 cm | 149 | 3.3, 5:68 / 3.3, 39* |
| 07E017.I | glass | vessel | rim of glass vessel | --- | --- / --- |
| 07E024.I | bronze | coin | bronze coin, diameter 2.8 cm; A: figure of standing king offering on the altar | --- | --- / --- |
| 07E024.II | bronze | sheet | Fragment of bronze sheet in 3 pieces. | --- | --- / --- |
| 07E024.III | bronze | coin | bronze coin, diameter 1.5 cm | --- | --- / --- |
| 07E028.I | pottery | button | round regular pottery sherd, worked for secondary use (button?) | 110 | --- / 3.1, 24* |
| 07E033.I | bronze | | fragment of round bronze object, diameter 0.55 cm | --- | --- / --- |
| 07E033.II | iron | | fragment of flat iron object | 128 | --- / 3.2, 41* |
| 07x000.I | bone | pin | fragment of the bone pin was found during constructing of topo-point on the summit of the Shakhristan (point 9001); 0.5 m under the surface | 143 | 3.3, 1:6 / 3.3, 89* |

| small find number | material | object | description | p. | tab. / fig. |
|---|---|---|---|---|---|
| 08A000.I | glass paste | bead | bead of cylindrical shape (made of greenish glass paste) | 99 | --- / --- |
| 08A002.I | limestone | spindle-whorl | | 99 | --- / 3.1, 20 |
| 08A003.I | bronze | | fragment of bronze object | 99 | --- / --- |
| 08A007.I | bronze | coin | Soter Megas | 173, 99 | 3.5, 25* and 26* |
| 08A009.I | stone | whetstone | fragment of an object made of greyish-black stone | 126, 99 | 3.2, 4:3 / 3.2, 65* |
| 08A012.I | bronze | coin | Kanishka II | 176 | 3.5, 88* |
| 09A013.I | stone | whetstone | rectangular worked stone, rounded corners, 9.2 × 9.9 × 4.3 cm (whetstone?) | --- | --- / --- |
| 09A015.I | bronze | coin | Kanishka I | 175 | 3.5, 47* and 48* |
| 09B002.I | stone | | fragment of black polished rounded stone (button?) | --- | --- / --- |
| 09B002.II | bronze | ear-ring | | 148 | 3.3, 4:38 / --- |
| 09B002.IV | bronze | coin | Kanishka II | 177 | --- |
| 09B009.I | bronze | | | --- | --- / --- |
| 09B009.II | bronze | arrow-head | bronze socketed arrowhead, three-sided in section | 122 | 3.2, 2:2 / 3.2, 14* |
| 09B010.I | bone | tool | | 114 | 3.1, 1:18 / 3.1, 72* |
| 09B012.I | bronze | | fragment of bronze pointed object (needle?, pin?) | 113, 155 | 3.3, 6:84 / 3.3, 76* |
| 09B015.I | bronze | | fragment of bronze pointed object (needle?, pin?) | 113, 155 | 3.3, 6:85 / 3.3, 77* |
| 09B016.I | | bead | lost? | --- | --- / --- |
| 09C000.I | bronze | coin | | --- | --- / --- |
| 09C001.I | bronze | | | 155 | 3.3, 6:92 / 3.3, 84* |
| 09C007.I | bone | pin | | 142 | 3.3, 1:14 / 3.3, 6a and 6b* |
| 09C015.I | bronze | arrow-head | bronze socketed arrowhead three-sided in section, with a triangular outline | 122 | 3.2, 2:2 / 3.2, 15* |
| 09C015.II | bronze | | | --- | --- / --- |
| 09C016.I | bronze | coin | | --- | --- / --- |
| 09C016.II | bronze | coin | | --- | --- / --- |
| 09C016.III | bronze | coin | | --- | --- / --- |
| 09C016.IV | bronze | | | --- | --- / --- |
| 09C016.V | bronze | pin? | | 128, 155 | 3.3, 6:86 / 3.2, 33* and 3.3, 78* |
| 09C016.VI | bronze | | | --- | --- / --- |
| 09C016.VII | iron | arrow-head | | 124 | 3.2, 2:08 / 3.2, 20* |
| 09C016.VIII | iron | | cylindrical perforated object | --- | --- / --- |
| 09C018.I | bronze | coin | | --- | --- / --- |
| 09C018.II | pottery | button | | 110, 114 | --- / 3.1, 42* |
| 09C021.I | pottery | button | | 110, 114 | --- / 3.1, 43* |
| 09C022.I | bronze | coin | | --- | --- / --- |
| 09C022.II | bone | pin | bone pin; V-shaped head for making thread?, 9.6 cm long | 142 | 3.3, 2:15 / 3.3, 7* |
| 09C022.III | teeth | | two worked animal teeth | 154 | --- / 3.3, 72* |
| 09C022.IV | clay | loom-weight | loom-weight of clay | 110, 115 | 3.1, 3:6 / 3.1, 43* |
| 09C022.V | clay | loom-weight | loom-weight of clay | 110, 115 | 3.1, 4:5 / 3.1, 45* |
| 09C022.VI | clay | loom-weight | a,b loom-weight of clay in two fragments | 110, 115 | 3.1, 4:4 / 3.1, 50* |
| 09C022.VII | clay | loom-weight | loom-weight of clay | 110, 115 | 3.1, 3:9 / 3.1, 54* |
| 09C026.I | bone | | lamb bone | --- | --- / --- |
| 09D001.I | bronze | sheet | fragment of a bronze sheet | --- | --- / --- |
| 09D001.II | bronze | coin | Vima Kadphises | 173 | --- / 3.5, 39* and 40* |

| small find number | material | object | description | p. | fig. |
|---|---|---|---|---|---|
| 09D003.I | glass paste? | bead | triangular perforated bead (?glass) | 153 | 3.3, 5:55 / 3.3, 51* |
| 09D007.I | bronze | needle or pin | 2 fragments of bronze pointed object (needle?, pin?) | 115 | --- / --- |
| 09D010.I | bronze | pin or rivet | bronze pin or rivet | 128 | 3.2, 5:1 / 3.2, *34** |
| 09D010.II | bronze | coin | bronze coin; d. 1.9–2 cm | 180 | cat. no. 119 |
| 09D010.III | bronze | coin | bronze coin; d. 2.1–2.2 cm | 177 | --- / 3.5, 104* and 105* |
| 09D033.I | clay | loom-weight | clay pyramidal loom-weight | 110, 115 | --- / 3.1, *55** |
| 09D033.II | clay | loom-weight | fragment of clay pyramidal loom-weight | 110, 115 | --- / 3.1, *51** |
| 09D033.III | bronze | ring | fragment of a bronze ring (finger or ear ring). d. 1.9 cm | 148 | 3.3, 4:36 / 3.3, 30* |
| 09E002.I | stone | whetstone ? | | --- | --- / --- |
| 09E002.II | stone | grindstone | | --- | --- / --- |
| 09E002.III | iron | tool ? | | 128 | --- / 3.2, 42* |
| 09E002.IV | stone | | | --- | --- / --- |
| 09E002.V | glass | vessel | | --- | --- / --- |
| 09E008.I | bone | tool | | 154 | --- / 3.3, 73* |
| 09E012.I | alabaster | spindle-whorl | spindle-whorl of alabaster | 108 | --- / 3.1, 22* |
| 09E013.I | shell | pendant | | 154 | --- / 3.3, 68* |
| 09E018.I | bronze | | | 155 | --- / 3.3, 79* |
| 09E020.I | stone | whetstone | | --- | --- / --- |
| 10C000.I | bronze | | two fragments of bronze object | --- | --- / --- |
| 10C000.II | stone | finger ring | | 146–147 | 3.3, 3:33 / 3.3, 27* |
| 10C001.I | stone | spindle-whorl | spindle-whorl, stone | 114 | --- / --- |
| 10C003.I | bronze | | | 155 | --- / 3.3, 80* |
| 10C003.II | bone | pin | | 143 | --- / 3.3, 17* |
| 10C003.III | stone | whetstone ? | | 126 | 3.1, 3:7 / 3.2, 28* |
| 10C005.I | alabaster | spindle-whorl | spindle-whorl, alabaster | 108 | 3.1, 2:10 / 3.1, 23* |
| 10C007.I | bronze | coin | | --- | --- / --- |
| 10C009.I | leaded bronze | tool | | 155 | 3.3, 6:89 / 3.3, 81* |
| 10C011.I | alabaster | spindle-whorl | spindle-whorl, alabaster | 108, 114 | 3.1, 1:6 / 3.1, 5* |
| 10C016.I | clay | loom-weight | loom weight, clay | 110, 115 | 3.1, 3:10 / 3.1, 47* |
| 10D002.II | bronze | coin | ? | 179 | --- / 3.5, 128* and 129* |
| 10D005.I | bronze | coin | Peroz? | 178 | cat. no. 87 |
| 10D013c.I | bronze | coin | ? | 180 | cat. no. 117 |
| 10D013c.II | bronze | coin | ? | 180 | cat. no. 116 |
| 10D018.II | clay | loom-weight | loom-weight | 110, 115 | --- / 3.1, 52* |
| 10D018.VI | bronze | coin | Kanishka II | 177 | --- / 3.5, 110* and 111* |
| 11C004.I | glass | bead | cylindrical hexagonal perforated bead (glass?) | 153 | 3.3, 5:59 / 3.3, 52* |
| 11C004.II | glass | bead | cut perforated black cylinder (glass bead?) | 153 | 3.3, 5:60 / 3.3, 50* |
| 11C005.I | stone | spindle-whorl | lenticular stone perforated spindle whorl | 108, 114 | 3.1, 2:8 / 3.1, 24* |
| 11C005.II | clay | loom weight | clay pyramidal loom-weight | 110, 115 | 3.1, 4:8 / 3.1, 57* |
| 11C005.III | clay | loom weight | clay pyramidal loom-weight | 110, 115 | 3.1, 4:9 / 3.1, 53* |
| 11C005.IV | iron | knife | tanged one-edged knife | 119 | 3.2, 1:1 / 3.2, 1* |
| 11C005.IX | iron | pole | little metal pole (iron) | 128 | --- / 3.2, 44* |
| 11C005.V | iron | knife | tanged one-edged knife | 119 | 3.2, 1:2 / 3.2, 2 |
| 11C005.VI | iron | rod | iron rod | 128 | 3.2, 5:6 / 3.2, 43* |

191

| small find number | material | object | description | p. | fig. |
|---|---|---|---|---|---|
| 11C005.VII | | bead | spherical perforated bead | 149 | 3.3, 5:61 / 3.3, 35* |
| 11C005.VIII | bronze | sheet | 2 fragments of bronze sheet | --- | --- / --- |
| 11C005.X | bronze | sheet | slightly bended bronze sheet | --- | --- / --- |
| 11C007.I | bronze | coin | Kanishka II | 176 | --- / --- |
| 11C008.I | glass paste | bead | glass spherical perforated bead | 149 | 3.3, 5:62 / 3.3, 36* |
| 11C009.I | bronze | coin | Vasudeva I | 176 | 3.5, 79* and 80* |
| 12C002.I | pottery | spindle-whorl | spindle-whorl, pottery | 108, 114 | 3.1, 1:16 / 3.1, 10* |
| 12C002.II | alabaster | spindle-whorl | spindle-whorl in two pieces, alabaster. | 108, 114 | 3.1, 2:11 / 3.1, 30* |
| 12C002.III | bronze | ladle | fragmentary bronze vessel – a ladle; handle is 15 cm long (0.6x0.7 cm), oval bowl 6.8 × 6.3 cm | --- | --- / --- |
| 12C002.IV | bone | astragal | | --- | --- / --- |
| 12C002.V | bone | astragal | | --- | --- / --- |
| 12C004.I | pottery | spindle-whorl | fragment of spindle-whorl, pottery | 108, 114 | 3.1, 2:15 / 3.1, 25* |
| 12C005.I | bronze | coin | Vasudeva II | 180 | --- / 3.5, 130* and 131* |
| 12C008.II | pottery | spindle--whorl | fragment of spindle-whorl?, pottery | 114 | --- / --- |
| 12C016.I | bronze | rod | | --- | --- / --- |
| 12C016.II | bronze | coin | | 179 | cat. no. 104 |
| 12C018.I | bronze | coin | Vasudeva II | 176 | --- / 3.5, 85* |
| 12D003.I | glass paste | bead | perforated (0,2 cm gap) bead made of red glass paste | 149 | 3.3, 5:63 / 3.3, 37* |
| 12D003.II | stone | slingshot | biconical to egg-shaped polished stone | 124 | 3.2, 2:12 / 3.2, 26 |
| 12D003.III | bronze | coin | Peroz | 178 | cat. no. 85 |
| 12D003.IV | bronze | coin | Peroz? | 178 | cat. no. 86 |
| 12D003.V | bronze | coin | | 179 | cat. no. 100 |
| 12D003.VI | animal bone | | lamb bone | --- | --- / --- |
| 12D003.VII | animal bone | | lamb bone | --- | --- / --- |
| 12D005.I | bronze | sheet | fragment of bronze sheet in two pieces | --- | --- / --- |
| 12D008.I | clay | spindle-whorl | spindle-whorl, clay, black surface | 108, 114 | 3.1, 2:13 / 3.1, 9* |
| 12D008.II | pottery | spindle-whorl | | 108, 114 | 3.1, 2:5 / 3.1, 18* |
| 20B001.I | iron | | fragment of an iron object | --- | --- / --- |
| 20C000.I | alabaster | spindle-whorl | spindle-whorl, alabaster | 108 | 3.1, 2:9 / 3.1, 26* |
| 20C001.I | bronze | coin | bronze coin | 52 | --- / --- |
| 20C001.II | alabaster | spindle-whorl | spindle-whorl in two pieces, alabaster | 108 | --- / 3.1, 27* |
| 20C004.I | bronze | coin | Kanishka II | 177, 43, 52 | cat. no. 70. |
| 20C004.II | bronze | coin | bronze coin | 43, 44, 52 | 2.1, 22 |
| 20C004.III | bronze | coin | bronze coin | 43, 52 | --- / --- |
| 20C004.IV | bronze | coin | bronze coin | 43, 52 | --- / --- |
| 20D001.I | metal, glass paste | ring | metal ring with glass paste, in five fragments, recent? | 146 | 3.3, 3:31 / 3.3, 24* |
| 20D002.I | bronze | vessel | fragment of bronze vessel | --- | --- / --- |
| 20D002.II | | blade | six fragments of a blade (?) | 124, 133 | 3.2, 3:2 / 3.2, 22* |
| 20D002.III | bronze | coin | Kanishka II | 178 | cat. no. 80 |
| 20E001.I | glass | vessel | fragment of glass vessel | --- | --- / --- |
| 20E004c.I | bronze | sheet | fragment of bronze sheet | 155 | --- / 3.3, 85* |
| 20E007.I | clay | spindle-whorl | spindle-whorl?, clay | 108 | --- / 3.1, 6* |
| 20F002.I | stone | spindle-whorl | spindle-whorl, black stone | 114 | --- / --- |
| 20F007.I | shell | shell | small shell | 154 | --- / 3.3, 67* |
| 20G001.I | clay | spindle-whorl | spindle-whorl?, clay | 108, 114 | --- / 3.1, 7* |

| small find number | material | object | description | p. | fig. |
|---|---|---|---|---|---|
| 20G002.I | clay | spindle-whorl | spindle-whorl?, clay | 108, 114 | --- / 3.1, 8* |
| 20G002.II | pottery | spindle-whorl | rounded smooth ceramic sherd, spindle-whorl or button | 110, 114 | --- / 3.1, 44* |
| 20G002.III | glass | goblet | fragment of glass goblet in seven pieces | --- | --- / --- |
| 20H002.I | bronze | ear ring | ear ring, bronze | 148 | 3.3, 4:37 / 3.3, 31* |
| 20H002.II | glass | vessel | fragment of glass vessel in three pieces | --- | --- / --- |
| 20H002.III | glass paste | bead | glass paste bead | 152 | 3.3, 5:64 / 3.3, 45* |
| 20H002.IV | clay | loom-weight | loom-weight, clay | 113, 115 | --- / 3.1, 58* |
| 20N001.I | bronze | | fragment of bronze object | 128, 130 | --- / 3.2, 46* |
| 20N001.II | bronze | sheet | fragment of bronze sheet | --- | --- / --- |
| 20N002.I | alabaster | spindle-whorl | spindle-whorl, alabaster | 108, 114 | --- / 3.1, 28* |
| 20N002.II | clay | spindle-whorl | spindle-whorl?, clay | 108, 114 | --- / 3.1, 15* |
| 20N002.III | bronze | | fragment of bronze object | --- | --- / --- |
| 20N002.IV | bronze | | fragment of bronze object | --- | --- / --- |
| 20N002.IX | glass paste | ball | small perforated glass paste ball | --- | --- / --- |
| 20N002.V | bronze | coin | bronze coin | 52 | --- / --- |
| 20N002.VI | bronze | coin | bronze coin | 179, 52 | cat. no. 97 |
| 20N002.VII | iron | knife | iron one-edged knife blade | 119 | 3.2, 1:3 / 3.2, 3* |
| 20N002.VIII | iron | | two fragments of an iron object | --- | --- / --- |
| 20N002.X | iron | rod | fragment of iron rod | 155 | --- / 3.3, 86* |
| 20N002.XI | bone | pin | fragment of bone pin, l. 4.76 cm | 143 | --- / 3.3, 14* |
| 20N002.XII | pottery | button | | 109, 110, 114 | --- / 3.1, 65* |
| 20N002.XIII | bronze | sheet | fragment of bronze sheet | --- | --- / --- |
| 20N002.XIV | terracotta | loom-weight | fragment of loom-weight, terracotta | 110, 115 | 3.1, 4:3 / 3.1, 46* |
| 20N003.I | bronze | buckle | rounded bronze object with tongue, a buckle? | 154 | 3.3, 6:78 / 3.3, 70* |
| 20N003.II | pottery | button | perforated pottery disc made of fragment of FW/RSW vessel | 110, 114 | --- / 3.1, 63* |
| 20N003.III | alabaster | spindle-whorl | fragment of spindle-whorl, alabaster | 108, 114 | --- / 3.1, 29* |
| 20O003.I | iron | knife | two fragments of an iron knife blade, both fitting together | 121 | 3.2, 1:5 / 3.2, 5* |
| 20O003.II | glass | vessel | fragments of bottom of glass vessel, 3 pieces | 73 | --- / --- |
| 20O004.I | bronze | hooklet | bronze hooklet | --- | --- / --- |
| 20O009c.I | alabaster | | raw alabaster | 110, 115 | --- / 3.1, 40* |
| 20O010.I | bronze | | fragment of bronze object | 130 | --- / 3.2, 47* |
| 20O010.II | clay | spindle-whorl | spindle-whorl, clay | 108, 114 | 3.1, 2:1 / 3.1, 12* |
| 20O010.III | carnelian | bead | carnelian object – worked and transpierced stone bead, 3 cm long | 154 | 3.3, 4:43 / 3.3, 63* |
| 20O010.IV | metal | sheet | 4 fragments of metal sheet | --- | --- / --- |
| 20O011.I | clay | | loom-weight or spindle-whorl?, clay | 108 | 3.1, 2:2 / 3.1, 13* |
| 20O011.II | iron | knife | iron knife-blade fragment | 121 | 3.2, 1:4 / 3.2, 4* |
| 20O013c.I | terracotta | figurine | terracotta figurine | 166 | 3.4, 2:2 / 3.4, 16 |
| 20O014.I | wood? | | fragment of an object of organic material, hollow cylindrical shape | --- | --- / --- |
| 20O018.I | bone | needle? | fragment of bone object, needle? | 115, 154 | 3.3, 6:79 / 3.3, 71* |
| 20O019.I | glass paste | bead | glass paste object in many fragments, many colors (black, red, white, yellow), bead | 153 | --- / 3.3, 59* |
| 20O019.II | shell | shell | fragment of shell | 154 | --- / 3.3, 66* |
| 20O020.I | clay | spindle-whorl | fragment of spindle-whorl? black, clay | 108 | 3.1, 2:14 / 3.1, 11* |
| 20O020.II | glass | sheet | fragment of glass sheet, recent? | --- | --- / --- |
| 20O020.III | iron | | fragment of iron object | 130 | --- / 3.2, 49* |
| 20O020.IV | glass paste | | fragment of yellow glass paste object | --- | --- / --- |

| small find number | material | object | description | p. | fig. |
|---|---|---|---|---|---|
| 20P002.I | bronze | coin | bronze coin | 179, 52 | cat. no. 108 |
| 20P002.II | bronze | sheet | tiny bronze sheet in 3 fragments | --- | --- / --- |
| 20P004.I | glass | vessel | fragment of glass vessel (light greenish blue) | --- | --- / --- |
| 20P006c.I | iron | knife | fragment of iron knife | --- | --- / --- |
| 20P009.I | glass paste | | yellow glass paste object in two pieces | --- | --- / --- |
| 20P014c.I | bronze | sheet | fragment of bronze sheet | --- | --- / --- |
| 20P015.I | glass | vessel | two fragments of glass vessel (rim) | --- | --- / --- |
| 20Q001.I | iron | hook | fragment of iron hook (?) | 128 | 3.2, 5:2 / 3.2, 35* |
| 20Q001.II | bronze | coin | bronze coin | 179, 52 | cat. no. 96 |
| 20Q001.III | stone | | fragment of worked stone | --- | --- / --- |
| 20Q001.IV | metal | | fragment of metal object (2.2 cm long) | 130 | --- / 3.2, 49* |
| 20Q001.V | glass paste | bead | black glass paste bead, perforated; with white dots | 153 | --- / 3.3, 46* |
| 20Q001.VI | glass | vessel | fragment of glass vessel | --- | --- / --- |
| 20Q001.VII | bronze | coin | bronze coin | 179, 52 | cat. no. 111 |
| 20Q002.I | clay | | clay perforated object | 153 | 3.3, 4:46 / 3.3, 47 |
| 20Q002.II | clay | | clay perforated object in two pieces. | --- | --- / --- |
| 20Q002.III | mother of pearl | bracelet | fragment of mother-of-pearl object, bent, perforated, decorated with holes | 148 | 3.3, 3:35 / 3.3, 29 |
| 20Q002.IV | bronze | coin | bronze coin | 52 | --- / --- |
| 20Q008.I | glass | vessel | rim of glass vessel, in two pieces | --- | --- / --- |
| 20Q011.I | bronze | sheet | fragment of bronze sheet | --- | --- / --- |
| 20Q011.II | bronze | | fragment of bronze object | --- | --- / --- |
| 20Q012.I | bronze | hook | fragment of bronze hook | 128 | 3.2, 5:3 / 3.2, 36* |
| 20Q012.II | terracotta | figurine | fragment of hand-made terracotta figurine, h. 5 cm; also 20Q012.20 | --- | --- / --- |
| 20Q012.III | clay | spindle-whorl | clay perforated object, spindle-whorl? | 108 | --- / 3.1, 1* |
| 20Q018.I | bronze | coin | bronze coin | 179, 52 | cat. no. 107 |
| 20Q020.I | carnelian | bead | long carnelian bead (2.1 × 0.9 cm) | 153 | 3.3, 4:48 / 3.3, 56* |
| 20Q038.I | bronze | coin | bronze coin | 179, 52 | cat. no. 96 |
| 20R001.I | --- | --- | --- | --- | --- / --- |
| 20R004.I | bronze | coin | bronze coin, modern – 20th c. (Sovyet) | 52 | --- / --- |
| 20R006.I | leather | sole | fragment of sole with hobnails (12 × 8 × 0.3 cm), recent | 53 | --- / --- |
| 20R012.I | glass paste | bead | fragment of glass paste bead in two pieces | 149 | 3.3, 4:49 / 3.3, 32* |
| 20S001.I | alabaster | spindle-whorl | spindle-whorl, alabaster | 108 | 3.1, 2:12 / 3.1, 31* |
| 20S002.I | bronze | coin | bronze coin | 179, 52 | cat. no. 112 |
| 20S002.II | bronze | coin | bronze coin | 180, 52 | cat. no. 115 |
| 20S002.III | bronze | coin | bronze coin of Kanishka II | 177, 52 | --- / 3.5, 99* and 99* |
| 20S003.I | bone | pin | fragment of bone pin, l. 7.8 cm | 142 | 3.3, 1:7 / 3.3, 4* |
| 20S003.II | iron | | fragment of pointed iron object in two pieces | 124 | 3.2, 3:3 / 3.2, 23* |
| 20Y002.I | bone | ring | fragment of bone ring, grooved, diameter 2 cm | 146 | 3.3, 3:28 / 3.3, 21* |
| 20Y002.II | stone | | flat object of white stone, perforated and drilled | 110, 115 | 3.1, 2:38 / 3.1, 38* |
| 20Y002.III | iron | knife | fragment of an iron knife: the tang and the lower part of the blade | 121 | 3.2, 1:6 / 3.2, 6* |
| 20Y002.IV | pottery | spindle-whorl | spindle-whorl?, pottery | 109, 115 | 3.1, 1:15 / 3.1, 35* |
| 20Y002.IX | bronze | coin | Vasudeva II (?) | 180, 52 | --- / 3.5, 132* and 133* |
| 20Y002.V | clay | | clay perforated object, spindle-whorl or loom-weight? | 108, 115 | 3.1, 2:4 / 3.1, 2* |
| 20Y002.VI | glass paste | | fragment of perforated dark glass-paste object | 153 | --- / 3.3, 60* |

| small find number | material | object | description | p. | fig. |
|---|---|---|---|---|---|
| 20Y002.VII | chalcedony | bead | | 153 | 3.3, 4:51 / 3.3, 33* |
| 20Y002.VIII | bronze | coin | bronze coin of Euthydemus | 173-4, 52 | --- / 3.5, 1* and 2* |
| 20Y002.X | alabaster | spindle-whorl | spindle-whorl, alabaster | 108, 115 | --- / 3.1, 32* |
| 20Y002.XI | bronze | | bronze "lentil", diameter 0.45 cm | --- | --- / --- |
| 20Y002.XII | wood? | | rounded perforated object of organic material (wood?, burned) | 153 | --- / 3.3, 62* |
| 20Y002.XIII | bronze | wire | fragment of bronze wire | --- | --- / --- |
| 20Y002.XIV | stone | whetstone | flat tool of black stone, whetstone | 126 | 3.2, 4:1 / 3.2, 29 |
| 20Y002.XIX | | bead | | 149, 152 | 3.3, 4:51 / 3.3, 33 |
| 20Y002.XV | | bead | | 149, 152 | 3.3, 4:51 / 3.3, 33 |
| 20Y002.XVI | | bead | | 149, 152 | 3.3, 4:51 / 3.3, 33 |
| 20Y002.XVII | | bead | | 149, 152 | 3.3, 4:51 / 3.3, 33 |
| 20Y002.XVIII | | bead | | 149, 152 | 3.3, 4:51 / 3.3, 33 |
| 20Y002.XX | | bead | | 149, 152 | 3.3, 4:51 / 3.3, 33 |
| 20Y002.XXI | | bead | | 149, 152 | 3.3, 4:51 / 3.3, 33 |
| 20Y002.XXII | | bead | | 149, 152 | 3.3, 4:51 / 3.3, 33 |
| 20Y002.XXIII | | bead | | 149, 152 | 3.3, 4:51 / 3.3, 33 |
| 20Y002.XXIV | | bead | | 149, 152 | 3.3, 4:51 / 3.3, 33 |
| 20Y002.XXIX | | bead | | 149, 152 | 3.3, 4:51 / 3.3, 33 |
| 20Y002.XXV | | bead | | 149, 152 | 3.3, 4:51 / 3.3, 33 |
| 20Y002.XXVI | | bead | | 149, 152 | 3.3, 4:51 / 3.3, 33 |
| 20Y002.XXVII | | bead | | 149, 152 | 3.3, 4:51 / 3.3, 33 |
| 20Y002.XXVIII | | bead | | 149, 152 | 3.3, 4:51 / 3.3, 33 |
| 20Y002.XXX | | bead | | 149, 152 | 3.3, 4:51 / 3.3, 33 |
| 20Y002.XXXI | | bead | | 149, 152 | 3.3, 4:51 / 3.3, 33 |
| 20Y002.XXXII | | bead | | 149, 152 | 3.3, 4:51 / 3.3, 33 |
| 20Y002.XXVIII | | bead | | 149, 152 | 3.3, 4:51 / 3.3, 33 |
| 20Y002.XXXIV | | bead | | 149, 152 | 3.3, 4:51 / 3.3, 33 |
| 20Y002.XXXV | | bead | | 149, 152 | 3.3, 4:51 / 3.3, 33 |
| 20Y002.XXXVI | | bead | | 149, 152 | 3.3, 4:51 / 3.3, 33 |
| 20Y002.XXXVII | | bead | | 149, 152 | 3.3, 4:51 / 3.3, 33 |
| 20Y002.XXXVIII | | bead | | 149, 152 | 3.3, 4:51 / 3.3, 33 |
| 20Y003c.I | | spindle-whorl | spindle-whorl | 108, 115 | 3.1, 2:3 / 3.1, 14* |
| 20Y005.I | glass paste | bead | dark glass paste bead, perforated | 149 | 3.3, 5:53 / 3.3, 34* |
| 20Y007.I | stone | | flat round object of white stone, drilled, but not perforated (button?) | 110, 115 | 3.1, 2:17 / 3.1, 39* |
| 20Y007.II | bronze | coin | Late Middle Ages | 181, 52 | --- / 3.5, 154* and 155* |
| 20Y010.I | | slag | piece of slag | --- | --- / --- |
| 20Y011.I | bronze | sheet | fragment of bronze sheet | --- | --- / --- |
| 20Y014.I | bronze | coin | Late Middle Ages | 181, 52 | --- / 3.5, 156* and 157* |
| 20Y022.I | stone | grindstone | grindstone, lower part, 25 × 22 × 12 cm | 50, 80 | --- / --- |
| 20Y022.II | stone | ring | fragment of stone ring, grooved, d. 2 cm | 146 | 3.3, 3:29 / 3.3, 22* |
| 20Y022.III | stone | quern stone | fragment of quern stone, perforated, 36.2 × 21 cm | 80 | --- / --- |
| 20Y023.I | iron | arrow-head | fragment of iron arrow-head. | 124 | 3.2, 2:9 / 3.2, 21* |
| 20Y026.I | clay | loom--weight | loom-weight, clay | 113, 115 | 3.1, 4:7 / 3.1, 59* |
| 20Y026.II | stone | whetstone or semi-finished spindle-whorl | flat perforated triangular stone object | 126, 110 | 3.1, 2:18 / 3.2, 30* |
| 20Y026.III | bronze | hook | | --- | --- / --- |

| small find number | material | object | description | p. | fig. |
|---|---|---|---|---|---|
| 20Y027.I | clay | stand? | cylindrical clay object, (h. 11 cm, diameter 8–10.5 cm) stand? | --- | --- / --- |
| 20Y027.II | stone | grindstone | fragment of grindstone, lower part, 22 × 18 × 5 cm | 50 | --- / --- |
| 20Z002.I | stone | quern stone | quern stone, perforated | 50, 78 | --- / 2.1, 30 and 31 |
| 20Z002.II | stone | quern stone | quern stone, perforated | 50, 78 | --- / --- |
| 20Z003.I | metal | slag | piece of metal slag | --- | --- / --- |
| 20Z004.I | metal | | piece of metal (bronze?) | --- | --- / --- |
| 20Z006.I | stone | bead | light red stone (?) bead, more times perforated | 152 | 3.3, 4:54 / 3.3, 43* |
| 20Z017c.I | metal | slag | piece of metal slag | --- | --- / --- |
| 20Z019.I | clay | | rounded clay object | --- | --- / --- |
| 21D001.I | glass paste | bead | polygonal perforated glass paste bead | 153 | 3.3, 4:39 / 3.3, 55* |
| 21D001.II | bronze | coin | bronze coin, d. 1.1–1.2 cm | 179, 52 | cat. no. 105 |
| 21D005.I | stone | | fragment of worked stone | --- | --- / --- |
| 21D007.I | | slag | slag in two pieces.(second: 35 × 25 × 20) | --- | --- / --- |
| 21D012.I | terracotta | figurine | terracotta figurine – horse rider | 161,163 | 3.4, 1:2 / 3.4, 8 |
| 21D017.I | bronze | coin | bronze coin, d. 1.4 cm | 179, 52 | cat. no. 103 |
| 21D019c.I | bronze | coin | bronze coin, d. 1.35–1.4 cm | 52 | --- / --- |
| 21D025.I | bronze | | fragment of bronze object | --- | --- / --- |
| 21D025.II | iron | | fragment of iron object | 130 | 3.2, 5:10 / 3.2, 50–54 |
| 21D025.III | bronze | | fragment of bronze object | --- | --- / --- |
| 21D025.IV | iron | | fragment of iron object | 130 | 3.2, 5:10 / 3.2, 50–54 |
| 21D025.IX | iron | | fragment of iron object | 130 | 3.2, 5:10 / 3.2, 50–54* |
| 21D025.V | | slag | slag, grey color | --- | --- / --- |
| 21D025.VI | iron | | fragment of iron object | 130 | 3.2, 5:5 / 3.2, 55* |
| 21D025.VII | iron | | fragment of iron object | 130 | 3.2, 5:10 / 3.2, 50–54 |
| 21D025.VIII | iron | | fragment of iron object | 130 | 3.2, 5:10 / 3.2, 50–54 |
| 21D025.X | iron | | fragment of iron object | 130 | 3.2, 5:10 / 3.2, 50–54 |
| 21E001.I | bronze | sheet | fragment of rounded bronze sheet, d. 1.1 cm | 21E001.I | --- / --- |
| 21E006.I | bronze | coin | Kanishka II | 177, 52 | --- / 3.5, 96* and 97* |
| 21E006.II | iron | | fragment of iron object | 130 | 3.2, 5:11 / 3.2, 56* |
| 21E010.I | bronze | sheet | fragment of bronze sheet | 130 | --- / 3.2, 57* |
| 21E010.II | stone | | fragment of worked stone | --- | --- / --- |
| 21E012.I | bronze | coin | mint of Southern Sogdia | 178 | --- / 3.5, 122* and 123* |
| 21E025.I | iron | | fragment of pointed iron object | 124 | 3.2, 3:4 / 3.2, 24* |
| 21E026.I | clay | spindle-whorl | spindle-whorl, clay | 108, 115 | --- / 3.1, 3* |
| 21E026.II | iron | | fragment of iron object | 130 | --- / 3.2, 58* |
| 21F001.I | bone | pin | fragment of bone pin | 139 | 3.3, 1:1 / 3.3, 1* |
| 21F001.II | bronze | rivet | bronze rivet | 154 | 3.3, 6:77 / 3.3, 69* |
| 21F001.III | pottery | spindle-whorl or button? | spindle-whorl or button, pottery | 109, 114 | --- / 3.1, 36* |
| 21F001.IV | bronze | coin | bronze coin | 179, 52 | cat. no. 95 |
| 21F001.IX | stone | tool | stone tool | --- | --- / --- |
| 21F001.V | bronze | | fragment of bronze object | --- | --- / --- |
| 21F001.VI | glass | vessel | fragment of glass vessel | --- | --- / --- |
| 21F001.VII | bronze | | fragment of bronze object | --- | --- / --- |
| 21F001.VIII | stone | tool | stone tool | --- | --- / --- |
| 21F005.I | clay | spindle-whorl | spindle-whorl, clay | 108, 115 | --- / 3.1, 16* |

| small find number | material | object | description | p. | fig. |
|---|---|---|---|---|---|
| 21F010.I | bone | pin | fragment of bone pin | 139, 142 | 3.3, 1:2 / 3.3, 2* |
| 21F010.II | bronze | coin | bronze coin | 179, 52 | --- / 3.5, 126* and 127* |
| 21F010.III | glass | | fragment of glass object, recent? | --- | --- / --- |
| 21F014.I | iron | | fragment of pointed iron object | 130 | 3.2, 5:4 / 3.2, 59* |
| 21F020.I | iron | | fragment of iron object | 130 | --- / 3.2, 60* |
| 21F023.I | glass paste | bead | fragment of bead made of blue glass paste | 153 | 3.3, 4:40 / 3.3, 58 |
| 21F023.II | glass | | fragment of glass object | --- | --- / --- |
| 21F024.I | bone | pin | bone pin | 142 | 3.3, 1:3 / 3.3, 3* |
| 21F024.II | glass paste | bead | fragment of bead made of yellow glass paste | 152 | 3.3, 4:41 / 3.3, 41* |
| 21F025.I | bone | plaque – finial of a bow | bone plaque – finial of a bow | 126, 134 | 3.2, 2:10 / 3.2, 27a* and 27b |
| 21O001.I | alabaster | spindle-whorl | spindle whorl, alabaster | 115 | --- / 3.1, 68 |
| 21O001.II | bronze | wire | fragment of bronze wire | 130 | --- / 3.2, 61* |
| 21O002.I | bronze | sheet | fragment of bronze sheet | 130 | --- / --- |
| 21P(z)001.I | clay | | fragment of perforated clay object | 115 | --- / 3.1, 67* |
| 21P(z)001.II | stone | | fragment of worked stone | --- | --- / --- |
| 21P(z)004.I | bone | pin | fragment of bone pin | 143 | 3.3, 1:5 / 3.3, 11* |
| 21P(z)004.II | bronze | coin | Vasudeva II or Kanishka II (?) | 177, 52 | --- / 3.5, 95* |
| 21P001.I | glass paste | bead | bead, green glass paste | 152 | 3.3, 4:42 / 3.3, 42* |
| 21P001.II | bronze | coin | bronze coin | 179, 52 | cat. no. 94 |
| 21P002.I | glass | | fragment of glass object | --- | --- / --- |
| 21P002.II | stone | tool | perforated stone tool | 114 | 3.1, 1:17 / 3.1, 62* |
| 21P002.III | iron | rod | fragment of iron rod | 130 | ---- / 3.2, 62* |
| 21P003.I | bronze | coin | Vasudeva II | 176, 52 | 3.5, 83* and 84* |
| 21P005.I | bronze | | fragment of bronze object | 130 | 3.2, 5:8 / 3.2, 64* |
| 21P005.II | | slag | slag | --- | --- / --- |
| 21P006c.I | iron | knife? | fragment of an iron one-edged knife (?) or another tool | 121, 131 | 3.2, 1:7 / 3.2, 7* |
| 21P006c.II | iron | knife | fragment of a one-edged iron knife | 121 | 3.2, 1:8 / 3.2, 8* |
| 21P006c.III | bronze | sheet | fragment of bronze sheet | --- | --- / --- |
| 21P007.I | iron | | fragment of iron object | 130 | 3.2, 5:8 / 3.2, 64* |
| 21P013.I | bronze | sheet | fragment of bronze sheet | --- | --- / --- |
| 21P016.I | bronze | coin | bronze coin | 180, 52 | cat. no. 121 |
| 21P018.I | bronze | coin | bronze coin | 52 | --- / --- |
| 21P023.I | bone | pin | fragment of bone pin | 143 | 3.3, 1:4 / 3.3, 10* |
| 30A004.I | bronze | | fragment of bronze object | --- | --- / --- |
| 30A013c.I | iron | razor? | group of iron items found together originally possibly making part of one object | 121, 130 | 3.2, 3:1 / 3.2, 12* |

[1]  This mark is used for the description of the walls in the text and in the general ground plan
[2]  Azimuth was measured in a south – north course of the longitudinal axis of the wall.
[3]  This mark is used for the description of the walls in the text and in the general ground plan
[4]  This value indicates the dimension of the bead in the direction of the threading hole. In the case of beads from Jandavlattepa it is also the maximum length.
[5]  In relation to the circular surfaces of the "disc" – diameter – perpendicular or parallel.

# JANDAVLATTEPA

The Excavation Report for Seasons 2002–2006
## VOL. 1

Editors
KAZIM ABDULLAEV
LADISLAV STANČO

Published by Charles University in Prague
Karolinum Press
Ovocný trh 3–5, 116 36 Prague 1, Czech Republic
Prague 2011
Vice-rector-editor Professor PhDr. Ivan Jakubec, CSc.
Cover and layout Kateřina Rezáčová
Printed by Karolinum Press
First edition

ISBN 978-80-246-1965-1